When the World Laughs

When the World Laughs

Film Comedy East and West

WILLIAM V. COSTANZO

OXFORD
UNIVERSITY PRESS

OXFORD
UNIVERSITY PRESS

Oxford University Press is a department of the University of Oxford. It furthers the University's objective of excellence in research, scholarship, and education by publishing worldwide. Oxford is a registered trade mark of Oxford University Press in the UK and certain other countries.

Published in the United States of America by Oxford University Press
198 Madison Avenue, New York, NY 10016, United States of America.

Library of Congress Cataloging-in-Publication Data
Names: Costanzo, William V., author.
Title: When the world laughs : film comedy East and West / William Costanzo.
Description: New York : Oxford University Press, 2020.
Identifiers: LCCN 2019032239 (print) | LCCN 2019032240 (ebook) |
ISBN 9780190925000 (paperback) | ISBN 9780190924997 (hardback) |
ISBN 9780190925024 (epub) | ISBN 9780190925017 (updf) | ISBN 9780190925031 (online)
Subjects: LCSH: Comedy films—History and criticism. |
Motion pictures—Social aspects.
Classification: LCC PN1995.9.C55 C683 2020 (print) |
LCC PN1995.9.C55 (ebook) | DDC 791.43/617—dc23
LC record available at https://lccn.loc.gov/2019032239
LC ebook record available at https://lccn.loc.gov/2019032240

1 3 5 7 9 8 6 4 2

Paperback printed by Marquis, Canada
Hardback printed by Bridgeport National Bindery, Inc., United States of America

For Diana, my treasured wife and constant muse, who has shared my labor and my laughter with love throughout the writing of this book.

Contents

Preface

As a young man back in the 1960s, I once found myself in a Manhattan art-house theater watching a short film titled *The Dove* (*De Düva*, 1968). It had English subtitles and came on before the main feature, a film by Ingmar Bergman. I still remember the car traveling through a desolate wintry landscape, a dark figure in a hood, and a lengthy close-up of a lone reed trembling in the wind. While I strained to read the subtitles, a titter of laughter reached me from behind, then another from my left. Gradually, more people in the audience joined in. It was not until the scene when a load of bird droppings landed on the car that I too got the joke. "The duve has y-crapped on der windershield," the driver said. He had been speaking in fake Swedish all along, with no need for translation.

It was my first real lesson in reading subtitles. Among other things, I learned not to glue my eyes to the bottom of the screen. I learned to free my focus, not to let that unrelenting crawl of English words distract me from the main point of a film. I also learned something about comedy. What I initially took for a serious art film was really a parody of the genre. The sly allusions to Bergman's celebrated imagery—the nostalgic road trip from *Wild Strawberries* (*Smultronstället*, 1957), the shrouded figure of death from *The Seventh Seal* (*Det sjunde inseglet*, 1957), the symbolic close-ups of nature—were all clues.

Understanding when a movie is a parody depends, of course, on one's familiarity with the target texts. The more movies I watched, the more alert I became to matters of cinematic style and intertextuality—those conversations that movies seem to carry on among themselves. But even if I had never seen a Bergman film before, or one like it, I might have picked up on other clues. One of these was the audience itself. People broke out laughing once they understood the joke. They became part of the in-crowd. Later, I began to pay attention to how jokes work. Like most jokes, *The Dove* had a setup and a reversal. The subtitles, the film's imagery and style, the theater itself had all set us up for some Swedish auteur cinema. The punchline undercut this expectation. For me, this was when the dove's droppings landed on the windshield, bringing any highbrow pretensions down to Earth. Jokes also have a social function. Those who laugh form of a kind of club; they are all in on the joke. In this case, the club was a temporary gathering of spectators with a shared interest in art-house movies. But in-groups can be broader and more lasting, like those who enjoy certain forms of ethnic humor or like members of a nation who share a common history and culture.

Humor, then, can be a ticket of admission, a key to access, a means for understanding other people, other groups. Writing this book has taught me how to laugh along with audiences from France and Italy, from China, Argentina, and Burkina Faso. Meanwhile, I have seen how many of my students, by meaningfully engaging with the world's great store of movie comedies, have become part of a growing international community.

To be sure, there are barriers to crossing borders. Some forms of humor stubbornly resist translation into other languages or fail to bridge cultural divides. One of my goals is to provide readers with the kind of knowledge that will help them understand what makes people laugh in different regions of the world. Even when we don't find the same things funny, we can learn something about the histories, lifestyles, and beliefs of others by studying the boundary lines of laughter. At the same time, I am mindful of the words of E. B. White, who warned that analyzing humor is much like dissecting a frog: Few people are interested and the frog dies. My hope is that you, dear reader, will not be left like those viewers in the Manhattan theater who took the whole film seriously and, straining to read the subtitles, never got to laugh. If I have done my job, you won't be left clueless in the dark with a dead frog.

Acknowledgments

I wish to express my deep appreciation to two special individuals. David Desser, renowned scholar and professor emeritus of cinema studies at the University of Illinois, understood my earliest notions for this book and helped to shape them into something more substantial through his unerring insight and wide-ranging knowledge of so many fields. Norman Hirschy, senior editor at Oxford University Press, saw promise in the fledgling manuscript and guided me along the winding road to publication with his consummate skill and delightful sense of humor.

Throughout the process of writing and revising, I have relied on the expertise of many distinguished faculty and researchers. I am especially grateful to the following for their professional judgment and collegial goodwill:

Dudley Andrew, Yale University
Salvatore Attardo, Texas A&M University-Commerce
Annie F. Berke, Hollins University
Stephanie Brown, University of Illinois at Urbana
Diane Carson, professor emeritus, Webster University and St. Louis Community College
Alex Clayton, University of Bristol, UK
Patrizia Comello, City University of New York
Maria Corrigan, Concordia University
Ken Feil, Emerson College
Lin Feng, University of Hull, UK
Michael Gott, University of Cincinnati
Maggie Hennefeld, University of Minnesota
Andy Horton, professor emeritus, University of Oklahoma
Daniel Johnson, Union College
Bruce Kawin, professor emeritus, University of Colorado at Boulder
Beck Krefting, Skidmore College
Peter Kunze, University of Texas at Austin
Manouchka Labouba, University of Southern California
Nadia Lie, KU Leuven, Belgium
Raphael Rafael, University of Hawaii at Manoa
Philip Scepanski, Marist College
Deborah Shaw, University of Portsmouth, UK
Robert Stam, New York University
Esi Sutherland-Addy, University of Ghana

Other colleagues, though not specialists in cinema or humor studies, also assisted me with their perceptive comments and moral support. For these contributions, I am indebted to Robert Diyanni, Roslyn Tanner-Evans, Peter Hawkins, Gloria Meisel, Marlene Rubins, Jed Stampleman, and Monique Citron-Stampleman.

Finally, I would to thank the publishing professionals at Oxford University Press and its production partners who worked with me on this project, including, Lauralee Yeary, Norm Hirschy's invaluable Assistant Editor; K. ShanmugaPriya, my graciously efficient project manager; K. Prabhakar, who performed minor miracles with the artwork; Wendy Lee Walker, my ever-vigilant, perceptive copy-editor; and Joyce H. Brusin, who created the index with meticulous care.

About the Companion Website

www.oup.com/us/whentheworldlaughs

Oxford has created a website to accompany *When the World Laughs: Film Comedy East and West*. This website complements the published edition with material that may be updated and expanded from time to time. Readers are encouraged to consult this resource in conjunction with Chapters 6 through 13. The following case studies of individual films, all available online, are indicated in the text with Oxford's symbol ▶.

Shaun of the Dead (UK, 1999)
Welcome to the Sticks/Bienvenue chez les Ch'tis (France, 2008)
Life Is Beautiful/La vita è bella (Italy, 1999)
Ivan Vasilievich Changes Profession/Ivan Vasilyevich menyayet professiyu (Russia, 1973)
Skirt Power/Taafé Fanga (Mali, 1997)
Elling (Norway, 2001)
Wild Tales/Relatos salvajes (Argentina, 2014)
Tampopo/Tanpopo (Japan, 1985)

Introduction

There's a joke about Europeans circulating on the internet and in various other forms:

> In heaven, the cooks are French, the policemen are English, the mechanics are German, the lovers are Italian, and the bankers are Swiss. In hell, the cooks are English, the policemen are German, the mechanics are Italian, the lovers are Swiss,and the bankers are French.

Like many witticisms, this one hinges on stereotypes. It assumes that we hold certain views of national character, and it reverses our expectations, or reshuffles them, for comic effect. It illustrates how all jokes are, in some sense, in-jokes: They work best among those who share a common past and common beliefs. Unpacking the assumptions about food, love, and engineering hidden in this anecdote would tell us volumes about European history and cultural development. At the same time, jokes can be dismissive or exclusionary. We can easily imagine times and places where any joke, including this one, would not seem funny. Humor, then, opens pathways to understanding national identities and our own place in the world.

There are good reasons for paying close attention to the world of movie comedies. Not only is comedy among the most popular cinematic forms for international audiences, it is also one of the most illuminating ways to explore issues of politics, social history, and aesthetics. What do people laugh at in Europe, Africa, or South America? What kinds of humor are universal? What gets lost in translation? Are there culturally specific cinematic styles for telling jokes or staging gags? What can the comic traditions of a nation or a region tell us about its most important values?

Such questions have been raised before, but more often in separate books or scattered essays. There are several illuminating volumes on British, French, Spanish, and Soviet comedy, and a few on humor in Asia, Latin America, and the Middle East, but none that brings together a truly global selection of film comedy within a single conceptual framework. The intent of this book is to deepen and widen the search for answers, not only East and West but also North and South of the equator.

Consider some examples. In Western Europe, the dry, detached qualities of much British humor and the cerebral wit of traditional Gallic comedy highlight certain differences between England and France. In Russia, musical comedy and political satire have served as important outlets or defensive weapons during eras of revolution and repression. In the Far East, centuries of Daoist, Confucian, and Buddhist thought have shaped the social roles of humor, which are now being reshaped by interaction with the West. Through the genre's many forms—from slapstick to parody, from lighthearted comedies of manners to the dark messages of black humor—film comedy registers the changing patterns of local anxieties and transnational trends.

My goal has been to present a work that is both instructive and entertaining, one that respects the profound importance of humor in the world without losing sight of the comic touch. I have also sought to keep alive the salutary benefits of laughter. Movies act like funhouse mirrors, reflecting realities through artful alterations. We laugh at the distorted image of ourselves, perhaps not entirely unaware that the license to laugher is also a corrective lens for our values and the times in which we live. We can learn much about other peoples, and ourselves, by comparing their comic screen reflections to our own. At a moment when nationalism and globalization have become pressing, serious issues, this approach seems timelier than ever.

When the World Laughs is divided into two sections. Section One provides a framework and introduces foundational concepts: tools for exploring the why, what, who, where, when, and how of movie comedy around the world. This section draws on the best studies of humor and applies them across national borders. Section Two focuses on four countries and four regions with strong, significant traditions of film comedy.

Section One comprises five chapters:

- Chapter 1, "Theories of Humor":What can we learn about humor from the works of Aristotle, Bergson, Freud, Confucius, or cognitive research?
- Chapter 2, "Comic Forms":Why does comedy take the form of satire, slapstick, parody, burlesque, or comedy of manners?
- Chapter 3, "Archetypes of Comedy":Why do clowns, tricksters, and comic pairs dominate so much of world comedy?
- Chapter 4, "Comedy, History, and Culture":How has comedy evolved around the globe from earliest times to today?
- Chapter 5, "Technique and Style":How do movies use the tricks of comedy to make us laugh?

Section Two comprises eight chapters:

- Chapter 6, "British Film Comedy":The English reputation for dry, reserved expressions of "humour" is the starting point for an exploration of the subgenres that typify Britain's comic legacy.

- Chapter 7, "French Film Comedy":If English humor tends to be understated and detached, how does the Gallic wit of French film comedies reflect their nation's politics and history?
- Chapter 8, "Italian Film Comedy":From Dante's *Divine Comedy* to the more human forms of *commedia all'italiana*, the varieties of humor in Italian movies follow the fortunes and misfortunes of the Italian people.
- Chapter 9, "Russian Film Comedy":Soviet and Russian cinemas offer unique opportunities to investigate the role of humor as an escape from oppression and an instrument for change.
- Chapter 10, "Film Comedy in Africa":The rich oral traditions of storytelling in sub-Saharan Africa have evolved into cinematic forms, adapting social satire and political humor to the realities of modern life.
- Chapter 11, "Film Comedy in Scandinavia":In the peculiar world of Nordic comedy, "quirky feel good" movies and their darker cousins perpetuate an offbeat brand of humor dating back to the Viking sagas.
- Chapter 12, "Film Comedy in South America":From Brazil's *Hello, Hello, Carnival!* to Argentina's *Wild Tales,* films from south of the US border have both adapted and defied Hollywood conventions for performing memorable comedy.
- Chapter 13, "Film Comedy in East Asia":Informed by centuries of Daoist, Buddhist, Shinto, and Confucian thought as well as the particularities of Eastern languages and customs, film comedy in China, Korea, and Japan offers fascinating new viewpoints for Westerners.

Throughout the book, I have sought to raise and answer fundamental questions about humor in general and cinematic comedy in particular:

- Theory (why?): Why do we laugh?
- Genre and Form (what?): What kinds of comedy (satire, parody, slapstick) are practiced in different parts of the world?
- History (when?): Does humor have a history? Has it evolved over time? What would a chronology of comedy reveal about the changing times?
- Culture (where?): How does comedy reflect its place of origin? To what extent is humor indigenous or universal?
- Archetypes (who?): What kinds of characters do people laugh at? Why do we find certain types funny no matter where we're from?
- Technique (how?): How does humor work? What are the mechanisms of a comic aesthetic?

To illustrate these points, I have made liberal use of screenshots throughout the text and, for convenience, added lists of important films at the end of every chapter in Section Two. I have also expanded the book with supporting material available online. This includes case studies of selected films that I believe to be most relevant for today's students of comedy, cinema, and culture. While any reader may enjoy these deeper forays into individual movies, I hope that they will also serve as instructive examples of close film analysis, applied theory, and further research—all of which, I believe, can lead to a richer film experience. References to these online resources are identified with the website icon ▶. Case studies available online are:

Shaun of the Dead (UK, 1999)
Welcome to the Sticks/Bienvenue chez les Ch'tis (France, 2008)
Life Is Beautiful/La vita è bella (Italy, 1999)
Ivan Vasilievich Changes Profession/Ivan Vasilyevich menyayet professiyu (Russia, 1973)
Skirt Power/Taafé Fanga (Mali, 1997)
Elling (Norway, 2001)
Wild Tales/Relatos salvajes (Argentina, 2014)
Tampopo/Tanpopo (Japan, 1985)

Victor Borge, the celebrated comedian-musician, once described humor as "the shortest difference between two people."[1] In my teaching and my personal life, I have come to appreciate how movie comedy can bring people together through the common bond of laughter. If every social group develops "a joking culture," one that embodies the spirit of its people, then understanding what makes people laugh in different regions of the globe can help us better understand each other. And if there is a "humor mindset," a state of mental and physiological receptivity—as this book amply illustrates—then gaining access to that state through international movie comedies can open us all to alternative ways of knowing and being in the world.

Notes

1. Quoted in Peter McGraw and Joel Warner, *The Humor Code: A Global Search for What Makes Things Funny* (New York: Simon & Schuster, 2014), 221.

SECTION ONE

FRAMEWORKS AND FOUNDATIONS

1
Theories of Humor

We all know that the best way to kill a joke is to explain it. Dr. Samuel Johnson, always a formidable admonisher, warned that "comedy is particularly unpropitious to definers."[1] Yet since ancient times, some of the world's greatest minds have tried to describe what humor is and why we laugh. Philosophers and scholars have offered definitions, explanations, and volumes of scrupulously analyzed evidence to support one theory or another. All this attention speaks to the importance of laughter in our lives. The Russian scholar Mikhail Bakhtin described laughter as "one of the essential forms of truth" during the European Renaissance, when it was given "a deep philosophical meaning."[2] Today's theorists, academic researchers, and neuroscientists continue to confirm the value of humor as a way of knowing and being in the world.

This chapter offers a survey of the best efforts to understand humor: what it is, how it works, and why it is important. We'll be examining the most prominent theories and significant research, applying these ideas and findings to a sampling of film comedies from around the world. While the movie samples will be treated only briefly here, more for illustration than analysis, the concepts introduced in this section will lay the groundwork for the many films discussed more thoroughly in Section Two.

At the center of our survey is a crucial distinction between comedy and tragedy. Those twin masks that still adorn our theaters—one mouth curved upward in a smile, the other twisted downward in a painful grimace (Figure 1.1a)—are a legacy of ancient Greece, but they have implications far beyond classical drama. It has been more common today to speak of tragedy and comedy in broader terms, not just as historical genres but as comprehensive visions of human existence. The tragic vision is serious, idealistic, more attuned to spiritual values than to bodily needs. It favors a traditional hierarchical order that is typically patriarchal and inflexible. Its heroes are driven by strong emotions and by principles like military prowess, bravery, retribution, and stubborn persistence. By contrast, the comic vision is playful, nonauthoritarian, and pragmatic. The comic hero, or anti-hero, has a high tolerance for disorder, is comfortable with ambiguity, can easily disengage from conflicts emotionally. This comic figure embraces bodily appetites, especially for food and sex, and solves problems with cunning rather than courage and brute force. While tragic stories typically end in the individual's demise, comic narratives tend to culminate in social

When the World Laughs. William V. Costanzo, Oxford University Press (2020). Oxford University Press
DOI: 10.1093/oso/9780190924997.001.0001

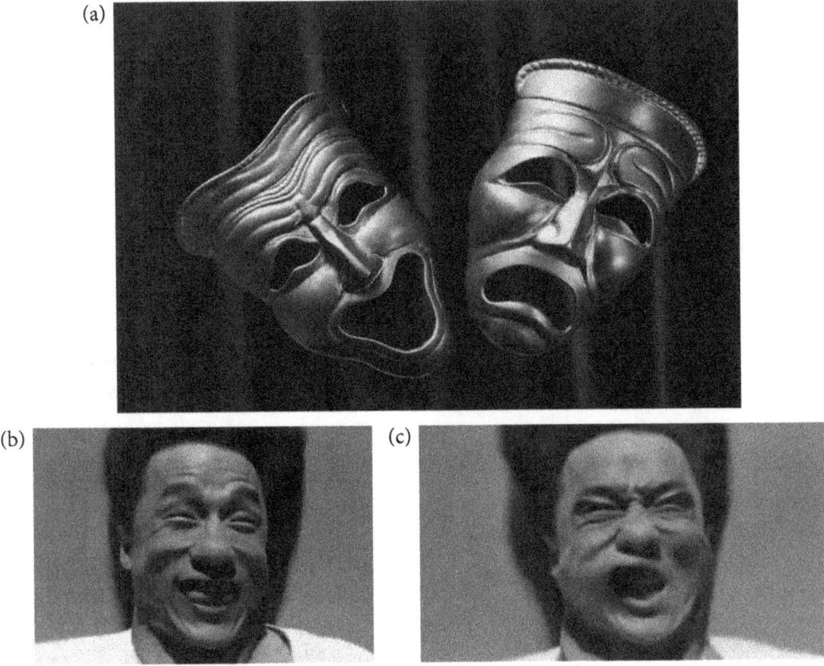

Figure 1.1a The twin masks of classical Greek comedy and tragedy. Courtesy of Oxford University Press. (b) A scene from *Armour of God 2: Operation Condor* (1991). Caught in the gusts of a giant Nazi wind machine, Jackie Chan's distorted face oscillates between the mask of comedy (ours) . . .; (c). . . and tragedy (his).

integration: a crowded scene of friendship, fun, and laughter. It is in such terms that scholars like John Morreall describe a fundamental division in our view of life.[3] Morreall, an American professor of religion, points out that "tragedy and comedy began as religious rituals and, like religions, focus on the problematic side of life."[4] They represent different ways of dealing with our problems. In his analysis of the world's religions, Morreall concludes that Eastern belief systems like Hinduism, Zen Buddhism, and Daoism are closely allied with comedy while the monotheistic creeds of Judaism, Christianity, and Islam are nearer to tragedy.[5] His observations will be particularly useful when we consider the place of humor in Eastern and Western traditions. As we'll see, scientists have also studied the distinction, citing evidence that it reflects a division in human nature itself, that our minds and bodies are wired to respond to outside stimuli in two different ways, through systems of response akin to comic and tragic modes of being. Filmmakers regularly exploit the tension between these two modes, as in the wind tunnel scene from *Armour of God 2: Operation Condor* (*Fei ying gai wak*, 1991), a Hong Kong comedy starring Jackie Chan (Figures 1.1b 1.1c).

For much of human history, tragedy received more critical attention—and respect—than comedy. When Aristotle analyzed these terms in his *Poetics*, around 335 BCE, he had a lot to say about the origins, forms, component elements, and purposes of tragic drama. For him, tragedy was a serious genre for representing human beings in action, "noble actions performed by noble men."[6] Aristotle famously observed that the plight of tragic heroes arouses fear and pity, purging the audience's emotions through *catharsis*. But he gave less attention to comedy, "a representation of men who are morally inferior"—that is, ludicrous in their intellectual and moral defects. If the influential Greek philosopher had much more to say about comedic forms and purposes, those words are lost.

Today, that imbalance is starting to change. Maurice Charney, the editor of a two-volume study of world comedy, notes that Shakespeare produced more comedies than tragedies, speculating that comedy covers a wider range of human (and literary) experience than does tragedy.[7] The thirty-eight essays in Charney's *Comedy: A Geographic and Historical Guide*, each written by a different specialist, offer instances of how seriously humor is being taken in recent times. In 2014, Salvatore Attardo edited an even more ambitious compendium of serious work. His impressive *Encyclopedia of Humor Studies* features over nine hundred pages of individual entries on topics ranging from "absurdist humor" to the history of Chinese *xiangsheng* comedy.[8] These collections demonstrate how many different fields are engaged in the study of humor. Cinema and literary scholars, cultural theorists and philosophers, sociologists and historians, cognitive psychologists and neuroscientists—an army of academics are contributing their knowledge and various perspectives to make this a truly interdisciplinary investigation.

Filmmakers around the world have also responded to Aristotle's oversight. Reading the *Poetics* in his native land of Cameroon, the African filmmaker Jean-Pierre Bekolo felt that "something was missing."[9] He moved to fill the gap with *Aristotle's Plot* (*Le complot d'Aristote*, 1996) and a string of brash, rollicking films that challenged Aristotle's thesis and opened the screens of African cinema to new perspectives in comedy. Hong Kong director Stephen Chow did something similar for Chinese audiences, bringing China's rich comic traditions to the screen with a distinctly modern, cinematic twist. In Europe, the Americas, and nearly everywhere else, movie comedies consistently top the charts as the most popular of all film genres.

With this mounting consensus on the importance of comedy come new questions, issues, and some lively debates. How well do conventional views of humor hold up under scrutiny? Do comedies by definition have a happy ending; does the comic hero always find a peaceful resolution and a comfortable place within society? Are ideological biases built into the genre? Is comedy inherently subversive and tragedy essentially conservative? Are there tragedies that challenge the status quo, comedies that support it?

And what about the darker comedies like *Dr. Strangelove* (1964) and *Catch-22* (1970), the jokes in *Ridicule* (1996) and *Life Is Beautiful* (*La vita è bella*, 1997), or the "gallows humor" so prevalent in Nordic comedies? In *Ridicule*, the witty repartee of King Louis's court is aggressive and demeaning, intended to gain social advantage in a cruel game of one-upmanship. Are we laughing with the characters, at them, or not at all? The first half of *Life Is Beautiful* abounds in entertaining antics and easy laughs, but the second half takes place in a Nazi concentration camp, where the protagonist's efforts to keep his son amused—diversions from the camp's grim realities—take on a stark, ironic tone. The jokes keep coming, but what is their intent and their ultimate effect on us? (▶ See Case Study for Chapter 8: *Life Is Beautiful* on the website.)

We'll be considering these questions and more in the context of world cinema. Although the many insights of humor studies have rarely been applied directly and systematically to movie comedies across transnational lines, we'll see how the two fields—recent humor research and international film comedy—can shed new light on each other.

Issues in Comedy and Humor

One issue that keeps coming up is the emotional ambivalence of humor. There seems to be a wicked spirit at the heart of certain comedies, a touch of malevolence in the laughter they provoke. The stinging pleasure of slapstick, the bittersweet revenge of witty repartee, the snowball that knocks the tycoon's top hat off his head may bring subtle smiles or belly laughs, but their delights come at a price. Nobody cares much when the tyrant and the hypocrite get their comeuppance. But watching the little guy get hammered, whacked, and repeatedly knocked down like a standup punching bag can make us wince, even if he keeps popping up for more. How many times can we watch Bud Abbot or Stan Laurel take it on the chin without feeling some sympathy or pity? Watch the swordfight in *Monty Python and the Holy Grail* (1975) when Arthur faces off with the Black Knight. Arthur lops off the knight's left arm, then his right one, then both legs, but the limbless man won't quit. "Come back here and take what's coming to you," he challenges. "I'll bite your legs off!" Or watch Jens Lien's *The Bothersome Man* (*Den brysomme mannen*, 2006), in which the sad-sack hero wants so desperately to fit in with his Norwegian peers. The indignities he suffers range from a missing finger, chopped off by the office paper trimmer, to an encounter with an oncoming train that runs over him and drags him along the tracks. Such scenes can be more discomforting than entertaining. All too often, comedy tests the limits of social correctness and audience response. Why do some of us laugh at ethnic stereotypes or dead baby jokes?

Humiliating laughter, the kind that villains discharge when torturing their victims, can be a barometer of power. The warrior triumphs over the foe with derisive mirth. The courtier insults his rival with the gleeful barb of ridicule. Yet if their smiles conceal a smirk, the reverse also may be true. Our capacity to laugh at the misfortunes of others, our *Schadenfreude*, is often mixed with our human aptitude for empathy. That could be us lying sprawled on the floor near the banana peel. But for the grace of circumstance or good luck, the butt of the joke could well be us. Are we always somehow laughing at a version of ourselves?

For Mel Brooks, whether we wince or laugh is a matter of personal involvement: "Tragedy is when *I* cut my finger," he once quipped. "Comedy is when *you* walk into an open sewer and die." But it can also be a matter of politics. Laughter and power make uncomfortable bedfellows. In the topsy-turvy realm of Carnival, for example, king and jester briefly exchange roles. The reigning monarch is unseated while the fool becomes king for a day: a license for hilarity and freedom, for rowdy communal mirth. Scholars like Jean Paul Simon believe that comedy is essentially seditious. Simon argues that comedy disrupts order, codes, and institutions. It shakes things up, opening the way for alternatives.[10] But does humor really undermine the status quo? This has been a big issue in Africa, where political and social change has been one of cinema's highest aspirations. Férid Boughédir, the Tunisian filmmaker and scholar, argues that comedies are intrinsically conservative.[11] In his view, comedy is a poor instrument for achieving real change because it blames individuals, not institutions, for serious problems, diverting attention and energy from the real, systemic causes of these problems. He faults comic films like Bekolo's for relieving pent-up frustration that could otherwise be channeled into action. This dispute over the political role of comedy runs through the whole history of film theory and practice. In 1930s Italy, Mussolini favored sunny *telefoni bianchi* films, so called because they featured white telephones and other symbols of the "good life" along with the conservative family values, respect for authority, and hierarchical social structure that supported fascist ideology. In 1930s Russia, Stalin promoted a cycle of bright musical comedies like *Jolly Fellows* (*Vesyolye rebyata*, 1934) and *Tractor Drivers* (*Traktorii*, 1939), which set workers to singing on the Soviet collective farms.

This pairing of comedy and song is nothing new. Some dictionaries trace the etymology of comedy back to the Greek term *komos*, a kind of revel. In Greek mythology, Comus is the joyful god of merriment, fond of wine and anarchy. Scholars like Mikhail Bakhtin who have studied this phenomenon link the bodily excesses of Rabelais, Shakespeare's Falstaff, and fraternity humor to ancient fertility rites and medieval Carnival. We can see this spirit of licentiousness in Ingmar Bergman's *Smiles of a Summer Night* (*Sommarnattens leende*, 1955), set during the summer solstice. Bergman, normally a sober-minded director of cinematic drama, allowed himself this foray into lighthearted comedy early in his career. In doing so, he was connecting with a Swedish tradition of *folklustpel*, or folk comedy, which itself derives from seasonal fertility rites.

Comic release and indulgence can entertain us with amusing romps, as they do in sophisticated bedroom farce or scatological teen movies. These forms are popular around the world. In Jean Renoir's *Boudu Saved From Drowning* (*Boudu sauvé des eaux*, 1932), a middle-class merchant saves a homeless man from suicide and takes him home. The shaggy vagrant's natural appetite for food and women wreaks havoc in the household—to the delight of most French moviegoers. In Mikkel Norgaard's *Klown* (*Klovn—The Movie*, 2010), two mismatched buddies set out on an adventure in search of freedom, sex, and booze, breaking every taboo they can. As crude and silly as its comedy may seem to some, *Klown* broke box-office records in Denmark and launched a popular television series. But what happens when the impulse to let loose, what Sigmund Freud might call *libido*, is pushed to the limit? In the French-Italian film *La grande bouffe* (*La grande abbuffata* in Italian, 1973), a group of friends meets in a villa to indulge their appetites. The four men begin binging on oysters, gourmet meals, fine wine, and women. The orgy continues through the weekend until they literally stuff themselves to death. *La grande bouffe* won an award at Cannes and was advertised in theaters as a comedy, but is it really funny?

The term *humor* has a notably different history and flavor from comedy. If we push back to that word's origin, we find its derivation in a Latin word meaning "moisture." The Greek physician Hippocrates (460–370 BCE) developed an elaborate theory of physiology based on the idea that human temperament depends on the distribution of a person's bodily fluids, or humors. An excess of bile produces a bilious disposition; too much phlegm makes one phlegmatic. By the Renaissance, humor came to be associated with an imbalance of character. The English playwright Ben Jonson wrote a pair of stage comedies based on this concept, *Every Man in His Humour* (1598) and *Every Man Out of His Humour* (1599). So historically, some humor is associated with physical and emotional equilibrium, all things in moderation, nearly the opposite of comedy's indulgence in excess. As we'll see, humor plays a similar role in some Eastern thought. East Asian languages have adapted the English word (*youmou* in Chinese, *yumou* in Japanese, *yumeo* in Korean), but China, Japan, and Korea have long traditions of comedy, and the European notion of balanced humors has a counterpart in Chinese medicine, where laughter helps to maintain a healthy equilibrium by unblocking the flow of *qi*, the body's vital spirit.

By the nineteenth century, a "sense of humor" meant seeing the funny side of things. A well-bred Englishman who possessed a healthy, self-deprecating form of humor (like Bertie Wooster, P. G. Wodehouse's comic creation in the popular book and television series) could laugh benignly at himself, restoring his composure and our confidence in the social order. The word *comedy* has similarly changed over time. For the most part, comedy identifies a genre, a way to classify artistic compositions. In ancient literature, it was used for plays written in a lighthearted, often preposterous style, like the Greek satires of Aristophanes or the Roman comedies of Plautus. In medieval times, it referred to works with a happy ending, like *The Divine Comedy*, Dante Alighieri's guided tour of the afterlife, which begins in hell, treks through purgatory, and ends favorably in paradise. Shakespeare's plays were divided into histories (based on real people and events), tragedies (with fictional characters headed for a fall), and comedies. This last category included entertaining fictions ranging in tone from farcical to romantic to emotionally mixed, but all ended more or less happily, typically with a lively marriage scene. Today, comedy can include movies, television shows, or live performances. The term covers parody and farce, jokes and witty sayings, almost anything that people find amusing.[12] Comedy can also point more broadly to a way of looking at the world, a comic perspective, a comic state of mind. Most of the theories we'll encounter in this chapter attempt to analyze these wider meanings of the term. But humor and comedy are frequently used interchangeably, even in scholarly work, a practice that we'll follow often in this book.

At the core of any global view of comedy is the issue of portability. To what extent is humor local or universal? What kinds of jokes, comic figures, or comic situations are able to cross frontiers and make people laugh in other regions of the world? What kinds defy translation? Roger Ebert, reviewing the Japanese comedy *Tampopo* (*Tanpopo*, 1985), wrote: "The humor that travels best, I sometimes think, is not 'universal' humor at all, but humor that grows so specifically out of one culture that it reaches other cultures almost by seeming to ignore them."[13] Exploring the geographic boundaries of humor can reveal much about national identity, about regional histories and cultures. Can it also clarify what makes people human at heart, united by global principles of laughter? To help us with this question, we turn to the world's most salient theories of humor, East and West.

Theorizing Laughter in the West: Superiority, Incongruity, Relief

Throughout the history of Western thought, philosophers have had much to say on the topic of comedy.

The most prominent Greek philosophers, who elevated reason above emotion, were generally suspicious of laughter because it springs from the body rather than the mind. Even when humor appears in the guise of wit, it runs the risk of being mocking and mean-spirited instead of entertaining for the common good. Aristotle, in addition to his analysis of comic plays in *The Poetics*, considered the social value of humor in his *Nicomachean Ethics*. He conceded that humorous amusement has a proper place in daily life but cautioned that obscene language and scornful wit are the province of vulgar boors and buffoons rather than of cultivated men.[14] This wary view is even more pronounced in Plato, who advised that people of importance should avoid laughter because "it almost always provokes a violent reaction."[15] Plato's main objection seems to focus on malicious laughter, which he found morally objectionable. His opposition extended even to the point of advocating censorship: "No composer of comedy . . . shall be permitted to hold any citizen up to laughter, by word or gesture, with passion or otherwise."[16]

This generally negative assessment continued in Europe through medieval times. Christian thinkers found little humor in the Bible. When God does laugh, he looks down on the kings of the earth and "laughs them to scorn."[17] Nor do the New Testament apostles show much inclination to tell jokes, although some of Christ's teachings take the form of witty parables. Later philosophers, notably René Descartes and Thomas Hobbes, further strengthened the case against comedy. In his study of emotions, Descartes noted that the joy of most laughter is mixed with hatred, an expression of disdain for people with disfigurements or minor faults.[18] Hobbes, who considered humans to be naturally selfish and competitive, observed how people "maketh those grimaces called laughter" when they feel "a Sudden Glory" at the expense of others.[19]

What Hobbes called "glory" has been linked to like-minded conceptions of humor reaching back to Plato and now called "superiority theory." This explanation holds that laughter expresses a sense of power over others. We laugh at the other guy's expense to feel better about ourselves. Perhaps that's why the fool, or dupe, is a perennial figure of fun in Russian folklore, literature, and movies. Much of the humor in Gogol's stories, from *Dead Souls* to *Nose*, comes from watching clever men exploit the credulity of others, a formula kept alive in film comedies like *Happiness* (*Schastye*, 1934) and *The Garage* (*Garazh*, 1980). It's a pattern that we also see in Italy, Africa, and China, where a lower-class conman usually outsmarts someone higher on the social ladder. But not always. In Lars von Trier's *The Boss of It All* (*Direktoren for det hele*, 2006), it's the boss who cons his underpaid employees. While we may feel superior to all the characters who are made into fools, by the film's end we're left wondering if we ourselves have been conned, if the director is laughing at us behind our backs (Figure 1.2).

Superiority theory withstood the test of time for centuries, but it began to weaken when an Irish philosopher challenged Hobbes's account. Writing in 1750, Francis Hutcheson gave examples of humor that had little or nothing to do with feelings of egoistic "glory." Why, he asked, do we laugh at quirky figures of speech that yoke together images of grandeur with images of meanness and profanity? Why is it funny to compare the sun to a lobster?[20] Immanuel Kant, Arthur

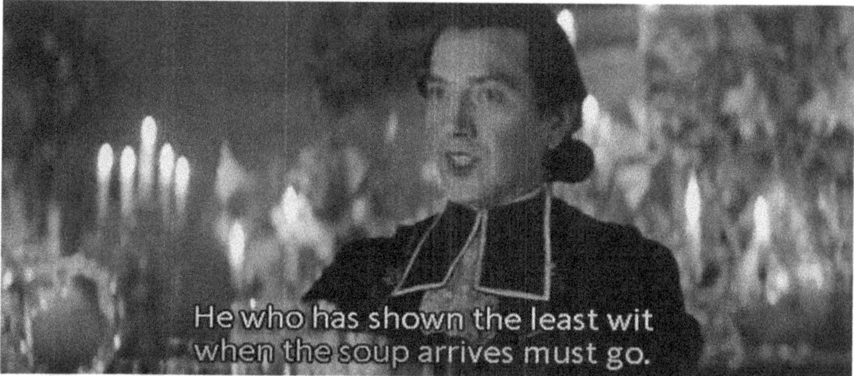

Figure 1.2 Superiority theory in film. The contest of wits in *Ridicule* (1996).

Schopenhauer, and Søren Kierkegaard elaborated on this idea, which came to be known as "incongruity theory." Their basic insight is that we laugh when something seems incongruous, when our usual expectations are undercut by a surprising turn in a new direction. Jokes and witty wordplay often work this way. Kant gives an example:

> The heir of a rich relative wished to arrange for an imposing funeral, but he lamented that he could not properly succeed; "for" (said he) "the more money I give my mourners to look sad, the more cheerful they look!"

"The joke amuses us by evoking, shifting, and dissipating our thoughts," notes Kant, concluding that "laughter is an affection arising from the sudden transformation of a strained expectation into nothing."[21]

Schopenhauer argues that the pleasure from this kind of humor springs from a "victory of perception over thought." It amounts to a kind of verbal sabotage. We enjoy the experience of undermining "the strict, troublesome governess of reason."[22] Kierkegaard finds something existential in the disparity between expectation and experience, which he calls "contradiction." "Humor," he asserts, "is the last stage of existential awareness before faith."[23] Kierkegaard goes on to reinterpret the Bible as a comic text. "The person with a religious view of life is likely to cultivate humor," he says, "and Christianity is the most humorous view of life in world history.[24] Thus armed with contradiction theory, seventeenth- and eighteenth-century philosophers overturned the prevailing Greek and Christian views of comedy, restoring laughter to a place of serious attention and respect.

Once aware of comic incongruity, we find it everywhere. In film comedies, the operative principle may take a verbal, conceptual, or situational form. Anyone who knows a little English can appreciate the wordplay in a British caper like

Carry on Spying (1964), with its goofy names (Agents Daphne Honeybutt and Harold Crump) and acronyms (STENCH for the preposterously overblown Society for the Total Extinction of Non-Conforming Humans). Some French is required to find humor in the ironic names of *Dancing in the Dust* (*Bal Poussière*, 1988), where a hunchback is known as Beau Goss (beautiful kid) and an arrogant thug calls himself Demi-Dieu (half-god). Puns, of course, are notoriously difficult to translate without losing the pleasure of instant gratification, although a clever subtitle artist may recreate that pleasure in the target language. In *The Visitors* (*Les visiteurs*, 1993), the character of Jacquouille (a coarse portmanteau of Jacques and "balls" in French) appears as Jacquasse in the English version.

Translation is usually no problem when disjunction is conceptual, as in the aphorisms of Oscar Wilde:

> Always forgive your enemies; nothing annoys them so much.
> Some cause happiness wherever they go; others whenever they go.
> When I was young, I thought that money was the most important thing in life; now that I am old, I know that it is.

Wilde's wit relies on that shift in conceptual continuity that Kant describes, in Schopenhauer's "triumph of perception over thought." Our delight comes when the sentence fails to end as we expected. The pious tone of "forgive your enemies" is delightfully undercut by an irreverent promise of annoyance. The usual platitudes about money and happiness turn into cynical jokes. We laugh at the moral twist and recover our balance. Of course, anyone who knows Wilde well soon comes to expect the unexpected, and this suggests a lesson about the volatility of incongruous humor. What one generation finds laughably clever can become stale and leaden to another: "Take my wife . . . please."

A good deal of comic dissonance in movies is situational. Time-travel comedies rely on anachronism for many of their gags. In *Ivan Vasilievich Changes Profession* (*Ivan Vasilyevich menyayet professiyu*, 1973), a modern Russian named Ivan finds himself back in the days of Ivan the Terrible, thanks to a malfunctioning time machine. Not only does Vasilievich share the tsar's first name, he also looks like him (and is played by the same actor). This leads to a series of hilarious misunderstandings in the sixteenth-century court, where Ivan's references to Hitler and Marlboro cigarettes are played for laughs. Meanwhile, the real tsar is transported to 1970s Russia, where he's taken for a madman. (▶ See "Case Study for Chapter 9: *Ivan Vasilievich Changes Profession*" on the website.) In *The Visitors*, a medieval French lord and his servant exchange places with their Parisian descendants from the 1990s. In a riotous bathroom scene, they mistake the toilet for a drinking fountain and dump a year's worth of expensive perfume in the tub, where they proceed to bathe fully dressed—nobleman first, of course (Figure 1.3). The contrast in eras provides a lot of slapstick humor, but it also offers food for thought about progress and privilege.

The possibilities of ludicrous incongruity have generated a whole sub-genre of fish-out-of-water comedies. *Bread and Chocolate* (*Pane e cioccolata*, 1974) begins with a bucolic moment. A guest worker from southern Italy is enjoying his day off in a Swiss park. The locals have spread their bounteous picnic lunches on the lawn and are listening to the peaceful strains of a string quartet. He's leaning against a tree about to bite into his sandwich. When he does, the crunch of crusty bread interrupts the public peace. The musicians stop abruptly and everyone looks at him in disdainful disapproval. So begins the hapless exploits of an Italian immigrant in a land of superior beings.

Often enough, the incongruity is personal, a matter of mismatched roommates and incompatible traveling companions. The spectacle of two people trying to live together—an obsessively neat Felix Ungar (Jack Lemmon) with an exuberantly untidy Oscar Madison (Walter Matthau) in *The Odd Couple* (1968)—has been repeated, and enjoyed, in Norway (*Elling*, 2001), England (*The Trip*, 2010), France (*The Intouchables*, 2011), India (*Singh Is Kinng*, 2008), China (*Lost in Thailand*, 2013), and nearly everywhere in between. Watching these comic duos go through their routines has entertained audiences since the days of vaudeville, which is where many of cinema's first paired comedians got their start. Abbott and Costello, Burns and Allen, Laurel and Hardy: All made the transition from stage to screen. Later, some crossed the line from simple slapstick to surrealist drama.

Exactly when mismatched tramps in bowler hats began to act like existential antiheroes is difficult to say, but by 1952 Samuel Beckett was pushing vaudeville routines into metaphysical realms. In some productions of his stage play *Waiting*

Figure 1.3 Incongruity theory at work. A medieval knight bathes the modern way in *The Visitors* (1993).

for Godot, the characters of Vladimir and Estragon behave and even look like Laurel and Hardy, but beneath the surface comedy is a dark vision of life's ultimate futility. They trade hats repeatedly, ramble on about ill-fitting boots, complain of boredom, dance, and decide to hang themselves more than once, but never quite succeed. Beckett labeled his play "a tragicomedy in two acts," and some audiences indeed did not know whether to laugh or cry; some did both. Critic Martin Esslin coined the term "theater of the absurd" to capture the peculiar tone of Beckett's work, its radical focus on the meaninglessness of existence. His characters perform much like circus clowns or puppets going through the motions of ordinary life. Their behavior would seem funny if it didn't also seem profoundly sad. Esslin noted that the word "absurd" originally meant "out of tune," eventually broadening to mean illogical, out of sync with reason.[25] Esslin applied his term to playwrights like Eugene Ionesco, Fernando Arabal, and Edward Albee. But while the theater of the absurd is a distinctly post–World War II phenomenon, existentially absurdist humor continues to be found in a range of movie comedies where bizarre juxtapositions, irrational behavior, and verbal non sequiturs express a fundamental contradiction at the heart of being human.

There is something of this quality in Roy Andersson's *Songs from the Second Floor* (*Sanger fran andra vaninger*, 2000). The protagonist wanders through a nameless city where inexplicable things take place as a matter of course. A stage musician saws through a screaming man's body while the audience applauds, an immigrant is kicked and stabbed in the street while someone blithely passes by on roller skates, a parade of groaning flagellants crosses heavy traffic on the highway. Lina Wertmüller's comedies often strike a similar tone. In her *Love and Anarchy* (*Film d'amore e d'anarchia*, 1972), a hapless Italian peasant stumbles into a plot to kill Mussolini. In *Seven Beauties* (*Pasqualino Settebellezze*, 1976), a smug ladies' man becomes the plaything of a sexually voracious female warden in a German concentration camp. Wertmüller pushes people's appetites for food, sex, and power to their absurd extremes, *reductio ad absurdum*, while we're tugged back and forth between laughter and lament. Such films share a comic consciousness with Franz Kafka and Søren Kierkegaard, who envisioned life as a ludicrous struggle between freedom and necessity, between a finite body and an infinite soul.[26] With them, absurdist comedy takes on the dimensions of a cosmic joke.

While incongruity theory led philosophers and theologians to explore the existential limits of absurdity, another approach to humor developed along different lines. Originally based on principles of hydraulic pressure, it has been called "relief theory." As early as 1709, Lord Shaftesbury (the first to use the word *humour* as a synonym for funniness) likened humor to a relief valve. In "An Essay on the Freedom of Wit and Humour," he proposed that animal spirits pent up in the body are released through laughter, easing pressure on the nerves.[27] This idea was later refined by men like Herbert Spencer and Sigmund Freud, whose understanding of human physiology was closer to our own. Spencer, who coined the term "survival of the fittest," wondered if humor has survival value. In his essay "On the Physiology of Laughter" (1911), he traced the physical pathways of emotions, which he believed function in the body as flows of nervous energy. In his analogy, emotions drive our muscles much like water vapor in a steam engine moves the pistons. If anger triggers aggressive action and fear activates the muscles associated with flight, he asked, what movement does laughter stimulate? Spencer concluded that unlike anger or fear, the anxiety that a joke might provoke has no practical object; it merely releases nervous energy through laughter.[28] Freud took this concept further. In his psychoanalytical account of laughter, an individual's hostile impulses (associated with the id) are blocked by societal taboos (internalized as the superego). One way that the individual psyche can mediate between these two opposing forces is through jokes, which disguise obscene or aggressive impulses as playful, seemingly meaningless expressions. Jokes allow us to give vent to primitive pleasures while circumventing censorship.[29]

Freud's focus on aggression and suppression brings to mind the many comedies that dance on the precarious brink of bigotry. Archie Bunker and his British cousin Alf Garnett could serve as case studies in relief theory. Archie Bunker's openly sexist, racist diatribes made *All in the Family* one of the most popular American sitcoms in the 1970s. Alf Garnett was renowned for his anti-foreign rants on the BBC and in the movie follow-up, *Death Us Do Part* (1969). Such unsavory characters have pushed the limits of political correctness throughout the world of comedy. While Archie and Alf gave vent to their hostile prejudices week after week, Uuno Turkhapuro was doing much the same in Finland. Crude in speech, behavior, and appearance (his name translates as Numbskull Emptybrook), thriving on junk food, beer, and chauvinistic sentiments, he starred in nineteen feature films from 1973 to 2004. Although Finnish culture critics regarded his popularity as a national embarrassment, Uuno continued to draw a faithful following, appearing in five of the ten most popular Finnish films since the 1960s.[30] Sitcoms and movie cycles thrive on characters that never change. Most one-of-a-kind movies, though, require some sort of resolution. Relief-valve comedies tend to end in social equilibrium. The protagonist gets to vent frustrations and act out antisocial fantasies, but once the hostile energy has been released, normalcy is restored. In *The Mad Adventures of Rabbi Jacob* (*Les aventures de Rabbi Jacob*, 1973), a blatantly anti-Semitic Frenchman must flee for his life from a band of terrorists. He manages to escape by disguising himself as a rabbi and learns a lesson in tolerance when a crowd of Jewish townsfolk mistake him for one of their own (Figure 1.4). In this way, comedic happy endings can work much like the catharsis in an Aristotelean tragedy, cleansing the audience of negative emotions.

Figure 1.4 Relief theory in action. An anti-Semitic Frenchman dances in a rabbi's shoes in *The Mad Adventures of Rabbi Jacob* (1973).

Thinking about Humor in the East

Plato and Aristotle, Hobbes and Descartes, Kant and Kierkegaard, Spencer and Freud: The list of Western thinkers who have theorized about humor is impressive. If there is a comparable body of serious thought about comedy in the East, it is less well known to English-speaking scholars. Those who have studied humor in South Asia, the Middle East, and the Far East have found fewer analytic texts. A sampling of these, and the works they draw from, suggest some similarities to European views and a few striking differences.

One of the few book-length studies of Middle Eastern movie comedies views them mostly in terms of European theoretical perspectives. While acknowledging a long tradition of humor (*fukaha*) in Arab literature, Gayatri Devi and Najat Rahman note that few critical studies of this humor have yet been translated into English.[31] One of the earliest comedic texts in Arabic is the *Kitab al-Bakhala* (*Book of the Misers*) by Al-Jahiz (776–869). Al-Jahiz satirizes those who turn the virtue of thrift into vice by hoarding wealth. One man diverts water from the ablutions fountain at the local mosque to his home, arguing that there are no prohibitions of this practice in the Quran. Another man makes a broth out of low-priced dates to cure his cough and discovers that it also suppresses his appetite, so he serves the broth to his family to save on food. Finally, he dries the dates and resells them in the market. Devi and Rahman see this brand of humor as a form of comic reversal (turning frugality into greed, good into bad) and find modern examples in satirical movies like Elia Suleman's *Divine Intervention* (2002).[32] Suleman's film is full of bizarre moments that reflect the absurdities of daily life for Palestinians in Israel. While the narrator is on the way to meet his girlfriend, who lives on the other side of a military checkpoint, he tosses an apricot out the window. The pit lands on a tank and destroys it. A foreign tourist asks a policeman for directions. Unable to help her, the Israeli cop brings out a blindfolded, handcuffed woman from his van to provide the requested information. Suleman's string of running sight gags has been compared to the comedies of Luis Buñiel and Jacques Tati, who also undercut the audience's expectations to emphasize the senselessness of modern life.

A recent Lebanese comedy, *Where Do We Go Now* (*Et maintenant on va où?*, 2011), uses humor to highlight the absurdities of war. Nadine Labaki sets her film in an unnamed village where Christians and Muslims live side by side in peace until the mayor installs a television in the community square. Everyone watches open-mouthed as a curvaceous commentator forecasts the weather and a romantic movie shows a couple in an intimate embrace. Then someone asks to change the channel; he wants to watch the news. Suddenly, the village starts to focus on the religious battles raging around them, and the men begin to take sides, Muslims against Christians. The women try to divert their men from fighting through a series of ingenious tactics that include wild parties, hashish desserts, and Ukrainian showgirls, all sources of broad comedy (Figure 1.5). But the film takes some surprising twists and turns, courting romance at one point, inserting a song-and-dance routine at another, veering toward dark satire. This mixture of genres and tones unsettled several critics, but Labaki had her reasons—and her precedents. A clear line can be traced from Labaki's film back to Aristophanes' *Lysistrata* (411 BCE) and the origins of Western comedy.

Figure 1.5 Lebanese women hatch a plan to pacify their warring menfolk in *Where Do We Go Now?* (2011).

Another tradition informs the role of comedy further east, in India. The seminal text of Indian aesthetics is the *Natyasastra*, a second-century treatise on theater and music attributed to Bharata Muni. Bharata used the metaphor of flavor (*rasa*) to explain artistic creativity. Just as a dish may be seasoned with spices that appeal to a variety of tastes, a play or a musical composition may arouse various emotions at different moments. Any work of art draws on a wide-ranging emotional palette, including fear, pity, eroticism, and humor. As Lee Siegel explains, this last emotion is regarded as a kind of seasoning: "The comic rasa is experienced when something tastes funny, when representations of the emotions of love or courage or sadness fail to produce the corresponding and expected amorous, heroic, or tragic rasas." "In the Indian context," Siegel continues, "comedy may be simply defined as that artistic form, regardless of genre, which has as its dominant aesthetic sentiment the theoretically codified and culturally conventionalized comic flavor, the *hasya-rasa*."[33] *The Natyasastra* lists trickery, tickling, excessive desire, lying prattle, inappropriate clothing, and deformities as possible causes of laughter. Audiences still laugh at these things in Indian movies today.

From the beginning, then, Western distinctions don't seem to apply. Those Greek masks representing comedy and tragedy as separate forms of theater fail to capture the way Indian plays by Bhasa (fourth century) or Sankara (seventh century) blended the tastes of sadness and hilarity. Nor does it make much sense to classify Bollywood films as melodramas, musicals, thrillers, mysteries, or comedies. Nearly every Bollywood production includes music and dance; moments of romance, excitement, and mirth; and an invariably happy ending. That's why reviewers speak of "masala," invoking the South Asian word for a mixture of spices, to describe films from India. Indian cinema has its genres, its categories, but these have more to do with subject matter (mythologicals, devotionals, Indian bandits, lost-and-found siblings) than with any dominant emotion.

Sholay (1975) features one of the funniest moments in Indian cinema, a side-splitting prison scene in which the warden, dressed like a British officer with a Hitler moustache, falls all over himself while trying to project an aura of authority. *Sholay* is a *dacoit* film, about Indian bandits. In addition to comedy, it also contains moments of unspeakable cruelty, brutal revenge, joyful celebration, somber spirituality, amorous play, and, of course, plenty of dancing and singing. In *Amar Akbar Anthony* (1977), a film about three siblings separated at birth, almost all of these emotional registers are activated in a single scene. The three brothers, now adults, have come to a wedding disguised as a caterer, a musician, and a priest. At first, they perform their phony roles in uproariously slapstick fashion. Amar (raised as a Hindu) treats the guests to a goofy vaudeville routine. Akbar (raised as a Muslim) entertains them as an overloaded one-man band. Anthony (raised as a Christian) officiates in the rites of matrimony with mock solemnity. But when their true intention becomes clear—to stop the wedding—the film runs through a gamut of emotional zigzags in a few frantic minutes: the melodrama of an unhappy bride, the outrage of a jealous husband, a profession of true love between secret admirers, and a lively round of hand-to-hand combat, all ending favorably for the brothers and their would-be brides. It's a generous serving of masala.

In addition to the lay literature, humor abounds in Indian religious texts and practices. Koenrad Elst finds lighthearted passages in the ancient Vedas, in the foundational *Mahabharata* epic, and in the behavior of the Hindu gods themselves. He notes that the deity Ganesha, depicted as a pot-bellied elephant riding on a rat, is known as "the laughing god." After remarking on the popularity of Brahmin jokes in India, Elst observes that "mockery and worship go together."[34] Some of this playful Hindu attitude can be seen in Hindi films today. In *Sholay*, a religious shrine becomes the site of an amusing exchange between young Jai and his girlfriend, who hides behind the statue of a deity pretending to be the voice of God. In contrast to Hinduism, Buddhism seems to take a more restrained view of comedy. In his book *Real Buddhas Don't Laugh*, Michel Clasquin quotes from the *Vinaya*, a code of conduct for Buddhist monks and nuns: "One should not go amidst the houses with loud laughter."[35] Yet Zen Buddhism, an offshoot that originated in China around the sixth century, uses paradox, puns, and riddles that defy logic to teach lessons about the absurdity of the human predicament.[36] In this respect, the non sequiturs of Zen koans, which may sound like contradictions (the sound of one hand clapping) or knock-knock jokes (Question: What is Buddha? Answer: Three pounds of flax), bring incongruity theory into a spiritual realm.

Before Buddhism arrived in the Far East, the two dominant systems of belief in China were Daoism and Confucianism. Essentially concerned with social conduct, Confucian teachings spelled out the appropriate uses of humor, advocating an "ethics of mirth." Respectable Confucians were advised to laugh gently, if at all, avoiding more boisterous, unseemly expressions of merriment. In contrast to this dignified restraint, the older Daoist tradition tolerated, even encouraged a broad spectrum of humor, much of it lighthearted. In the *Zhuangzi* (476–221 BCE), one of Daoism's basic texts, there is the story of a man who dreamed he was a butterfly. Happily, he fluttered about, not knowing he was a man. Suddenly, he awoke, wondering if he had dreamed he was a butterfly or if he was now the butterfly dreaming he was a man.[37] The humor here is based on ironic incongruity, in this case between the man's perspective and the insect's, but Daoists believe that the incongruities of life are built into the nature of the universe. While Western irony depends on an awareness of two seemingly contradictory ideas, placing the perceiver in an external and usually superior position, "for the Daoist who mirrors the parity of things, there can be no final distinction between the joker and the 'jokee.' Humor must be based upon parity, and this means that the joke is always pretty much on everyone," as David Hall and Roger Hanes point out in their study of Daoist thought.[38] In this respect, the paradoxical ripostes of Zen masters are more akin to Daoism than to Confucianism and quite different in character from the incongruity of European humor.

The foundation texts of Chinese religious and social thought did not elaborate on humor per se. It was not until much later that theoretical works comparable to Aristotle's *Poetics* or Cicero's treatise on the rhetoric of wit in *De Oratoria* (55 BCE) appeared. Liu Xie's *Wenxin diaolong*, a classic of literary criticism that confirmed Confucian attitudes toward jesting, was written at the turn of the sixth century. Xie disapproved of humor except as a vehicle for moral education. It was even later, during the Ming-Qing period (1368–1911), that Chinese literati began validating irony, satire, and even doggerel verse as legitimate expressions of humor.[39] In 1953, C. T. Hsia published an essay on "The Chinese Sense of Humor" in which he distinguished among several kinds of laughter. One form occurs as "malicious self-assertion," a primitive sign of victory over an injured foe, which later transformed into sophisticated ridicule through the wit of Mandarin intellectuals. Another form, directed at authority, enables those who feel oppressed to vent pent-up feelings and maintain their mental health. A third form treats its object with affection, a gentle laughter tempered by goodwill. The first two varieties of laughter correspond roughly to Western theories of superiority and relief. In addition, humor of the witty kind often depends on incongruity since, like the riddles of court jesters, it uses "farfetched analogies" to point out the absurdities of tyrannical actions and ill-advised ideas.[40] Scholars and retired officials used clever anecdotes and fables in this way to entertain misguided rulers while pointing them in wiser directions.[41]

All these forms of laughter are alive and well in Chinese cinema. There is a good deal of rapid-fire wit and malicious self-assertion in the Hong Kong comedies of Stephen Chow, whose *Kung Fu Hustle* (*Kung fu*, 2004) and *The God of Cookery* (*Sik san*, 1996) roil with manic wordplay and high-testosterone competition. Taiwan-born Ang Lee prefers a gentler kind of humor. His father figures in *The Wedding Banquet* (*Xi yan*, 1993) and *Eat Drink Man Woman* (*Yin shi nan nu*, 1994) exemplify the humanistic wisdom of Confucian ethics. And on the mainland, a special genre known as "New Year's celebration movies" (*hesui pian*) marks the start of every year, inviting millions of Chinese to let off steam with a rousing, typically comic blockbuster. These lively observances of the Chinese New Year, based on a lunar calendar, remind us that comedy can embody the spirit of revelry and renewal almost anywhere on Earth.

Japan and Korea share many of China's cultural traditions, including comicality, but laughter takes some uniquely local forms in these two countries. Outsiders may think of Japanese society as decorous and polite, and they will find much gentle laughter in Yasujiro Ozu's *Good Morning* (*Ohayo*, 1959) or Masayuki Suo's *Shall We Dance?* (*Sharu wi dansu?*, 1996). But a good deal of humor in Japan is sharply satirical, crudely farcical, and even obscene. Marguerite Wells traces the bawdy strain back to the island's early animist religion, Shintoism. There is a mythic story in the *Kojiki*, Japan's oldest chronicle (712 BCE), in which the sun goddess retreats into her dark cave. The other gods trick her into coming out and performing a crude striptease, which drives them to laughing fits, thus ensuring another harvest through laughter. Wells considers this to be Japan's first comedy performance, celebrated in annual rituals to this day.[42] Traces of the Shinto tradition can be found in films like Hayao Miyazaki's *Spirited Away* (*Sen to Chihiro no Kamikakushi*, 2001), in which a ten-year-old girl enters the spirit world to find her parents transformed into pigs. The humor in Juzo Itami's satires (*Tampopo* [*Tanpopo*], 1985; *A Taxing Woman* [*Marusa no onna*], 1987) is anything but decorous. His characters eat oysters at the movies and pass a raw egg yolk from mouth to mouth while kissing. Korea's history also diverges from China's, notably in its lengthy subjugation by powerful neighbors and the internal struggles endured during its transformation into a modern state. (▶ See "Case Study for Chapter 13: *Tampopo*" on the website.) The scars of a high-pressure society whose energy is born of deep-seated struggle and oppression are evident in dark and violent comedies like *The Good, the Bad and the Ugly* (1966) and *Attack the Gas Station!* (*Juyuso supgyoksagon*, 1999).

More Theories in Action: Bergson, Frye, Bakhtin

Before moving on to the most recent views of comedy put forward by modern scientists, we should acknowledge the ideas of three more theorists who have shaped the way humor is understood around the world: Henri Bergson (a French philosopher), Northrop Frye (a Canadian literary critic), and Mikhail Bakhtin (a Soviet scholar interested in semiotics, literature, and ethics).

Bergson (1859–1941) proposed his influential theory in a 1900 publication, "Laughter: An Essay on the Meaning of the Comic." Without defining the comic spirit itself, which he regarded as "a living thing," he enumerated three starting points of inquiry. First, humor is uniquely human, the peculiar trait of "an animal that laughs." Second, humor requires emotional distance, a "momentary anesthesia of the heart." Situations that might otherwise evoke pity or fear become comic when viewed with a certain indifference. Third, humor is essentially a social phenomenon. He disagrees with those who define it in abstract terms, as "an intellectual contrast" or "a palpable absurdity," arguing that "laughter is always the laughter of a group." Building on these observations, Bergson considered moments when we laugh—at someone stumbling in the street or at the victim of a practical joke whose inkwell has been rigged—concluding that what these and other instances of comedy have in common is a certain mechanical inelasticity.[43] We laugh when people behave like machines: slipping on banana peels like mindless objects, inappropriately following old habits when conditions have changed, foolishly pursuing the *idée fixe* of avarice or jealousy. Watch the mechanical motions of Jacques Tati's summer crowds in *Mr. Hulot's Holiday* (*Les vacances de Monsieur Hulot*, 1953). They cram themselves into a bus like so much luggage, colliding and tangling with each other's arms and legs as if driven by a hyperactive engine. At the train station, they rush together in a pack from one track to another, mindlessly heeding a disembodied, incoherent voice on the loudspeaker that announces last-minute changes. What makes these throngs so ludicrous is their robotic inflexibility: They act as if they have no mind of their own. At the core of comedy, then, is an anxiety about free will, determinism, and the need to adapt to a changing world. Bergson's ideas go a long way toward endowing certain kinds of comedy, like slapstick, with moral, even metaphysical significance. Consider Buster Keaton as he ingeniously evades the laws of physical probability in *The General* (1926), beating the mechanical world at its own game. Or watch the prisoners escape from the assembly line in René Clair's *Freedom for Us* (*À nous la liberté*, 1931) (Figure 1.6). In these instances of human elasticity and self-assertion, we laugh *with* the characters, not *at* them.

Figure 1.6 Henri Bergson. We laugh when men act like machines. A scene from *Freedom for Us* (1931).

The human spirit triumphs over the tyranny of machines and the soul is released from the body's bondage.

Bergson's emphasis on the social contexts of laughter became even more central in Northrop Frye's *Anatomy of Criticism*, published in 1957. Frye offered a new "poetics" in Aristotle's sense of the word: a coherent, systematic analysis of literature. Deliberately avoiding moral judgments, Frye based this analysis on the fictional hero's relationship to power, distinguishing between mythic, romantic, mimetic, and ironic modes. Comedy, he concluded, is related to the low mimetic and ironic modes, in which the hero is equal or inferior in power to other men and nature. In this respect, he returned to Aristotle's dichotomy between characters superior to the audience (in tragedy) and those equal or inferior to the audience (in comedy). But to account for the proliferation of literary forms since ancient Greece, Frye made finer distinctions in terms of social reconciliation. In mythical comedy, the hero is accepted into the society of the gods, as in the myth of Zeus's son Hercules, Dante's *Commedia*, and other Christian stories of salvation. In romantic comedy, the hero seeks temporary escape from a society that thwarts his dreams. He may rebel against the society of his elders, replacing it with one that reverses their social standards (Frye called this alternative society a Saturnalia) or that restores the proper standards of a previous golden age. In the mimetic comedy of Aristophanes, Plautus, Shakespeare's *The Tempest*, or Balzac's novels, a new society forms around the comic hero, typically an ordinary person who rises in status like Horatio Alger. In sum, "the theme of the comic is the integration of society."[44]

While Frye rarely mentioned movies, his insights can be applied productively to cinematic comedy as well as to literary forms. The mythic mode is still popular in India, where mythologicals have always been a favorite genre. *Sita Sings the Blues* (2008) blends scenes from the Sanskrit epic *Ramayana* with the director's private life in a lively tale of exile, abduction, and redemption. Although the movie's ending is no happier than it is in the original text, the whole story is presented in the lighthearted spirit of an animated film (Figure 1.7). In Africa, where the spirit world still regularly interacts with daily life, mythic elements abound in many films. Adam Drabo's *Skirt Power* (*Taafé Fanga*, 1997) is based on a nineteenth-century Dogon tale in which the village women wrest power from the men with the help of an enchanted mask. The scenes of men carrying babies on their back and pounding yams for dinner while the women chat and smoke are hilarious reversals of gender roles. But while this may seem like a radical departure from the norm (inspired, incidentally, by the actual role that women played in Mali's 1991 revolution), both sexes return to their traditional place within society by the end. The difference is that the men have learned a lesson about abusing their position. (▶ See "Case Study for Chapter 10: *Skirt Power*" on the website.)

Figure 1.7 Northrop Frye. Mythic comedy animates a cartoon in *Sita Sings the Blues* (2008).

The romantic mode offers another opportunity to understand the mechanics of social integration. How many romantic comedies end in weddings or some other social ritual that ties together the fabric of the plot and of the community? The problem may be social taboos (like the traditional Indian ban on second marriages in *Sometimes Things Do Happen* [*Kuch Hota Hai*], 1998), ethnic differences (in *My Big Fat Greek Wedding*, 2002), or comic misunderstandings (in *The Wedding Banquet* [*Xiyan*], 1993, where the groom tries to hide the fact that he is gay from his old-fashioned Chinese parents), but these stories typically end in reconciliation and a big celebration. American wedding films tend to be upbeat romantic comedies, bolstered by a view of the nation as a melting pot. Romantic love can conquer all obstacles regardless of religion, ethnicity, or mismatched bank accounts. In *My Big Fat Greek Wedding*, Toula Portokalos is the daughter of Greek orthodox immigrants while Ian Miller is an upper-middle-class white Anglo-Saxon Protestant, a WASP. Yet, as Toula's father explains at the banquet, the name Miller comes from the Greek word for apple, Portokalos means orange, "but in the end we all fruit."

"In ironic comedy," Frye noted, "the demonic world is never far away."[45] As examples of "pure" comedy become harder to find, especially abroad, the lighter moments in movies are increasingly mixed with darker elements. Sometimes social integration requires an expulsion, the removal of a fool or clown figure who must be sacrificed, like Shakespeare's Falstaff, Shylock, or Malvolio, for the common good. In *Xala* (1974), Ousmane Sembène's satire of corruption in modern Senegal, the protagonist is treated as a ludicrous character. His Western affectations are continually mocked, his inflated sense of self-importance is belied by a diminutive stature, and his pretensions to male prowess are undercut by the curse of impotence. Finally expelled from the business council for misappropriating funds, abandoned by his family, and driven to seek help from a local shaman for his impotence, he submits to the shaman's cure by allowing the beggars he has denigrated throughout the film to spit on his naked body. This degrading end has all the hallmarks of a sacrificial rite. Frye took pains to separate the ironic treatment of the scapegoat in fiction from the barbarism of historical sacrifice. What distinguishes ironic comedy, he argued, is a certain sense of play. The clown figure is rejected in a playful manner, without malice or true violence, he explained, just as theatergoers may hiss the stage villain or fans may boo the umpire at a baseball game: "The element of play is the barrier that separates art from savagery."[46] We can find this playful quality, of all places, in the musical comedies of Stalin's Russia. Grigori Aleksandrov launched this cycle of lighthearted crowd pleasers with *Happy Guys* in 1934. The fun begins when Kostya, a shepherd on a bucolic collective farm, leads a parade of livestock into a nearby hotel, where the animals run amok. The Westernized bourgeoisie who live there in high style are made to look like pretentious fools. In the real Russia of the 1930s, those who clung to outmoded Western ways were purged by Stalin as "the enemy within." But in the movies, they are simply laughed out of the picture. *Happy Guys* ends with a rousing chorus of social(ist) solidarity: "We sing and laugh like children," sing the joyful masses, "through the unending struggle and toil."

This brings us to the remarkable research and insights of Mikhail Bakhtin. Working independently in the academic world of Soviet Russia, Bakhtin was also interested in social integration and the collective spirit of jollity found in Carnival and other forms of ritualized laughter. Like Frye, he was less interested in the ceremonial roots of this spirit than its implications for literature. In *The Dialogic Imagination*, first published as a whole in 1975, he introduced his thoughts on parody and polyglossia. Bakhtin noticed that the history of the novel starts with parodies of epic style. Miguel Cervantes in Spain and Henry Fielding in England began their great works of fiction by making fun of the prevailing genres, infusing the high-toned language of epic with elements of laughter, irony, and self-conscious parody. This "ability of the novel to criticize itself" creates a dialogic imagination, a flexibility of mind and an ambivalence of language that put it in "living contact with unfinished, still-evolving contemporary reality."[47] Bakhtin argued that this cognitive elasticity opened a new "polyglot world" that was larger and more dynamic than the world of a national genre like the epic, with its "firsts," "bests," and "forevers." In contrast to the timeless, hierarchical, holistic realm of gods and heroes, parody dismantles and dissects, reveals the seams, views the gods and heroes in close-up, allows them to be handled and examined, often with irreverence.

This opens the space of literature for the sideward glance of irony, "the corrective of laughter."[48]

Bakhtin rarely applied his ideas to cinema, but it's not difficult to find the principles of polyglossia at play in almost any movie comedy that depends on incongruity for its humor. In time-travel comedies like *The Visitors* and *Ivan Vasilievich Changes Profession*, the contrast between two eras provides rich material for laughter. It's not only a matter of playing with anachronisms; the cognitive dissonance involved in being transported to a different time in history provides opportunities for dissecting cultural beliefs and economic systems. When Sir Godefroy and his lowly servant Jacquoille in *The Visitors* take the leap from feudal France to modern Paris, they mistake a dark-skinned postal worker for a Saracen riding the devil's chariot. The humor works two ways: We can laugh at their ignorance and at our own prejudices at the same time. How much have European attitudes toward Africans and Muslims really changed since the Middle Ages? Likewise, in *Ivan Vasilievich*, when Ivan the Terrible finds himself in 1970s Russia, he continues to act like a tsar, inviting us to laugh at his arrogance and sense of privilege. Meanwhile, his modern counterpart enjoys a temporary promotion to the medieval Russian throne, a slap at Soviet ideals. In both films, the solid belief system of a heroic age crashes against the realities of a less heroic one, exposing both ages to "the corrective of laughter."

Bakhtin went on to explore the topsy-turvy world of Carnival as a social institution in *Rabelais and His World* (completed in 1940, published in 1965). Using the French writer's sixteenth-century text *The Life of Gargantua and Pantagruel* as the starting point for his analysis, Bakhtin described the spirit of Carnival as a liberating force, enabling celebrants to obscure their individuality behind costumes and masks and to assume a new collective identity. While Bakhtin viewed the Carnivalesque from a Marxist perspective, as a form of resistance against class oppression, the concept has been studied by anthropologists as a cultural ritual enacted around the world. The fool is crowned king for a day as the Lord of Misrule, liberating the community from its usual hierarchies and proprieties. In this sense, such customs are rebellions against dogma and authority. On the other hand, some argue that they are more conservative than subversive, releasing pent-up feelings only briefly before the inevitable return to the status quo.

This liberating spirit is alive in comedies like *Passport to Pimlico* (1949), set in London just after World War II. Fed up with food rationing and other government regulations, the citizens of Pimlico declare themselves independent from Great Britain. A young man with a French accent becomes their head of state, basing his claim on a long-lost document that links him to the dukedom of Burgundy. Without the usual restrictions, Pimlico quickly devolves into an exuberant state of anarchy (Figure 1.8). Streams of venture capitalists, bargain hunters, and conmen of all kinds pour in. Neighboring nations offer treaties and

Figure 1.8 Mikhail Bakhtin. The liberating spirit of Carnival in *Passport to Pimlico* (1949).

emergency aid. Trucks deliver milk through hoses. Pigs are parachuted to the populace. All this cheerful chaos doesn't last, however. By the end of the movie, Pimlico returns to normalcy, as does any Carnival, after a moment of comic release for the Pimlico community and the audience.

In addition to the Carnivalesque reversal of social roles and rules, Bakhtin found in Rabelais an upending of the human body itself. In *The Life of Gargantua and of Pantagruel*, Rabelais (a doctor and former friar) turns the body upside-down, giving top billing to the "lower" functions of eating, fornicating, and excreting. His prose is inventive, excessive, and energetically obscene. It was also strategic in its time: a humanist's challenge to the medieval order of spirituality. Bakhtin described the earthy imagery of Rabelais as "grotesque," linking it to rituals of death and rebirth. The laughter released in *Gargantua and Pantagruel* is the liberating laughter of renewal.

We still hear echoes of that laughter today. It is possible to view gross-out comedies, with their grotesque bodily imagery and crude language, as heirs to Rabelais. The mischievous mirth unleashed from *National Lampoon's Animal House* (1978) to *Porky's* (1982) and from *Numbskull Emptybrook in the Army* (*Uuno Turhapuro armeijan leivissa*, 1984) to *Klown* (2010) may not be consciously calling for death to the old order or for the birth of a new one, but it is part of a long historical trajectory that takes a more pointedly rebellious and decidedly Rabelaisian turn in the films of Roberto Benigni. As a young man, Benigni was fascinated by the troubadour tradition of improvising bawdy lyrics at *fescennini* festivals in his native Tuscany. Dating from Etruscan times, these festivals hark back to ancient fertility rites and pre-Roman saturnine verse, among the oldest forms of poetry in Italy and a forerunner of modern satire. In his study of Benigni, Carlo Celli finds allusions to Gargantua throughout the filmmaker's early works.[49] As Benigni honed his craft for an ever-widening audience, he continued to deploy the coarse, frequently grotesque weaponry of Rabelaisian humor to undermine religious posturing and ideological elitism. Although much of the comedy in *The Monster* (*Il Mostro*, 1994), *Johnny Toothpick* (*Johnny Stecchino*, 1991), and even *Life Is Beautiful* may seem like innocent fun to many viewers, it flows from sources that are, from a Bakhtinian perspective, deeply and shrewdly subversive.

The Science of Comedy: Laughter and the Brain

So far, we've been reviewing theories, past and present, that seek to explain what humor is and how it works. The thinkers behind these theories have been mostly philosophers, literary scholars, writers on aesthetic and religious thought, and a few early psychologists. Only recently have scientists begun to apply more rigorous methods of inquiry to the field. Using the tools of behavioral, cognitive, and social psychology as well as neuroscience and biology, they have questioned some of the earlier theories and corroborated others. They have also posed new sets of questions. What mental processes are involved in understanding jokes? How does the brain respond to humor and how does humor affect our bodies? Are humans the only animals that laugh? What purposes does laughter serve in our evolution as a species?

In his wide-ranging survey of the empirical research, Rod A. Martin finds much support for Bergson's emphasis on the social roles of humor: "Humor is fundamentally a social phenomenon . . . essentially a way for people to interact in a playful manner."[50] Martin cites multiple studies that demonstrate how humor is used in relationships. It can facilitate bonding with other individuals or groups (people often cite a "sense of humor" as a valued trait), and it can probe their reactions to ideas without seriously committing to those ideas ("only kidding"). People use humor to impose their will on others (bosses tend to use humor at meetings more than underlings); to smooth over conflicts, reducing tension (comic relief); and to get away with breaking various taboos (as in politically incorrect bar jokes). Developmental psychologists note that children begin to respond to humor at age four and go through stages of progressively complex cognitive capacities, enabling them to understand increasingly sophisticated forms of joking. Like other forms of play, playful humor is a safe way to test their mental abilities through riddles, puns, and other forms of conceptual ambiguity as they prepare for adulthood. Some biologists believe that humor may have contributed to human evolution, accelerating our social and cognitive development through play.[51] Contrary to Bergson's claim that humor is uniquely human, it turns out that members of the ape family laugh too. Martin presents the findings of recent primate research, which suggest that human laughter has the same evolutionary origin as the relaxed, open-mouth display or "play face" seen in bonobos, orangutans, and gorillas.[52]

How well do the discoveries of science square with earlier, less empirically grounded theories? The oldest of those theories, the view that humor is an aggressive assertion of superiority, has largely fallen out of favor. Psychologists today still find plenty of negativity, humor aimed at putting others down, but they also find many types of humor, like riddles and puns, that have nothing to do with domination. Most believe that humor is inherently neither friendly nor hostile. The relief theory and Freud's psychoanalytic view, which dominated psychological humor research during the mid-twentieth century, have also lost much of their hold. Freud's distinctions among wit (a release of sexual or aggressive impulses through jokes), humor (a defense mechanism for redirecting anxiety away from pain), and the comic (nonverbal antics involving slapstick, clowns, and banana peels) have been replaced by other categories. Nor is there much talk of egos, superegos, and ids among psychologists today.

What seems to have held up best is the concept of incongruity, the view that humor involves some sort of conceptual disparity, a mismatch between conflicting ideas. This approach enjoys a boost from the relatively new field of cognitive psychology, "the study of mental processes and their role in thinking, feeling, and behaving."[53] Cognitive scientists build on information processing theory. They are interested in how the human brain represents information internally and how it manipulates (processes) that information to store memories, redirect attention, or solve problems: in brief, to think. According to the terminology of this field, the brain represents the outside world in *schemas* and *scripts*, dynamic patterns of thought or behavior that capture information and relationships. These patterns may serve as models for behavior, much as a movie script might provide instructions for appropriate action.

Victor Raskin offers the following example:

> "Is the doctor at home?" the patient asked in his bronchial whisper.
>
> "No," the doctor's young and pretty wife whispered in reply. "Come right in."[54]

The joke hinges on a conflict between two competing scripts. In the doctor script, the patient's whisper implies that he is seeking medical help for a bronchial condition. In the lovers script, his low voice suggests a secret tryst, confirmed by the pretty wife's discreetly whispered invitation. Following the first script, we expect her answer, "No," to come as a disappointment, but that expectation is derailed by the punchline, "Come right in." Script theory helps to explain the mechanism of incongruity at work in jokes like this. Humor arises with the shift in perspective, a conceptual reversal. Some cognitivists have run experiments to study the degree to which activated scripts play against each other, positing a direct correlation: the more investment in the scripts, the more "cognitive elaboration," the more the joke will be enjoyed.

Scott Weems, a cognitive neuroscientist with a specialty in humor, postulates three stages for understanding jokes: constructing, reckoning, and resolving. Construction is the act of generating possibilities, theories that account for our perceptions, like the doctor script that "explains" the first part of Raskin's joke. Reckoning is what forces us to reexamine misleading expectations, which is what happens when we come up against the joke's second part. The process of resolving, in turn, activates a new frame of reference, opening a larger picture that takes both parts into account. Unless we resolve the incongruity, Weems believes, we won't find the joke pleasurably funny. Weems the scientist points out that pleasure is induced by a rush of dopamine, the brain's "reward chemical," which stimulates physiologic arousal and expresses itself through smiling and laughter.[55]

The cognitive approach tends to favor theories of conceptual disparity, perhaps because it focuses on mental processes. But humor has other dimensions too, including its relationship to mood. Neuroscientists who study the nervous system with electroencephalography (EEG), magnetic resonance imaging (MRI), positron emission tomography (PET) scans, and other neuroimaging tools are learning that humor is connected to a range of biochemical changes in the body and the brain. Laughter is associated with an emotional high, that subjective feeling of pleasure that resonates throughout the autonomic nervous, endocrine, cardiovascular, digestive, and immune systems.[56] This pervasively buoyant effect is, perhaps, the biological basis of what Hobbes called "sudden glory." It may also be related to the joyful sense of release described by relief theory. Some research indicates that positive emotions like mirth broaden one's attention, in contrast to negative emotions like fear and anger, which narrow a person's range of options.[57] While a negative stimulus might lead directly to flight or fight, humor opens paths to creativity and a greater tolerance for ambiguity. This concept of "broaden and build" is consistent with Morreall's description of comedy as a flexible, nonauthoritarian, open-ended state of mind, at ease with disorder and diversity. It also suggests that there may be physiologic dimensions to the division between tragedy and comedy that has preoccupied literary theory from Aristotle to Frye.

Laughter also is contagious, inciting similar responses in others. Research indicates that people are thirty times more likely to laugh when they are with other people than when they are alone.[58] It's no wonder that so many television sitcoms add recorded laughter to their soundtracks. Yet laughter is not necessarily a sign of mirth. There is nothing particularly funny about tickling. Even rats can be tickled into giggles.

So far, psychologists and other scientists have advanced no conclusive evidence to resolve some of the other issues debated in the field of humor studies. Whether humor is essentially conservative or subversive, for example, and whether sexist and racist humor actually promotes prejudice are still open questions.[59] Nor do they have much to say about the humor in movie comedies, aside from using Mr. Bean or Monty Python films to stimulate laughter in their subjects. Even practitioners of cognitive film research, a growing new field within cinema studies, have just begun to focus on the way comedies work on the human nervous system. One of the most promising accounts is Torben Grodal's PECMA flow model, short for Perception, Emotion, Cognition, and Motor Action. Among other things, Grodal's model helps to explain why we laugh when a clown falls on a banana peel but we feel sympathetic pain if our neighbor falls on the ice. Grodal notes that external stimuli arouse emotional responses in the brain. The perception (P) of a wolf close by arouses the emotion (E) of fear, triggering a cognitive (C) judgment to escape or confront the wolf. This in turn is followed by an implementation of the flight-or-fight options through muscular activation (MA).[60] The PECMA model accounts for the internal mechanism when we encounter a real wolf. But if the stimulus is a cartoon wolf, the banana-peel gag, or some other form of comic entertainment, the pathway may diverge. In that case, the prefrontal cortex makes a different judgment. It redefines the situation as playful and comic, triggering a different set of events that reduces the tendency to act. Instead of stimulating muscles, the impulses are diverted to the brain stem, limbic system, and cerebellum, eliciting laughter. The arms and legs that might otherwise send us running for safety or reaching out to our fallen neighbor remain inactive, blocked from action. We become "self-directed" rather than "world-directed." Bergson may not have been far off when he spoke of "a momentary anesthesia of the heart." Interestingly, something like this also occurs during dreams, when we don't act on perceptions as we would in waking life. Similar pathways are activated when dental patients are given laughing gas (nitrous oxide) to reduce pain.

A key biologic difference, then, between serious and playful situations may be attributed to cognitive interpretation, a judgment in the brain's prefrontal cortex to treat the perception as real or unreal. This interpretation puts the whole system in a particular state of readiness (to respond to an actual threat) or relaxation (in the case of mirthful entertainment). The mechanism by which laughter initiates or accompanies a pervasive state of mirth ("it's all in fun") may be why so many theorists speak broadly of a "comic view" or "the comic mind."

Like many others, Grodal acknowledges the communal significance of comedic entertainment, which in his words serves as "a kind of frame for social grooming and bonding." He also points out that comedies typically appeal to narrower groups than do genres like action or animation. Although the sounds of laughter are indistinguishable from one culture to another, what triggers that laughter is often culturally specific.

The cultural dimensions of humor have been analyzed in different ways. Some scholars distinguish between "high- and low-context" societies. In the high-context cultures of Africa, Asia, South America, and the Middle East, messages rely heavily on nonverbal information, such as body language and shared cultural knowledge. In low-context cultures, such as those in North America and most of Western Europe, messages depend more on explicit verbal communication than on implied meanings.[61] This may explain why so much of the humor in an African film like *Taafe Fanga*, which relies largely on visual cues and the particularities of local village life, is lost on European audiences (Figure 1.9). On the other hand, American slapstick is almost universal, while Western comedies that trade heavily in dialects and puns, like France's *Welcome to the Sticks* (*Bienvenue*

Figure 1.9 High-context comedy relies heavily on shared visual cues: Two village men tease each other for doing women's work in *Skirt Power* (1997).

chez les Ch'tis, 2008) and Italy's *Welcome to the South* (*Bienvenuti al sud*, 2010; Figure 1.10), are significantly less entertaining in translation, especially when the subtitles are in Hindi or Chinese. Other cultural scholars point out that the social value of humor differs from region to region. According to Liisi Laineste, humor is more highly valued in Europe and North America than it is in East Asia. In addition to highlighting the relative importance of humor in different cultures, Laineste offers explanations to account for different national tastes. Britain, a generally stable society free from invasion, developed an appreciation for class-based ridicule, sexual innuendo, and satirical takes on the absurdity of everyday life. Examples of these preferences abound in the Ealing comedies, the Carry On cycle, and Monty Python films. Russian humor, honed during times of totalitarian oppression, produced the biting political satire of the *anekdot*. The bite is sharpest in Soviet-era jokes and in movies of the Thaw and Stagnation periods, like *The Garage* (1980) and *Repentance* (*Pokanyaniye*, 1984).[62]

What emerges from all these theories and ongoing studies is a deeper understanding of what humor is and what it means for us as biologic and social beings. Since Aristotle's early efforts to explain tragedy and comedy, the varieties of imaginative literature—and, later, cinema—have multiplied exponentially. Over the centuries, humor in art and daily life has assumed an array of forms so broad in scope and richly layered as to require new explanatory theories and research. One school of thought has supplanted another. The long-held explanations of humor as an expression of superiority (Plato, Hobbes) or a release mechanism (Spencer, Freud) have given way to incongruity theory (Kant, Kierkegaard), now supported by more recent empirical research. This idea that humor hinges on a sudden, unexpected shift in mental concepts, what cognitivist psychologists

Figure 1.10 Low-context comedy depends more on explicit verbal humor: "When you strike it lucky, you say 'Uaaa!'" Southern Italians treat their northern boss to a language lesson in *Welcome to the South* (2010).

call scripts, helps to explain the shape of jokes and the appeal of absurdist comedy. Social psychologists confirm the vital role that humor plays in interpersonal communication and community cohesion explored by Bergson and Frye. Anthropologists link Bakhtin's insights about Rabelaisian humor and the Carnivalesque to age-old rituals of laughter and renewal. Those who argue that humor is politically subversive or conservative will probably continue their debate, since there is evidence for both. Those who stress the local or universal nature of humor will likewise find support for either claim. More important is the view that comedy is much more than a genre. It turns out that those two masks of Greek drama, the scowl and the smile, represented something greater and more deeply engrained in the human psyche. If there is a "comic mind," a counterweight to the "tragic vision" of life, the evidence may be found both in the wide-ranging spectrum of the comic arts and in the findings of modern science. Morreall summed up the tragic view as being serious, idealistic, hierarchical, and single-mindedly fixed on goals. In contrast, the comic spirit is playful, pragmatic, democratic, and elastic. This description captures the essence of what Johan Huizinga called *homo ludens*, humanity at play.[63] Biologists who trace the circuitry of laughter back to interpretations in the brain, decisions in the prefrontal cortex to treat perceptions as unreal, as "just for fun," remind us that a playful state of mind affects our entire physical being, releasing dopamine throughout the body to induce a holistically pleasurable state of mirth. A funny movie or a comic episode engages this lightness of being. It allows us to let down our guard and entertain matters of life and death with flexibility and freedom in the playground of comedy.

Notes

1. Samuel Johnson, "'The Difficulty of Defining Comedy,' *The Rambler* (1971)," in *Reader in Comedy: An Anthology of Theory and Criticism*, ed. Magda Romanska and Alan Ackerman (London: Bloomsbury, 1988), 150.
2. Mikhail Bakhtin, *Rabelais and His World*, trans. Hélène Iswolsky (Bloomington: Indiana University Press, 1984), 66.
3. John Morreall, *Comedy, Tragedy, and Religion* (Albany: State University of New York Press, 1999), 41–48.
4. Morreall, *Comedy, Tragedy, and Religion*, 41.
5. Morreall, *Comedy, Tragedy, and Religion*, 74.
6. Aristotle, "The Art of Poetry," in *Selected Works*, trans. Philip Wheelwright (New York: Odyssey Press, 1951), 291–325.
7. Maurice Charney, ed., *Comedy: A Geographic and Historical Guide*, vol. 1 (Westport, CT: Praeger, 2005), 1.
8. Salvatore Attardo, ed., *Encyclopedia of Humor Studies* (Los Angeles: Sage, 2014).

9. Qtd. in Nwachukwu Ukadike, *Questioning African Cinema: Conversations with Filmmakers* (Minneapolis: University of Minnesota Press, 2002), 229.
10. Jean Paul Simon, *Le Filmique et le comique* (Paris: Méridien Klinsieck, 1979).
11. See June Givanni, ed., *Symbolic Narratives/African Cinema: Audiences, Theory and the Moving Image* (Cambridge: Cambridge University Press, 2000), 117.
12. Adrian Bardon, "The Philosophy of Humor," chap. 30 in *Comedy: A Geographic and Historical Guide*, vol. 2, ed. Maurice Charney (Westport, CT: Praeger, 2005), 462.
13. Roger Ebert, "Review of *Tampopo*, Directed by Juzo Itami," *Chicago-Sun Times*, September 11, 1987, https://www.rogerebert.com/reviews/tampopo-1987.
14. Aristotle, *The Nicomachean Ethics*, trans. with commentaries by Hippocrates G. Apostle (Dordrecht, Holland: D. Reidel, rpt. 1980), 75–76.
15. Plato, *The Republic*, trans. Richard Sterling and William Scott (New York: Norton, 1985), 85.
16. Plato, "Laws," in *The Collected Dialogues of Plato*, trans. E. Hamilton and H. Cairns (Princeton, NJ: Princeton University Press, 1978), 7: 816e; 11: 935e.
17. Psalms 2:2–5 (King James version).
18. René Descartes, "The Passions of the Soul" [1649] Part III, in *Philosophical Works of Descartes*, vol. 1, trans. Elizabeth Sanderson Haldane and George Robert Thomson Ross (Cambridge: Cambridge University Press, 1975), 178–179.
19. Thomas Hobbes, *Leviathan* [1651] (New York: Penguin, 1982).
20. Francis Hutcheson, *Reflections upon Laughter, and Remarks upon the Fable of the Bees* [1750], ed. Peter Kivy (The Hague, Holland: Martinus Nijhoff, 1973).
21. Immanuel Kant, *Critique of Judgment* [1790], First Part, sec. 54, trans. James Creed Meredith (Oxford: Clarendon Press, 1911).
22. Kant, Supplement to Book I, chap. 8.
23. Søren Kierkegaard, *Concluding Unscientific Postscript* [1846], trans. D. Swenson and W. Lowrie (Princeton, NJ: Princeton University Press, 1941), 259, 448.
24. Søren Kierkegaard, *Journals and Papers*, vol. 2, trans. and ed. H. Hong and E. Hong (Bloomington: Indiana University Press, 1970), entries 1681–1682.
25. Martin Esslin, *The Theatre of the Absurd* (New York: Doubleday, 1961), xix.
26. See Thomas C. Oden, ed., *The Humor of Kierkegaard: An Anthology* (Princeton, NJ: Princeton University Press, 2004), 27.
27. Lord Shaftesbury, "*Sensus Communis*: An Essay on the Freedom of Wit and Humour," in *Characteristicks of Men, Manners, Opinions, Times* [1709], ed. Lawrence E. Klein (Cambridge: Cambridge University Press, 2003), 29–69.
28. Herbert Spencer, "On the Physiology of Laughter" [1911], in *Essays on Education, the Philosophy of Style, and Kindred Subjects* (London: Dent, 1914), 301–312.
29. Sigmund Freud, *Jokes and Their Relation to the Unconscious* [1905], trans. and ed. James Strachey (New York: Norton, 1960).
30. John Sundholm, Isak Thorsen, and others, *Historical Dictionary of Scandinavian Cinema* (Lanham, MD: Scarecrow Press, 2012), 387.
31. Gayatri Devi and Najat Rahman, eds., *Humor in Middle Eastern Cinema* (Detroit: Wayne State University Press, 2014), 6.
32. Devi and Rahman, *Humor in Middle Eastern Cinema*, 18.

33. Lee Siegel, *Laughing Matters: Comic Tradition in India* (Delhi: Motilal Banarsidass, 1987), 7–9.
34. Koenrad Elst, "Humour in Hinduism," chap. 3 in *Humour and Religion. Challenges and Ambiguities*, ed. Hans Geybels and Walter Van Herck. Continuum Religious Studies (London: Continuum International, 2011), 35–53.
35. Michel Clasquin, "Real Buddhas Don't Laugh: Attitudes towards Humour and Laughter in Ancient India and China," *Social Identities* 7 (2001): 1.
36. See Conrad Hyers, *Zen and the Comic Spirit* (Eugene, OR: Wypf and Stock, 1974).
37. *The Complete Works of Chuang Zu*, trans. Burton Watson (New York: Columbia University Press, 1968), chap. 2.
38. David L. Hall and Roger T. Ames, *Thinking from the Han: Self, Truth, and Transcendence in Chinese and Western Culture* (Albany: State University of New York Press, 1998).
39. Jessica Milner Davis and Jocelyn Chey, *Humour in Chinese Life and Culture* (Hong Kong: Hong Kong University Press, 2013).
40. C. T. Hsia, "The Chinese Sense of Humor," *Renditions* 9 (1978): 72–84. https://www.cuhk.edu.hk/rct/renditions/sample/b09.html accessed 4 April 2019.
41. See *Everyday Chinese: 60 Fables and Anecdotes*. ed. Zhong Qin (Beijing: New World Press, 1983).
42. See Marguerite Wells and Ronald Stewart, "History of Humor: Premodern Japan," in *Encyclopedia of Humor Studies*, ed. Salvatore Attardo (Los Angeles: Sage, 2014), 320–326 and Jessica Milner Davis, ed., *Understanding Humor in Japan* (Detroit: Wayne State University Press, 2006), 4.
43. Henri Bergson, *Laughter: An Essay on the Meaning of the Comic* [1900], trans. Cloudesley Brereton and Fred Rothwell, chap 1. https://www.gutenberg.org/files/4352/4352-h/4352-h.htm.
44. Northrop Frye, *Anatomy of Criticism: Four Essays* [1957] (New York: Atheneum, 1967), 43.
45. Frye, *Anatomy of Criticism*, 178.
46. Frye, *Anatomy of Criticism*, 45–46.
47. Mikhail Bakhtin, *The Dialogic Imagination: Four Essays by M. M. Bakhtin*, ed. Michael Holquist, trans. Caryl Emerson and Michael Holquist (Austin: University of Texas Press, 1981), 6–7
48. Bakhtin, *Dialogic Imagination*, 55.
49. Carlo Celli, *The Divine Comic: The Cinema of Roberto Benigni* (London: Scarecrow Press, 2001).
50. Rod A. Martin, *The Psychology of Humor: An Integrative Approach* (Amsterdam: Elsevier Academic Press, 2007), 5.
51. Martin, *Psychology of Humor*, 10.
52. Martin, *Psychology of Humor*, 165.
53. Martin, *Psychology of Humor*, 83.
54. Victor Raskin, "Semantic Mechanisms of Humor," *Proceedings of the Fifth Annual Meeting of the Berkeley Linguistics Society* (1979): 325–335. https://journals.linguisticsociety.org/proceedings/index.php/BLS/article

55. Scott Weems, *Ha! The Science of When We Laugh and Why* (New York: Basic Books. 2014), 31–37 and Rod A. Martin, "Psychology," in *Encyclopedia of Humor Studies*, ed. Salvatore Attardo (Los Angeles: Sage, 2014), 604–607.
56. W. F. Fry, "The Body of Humor," *Humor: International Journal of Humor Research* 7, no. 2 (1994): 111–126.
57. B. L. Fredrickson, "The Broaden-and-Build Theory of Positive Emotions," *American Psychologist* 56, no. 3 (2001): 218–226.
58. Robert Provine, "Contagious Laughter," *Bulletin of the Psychonomic Society* 30, no. 1 (1992): 1–4.
59. Martin, 138–153.
60. Torben Grodal, "A General Theory of Comic Entertainment: Arousal, Appraisal, and the PECMA Flow," chap. 10 in *Cognitive Media Theory*, ed. Ted Nannicelli and Paul Taberham (New York: Routledge, 2014), 177–195. See also his *Embodied Vision: Evolution, Emotion, Culture and Film* (Oxford: Oxford University Press, 2009).
61. Audrey C. Adams, "High-Context Humor," in *Encyclopedia of Humor Studies*, ed. Salvatore Attardo (Los Angeles: Sage, 2014), 288–289.
62. Liisi Laineste, "National and Ethnic Differences," in *Encyclopedia of Humor Studies*, ed. Salvatore Attardo (Los Angeles: Sage, 2014), 541–542.
63. Johan Huizinga, *Homo Ludens: A Study of the Play-element in Culture* (London: Routledge & Kegan Paul Ltd., 1949).

2
Comic Forms

The profusion of competing theories discussed in Chapter 1 suggests that humor comes in many diverse forms. It makes a difference whether people are laughing at a literary satire, a stage farce, a knock-knock joke, or the gross-out humor in a fraternity-house movie. Understanding comedy, then, requires some attention to categories, the various purposes and expectations associated with comic genres and sub-genres. The intent of this chapter is to clarify the most important generic distinctions that we will be encountering in our survey of the world's movie comedies.

Slapstick

Slapstick is probably the oldest and most persistent form of movie comedy. The madcap chases of the Keystone Cops, Charlie Chaplin's hapless pratfalls and well-directed kicks in the pants, the incessant mutual thrashings of the Three Stooges: All helped to set in motion an unending spectacle of horseplay, boisterous gymnastics, and ludicrous, sometimes vulgar sight gags on the screen. The silent-movie clowns were already part of a long tradition of physical comedy, borrowed from the vaudeville stage and, before that, from theatrical sources like Shakespeare's *Comedy of Errors* (1594) and Aristophanes' *Lysistrata* (441 BCE).

The term *slapstick* has been traced back to the sixteenth-century Italian entertainment *commedia dell'arte*, in which one of the stock characters, Arlecchino, used a prop made of two flat wooden paddles to whack unwary victims. The loose ends of this contrivance flapped together loudly on impact, producing more laughter than pain.[1] It is this *semblance* of violence, extravagant ferocity with no real damage done, that drives the machinery of slapstick humor. It can be seen as a form of play, a harmless way to exercise aggressive energies, much as bear cubs spar with one another, which may explain why practitioners from the Marx Brothers to Jerry Lewis act so much like children. Scientists who have studied the phenomenon of laughter among primates underscore the social and developmental value of such play in apes as well as humans. We get to act out hostile behavior "all in fun," to test the limits of acceptable conduct while maintaining that we're "only kidding."

When the World Laughs. William V. Costanzo, Oxford University Press (2020). Oxford University Press
DOI: 10.1093/oso/9780190924997.001.0001

Since "pure slapstick" is hard to take in lengthy doses, its guilty pleasures are often mixed with other genres. We find some in the anarchic satires of the Marx Brothers, in the combative romances of screwball comedy, in Westerns, kung fu movies, and horror films. Slapstick is enjoyed around the world. Silly walks and goofy stunts are the stock and trade of Italy's Roberto Benigni (*Johnny Stecchino*, 1991), Britain's Rowan Atkinson (*Mr. Bean's Holiday, 2007*), and Hong Kong's Stephen Chow (*Tricky Brains* [*Jing gu jyun ga*], 1991) (Figure 2.1a). But while slapstick's appeal is universal, it often reflects the cultural background of its local audience. So Jackie Chan's performance in *Drunken Master* (*Zui quan*, 1978) displays the hallmarks of his acrobatic training for the Peking opera. The Gallic grunts and gestures of Louis de Funès in *The Mad Adventures of Rabbi Jacob* (*Les aventures de Rabbi Jacob*, 1973) express the peculiar peccadillos of his native France (Figure 2.1b). And the scenes of ludicrous inanity in *Amar Akbar Anthony* (1977) are part of the multi-genre tapestry of humor, action, and melodrama that is expected by most Bollywood fans (Figure 2.1c).

Although critics regularly regard slapstick as lowbrow, professional comedians consider it one of the most demanding of theatrical forms. Successful stunts require flawless timing and well-practiced performance skills. Anyone can throw a cream pie or slip on a banana peel, but making it funny is an art.

Moreover, recent studies of the genre point out how complex slapstick can be in its uses and misuses. Through a process of cultural transformation, avant-garde writers of the early twentieth century turned the disruptive absurdities of Harold Lloyd and Harry Langdon into darkly comic critiques of technology and capitalism, introducing a form that William Solomon calls "slapstick modernism."[2] Solomon cites Walter Benjamin, who warned that "the laughter [slapstick] provokes hovers over an abyss of horror," a grim vision of mechanized humanity that displays itself in the form of assembly-line labor and mindless military squadrons.[3] It's only a short hop from the farcical clowning in Sergei Eisenstein's first film, *Glumov's Diary* (*Dnevnik Glumova*, 1923), to the horrific Odessa Steps sequence in his *Battleship Potemkin* (*Bronenosets Potyomkin*, 1925). Another dark side of the genre can be seen in *Dying of Laughter* (*Muertos de risa*, 1999), a Spanish film in which a standup comedian gains fame and fortune by slapping his partner on the stage. The slaps become so fierce and humiliating that the duo begin a personal battle (Figure 2.2). Their feud ends in real violence, but the audience is laughing. Joshua Moss finds a related trend in the unscripted moments of reality television shows like *Jackass* and *America's Funniest Home Videos* when foolish behavior results in genuine injury. He calls this "crisis slapstick."[4]

(a)

(b)

(c)

Figure 2.1 Slapstick around the world. Innocuous diversions in Hong Kong, France, and India. (a) Stephen Chow dons a birdcage hat in *Tricky Brains* (1991). (b) Louis de Funès leads a chase through the bubblegum factory in *The Mad Adventures of Rabbi Jacob* (1973). (c) Vinod Khanna performs a goofy vaudeville routine in *Amar Akbar Anthony* (1977).

Figure 2.2 Slapstick turns deadly serious in *Dying of Laughter* (1999).

Farce

Slapstick shares its lowly status with farce, a dramatic cousin. If the former term draws attention to the genre's stylized actions, the latter emphasizes the nature of its plots. *The Oxford English Dictionary* defines farce as "a comic dramatic work using buffoonery and horseplay and typically including crude characterization and ludicrously improbable situations." The French word *farcir*, "to stuff," was applied metaphorically to comic interludes stuffed between more serious religious plays in early sixteenth-century Europe.[5] The metaphor is also apt for a dramatic form overflowing with exaggerated gestures, overblown characters, and stories that indulge our appetite for outrageous scenes.

French works of cinematic farce like René Clair's *The Italian Straw Hat* (*Un chapeau de paille d'Italie*, 1928) and Jean Renoir's *Elena and Her Men* (*Elena et les Hommes*, 1956) draw inspiration from the popular plays of Georges Feydeau (1862–1921), who perfected the conventions of stage farce for middle-class Parisian audiences during the Belle Époque. Feydeau's tightly crafted plot structures, honed in more than sixty plays, balanced the requirement of credulity and pleasure, of respectability and entertainment. For five amusing acts, his characters struggle to preserve their dignity while feeding their basic human appetites. Although hypocrites and figures of authority usually get their comeuppance by Act Four, the social order is happily restored by the final act.

Other national traditions of movie farce trace their roots to native theatrical and literary sources. The British Carry On series and Monty Python films owe a debt to the lively farces of London's Aldwych Theatre and to shrewd playwrights like Oscar Wilde. Benigni was schooled in the vulgarities of Tuscan *Fescennine* verse and the bawdy Roman comedies of Plautus and Terence. The master of Soviet laugh-aloud comedy, Leonid Gaidai, drew on Mikhail Bulgakov's wacky stories and Chekhov's early, lighthearted stage plays. Their influence runs through scene after madcap scene of Gaidai's *Operation Y and Shurik's Other Adventures* (*Operatsiya 'Y' i drugie priklyucheniya Shurika*, 1967), *The Diamond Arm* (*Brilliantovaya ruka*, 1968), and *Ivan Vasilievich: Back to the Future* (*Ivan Vasilyevich menyayet professiyu*, 1973).

Similar pathways of influence can be found in the East. Some Indian comedies hark back to the farcical Sanskrit texts (*prahasana*) of the seventh century, which took the upper castes and holy men as their targets. Much of the mirth in Japanese films dates back to the Kyogen farces of the fourteenth through seventeenth centuries, which lampooned the landed *daimyo*. Like the humorous interludes of late medieval European drama, which offered unruly sketches of a drunken Noah between solemn mystery plays on the cathedral steps, Kyogen skits served as comic relief from the weightier pageantry of Noh drama, performed on the same stage.[6]

Farce reminds us that all humans are at the mercy of their animal drives. However much we try to appear pious or noble, our pretensions to dignity and social standing can slip away at any moment like papier-mâché masks. Yet in its purest form, farce is basically conservative: At the end of day, the status quo is essentially restored and the audience leaves with a smile, having been more entertained than instructed. Today, pure farce is still served up in theaters and on screen. Accomplished playwrights like England's Michael Frayn (*Noises Off*, 1982) and French filmmakers like Michel Hazanavicius (*OSS 117: Cairo, Nest of Spies*/*OSS 11: Le Caire, nid d'espions*, 2006; *The Artist*, 2011) follow the old formulas with admirable success. More often, though, the machinery of farce serves satirical or absurdist agendas in contemporary film and drama. It may offer the comic spectacle of people reduced to acting like physical objects, a concept explored at length in Henri Bergson's *Laughter*. It may enact the spirit of Carnival, indulging the pleasures of the lower body, as Mikhail Bakhtin proposed in *Rabelais and His World*. And it may provide opportunities to release the kind of repressed energies that Sigmund Freud analyzed in *Jokes and Their Relation to the Unconscious*. These three most-often-cited theorists of humor only begin to explain this seemingly simple comic genre.

Satire

If slapstick sometimes bumps into farce and vice versa, both forms of comedy often merge with satire, a more pointed use of humor that takes aim at particular targets. The targets may be social, political, or cultural institutions. They also may be individuals. Typically, the people being satirized are those in power whose pretensions and hypocrisy are exposed, to the delight of those who have the wit to recognize that the emperor is just an ordinary man (rarely a woman) without his crown and fancy clothes.

In *Whiskey Galore!* (1949), the stuffy English commander of the Home Guard tries to confiscate a stash of whiskey from the Scottish locals who have salvaged several cases from a ship just run aground on their isolated island. The war is nearly over, so there's no real need to ration alcohol or prepare for an invasion, but Captain Waggett insists on keeping up the wartime spirit, proudly asserting his stiff upper lip. "They're so unsporting," he complains about the Scots. "They don't do things like the English. We play the game for the sake of the game. Other nations play for the sake of winning it." Alexander Mackendrick's film mocks Waggett's superior attitude and the British arrogance he represents (Figure 2.3a). *The Man in the White Suit* (1951), another Ealing Studios comedy, satirizes corporate capitalism and the labor unions that are quick to shed their principles and the trust of their most deserving members for profit and self-interest. In *3 Idiots* (2009), a Hindi film, the target is a pompous professor and the principles of cut-throat competition and rote learning that govern his elite engineering school. In the course of the three-hour film, a group of students led by their ingenious schoolmate cut the professor down to size and expose flaws in the school's philosophy of education. *3 Idiots* was a huge hit in India and helped to reform the Indian system of higher education (Figure 2.3b).

It might be tempting to trace the term *satire* back to the so-called satyr plays of ancient Greece, a rowdy form of burlesque comedy, rife with bawdy sight gags and mock drunkenness, that was performed between more serious dramatic fare. The dual nature of satyrs—half human and half beast—accentuates the animal in man. However, most scholars today have concluded that the word more properly derives from the Latin word *satur* or *satira*, meaning "full." It refers to a Roman tradition of poetic medley (*lanx satura*), metaphorically conceived as a platter of mixed fruits and nuts, suggesting a variety of styles and subjects, a fitting food for thought.[7]

While satire in literature, cinema, or the other arts is often studied as a genre, the term is such a slippery one that some consider it more of a mode or style. Satires range widely from the cheerful ironies of *The Gods Must Be Crazy* (1980), in which a Coke bottle tossed from an airplane over the Kalahari Desert is worshipped by a tribe of bushmen as a gift from the gods (Figure 2.3c), to the bitter cynicism of *Xala* (1975), in which a Senegalese businessman is cursed for his mistreatment of women and the poor. Satires may be uproariously funny, like *The Mad Adventures of Rabbi Jacob*, or darkly humorous, if humorous at all, like *La Grande Bouffe* (1973), in which the protagonists eat themselves to death.

Figure 2.3 Three targets of film satire. (a) British arrogance in *Whiskey Galore!* (1949). (b) Competitive education in *3 Idiots* (2009). (c) Coca-Cola culture in *The Gods Must Be Crazy* (1980).

In contrast to slapstick and farce, which are identified by their techniques and plot devices, satire hinges on intention. In broad terms, the purpose of satire is to hold human folly up to ridicule. This is often achieved through the use of irony, exaggeration, contrast, and double entendre, all instruments of incongruity. The very title of Stanley Kubrick's *Dr. Strangelove or: How I Learned to*

Stop Worrying and Love the Bomb (1964) is ironic. Affection for a nuclear warhead is a strange love indeed. But what makes the film satiric are the consistently ironic and exaggerated portraits of characters like General Jack D. Ripper, who believes the Soviets are using fluoridation to pollute the "precious bodily fluids" of Americans, and Dr. Strangelove himself, a German scientist whose prosthetic right arm keeps snapping into a Nazi salute. Caricature after caricature, image after ironic image, the elements of Kubrick's film add up to a dark satire on the insanity of war, right up to the final scene when a pilot in a Texan hat leaps astride a nuclear bomb and rides it toward its Russian target like a cowboy at a rodeo, to the buoyant tune of "We'll Meet Again."

Parody

Satire bears a family resemblance to parody, but their kinship is not a simple one. Some satires, like the Monty Python films, are also parodies. *Monty Python and the Holy Grail* (1975) parodies movies about heroic knights in armor while taking satiric aim at contemporary British politics. *Monty Python's Life of Brian* (1979) parodies biblical epics at the same time that it satirizes blind faith and religious fanaticism. In his study of *Film Parody*, Dan Harries includes all parody under the general heading of satire because he considers parodies, like satires, to be critiques.[8] But in *A Theory of Parody*, Linda Hutcheon carefully distinguishes parody from satire because "they have different targets and different affinities with the rhetorical trope common to both: Irony."[9]

Strictly speaking, parody is a comic form of imitation. A movie parody imitates the style and structure of another film, typically a genre film. Mel Brooks made a career of spoofing Westerns (*Blazing Saddles*, 1974), horror films (*Young Frankenstein*, 1974), thrillers (*High Anxiety*, 1977), and science fiction (*Spaceballs*, 1987), among other popular genres. Literary parodies emulate literary models, as Henry Fielding did when he made fun of the epistolary style and sappy sentiment of Samuel Richardson's *Pamela* (1740) by transforming the protagonist, a virtuous servant girl, into a calculating gold-digger in his witty *Shamela* (1741).

The term *parody* emerged during the sixteenth century with a form of burlesque poetry known as *paroidia*, from the Greek words *para* (beside) and *oide* (ode, or song). At heart, a parody is a kind of counter-song, a facetious facsimile intended to be read or seen alongside the original text. In contrast to homage, which pays respectful tribute to its source material, parody is typically irreverent, often subversive. So while the Australian release of *Snow White and the Huntsman* (2012) is a deferentially updated homage to Walt Disney's classic *Snow White and the Seven Dwarfs* (1937), the Disney Studio's own *Enchanted*

(2007) pokes fun at Snow White's old-fashioned notions of female domesticity and romance in a hip, tongue-in-cheek retelling of the tale. Parody may also be distinguished from the postmodern concept of "pastiche," another kind of imitation that celebrates the text or texts it replicates without the mocking tone. Quentin Tarantino's hybrid genre films are often cited as examples of pastiche.

Cinematic parody is almost as old as cinema itself. A week after the Lumière brothers released their comic gag film, *The Sprinkler Sprinkled* (*L'arroseur arrosé*, 1985), Edison made fun of it with *Garden Scene*. A few years later, Buster Keaton was spoofing early Westerns in *The Frozen North* (1922), in which he arrives in Alaska by way of the New York City subway. The American Western proved to be particularly ripe for emulation around the world. Directors in Italy, England, Germany, and India appropriated its imagery and stories, adapting them to local tastes. Many of these overseas Westerns (like Sergio Leone's *A Fistful of Dollars* [*Per un pugno di dollari*], 1964 and Ramesh Sippy's *Sholay*, 1975) were serious efforts to exploit a popular film form, more homage than parody. It was a different matter east of the Iron Curtain. In Soviet Czechoslovakia, Oldřich Lipský scored a big hit with *Lemonade Joe, or the Horse Opera* (*Limonádový Joe aneb Koňská operá*) in 1964. The eponymous hero is a clean-living gunslinger who sets out to reform a town full of hard-drinking cowboys. Dressed in a white outfit, his guns slung low over the hips, Joe saunters into the Trigger Whiskey Saloon and orders a glass of lemonade. When someone scoffs, he quickly demonstrates how lemonade makes for sharper shooting than does whiskey. The film features the genre's usual characters—a handsome hero, a shifty villain, a revivalist's virtuous blonde daughter, a dark-haired saloon singer named Tornado—all delivering the Western clichés in Czech. This would be simply good fun, pure parody, if not for the critical elements of satire. It turns out that Joe has a secret motive. He has really come to promote his lemonade, which bears the brand name of Kolaloka. He courts the blonde evangelist and makes a deal with her father to set up a lemonade saloon in competition with the Trigger Whiskey, offering the man 4% of the business. So, serious or not, *Lemonade Joe* ends up as a Soviet critique of Western, Coca-Cola capitalism (Figure 2.4a).

Red Western parodies gained popularity in another part of Eastern Europe, Soviet-controlled Romania. From 1978 to 1981, Dan Pita directed a set of comedies known as the Transylvanian Trilogy. The first of these (*The Prophet, the Gold and the Transylvanians* [*Profetul, aurul şi ardelenii*], 1978) is set in Cedar City, Utah, where a pair of Transylvanian immigrants have come to meet their brother. Instead, they're greeted by gunfire. The newcomers speak no English and their only weapon is a Turkish gun taken from the siege of Plevna. What follows is an entertaining romp through the familiar territory of the Wild West seen through the eyes of Romanians (Figure 2.4b). Many of the stereotypes are here—the reluctant marshal, the crooked ex-cavalry officer, shootouts in

(a)

(b)

(c)

(d)

Figure 2.4 Parodies of the Western, east and south. (a) *Lemonade Joe, or the Horse Opera* (1964)—Czechoslovakia. (b) *The Prophet, the Gold and the Transylvanians* (1978)—Romania. (c) *The Return of an Adventurer* (1966)—Niger. (d) *Sholay* (1975)—India.

saloons and on the street, with plenty of villains—but much of the humor turns on Eastern European politics, history, and culture. The Romanian brothers and their Hungarian neighbors are still feuding under the banners of Kossuth and Iancu, two dead heroes from the old country. Even the American-born cowboys speak with foreign accents. The film reminds us how many of the pioneers who tamed the West were immigrants. For Romanians who watch the trilogy nostalgically today, it's a reminder of a time when the most readily available Westerns behind the Iron Curtain were local parodies.

Elsewhere in the world, Westerns were parodied with more satiric intensity. Alassane Moustapha, one of black Africa's first film directors, made *The Return of an Adventurer* (*Le retour d'un aventurier*) in Niger in 1966 (Figure 2.4c). It begins innocently enough when a young man named Jimmy returns from the United States with a suitcase full of cowboy gear for his friends. But when they start to act like the gambling, whiskey-drinking, rough-riding characters they've seen in movies, their disruptive behavior threatens the peace of village life. Moustapha allows his audience to have fun with the clichés, but his intentions are clearly polemical: Hollywood's fantasies have no place in traditional African culture. Thirty years later, Jean-Pierre Bekolo released *Aristotle's Plot* (*Le complot d'Aristote*, 1996) in Cameroon. More complex than Moustapha's parody-satire, Bekolo's film centers on a movie theater where a gang of African youths have grown up on Hollywood fare. Like the young men in *The Return of an Adventurer*, they try to emulate the actors they admire, with disastrous results. Bekolo's target here is not just the American Western genre but the whole canon of Western storytelling and its roots in Aristotle's *Poetics*. Countering this tradition, Bekolo proposes a radical new form of film narrative that he believes authentically reflects the peoples and cultures of Africa.

Making parodies invokes the creative spirit of rebellion, a way to topple old genres and clear the way for new ones. The European novel was born this way. Cervantes and Fielding began by making fun of medieval romance (in *Don Quixote*) and the classical epic (in *Tom Jones*), inventing a new form of modern narrative in the process. For readers and for viewers, parodies offer the pleasure of recognition. To the extent that we know the target texts, we enjoy being in on the joke. From an international perspective, parodies demonstrate the flow of media images, stories, and ideas across national boundaries. In addition to the Western, the genres most often spoofed abroad include James Bond spy flicks (France's *OSS 117: Cairo, Nest of Spies*, Britain's *Carry On Spying* [1964], Hong Kong's *Aces Go Places* [*Zui jia pai dang*], 1982), horror films (Hong Kong's *Encounters of the Spooky Kind* [*Gui da gu*], 1980, and *Mr. Vampire* [*Geung si sin sang*], 1985), Norway's *Trollhunter* [*Trolljegeren*], 2010), and Chinese martial arts films (Hong Kong's *Drunken Master*; Mainland China's *Just Call Me Nobody* [*Da xiao jiang hu*], 2010). Indian films are rife

Figure 2.5 Ansari mimics Chaplin imitating Hitler in a scene from *Sholay* (1975).

with parody, like the sidesplitting prison scene in *Sholay* when Ansari mimics Charlie Chaplin mimicking Hitler (Figures 2.4d and 2.5). Genres seem to get tossed back and forth like beach balls in a transnational game of harmless fun, but also as a way for one region to cash in on another's success while adding a local spin to the sport.

More Forms of Comedy

In Section Two of this book, we'll be encountering all the comic forms described above and several more specialized formulas.

The "comedy of manners" is a subspecies of satire that focuses on the behavior of a social class. It boasts a literary ancestry dating back to Shakespeare, English Restoration comedy, and, more recently, the plays of Oscar Wilde and Noël Coward. In modern times, comedies of manner are likely to spoof the upper crust on British television (in *Jeeves and Wooster*, it's the wily servant Jeeves who gets the better of his master), but they may also take aim at the smug self-satisfaction of France's bourgeoisie (Jean Renoir's *Boudu Saved from Drowning* [*Boudu sauvé des eaux*], 1932) or the rising middle class in postwar Japan (Yasujiro Ozu's *Good Morning* [*Ohayo*], 1959).

Military comedies tend to emerge once the censorship and propaganda of actual wartime subside. From the United States (*Stalag 17*, 1953; *M*A*S*H*, 1970) to France (*Don't Look Now . . . We're Being Shot At!* [*La grande vadrouille*], 1966) and Italy (*The Great War* [*La grande Guerra*], 1959) to China (*Off to Success* [*Chen gong ling shang*], 1941) and Korea (*Joint Security Area* [*Gongdong gyeongbi guyeok*], 2000), these films may revive the jocular camaraderie of military life for many veterans but also often ridicule the darkly risible absurdities of war.

Romantic comedy can flourish anywhere and anytime the unsmooth course of true love seems fair game for a humorous appraisal. In 1930s Hollywood, the rocky road of romance took the form of "screwball comedy," which plays the romantic leads against each other in a mock battle of the sexes. *It Happened One Night* (1934) puts a spoiled socialite (Claudette Colbert) together with a roguish working-class reporter (Clark Gable) on a bus trip down the East Coast. By the time they reach the journey's end, both have overcome the barriers of class, gender politics, and ego to find common ground and the inevitable happy ending. In England, Richard Curtis scored a series of successes as the writer for witty rom-coms like *Four Weddings and a Funeral* (1994), *Notting Hill* (1999), *Bridget Jones's Diary* (2001), and *Love Actually* (2003), which he also directed. In France, rom-coms tend to be more talky (Éric Rohmer's *Claire's Knee* [*Le genou de Claire*], 1970; Agnès Jaoui's *The Taste of Others* [*Le goût des autres*], 2000) or quirky (Jean-Pierre Jeunet's *Amélie* [*Le fabuleux destin d'Amélie Poulain*], 2001). Italians like their romance bawdy, at least they seemed to during the *commedia sexy* craze of the 1970s, when directors like Pier Paolo Pasolini drew on the earthy tradition of Boccaccio in *The Decameron* (*Il Decameron*, 1971). From Scandinavia (*Italian for Beginners* [*Italiensk for begyndere*], 2000) to Africa (*Sex, Okra and Salted Butter* [*Sexe, gombo et beurre salé*], 2008), from South Asia (*Who Am I to You?* [*Hum Aapke Hain Koun . . .!*], 1984) to East Asia (*Shall We Dance?* [*Sharu wi Dansu?*], 1996), every corner of the planet adds its own regional flavor to the universally cockeyed concoction of romance.

One of the most fascinating developments in global comedy is the trend toward black comedy, which seems to have reached a critical mass in recent times. To be sure, taboo subjects like suicide and sexual violence were treated earlier with satirical intent. It was the surrealist theorist André Breton who coined the term *humour noir* in his 1935 *Anthology of Black Humor*. Breton cited writers like Jonathan Swift, who published *A Modest Proposal For preventing the Children of Poor People From being a Burthen to Their Parents or Country, and For making them Beneficial to the Publick* in 1729. The mock modesty and the verbosity of Swift's title underscore the irony in his proposal. By offering to solve both the Irish food shortage and the overpopulation problem by serving surplus children as food for wealthy ladies and gentlemen, he expressed his scorn for the heartless attitudes of the upper class toward the poor.

Something like this scornful humor is at work in films like *Dr. Strangelove, M*A*S*H, La Grande Bouffe*, and *Seven Beauties*. A dark strain of comedy also runs through Norway's *The Bothersome Man* (*Den brysomme mannen*, 2006) and South Korea's *Oldboy* (*Oldeuboi*, 2003), where the violence ranges from a cut finger, self-flagellation, and a man run over by a train to predatory sex and torture. In *Wild Tales* (*Relatos salvajes*, 2014), an anthology film from Argentina, a man threatens to destroy an entire airplane full of people as revenge for past events and two men caught in the throes of road rage chase each other to a fiery death. What is troubling about these movies is not just the level and variety of man's inhumanity to man, but the way these violent acts are staged for laughs. The airplane story comes across as a single punchline joke and the charred, entangled corpses of the two male drivers are ironically mistaken for entwined lovers. (▶ See "Case Study for Chapter 12: *Wild Tales*" on the website.)

Some cultural analysts relate these films to the sick comedy and dead-baby jokes that emerged in the 1950s. (Question: What is red and silver and spins around? Answer: A baby in a blender.) Freudians evoke release theory to explain what they regard as a way to vent anxiety in the form of nervous laughter. Freud used the term *gallows humor* to describe jokes that people tell in the face of extreme trauma, like the discomforting jokes Jews tell about the Holocaust. There is plenty of grim gallows humor in Nordic movies like *101 Reykjavík* (2000), where it sometimes goes by the Icelandic label *Gálgahúmor*. But Freud limited his term to jokes told by the victims, those whose neck is in the noose, not to the hangman's sense of humor. Much of the dry wit in Scandinavian cinema seems more akin to the sarcastic repartee of the Old Norse heroes, who used humor to bait their foes and crow about their conquests. This aggressive form of laughter, intended to establish dominance, is more aptly explained by the superiority theory of humor espoused by Plato and Hobbes. It may even be related to the guilty pleasures of slapstick, especially the "crisis slapstick" that Joshua Moss finds in *Jackass* videos. After a chapter-long analysis of the phenomenon, Benjamin Schachtman makes a distinction that pivots on ambivalence. He concludes that sick humor and absurd humor (the existential comedy of Samuel Beckett, which underscores the meaninglessness of life) lack the instability of dark humor, which "represents the natural ambivalence of comedy and tragedy." Schachtman argues that the darkness comes from "the anxious coexistence of two opposing emotional responses toward a stimulus."[10]

Viewed this way, black humor answers to the incongruity theory associated with Immanuel Kant and Arthur Schopenhauer, supported further by neuroscientists who find evidence that an individual's response to stimuli can take two paths. One path follows the primal limbic system, preparing us to fight or flee. This mirrors the seriously single-minded arc of tragedy. The other response, processed in the brain's prefrontal cortex as nonserious, follows a different set of pathways, circumventing the impulses to action and diverting energy to laughter. This roundabout route, described by Torben Grodal's PECMA flow model,[11] mirrors the elastic, multifaceted, playfully indirect trajectories of comedy.

Like all genres and sub-genres, comic forms go in and out of fashion with the times. They also arise in certain places or adapt themselves to local conditions, like the *folklustpel* films of Sweden or the kung fu comedy of Hong Kong. The kinds of humor we prefer—cynical or joyful, malicious or benign—may appeal to us at different moments in our lives, much as comic forms do at different eras in a nation's history. Understanding these forms and their traditions is one more way to help us place ourselves within the vast and ever-shifting spectrum of world comedy.

Notes

1. Terry Lindvall, "Movie Humor Types," in *Encyclopedia of Humor Studies*, ed. Salvatore Attardo (Los Angeles: Sage, 2014), 520–522.
2. William Solomon, *Slapstick Modernism: Chaplin to Kerouac to Iggy Pop* (Champaign: University of Illinois Press, 2016), 7.
3. Solomon, *Slapstick Modernism*, 8.
4. Joshua Moss, "Punching Snook: Crisis Slapstick and Geo-Violence in Contemporary Humor." Paper presented at the Society for Cinema and Media Studies Conference in Toronto, March 14, 2018.
5. "Farce," *Oxford Living Dictionaries*, continually updated at https://en.oxforddictionaries.com/definition/farce.
6. Jessica Milner Davis, "Farce," in *Encyclopedia of Humor Studies*, ed. Salvatore Attardo (Los Angeles: Sage, 2014), 233–236.
7. See Dustin Griffin, *Satire: A Critical Reintroduction* (Lexington: University Press of Kentucky, 1994), 6–10; Catherine M. Schlegel, *Satire and the Threat of Speech: Horace's Satires, Book 1* (Madison: University of Wisconsin Press, 2005), 4.
8. Dan Harries, *Film Parody* (London: British Film Institute, 2000), 32.
9. Linda Hutcheon, *A Theory of Parody: The Teachings of Twentieth-Century Art Forms* (New York: Methuen, 1985), 104.
10. Benjamin Nathan Schachtman, "Black Comedy," chap. 12 in *Comedy: A Geographic and Historical Guide*. vol. 2, ed. Maurice Charney (Westport, CT: Praeger, 2005), 169.
11. Torben Grodal, "A General Theory of Comic Entertainment: Arousal, Appraisal, and the PECMA Flow," chap. 10 in *Cognitive Media Theory*, ed. Ted Nannicelli and Paul Taberham (New York: Routledge, 2014). See also his *Embodied Vision: Evolution, Emotion, Culture and Film* (Oxford: Oxford University Press, 2009).

3
Archetypes of Comedy

In Chapter 1, we traced a number of theories and studies to explore *why* people laugh. In Chapter 2, we considered the most popular comic genres, or forms, that help to classify *what* they laugh about. In this chapter, we'll be asking questions about *who*. Who are the people we laugh at or with in movie comedies? What kinds of individuals are the most frequent targets or perpetrators of cinematic mirth? A great many figures of fun populate our jokes and literary humor, our television shows and movies, but only a few have persisted through the centuries and across cultural boundaries to be considered comic archetypes. We will be focusing on three of these: the clown, the trickster, and the comic duo.

Here Come the Clowns

The word *clown* may derive from a Scandinavian term (Icelandic *klunni*, Swedish *kluns*) meaning "clumsy." Or it might come from the Latin word *colonus*, for "farmer."[1] In either case, the clown's etymological roots underscore his lowly status as a creature of the country, ignorant and boorish.

We laugh at clowns to feel superior, perhaps, or to laugh by proxy at ourselves. The red nose and big feet of the circus clown exaggerate the physical aberrations of the "other," what makes him (for clowns are most often male) funny looking, at odds with the norm. But his differences from the rest of us also give him license to flout the rules of normal behavior. He acts like a spoiled child, gooses the emcee in the high hat, breaks balloons and taboos, is funny in another sense, creating a light-hearted mood that is more receptive to reproach. In this role of the jester, the clown performs an age-old ritual, revealing truths about society that can only be said in jest. The clown gets to be both entertaining and subversive.

This clown figure seems to be an ancient, universal character. In his book on *Clowning as a Ritual Practice*, William Mitchell finds examples among the Mayans of Mexico, the Melanesians of Papua New Guinea (where women often play the role), and the Hopi Indians of North America (where they act as "contrary" individuals to poke fun at the group). Mitchell notes that clowning "creates mayhem by dismantling cognitive coherence and continuity" and consequently serves as social criticism.[2]

When the World Laughs. William V. Costanzo, Oxford University Press (2020). Oxford University Press
DOI: 10.1093/oso/9780190924997.001.0001

Circus clowns may come in two varieties. The Whiteface, smartly dressed and eminently clever, carries the slapstick and plays the pranks. The Auguste, or red-nosed clown, is clumsy and incompetent; he is invariably the butt of the jokes, the one who gets slapped. The boorish Auguste has been traced back to the sixteenth-century *zanni* (zany) figure of the *commedia dell'arte* and before then to the rustic fools of Greek and Roman comedy. The Whiteface has its origins in the figure of the harlequin, with his diamond-patterned costume and nimble wit, a later cousin of the clever servant in plays by Aristophanes and Plautus. In Shakespeare's works, the two figures appear as the natural (simpleton) and the artificial (witty, verbal) fools. Lear's Fool, one of the shrewdest and wiliest in literature, still wears the motley clothing of his ancestor.[3] In the global literature of movie comedy, clowns of both varieties abound.

Clowning around has always been a popular entertainment in the United States, where the film industry set standards for the business early on. More books have been written about Hollywood's movie comedians than about comic film actors from elsewhere in the world.[4] The classic American film clowns often worked alone (Buster Keaton, Harold Lloyd, Harry Langdon), sometimes in pairs (Abbott and Costello), occasionally in threes (the Three Stooges) or more (the Marx Brothers, Max Sennett's Keystone Cops). While all of them could do a pratfall when needed, each cultivated a recognizable comic style. Keaton was the stone-faced stoic improvising success out of chaos (and sometimes the reverse) with an American can-do ingenuity. Harold Lloyd fashioned a straw hat, a pair of horn-rimmed glasses, and a penchant for daredevil stunts into a prolific career. These movie clowns were followed by a long line of successors known for their distinctive styles, among them Mae West's campy wisecracks, Lucille Ball's zany timing, Robin Williams's manic improvs, Steve Martin's absurdist wit, Woody Allen's neurotic fretting, Eddie Murphy's street-smart rowdiness, Jim Carrey's energetic slapstick, and Whoopi Goldberg's brassy sass.

In England, the tradition of clown-based comedy stretches from Charlie Chaplin's silent frolics to Mr. Bean's visual and verbal inanities. In the early days of sound film, regional comedians from vaudeville like George Formby and Gracie Fields brought their local accents and their antics to the screen. This proved to be particularly popular with British audiences and helped the British film industry gain traction at home. Later comic Brits like Peter Sellers, John Cleese, Stephen Fry, and Steve Coogan indulged their countrymen's partiality for eccentric characters, honing their peculiarities into a kind of national brand. Unlike most of their American counterparts, they seemed to be more interested in getting laughs than in being liked. Chaplin understood this when he moved to the United States, where he developed his Little Tramp figure as a sympathetic outsider. Compare this to Rowan Atkinson's Bean, who has a certain nasty streak that keeps him at a distance.

In France, the launch site of world cinema, the clown tradition dates back even earlier. Max Linder preceded Chaplin as an international star of silent comedy. Gabriel-Maximilien Leuvielle (Linder's real name) was already an award-winning performer of stage comedy when Georges Méliès gave him a chance to enter the new medium of motion pictures. His screen persona, Max, channeled the Whiteface clown into an upper-class dandy whose desire for women and the high life invariably led to trouble and loads of laughs. Max wielded his swagger cane for comic effect before Chaplin's tramp adopted the same prop, and like Chaplin, Linder went to Hollywood, but his films were less successful there. Dogged by his declining popularity and by fits of depression after injuries sustained during World War I, Linder, once the highest-paid entertainer in the world, ended his life sadly, in what may have been a double suicide with his wife. This unhappy ending has become commonplace in comedians' biographies, underlying a persistent link between laughter and depression.

Linder was succeeded by the great Fernandel, who dominated French comedy for more than forty years, from 1930 on, starring in some 150 films. His persona, in contrast to Lindner's Max, was more in line with the Auguste character: badly dressed, uncouth in speech, and distinctly lower class. Yet he always managed to persevere over his betters. Fernand Joseph Désiré Contandin (his name at birth) was likeable both on and off the screen. He was reportedly so attentive to his wife that her mother nicknamed him *Fernand d'elle* (Fernand of her), thus giving him his stage name. Max Linder and Fernandel excelled in physical comedy, a practice continued by the likes of Louis de Funès, a master of comic groans and grimaces, by Jacques Tati, Pierre Étaix, Jean Dujardin, and Jacques Villeret. This may be a clue to why the French are so fond of Jerry Lewis.

Nearly every country seems to have its favorite national clowns (Figure 3.1). In Italy—the land of Totò, Alberto Sordi, Nino Manfredi, and Roberto Benigni—he is typically a *chiacchierone*, a congenial nonstop talker with a big heart who all too often acts like a buffoon. In Russia, he is apt to be a charming schemer, like Chichikov in Gogol's classic *Dead Souls*, or a guileless dupe, like Pyotr Zinovyev's Khmyr in *Happiness* (*Schastye*, 1934). Karl Valentin, a Bavarian comedian, made his mark in Weimar Republic cabaret culture and silent films, combining a Dadaist form of wordplay with gallows humor into routines that would inspire works by Bertolt Brecht and Samuel Beckett. Brecht considered him "probably the greatest clown Germany ever produced."[5]

In every region of the world, movie clowns bring the native styles of earlier traditions to the screen. Jackie Chan's roles as a much-battered but ultimately triumphant kung fu clown reflect the acrobatic energy of Peking opera, in which he was originally trained. Toshiro Mifune's parodic performances as the boorish, would-be warrior in *Rashomon* (1950) and *Seven Samurai* (*Shichinin no samurai*, 1954) incorporate visual and dramatic elements of the demonic ogres

Figure 3.1 A global gallery of clowns. (a) France's Fernandel in *Heartbeat* (1938). (b) Italy's Roberto Benigni in *Life Is Beautiful* (1997). (c) Hong Kong's Stephen Chow in *The God of Cookery* (1996).

(*oni*) from Japanese folklore. In African satires, from Sembène's *Xala* (1975) to Mambéty's *Touki Bouki* (1973), many of the comic figures are modeled on the shifty animals—hares, spiders, and hyenas—that abound in local trickster tales. Further north, in Scandinavia, film comedians combine the irreverent humor of Loki, the wily trickster god of Old Norse mythology, with a tight-lipped detachment that seems to be in keeping with the dark, desolate winters of Norway, Sweden, or Finland.

Although comedy is regularly seen as the opposite of tragedy, its laughing twin, the clown may function psychologically much like the tragic hero. Freud regarded Oedipus as a dramatic representation of unconscious drives. On the stage, Oedipus the King acts out every man's deep-seated desire to kill his father and sleep with his mother. When he is finally punished in Sophocles' play, the audience experiences a vicarious catharsis. Oedipus dies, but we get to leave the theater cleansed of our guilty impulses. Something like this happens in *Till Luck Do Us Part* (*Até que a Sorte nos Separe*, 2012), a Brazilian comedy directed by Roberto Santucci. The film opens in the living room of an ordinary family. Faustino (known as Tino) barely earns enough money as a fitness trainer to support his wife and kids, but they are generally happy. All this changes when he wins the lottery. Sometime later, they are living a life of conspicuous consumption. Their spending is out of control and everything is oversize, from their home to their meals. Leandro Hassum plays the lead as a clownish but lovable buffoon. He's larger than life, everything in excess, but he also has a big heart. When he finally learns that he has overspent his budget, that he's flat broke, he struggles to explain this to his wife, who is pregnant and may lose the baby if she has a sudden shock. Now Tino must economize, get a job, become responsible, and keep one step ahead of his wife's carefree shopping binges. His preposterous efforts to do so keep the comedy in high gear. For Brazilians in 2012 this whiplash ride from rags to riches and back again had special meaning: After a brief period of heady prosperity in the 2000s, the country was plunged back into an era of scandal and recession. Like Faustino (a wry allusion to Faust's bargain with the devil in Goethe's tragic play), the people of Brazil now had a lot of belt tightening to do. Watching Leandro Hassum enact a version of their own predicament on the screen, they could experience the cleansing work of comedy. In this way, the clown embodies our failings and our fears in exaggerated forms. In his excesses we recognize something of ourselves and laugh away the pain, a form of comedic catharsis.

Tricksters of the World

As we've seen, some clowns may be tricksters. Nineteenth-century anthropologists used the term *trickster* to denote a certain kind of character that populates the myths and folktales of traditional societies. Whether it's a spider in the oral narratives of West Africa or a coyote in North American Indian lore, the trickster (usually, but not always, male) delights in poking fun at the bigger creatures in its neighborhood, using wit and imagination to outsmart established power and authority. In his study of West African societies, Robert Pelton describes the trickster as "loutish, lustful, puffed up with boasts and lies, ravenous for foolery and food, yet managing always to draw order from ordure."[6] At the same time, Pelton finds a sacred dimension in this slippery figure, "a vivid and subtle religious language, through which he links animality and ritual transformation."[7] Pelton's findings echo earlier observations by Carl Jung, who regarded tricksters as "cosmic beings" bridging the animal and divine aspects of mankind. For Jung, the trickster spirit is "a 'psychologem,' an archetypal psychic structure of extreme antiquity," "the reflection of an earlier, rudimentary stage of consciousness," "a collective personification."[8] It's no wonder, then, that versions of this mischievous, elusive figure appear throughout the history of humanity, reflected in stories that societies everywhere tell themselves.

We find traces of his crafty conduct in Enki, the impish Sumerian god; in the prank-loving giant Loki of Old Norse mythology; in the exploits of Turkey's Nasreddin Hodja; and in the rollicking adventures of Sun Wukong, China's irrepressible Monkey hero. He appears in the Old Comedy of Aristophanes as the cunning servant who outsmarts his social betters, in a sixteenth-century German chapbook as Till Eulenspiegel, as the picaresque rogue of seventeenth-century Spanish novels, as Br'er Rabbit in the Uncle Remus stories, and as Shakespeare's Puck in *A Midsummer Night's Dream*. Not surprisingly, the trickster spirit continues to inspire the storytellers of the world, most notably through the modern medium of movie comedy.

In her book *The Trickster in Contemporary Film*, Helena Bassil-Morozow finds examples of cinematic tricksters in Jack Nicholson (*One Flew Over the Cuckoo's Nest*, 1975), Tim Burton's *Batman* (1989), Jim Carey (*Dumb and Dumber*, 1994), and Ben Stiller (*The Cable Guy*, 1996), among others. Bassil-Morozow builds on Jung's belief that tricksters bear traces of our species' earlier development, the animal in us linked to a sense of the divine, a reminder from the unconscious. She stresses that tricksters are liminal figures, ignoring boundaries set by the authorities, forever playing in the margins of society.[9]

While most of Bassil-Morozow's analysis focuses on American movies, tricksters can be found throughout world cinema (Figure 3.2). This is particularly true in Africa, where so much filmmaking is still close to the traditions of oral storytelling. The female protagonist in Mambéty's *Hyenas* (*Hyènes*, 1992) acts much like the animal of its title does in West African tales, misleading the men who have mistreated her with elaborate deceptions. Like the beast that personifies scornful intelligence and guile in Africa, she devours her wrongdoers

Figure 3.2 Cinematic tricksters, north, east, and south. (a) A Danish boss tricks his employees in *The Boss of It All* (2006). (b) China's mythical Monkey does a tricky dance in *Journey to the West: Conquering the Demons* (2013). (c) Africa's animal tricksters are personified in *Hyenas* (1992).

with ferocious, mocking laughter. In Jean-Pierre Bekolo's *Quartier Mozart* (1992), a sassy schoolgirl called "Queen of the Hood" inhabits a male body in order to experience sexual politics from a different point of view. Assisting her in this deception is a shape-shifting trickster known as Panka. As in *Hyenas*, it is the women who overturn the status quo by crossing boundaries of gender and power with hilarious results. The comic potential of upsetting cosmic order is even more apparent in Adama Drabo's *Skirt Power* (*Taafé Fanga*, 1997), in which a whole village of women exchange roles with their menfolk. By setting his film in Mali, Drabo accentuates Jung's point that tricksterism evokes a primal link between comedy and divinity. (▶ See "Case Study for Chapter 10: *Skirt Power*" on the website.) While some of the trickster's cosmic origins may be missing from more modern stories, the figure's trickery is often a matter of survival. The comic hero in *Life Is Rosy* (*La Vie est belle*, 1987) practices a form of *débrouillardise*, the art of being resourceful to get by, outwitting others and ridiculing authority on the way to fast money and/or sex. The ludicrous protagonist of *Osuofia in London* (2003) acts and dresses like a clown in the mismatched clothing of a country rube, but he manages to outsmart an unscrupulous London lawyer and his haughty white wife, returning to his African village in triumph. These films from Senegal, Cameroon, Mali, Zaire, and Nigeria illustrate the widespread persistence of trickster characters in what is arguably their place of origin. But they also inhabit the cinemas of Asia, Europe, and the Americas as if these continents were their native habitats.

The oldest chronicle of Japan, the *Kojiki*, further attests to the trickster's spiritual origins. Among the oral narratives that it records is the story of Amaterasu Omikami, the sun goddess who disappears during an eclipse. With trickery and burlesque laughter, the other gods draw her out of her dark cave and watch her perform a comical striptease, establishing connections between comic pranks and sexuality, laughter and fertility that continue to be celebrated in modern rituals.[10] Elements of this folkloric tradition may be found in the shape-shifting trickery of anime films like *Spirited Away* (*Sen to Chihiro no Kamikakushi*, 2001). China's most celebrated trickster, Monkey, survives his mythical origins in the many feature films and cartoons that have entertained children and adults for generations. A master of disguises and ingenious pranks, this childlike simian figure of fun runs amok in heaven and on earth, gleefully creating chaos and upsetting the established order wherever he goes. Monkey possesses all the attributes of tricksters listed by William Hynes and William Doty in *Mythical Trickster Figures*: a semi-godly birth; an aptitude for changing shape at will; a gift for imaginative deceptions; a proclivity to mix the sacred and profane, to turn hierarchies upside down, and to cloud the air with ambiguity.[11] Stephen Chow gives the legend a cinematic twist in *Journey to the West: Conquering the Demons* (*Xi you: Xiang mo pian*, co-directed with Derek Kwok in 2013), cutting a tricky path between wacky comedy and grotesque satire. Chow himself, known for his special brand of Hong Kong "tricky-brain humor," has directed and starred in some of China's most popular comedies, including *The God of Cookery* (*Sik san*, 1996) and *Kung Fu Hustle* (*Gung fu*, 2004), all of which spin around the exploits of fast-talking, manic, devious protagonists.

Chow's character might be called a conman in the West, where trickster figures regularly take the form of charismatic cheats and rip-off artists. We see them trying to pull off petty thefts and scams (usually without much success) in Italian comedies like *Big Deal on Madonna Street* (*I soliti ignoti*, 1958) and *Divorce Italian Style* (*Divorzio all'italiana*, 1961), in French films like *The Swindle* (*Rien ne va plus*, 1997), and in Danish movies like *The Boss of It All* (*Direktøren for det hele*, 2006). They also abound in South American comedies, from *The Little Liar* (*La mentirosa*, 1942) to *Macunaíma* (1969) and *Nine Queens* (*Nueve reinas*, 2000).

The Boss of It All is about an actor hired to impersonate a corporate CEO who turns out to be using the hapless man for his own con game. It was directed by Lars von Trier, who has been called "one of the foremost tricksters of world cinema,"[12] reminding us that filmmaking itself can be a tricky business. Trier delights in playing clever pranks on his audience, manipulating their perceptions with crafty editing and camerawork. He works in the tradition of cinematic illusionists like Georges Méliès, who, back in the earliest days of motion pictures, discovered that movie tricks could be entertaining and profitable.

Comic Duos

Clowns and tricksters often work alone, but they sometimes need a foil to bring out the comedy. We have seen this with the Auguste and Whiteface clowns, who work against and with each other. The red-nosed Auguste's goofy buffoonery seems funnier when set off against the reserved behavior of the well-dressed Whiteface. Together, these two circus types perform a double act that entertains live audiences with comic contrasts in character and social status. In one form or another, they have appeared on the vaudeville stage, radio, television, and the internet and in movies and standup.

Nearly every national tradition seems to have its equivalent of Laurel and Hardy (Figure 3.3a). In the United States the list includes Abbott and Costello, Dean Martin and Jerry Lewis, Lucille Ball and Desi Arnaz, Cheech and Chong, Tina Fey and Amy Poehler, Key and Peele, and Bert and Ernie. In Denmark, a comic vagabond team known as Doublepatte and Patachon entertained local film audiences with their slapstick routines even before Laurel and Hardy. The comedy twosome of Olmedo and Porcel was a big hit in Argentina during the 1970s and 1980s. While the laughter sparked by these duos invariably comes from a clash of personalities, it is usually fed by certain cultural assumptions. When British viewers enjoy an episode of *Jeeves and Wooster*, they are laughing at the same interaction between a wily servant and his foolish master that once entertained audiences in ancient Greece and the Italian *commedia dell'arte*, but their laughter is filtered through the particularities of the English language and the British class system. When French filmgoers watch an African immigrant from the banlieues trying to take care of a wheelchair-bound Parisian aristocrat in *The Intouchables* (*Intouchables*, 2011), it is their day-to-day familiarity with the plight of migrants in modern France that gives this mismatched buddy film its comic edge.

In Japan, a form of comic scuffling between a witty character (*tsukkomi*) and a fool (*boke*) grew popular in variety halls in the late 1920s, becoming a mass-media, commercial genre in the age of radio and film. Known as *manzai*, the act alternated between verbal sparring and whacks on the head and has been traced back to traveling teams who performed at New Year's festivals during the Middle Ages.[13] In China, a similar phenomenon is known as *xiangsheng* (literally "face and voice"). Here, the comic appeal lies in a rapid-fire banter, typically between an exasperatingly thick-headed clown and a frustrated straight man, much like Abbott and Costello's "Who's on first?" routine. Traditionally delivered in the Beijing dialect, the dialog is rich in puns and contemporary allusions. With origins in the Qing Dynasty, some two hundred years ago, *xiangsheng* has evolved from a low-class street entertainment into an alternately bawdy and sophisticated art form comparable to Western standup. During the Communist era, crosstalk performances were sanitized and repurposed to promote Mao Zedong's program for a common people's language, *putonghua*. During the Cultural Revolution, they were used as a blatant propaganda tool. More recently, the form has acquired new energy and satirical bite on television and the internet.[14]

Buddy movies offer various versions of the comic duo, usually two men with opposing goals and dispositions, like the incompatible roommates in *The Odd Couple* (1968). Walter Matthau's Oscar is sloppy and carefree while Jack Lemmon's Felix is fussy and high-strung, a perfect recipe for predictable laughs. Much of the humor in these films depends on viewers being familiar with home-grown actors and their screen personas. British fans of Michael Winterbottom's road movies, *The Trip* (2010) and *The Trip to Italy* (2014), recognize that Steve Coogan and Rob Brydon are playing self-ironic versions of themselves. The same is true of the Taiwanese comedians in Lee Hsing's *Brother Wang and Brother Liu on the Road in Taiwan* (*Wang Ge Liu Ge You Taiwan*, 1959), which follows the escapades of two working-class buddies (Figure 3.3b). The heavy-set shoe-shiner (Wang) and the scrawny rickshaw driver (Liu) strike it rich and live it up like

Figure 3.3 Comic duos on the world's screens. (a) Laurel and Hardy in *Thicker Than Water* (1935). (b) Taiwan's *Brother Wang and Brother Liu on the Road in Taiwan* (1959). (c) Argentina's Olmedo and Porcel in *Los extraterrestres* (1983).

an Asian Laurel and Hardy. Wang Ge and Liu Ge became so popular that they performed in several sequels. Familiarity and predictability are part of the fun.

Important, too, is the way these movies mirror a particular time and culture. For Petter Næss's *Elling* (2001), Næss cast the two leads, Per Christensen and Sven Nordin, from an earlier stage play, itself based on a bestselling novel. Elling (Christensen) is a technophobic fusspot who is paired with a burly, boisterous man named Kjell Bjarne (Nordin). The Norwegian government has removed them from an institution and placed them in their own apartment, hoping to integrate them back into society. Much like Felix and Oscar, they become ludicrously incompatible roommates, but while *The Odd Couple* is a comedy about two Hollywood celebrities working through the predicaments of single men in 1960s America, *Elling* has a lot to say about the Norwegian welfare system at the start of a new era of social politics. (▶ See "Case Study for Chapter 11: *Elling*" on the website.)

The dynamics between Olmedo and Porcel likewise reflect the social context of Argentina during the times in which their films were made (Figure 3.3c). In their earlier films, both actors played middle-class married men in hot pursuit of other women. Olmedo is the mustached Lothario, Porcel ("*el gordo*") his overweight companion in preposterous crimes of infidelity. Their elaborate sexploits invariably fail, landing them back home where they belong. Sexual transgression is thwarted and the institution of marriage is saved. In his study of the team's joint career, Fernando Pagnoni concludes that these adult films served a conservative agenda, functioning as "safety valves" during the 1970s, an era of harsh Argentinean dictatorships and strict oversight of moral values by the Catholic Church. Their later films, Pagnoni argues, introduce a more subversive tone as the political climate grew more volatile. In the late 1970s and early 1980s, their escapades become more absurd as the duo adopts improbable disguises (usually of their social betters) in pursuit of their illicit desires. The duo keeps falling prey to their own absurdities, but they come closer to their goal. As Porcel says to Olmedo in *Las mujeres son cosa de guapos* (1981), at the very point when both are finally about to realize their dreams of sexual conquest, "We have been waiting for this moment for 20 movies."[15]

While clowns, tricksters, and comic duos form the lion's share of comedic archetypes, these overlapping figures of fun have many relatives. The Italian *commedia dell'arte* fine-tuned its stock characters into local specialties, like the bombastic soldier (*miles gloriousus*), the miserly merchant (*Pantalone*), or the pedantic scholar (*il Dottore*), types that can still be found throughout the world. Other laughingstocks from literature and film have found their way into American television sitcoms and standup comedy teams, including dreamers (Don Quixote, Candide, Lucille Ball in *I Love Lucy*), neurotics (Philip Roth's Portnoy, Woody Allen, David Hyde Pierce's Niles Crane on *Frasier*), and eccentrics (Dickens's Mr. Grimwig, Rowan Atkinson's Mr. Bean, Lisa Kudrow's Phoebe Buffay on *Friends*). Some characters, however, seem less universal. Lin Feng, a film scholar in England, has explored the image of the *choujue* (ugly character) in Chinese cinema, noting how the performances of Ge You in movies like *Big Shot's Funeral* (*Dawan*, 2001) and *If You Are the One* (2008) have elevated him to star status in his own country but not in the West. Lin Feng contrasts the way beauty and ugliness are viewed as opposites in the West while there is a tendency to regard them not in binary terms but as acceptable features of normal life within Chinese culture.[16]

Women are more prominent among comic figures than might be inferred from this brief and incomplete survey. Recent studies by scholars like Susan Horowitz, Gail Finney, and Linda Mizekewski are helping to revise our understanding of the many ways that female characters and caricatures contribute to the world of comedy.[17] As this kind of scholarship advances, and as women keep expanding our notions of humor, we can look forward to a richer, more varied balance of comic archetypes on stage, in our literature, and on our screens.

Notes

1. "Clown," *Shorter Oxford English Dictionary*, 6th ed. See also Louise Peacock, "Clowns," in *Encyclopedia of Humor Studies*, ed. Salvatore Attardo (Los Angeles: Sage, 2014), 131.
2. William E. Mitchell, ed., *Clowning as Critical Practice: Performance Humor in the South Pacific* (Pittsburgh, PA: University of Pittsburgh Press, 1992), 19.
3. See Norrie Epstein, "Lear's Fool," in *The Friendly Shakespeare: A Thoroughly Painless Guide to the Best of the Bard* (New York: Viking, 1993), 409–415.
4. For example, see Gerald Mast, *The Comic Mind: Comedy and the Movies* (Chicago: University of Chicago Press, 1979; Ed Sikov, *Laughing Hysterically: American Screen Comedy of the 1950s* (New York: Columbia University Press, 1994); Kristine Brunovska Karnick and Henry Jenkins, eds., *Classical Hollywood Comedy* (New York: Routledge, 1995); Alan Dale, *Comedy Is a Man in Trouble: Slapstick in American Movies* (Minneapolis: University of Minnesota Press, 2000); Frank Krutnik, ed., *Hollywood Comedians, the Film Reader* (New York: Routledge, 2003); Bambi Haggins, *Laughing Mad: The Black Comic Persona in Post-Soul America* (New Brunswick, NJ: Rutgers University Press, 2007); Scott Balcerzak, *Buffoon Men: Classic Holiday Comedians and Queered Masculinity* (Detroit: Wayne State University Press, 2013); Linda Mizejewski, *Pretty/Funny: Women Comedians and Body Politics* (Austin: University of Texas Press, 2014).
5. Maurice Charney, ed., *Comedy: A Geographic and Historical Guide*, vol. 2 (New York: Praeger, 2005), 355.
6. Robert D. Pelton, *The Trickster in West Africa: A Study of Mythic Irony and Sacred Delight* (Berkeley: University of California Press, 1980), 1.

7. Pelton, *Trickster*, 5.
8. Carl Jung, "On the Psychology of the Trickster-Figure," in *Four Archetypes: Mother, Rebirth, Spirit, Trickster*, trans. R. F. C. Hull (New York: Routledge, 1972); originally published as part 5 of *Der Goetliche Schelm*, by Paul Radin (Zurich, 1954), 165–167.
9. Helena Bassil-Morozow, *The Trickster in Contemporary Film* (New York: Routledge, 2012).
10. Jessica Milner Davis, *Understanding Humor in Japan* (Detroit: Wayne State University Press, 2006), 4.
11. William J. Hynes and William G. Doty, eds., *Mythical Trickster Figures: Contours, Contexts, and Criticisms* (Tuscaloosa: University of Alabama Press, 1993).
12. Stephen Holden, "It's Not That the Boss Seems Distant. It's Just That He Doesn't Exist," *New York Times*, May 23, 2007. http://www.nytimes.com/2007/05/23/movies/23boss.html.
13. Joel Stocker, "Manzai: Team Comedy in Japan's Entertainment Industry," in *Understanding Humor in Japan*, ed. Jessica Milner Davis (Detroit: Wayne State University Press, 2006), 51–74.
14. See David Moser, "Xiangsheng," in *Encyclopedia of Humor Studies*, ed. Salvatore Attardo (Los Angeles: Sage, 2014), 808–812.
15. Fernando Gabriel Pagnoni, "Enrique Cahen Salaberry and Hugo Sofovich: Humor Strategies in the Films Featuring the Duo Alberto Olmedo and Jorge Porcel," in *Humor in Latin American Cinema*, ed. Juan Poblete and Juana Suárez (New York: Palgrave Macmillan, 2016), 129–154.
16. See Lin Feng, "'I'm Ugly but Gentle': Performing Xiaorenwu in Chinese Comedies during the Post-Mao Era," *Transnational Cinemas* 5, no. 2 (2014): 127–140.
17. See Susan Horowitz, *Queens of Comedy: Lucille Ball, Phyllis Diller, Carol Burnett, Joan Rivers, and the New Generation of Funny Women* (New York: Routledge, 1997); Gail Finney, ed., *Look Who's Laughing: Studies in Gender and Comedy* (New York: Routledge, 2004); Mizejewski, *Pretty/Funny*.

4
Comedy, History, and Culture

After considering the why, what, and who of movie comedy, we are ready to take up questions about when. If humor has a history, at what point did it begin? Is there a reliable chronology of laughter? Just when did *homo erectus* become *homo ludens*?

Many have tried to put a starting date on the evolution of human comedy, seeking evidence in the archeologic record, ancient texts, and genetic research. Pointing to prehistoric masks and sculptured faces, Carolyn Wells sees comic figures—fools and buffoons—as early as 11,000 BCE.[1] Thomas Wynn goes even further back in time. With less evidence and a good deal of circumstantial speculation, Wynn theorizes that Neanderthal communities may have had designated clowns, individuals who performed physical humor to amuse the group and relieve stress, a social function similar to medieval court jesters and comedians today.[2] Frank Machovec stands on more solid ground when he cites examples of 3,500-year-old riddles from the Nippur tablets of Sumeria or quotes from the Chinese *Book of Changes* (possibly the oldest book in the world, dating back to 1000 BCE) or points out whimsical images of animals playing human roles in Egyptian hieroglyphs from about the same era.[3] In fact, the lighter side of life in ancient Egypt is illustrated again and again in comic sketches and graffiti left by artisans on the walls of tombs. It can even be argued that the concept of "lighthearted" has pharaonic origins. The *Book of the Dead* describes how each person's heart is weighed in the balance at death. If it weighs less than an ostrich feather, the person enters the everlasting afterlife. Otherwise, the heart is consumed by vicious beasts and its bearer ends up in a kind of eternal chaos (Figure 4.1).[4] Lightheartedness has continued to be a preferable option for many people in many cultures since that time.

Before attempting an historical account, we should review a few key definitions. The word *laughter* describes physiologic behavior, a response to certain stimuli. Although we commonly attribute human laughter to jokes and funny stories, scientists who specialize in laughter and its biologic effects (they call themselves gelotologists) point out that people laugh for reasons that are not particularly funny, like tickling and neurologic disorders. As we learned in Chapter 1, apes, bonobos, and even mice can laugh. So constructing a chronology of laughter, strictly speaking, would be a tenuous undertaking at best. Humor and comedy are more helpful terms. The word *humor*, as it is generally

When the World Laughs. William V. Costanzo, Oxford University Press (2020). Oxford University Press
DOI: 10.1093/oso/9780190924997.001.0001

Figure 4.1 Weighing the heart in ancient Egypt. Only the lighthearted go on to the afterlife. From *Book of the Dead*, circa sixteenth century BCE. Courtesy of Oxford University Press.

used today, refers to things that we find funny, lightheartedly entertaining. Someone with a sense of humor appreciates witty comments, clever jokes, and amusing situations. In earlier times, the term was associated with theories of medicine dating back to ancient Greece and widely believed during the European Renaissance (Figure 4.2). According to that belief, the body's equilibrium depends on four vital fluids (called humors, or humours) in the bloodstream. Physical, emotional, and mental health require a harmonious balance of these fluids. Our modern usage bears traces of these theories when we say a healthy sense of humor is the mark of a balanced personality. There is a similar concept in traditional Chinese medicine, which links wellness to the flow of *qi*, a vital energy or spirit. The free, unobstructed flow of *qi* through the body ensures one's physical health and mental stability. When we revisit this concept in Chapter 13, we will see that the earliest terms for "funny" in Chinese, Japanese, and Korean were reserved for intellectual, often satirical forms of wit. It was not until much later that English loan words like *yumou, youmo*, and *yumeo* entered East Asian languages to describe the more amiable, lighthearted forms of humor associated with the British ideal of a well-mannered individual.

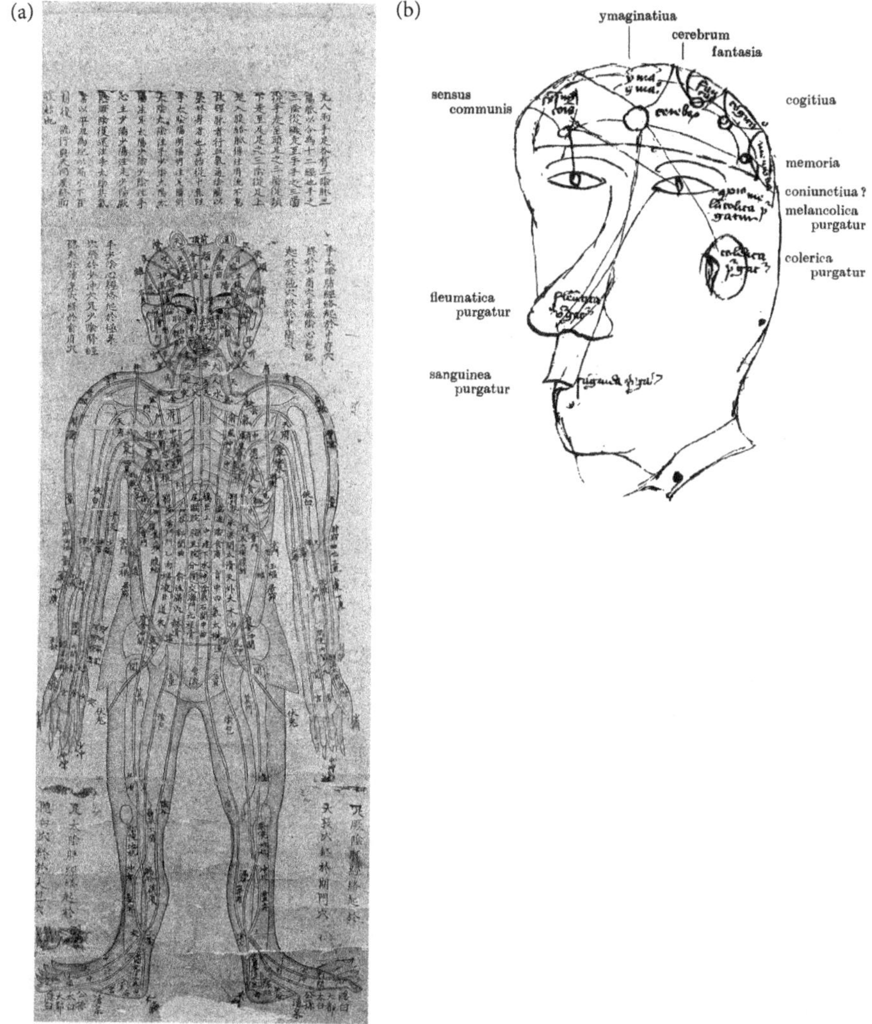

Figure 4.2 Traditional Asian and medieval European medicine focus on the body's equilibrium. (a) Chinese acupuncture chart. Courtesy of Oxford University Press. (b) European drawing. Courtesy of The Wellcome Trust.

A third important term is *comedy*. While comedy and humor are regularly used interchangeably today, comedy originally referred to a literary genre. In Aristotle's day, drama and poetry were classified as comic or tragic, with tragedy enjoying the major share of serious critical attention. In our own time, comedy is regarded as more substantial and complex, as attested by the many sub-genres of comedy described in Chapter 2. In this sense, a global history of comedy is both conceivable and instructive. The brief survey offered in this chapter traces some of the crisscrossing paths of comic storytelling and performance that prepared the way for movie comedies around the world.

Comedy in Ancient and Medieval Times

Before the comic spirits of India, Africa, or China found their way into written texts, before the dramatic comedies of ancient Greece and Rome set the stage for Western literature, people everywhere celebrated the joys of mirth in ritual festivals. These were social events, brimming with revelry and laughter, typically linked to fertility and the community's well-being. The colorful Holi festival in India, the Jewish holiday of Purim, the Roman Saturnalia, the Odwira celebration in Ghana, the Shinto ceremony honoring the Goddess Amaterasu in Japan: Joyous festivals like these are still observed in every continent where human life abounds. The Carnivalesque vitality that animates them lives on in folktales, popular novels, and much of modern literature, often taking the absurd and grotesque forms described by Mikhail Bakhtin in his landmark study of Rabelais.[5] The carefree spirit of Carnival, with its unrestrained indulgences and subversive laughter, is a mainstay of world comedy. We will encounter it in one form or another: in the amatory mischief of Ingmar Bergman's *Smiles of a Summer Night* (*Sommaranatten leende*, 1955), in the carefree exuberance of Brazilian *chanchadas* like *Hello, Hello, Carnival!* (*Aló, Aló, Carnival!*, 1936), in the seditious politics of Joaquim Pedro de Andrade's *Macunaíma* (1969), and the adolescent gross-out jokes of *National Lampoon's Animal House* (1978).

When Greek comedy began to flourish in the fifth century BCE, it still bore the imprint of its prehistoric origins in Dionysian rituals. Dionysius, later called Bacchus by the Romans, was a fertility god, a deity of wine, song, and sacred ecstasy. Like Greek tragedy, its dramatic counterpart, comedy was first performed during religious festivals along with satyr plays, bawdy satires that emphasized the animal side of human life. They abound in frank sexuality, intoxicated gaiety, and all manner of mischievous merriment. Satyr plays were brief interludes, moments of comic relief from the serious, high-minded stuff of tragedy. The comedic plays we know from the collected work of Aristophanes (only eleven of his forty plays survive) are classified as Old Comedy to distinguish them from the New Comedy of Menander. Old Comedy was pungently satiric and rich in lower-body humor, much like the works of Rabelais, Swift, and Voltaire that continued this tradition. New Comedy was less biting and less farcical, centering more on stock characters and their calamitous encounters with the social morality of the day. Its legacy lives on in the Roman plays of Plautus and Terence, in the *commedia dell'arte* of sixteenth-century Italy, in Shakespeare and Molière, in Oscar Wilde's comedies of manners, and in modern sitcoms.

It is difficult to find anything comparable to Greek dramatic comedy in other ancient or medieval cultures, but a lively sense of play runs through the world's earliest writings, from the cuneiform tablets of Mesopotamia to the Sanskrit poetry of India and the works of Chinese literati. This often took the form of riddles, puns, and entertaining tales of trickery. A Sumerian scribe in 1500 BCE asked, "Can you have children without sex?" His answer has the ironic tone of many ribald jokes today: "Can you get fat without eating?"[6] Ancient Sanskrit poets and Chinese scholars were as fond of wordplay as Ugaritic scribes, all of whom delighted in the ambiguous relationships of sound and meaning in their ancient languages.[7] A clever Sanskrit verse addressed to an early Indian ruler plays on the fact that one word, *varna*, refers to both "color" and the basic class system of Indian society:

> You are *rakta* (red, loving) toward good men, *kala* (black, death) toward your enemies, *pita* (yellow, drunk) by women's glances, and possessed of white game. So truly you are the support of the four varnas.[8]

A Song Dynasty wit used the peculiar graphic nature of Chinese to answer the question, "Why does using bamboo to beat a dog result in laughter?"[9] It turns out that the written character for laughter (笑) combines the written characters for dog (犬) and bamboo (竹). As with puns in Sanskrit or any other language, the humor here is confined by linguistic boundaries as well as matters of taste. Outsiders will derive little laughter from these in-jokes.

More accessible is the mocking wit of Dongfang Shuo, the legendary Chinese jester who tickled Emperor Wu (141–87 BCE) into acting sensibly with humorous accounts of royal vanity and imprudent policies. Like court jesters in Africa and Europe, Shuo nimbly strolled along the fine line between amusement and critique. He cleverly couched his reproaches of the emperor in entertaining metaphors and diverting quips. Universal too is the crafty jocularity of Al-Jahiz (776–868), the Arabic prose writer whose *Book of Misers* made fun of his greedy contemporaries, from beggars to schoolmasters. Al-Jahiz's *Book of Animals* may owe some of its satirical humor to *The Panchatantra* (circa 300 BCE), a collection of entertaining Hindu tales in which animals act like people, illustrating greed, lust, vanity, and other all-too-human foibles. This tradition, allied to the spoken stories of preliterate Africa and North America, spread through early medieval Europe as beast fables and later influenced Boccaccio's *Decameron* and Chaucer's *Canterbury Tales* during the fourteenth century in the form of *fabliaux*.

Early Modern Stage Comedy and Precursors of the Comic Novel

The sixteenth century is generally regarded as a turning point in global history. In Europe, an intellectual Renaissance recovered and revived the cultures of classical Greece and Rome. The Protestant Reformation challenged the supremacy of Roman Catholic authority that had dominated medieval life and thought. A new era of exploration and conquest opened trade links from Europe to the New World and the Far East. In the Middle East, where Muslim art and science had already surpassed much of Europe's during the Middle Ages, the Ottoman empire continued to expand the reach and progress of Islam. In Asia, the Indian subcontinent was ruled by Akbar's Mughal empire while the Japanese invaders of Korea were forced to withdraw by China's Ming dynasty troops, restoring Korea's Joseon dynasty as China's traditional ally. In Africa, Islam had built a solid base along the northern coast and was reaching into the established empires and kingdoms of the southern heartland. In the Americas, native peoples like the Algonquians, Sioux, and Navajo had flourished in the northern hemisphere for millennia, and others, like the Arawak, Caribs, Aztecs, and Incas, built sophisticated civilizations further south. These cultures would soon be challenged and overwhelmed by the new arrivals from Western Europe.

During this period and continuing into the next four centuries, people's sense of humor found many outlets as they expressed themselves in performance and in print. We will follow these two strands as they crisscross the planet from place to place, shaping the evolution of stage comedy and the modern novel.

The phenomenon that we call *commedia dell'arte* first appeared in sixteenth-century Italy as troupes of actors plied their trade throughout the countryside. They were professional players, small ensemble groups who performed indoors using masks to represent stock characters (Figure 4.3). At first, few of their plots were scripted. Actors drew from a wide range of known scenarios, relying on their wits to embellish scenes and improvise dialog, which they often delivered in regional dialects to amuse the local crowds. Some of their roles and stories have been traced back to Greek and Roman models, like the clever servant who outwits her overbearing master or the young lovers who try to outmaneuver their old-fashioned elders. Other roles, like the braggart Capitano (a descendant of Plautus's *Miles Gloriosus*) and the pedantic Dottore (associated with Bologna, the home of Europe's oldest university), were honed into hilarious caricatures that remained popular for centuries. Women were important members of these troupes both as actors and as innovators. They are credited with elevating the language and plot material to a higher level. By the middle of the eighteenth century, Italian theater had achieved a literary status under the reforms of Venetian playwright Carlo Goldoni, who introduced elements of realism and rigor. While

Figure 4.3 Stock characters from *commedia dell'arte*. Courtesy of Oxford University Press.

his plays pleased a more sophisticated audience, they sucked much of the vitality from Italy's two-hundred-year-old tradition of masks and impromptu contrivances.

Meanwhile, *commedia dell'arte* helped to fan the flames of national comedic drama throughout Europe. As their reputation grew, troupes spread into Spain, Bavaria, Eastern Europe, England, and France. Louis XIV invited a group of Italian players to Paris, where their recipe of improvised dialog, acrobatic slapstick, and pantomime was called *Comédie-Italienne*. Eventually, this mélange became increasingly French in language and in style, an alternative to the *Comédie-Française* (founded in 1680 as the French state theater), and was itself replaced by the *Opéra-Comique* in 1801. The great French playwright Molière (1622–1673) absorbed the Italian style into his comedies and farces. Lope de Vega (1562–1635) and Pedro Calderón de la Barca (1600–1681) did much the same in Spain. In England, William Shakespeare (1564–1616) and Ben Jonson (1572–1637) borrowed elements of *commedia*, each in his own way. Whole books have been written about Shakespeare's debt to Italian models.[10] Jonson seized on the medieval theory of humors and applied it metaphorically to comedy. In the introduction to his play *Everyman out of His Humour* (1600) he wrote,

"When some one peculiar quality doth so possess a man that it doth draw all his affects, his spirits, and his powers in their confluxions all to run one way: this may be truly said to be a *humour*."[11] This notion, that the natural balance of internal drives goes awry when a person's entire psychological energy flows in a single direction, is central to much comedy. Today, we might call it a ludicrous obsession. *Commedia dell'arte* figured the obsession in masks, each representing a dominating trait, and in the gestures of stock caricature. Later playwrights ridiculed characters possessed by greed (Molière's *The Miser*, Jonson's *Volpone*, Shakespeare's *Merchant of Venice*), vanity (William Congreve's *The Way of the World*), or lust (William Wycherley's *The Country Wife*). We still laugh at these types because we recognize their distorted values and behavior in our neighbors and ourselves.

At roughly the same time, performance comedy gained popularity in East Asia. The Kabuki theater that arose in seventeenth-century Japan drew laughs with its distinctly ribald jokes. Like *commedia*, Kabuki relied on well-defined role types and physical clowning, but it eventually developed more complex characters and elaborate staging that involved trapdoors and wire tricks. In this respect, it is closer to the stylized figures and acrobatic stunts of Peking opera that entertained crowds in eighteenth-century China and continue to this day on stage, in television programming, and in Jackie Chan movies.

While the comic muse of the European Renaissance was expressing itself on stage, it was also finding outlets in prose narration. Sometimes this took the form of satirical stories written by learned men who were familiar with Horace, Juvenal, and other Roman models. The Dutch humanist Desiderius Erasmus wrote *The Praise of Folly* (1509) in Latin. Sir Thomas More, an Englishman, used Latin for his *Utopia* (1516), although his title is a Greek pun combining *ou-topos* (no place) and *eu-topos* (good place). Sometimes the comic impulse took the form of picaresque novellas like *The Life of Lazarillo de Tormes* (1554), published anonymously in Spanish. Like his crafty cousins in trickster tales around the world (Germany's Til Eulenspiegel, France's Reynard the Fox), the Spanish *picaro* (rascal) amused readers with his meandering adventures while exposing injustice and hypocrisy along the way. The roguish hero continued to serve as a playful protagonist for social satire in Henry Fielding's *Tom Jones* (1743) and Laurence Sterne's *Tristram Shandy* (1761–1767), precursors of the modern novel and a major genre of film comedy.

Elements of picaresque humor run through Eastern fiction too, in China's *Journey to the West* (1590), for example, or in the "floating world" literature of Japan, an urban genre that flowered in the 1600s as a new mercantile middle class was emerging.[12] As in the West, these works contributed to the modern novel along with classics like *The Tale of Genji* (eleventh-century Japan) and *Dream of the Red Chamber* (eighteenth-century China), with their gentler forms of social satire more akin to comedy of manners.

The Nineteenth and Twentieth Centuries: Modern Comedy

The nineteenth century has been called the age of nationalism, a time when people who shared a common border, language, political ideals, and cultural traditions focused on their collective identity. The feeling was especially strong in Europe, where like-minded compatriots fought to unify populations within Germany and Italy or to free Greece and Poland from foreign domination. Liberation movements also spread through Latin America, Africa, Asia, and the Middle East as Argentinians, Ghanaians, Indians, Han Chinese, Egyptians, and Syrians sought freedom from colonial control as independent nations.

The history of humor reflects this new direction in important ways. From the1800s onward, it became increasingly common to speak of German drama or the English novel or modern Japanese literature. While the spirit of *homo ludens* continued to express itself in festivals and through personal interactions, more and more humor took written forms, as literacy and printing technologies grew more widespread. American writers like Mark Twain and James Thurber became known as humorists. Others, like Jane Austen in England, Honoré de Balzac in France, and Heinrich von Kleist in Germany—though not known primarily for their comic sensibility—wrote novels and plays that advanced earlier literary traditions of satire, parody, and comedy of manners. In each case, their works are closely tied to the conditions and social orders of a particular time and place.

English humor of the time gained worldwide recognition as being culturally distinct. There was nothing quite like the witty social critique of Jane Austen's *Pride and Prejudice* (1813) or *Mansfield Park* (1814). While her comic characters might reveal their foolishness through their own delightful dialog (sometimes as high-spirited and coarse as if they were acting in a farce), it is Austen's restrained and subtle narrative voice that chides them and their milieu with gentle (and sometimes not-so-gentle) gradations of irony. The social satire in William Thackeray's *Vanity Fair* (1847–1848) and Samuel Butler's *Erewhon* (1872) turned darker and more scathing as England entered the Victorian era. George Meredith noted this English taste for satire, which he considered antisocial. In *An Essay on Comedy* (1877),[13] he described Swift as "savage" and Gibbon as "malicious," contrasting their misogamist form of ironic humor with "the Comic spirit," a more accepting form of humor that underlies the comic works of Shakespeare, Austen, and Fielding. Whereas satire condemns mankind for its faults, the Comic ridicules characters for their unhealthy behavior, their affectations. English humor delights in eccentricity, which is both ludicrous and optimistic,

optimistic because an eccentric individual is not incurably wicked but merely out of balance.

Across the English Channel, in France, comedy also took distinctive paths. Guy de Maupassant's short stories and the novels of Balzac and Gustave Flaubert are rife with satirical Gallic wit. On stage, the taste for biting satire found expression in Henri Bonaventure-Monnier's burlesques and vaudevilles, which caricatured bourgeois mediocrity in the likes of Monsieur and Madame Prudhomme. The vaudevilles of Georges Feydeau and the "well-made" plays of Eugène Scribe treated the middle class more gently; they drew more laughs from the misjudgments and misunderstanding among characters than from fundamental failings in the characters themselves. The calculated absurdities in these plays gave French farce its national flavor and influenced Alfred Jarry's *King Ubi* (1895), a forerunner of the modernist theater of the absurd.

Spanish-language comedy flourished during the first half of the century. Fernández de Moratín, Spain's Molière, brought more realism to the stage in *El baron* (*The Baron*, 1803) and *El sí de las niñas* (*The Maiden's Consent*, 1806) as did Manuel Eduardo de Gorostiza in Mexico. Meanwhile, on the Italian peninsula, young intellectuals were struggling to define a national identity. Writers like Carlo Righetti, Giuseppe Rovani, and Arrigo Boiti formed a movement known as *scapigliatura* (disheveled). Their bohemian brotherhood sought to rejuvenate Italian culture by incorporating foreign influences from Germany, France, England, and America. Writers in the German-speaking lands were also forging a sense of national unity. While Wolfgang Goethe tended to be more seriously satiric, Heinrich von Kleist drew on the Carnivalesque tradition of *Fastnachtspiel* in *The Broken Pitcher* (*Der zerbrochne Krug*, 1807), and Heinrich Heine, who lamented the German reputation for ponderous prose, added flourishes of wit and graceful humor in his verse. Several currents of humor also run through Russian literature of the period, notably in Ivan Goncharov's satirical novel *Oblomov* (1859), Nikolai Gogol's sardonic story "The Overcoat" (1842), and Anton Chekhov's plays, in which the characters are all too human, largely unaware of their flaws and the illusions that skew their lives.

Some of these comic forms and the beliefs that sustain them continued on into the twentieth century and our own times. In the early 1900s, the popular demand for live comic entertainment found outlets in the music halls of England, in American revues and French vaudeville, in the smoky cabarets of Vienna and Berlin. Later on, as new technologies opened more venues, variety shows on radio and television catered to mass audiences looking for some comic relief from their daily lives. Much of the humor in these shows was topical, playing on local stereotypes and issues, mixing physical gags and wordplay just as *commedia* players had done in the sixteenth century. Some of the same humor can be found in today's standup comedy, performed live or on the internet.

A good deal of modern late-night television and standup comedy trades in satire, continuing another thread of comedy that can be traced back through more literary forms to Swift, Voltaire, Gogol, Erasmus, and Horace. Satirical newspapers and weekly periodicals like France's *Charlie Hebdo* and *Mad* magazine in the United States hark back to *The Spectator*, an eighteenth-century broadsheet published several times a week by Joseph Addison and Richard Steele and read in London's coffeehouses. Such precursors can be found for nearly every form of humor in contemporary life. Ralph Mueller points out that *The Boys from Syracuse*, the Rodgers and Hart musical of 1938, was based on Shakespeare's *Comedy of Errors*, itself adapted from Plautus's *plautusenaechmi*. Mueller traces the precisely timed, coincidental comedy of Michael Frayn's *Noises Off* (1982) back to eighteenth-century French and English farce. He even suggests that the comic triumph of young love over age, a recurring plot in modern soaps and sitcoms, has its origins in ancient fertility rituals.[14]

Despite these threads of continuity, the twentieth century disrupted the parade of human history with its own unique anxieties. The massive devastation of two world wars, the rise of ideologies like Fascism and Communism, advances and setbacks in science and technology, Freudian psychology, and a robust momentum toward transnational interdependence: These transformative forces caused major shifts in the global zeitgeist. A universal faith in God or in rational man no longer seemed possible. Some forms of comedy acquired a noticeably different tone, becoming darker, more grotesque. Avant-garde artists began to explore the implications of a fundamentally purposeless existence. Dadaists and surrealists opened pathways to the unconscious drives underlying and undermining rational thought. This new form of comedy became known as absurdist. Martin Esslin popularized the term in his 1961 book, *The Theatre of the Absurd*, in which he grouped playwrights like Samuel Beckett, Eugène Ionesco, and Jean Genet. Their work, Esslin argued, describes a world that is "absurd" in Albert Camus's sense of the word, an existence "devoid of purpose . . . cut off from [mankind's] religious, metaphysical, and transcendent roots."[15] In Ionesco's *The Bald Soprano* (1950) and Beckett's *Waiting for Godot* (1952), there is no plot, the characters lack human depth, their speech is riddled with clichés and non sequiturs. There seems to be no hope for a happy ending to their meaninglessly circular bustling and chattering, yet the audience is laughing. While the existential underpinning of these plays may be new, much is still familiar. Didi and Gogo, the central characters in *Waiting for Godo*t, talk and act like old vaudeville clowns. Other precedents can be found in the illogicalities of Lewis Carroll's *Through the Looking Glass*, the perplexing circularities of Franz Kafka's *The Castle*, or the grotesqueries of Alfred Jarry's *Ubu Roi*.

While these recent trends in literary humor have been well documented in Europe, much less has been written in English about comedy in Asia, Africa, or the Middle East. One place to look for examples is in Japan during the Tokugawa period (1603–1868) and the ensuing Meiji Restoration. Several Japanese studies of comic literature appeared during that time. Some focused on the evolution of *kyogen* drama from its native roots as a crude form of popular entertainment to its acceptance as an bona fide art form, an everyday-life alternative to the ideal world of No drama. Other studies sought to explain Western literary forms to Eastern readers in terms of Japanese models. Parallels might be made between the earthy comedy of medieval verse and sixteenth-century haiku or between English comedy of manners and the urbane satire of *The Tale of Genji*. But Joel Cohn, who cites these references in his *Studies in the Comic Spirit of Modern Japanese Fiction*, finds a general lack of congruence between Western and Asian categories.[16] Cohn identifies two major strains of humor in Japan: a lowbrow spirit of jovial mockery and an elite culture, generally conservative and inhospitable to satire unless directed at individuals rather than the status quo. That is what makes Edo Japan such a rarity, "an outburst of boldly freewheeling parody, extravagant wordplay, and incisive satire that has had few if any equals in Japanese culture before or since."[17] The rare works of comic literature that do appear in twentieth-century Japan are exceptions that prove the rule. Shikitei Sanba's *The Bath-House of the Floating World* (1809–1813) used coarse humor to poke fun at members of the lower classes. Natsume Soseki's *I Am a Cat* (1905–1906) and *Botchan* (1906) offered deft satirical portraits of vanity and folly among the upper crust in the manner of Fielding and Meredith. Ibuse Masuji (*The Bill Collecting Trip*, 1937) and his protégé Dazai Osamu (*New Tales of the Provinces*, 1944) adapted Western models to Japanese culture and society, creating some of East Asia's most universal works of comic literature. As travel and cultural exchange became more commonplace, writers in China, Africa, and India began to follow suit.

Enter the Movies

The new medium of motion pictures proved particularly well suited to comedy of all kinds. Here was an art form that could tell stories in realistic or imaginative modes. It could combine whimsical music with uproarious chase scenes, could crack droll jokes, perform slapstick routines, and engage in witty wordplay. It could entertain the masses with crude clowning or appeal to subtler sensibilities through cunning satire and amusing pleasantries. As cinema evolved and traveled across borders, it absorbed traditions of humor from all parts of the globe.

Early cinema borrowed freely from the stage, especially vaudeville. The silent gags of a Charlie Chaplin or Stan Laurel had universal appeal. When movies added synchronous sound, local favorites from the music-hall tradition brought

Figure 4.4 British vaudeville moves from stage to screen: Benny Hill on TV, season 1, episode 1, "European Song Contest" (1969).

their homespun humor and their dialects to the screen: George Formby and Gracie Fields in England, Max Linder and Fernandel in France, Karl Valentin from the German cabaret, Mae West from American burlesque, Niní Marshall and Luis Sandrini from Argentinian radio. These first comedians of cinema revealed a pattern that would persist throughout the history of the medium: While physical comedy appeals to audiences everywhere, humor based on language and culture tends to be limited to niche markets.This is largely true of comedies that continue the Carnivalesque spirit of mischief and mayhem. In the coming chapters, we will see how Ealing Studios comedies like *Passport to Pimlico* (1948) and *Whiskey Galore*! (1949) provided timely relief for Britons after years of wartime sacrifice. Eldar Ryazanov's *Carnival in Moscow* (*Karnavalnaya noch*, 1956) did something similar for Russians, managing to make fun of Soviet life without offending Soviet authority. In Brazil, a *chanchada* like *Hello, Hello, Carnival!* (*Aló, Aló, Carnival!*, 1936) invited audiences to let off steam with carefree displays of music and spectacle while a tropicalist satire like *Macunaíma* (1969) evoked the more subversive side of Carnival with its challenges to conventional filmmaking and the status quo.

While satire has always gone hand in hand with Carnivalesque hilarity—from Japan's fertility festivals through Rabelais's *Gargantua and Pantagruel* to the masks and stereotypes of *commedia dell'arte*—it becomes more pointedly social and political in satirical comedies like Pietro Germi's *Seduced and Abandoned/ Sedotta e abbandonata* (Italy, 1964), Tengiz Abuladze's *Repentance/Pokanyaniye*

Figure 4.5 The Carnival spirit animates Brazilian *chanchadas* like *Entrei de Gaiato* (1959).

(Soviet Russia, 1984), Juzo Itami's *Tampopo/Tanpopo* (Japan, 1985), and Ra'anan Alexandrowicz's *James' Journey to Jerusalem/Massa'ot James Be'eretz Hakodesh* Israel, 2003). We will see how Djibril Diop Mambéty's *Hyenas/Hyènes* (Senegal, 1992) and Adama Drabo's *Skirt Power/Taafe Fanga* (Mali, 1995) drew on the oral traditions of West Africa to criticize modern Africans. We will watch how Fernando Solanas used surrealist aesthetics to critique the grand narratives of South American history in *The Voyage/El viaje* (Argentina, 1992). We will follow a trend toward darker forms of satire, more akin to Juvenal than Horace, in Jiři Menzel's *Closely Watched Train/Ostřo sledované vlasky* (Czechoslovakia, 1966; Figure 4.6), Hong Sang-soo's *The Day a Pig Fell into the Well/Daijiga umule pajinnal* (South Korea, 1996), and Marco Ferreri's *La Grande Bouffe/La grande abbuffata* (Italy and France, 1973).

The other comic traditions explored in this chapter may also be traced forward to the movies in Section Two. We will find some of the freewheeling, picaresque adventures of Til Eulenspiegel, Lazarillo, Tristram Shandy, and China's Monkey in episodic films like *Bye Bye, Brazil/Bye Bye, Brasil* (Brazil, 1979), *Leningrad Cowboys Go America* (Finland, 1989; Figure 4.7), and *The 100-Year-Old Man Who Climbed Out of a Window and Disappeared/Hundraåringen som klev ut genom fönstret och försvann* (Sweden, 2013). Fans of Jean Renoir's *Boudu*

Figure 4.6 The tradition of satire lives on in Czech films like *Closely Watched Trains* (1966).

Figure 4.7 A Finnish rock band's picaresque adventures in *Leningrad Cowboys Go America* (1989).

Figure 4.8 Ozu's *Good Morning*, a gentle comedy of manners.

Saved from Drowning/Boudu sauvé des eaux (1932), Jacques Tati's *Mr. Hulot's Holiday/Les vacances de Monsieur Hulot* (1953), Yasujiro Ozu's *Good Morning/ Ohayo* (1959; Figure 4.8), and Ang Lee's *Eat Drink Man Woman/Yin shi nan nu* (1994) will find much of the gentler, ironic comedy of manners that sophisticated eighteenth-century readers appreciated in China's *Dream of the Red Chamber* and Jane Austen's novels. The nationalist impulses that fueled much nineteenth-century literature are still active in films like South Korea's *Joint Security Area* (2000) and Uruguay's *The Last Train* (2002) (Figure 4.9). Romantic comedy too, a legacy of Shakespeare and his Italian sources, thrives in films from Germany (*Mostly Martha/Bella Martha*, 2001), England (*Love Actually*, 2003), Lebanon (*Caramel/Sukkar Banat*, 2007), and the People's Republic of China (*Ex-files/Qianren gonglue*, 2014). Meanwhile, the absurdist sensibility that Martin Esslin identified in Beckett and Ionesco still animates films from France (*The Discreet Charm of the Bourgeoisie/Le charme discret de la bourgeoisie*, 1972) and Czechoslovakia (*Daisies/Sedmikrásky*, 1966; Figure 4.10) to Bosnia (*Underground/Podzemlje*, 1995) and Belgium (*The Brand New Testament/Le tout nouveau testament*, 2015).

As the world shrinks, as our global economy stirs the cross-currents of cultural exchange, questions of origin and influence grow more complex. Just as evolutionary biologists debate how species adapt to local habitats and diverge—which species spring from common ancestors, which develop through crossbreeding

Figure 4.9 "Our patrimony is not for sale." Nationalist sentiment in *The Last Train* (2002).

Figure 4.10 Humor takes an absurdist twist in *Daisies* (1966).

and convergence, which arise independently or go extinct—we will see how some film scholars disagree about the precise lineage of movie genres. Most, however, concur that while the uses and expressions of comedy may differ from time to time and place to place, the need to laugh is global and genetic. It's in our DNA.

Notes

1. Carolyn Wells, *An Outline of Humor, Being a True Chronicle from Prehistoric Ages to the Twentieth Century* (New York: Putnam, 1923).
2. Thomas Wynn and Frederick L. Coolidge, "A Neanderthal Walked into a Bar," in *How to Think like a Neanderthal* (Oxford: Oxford University Press, 2012), 134–145.
3. Frank Machovec, "Humor in History," chap. 7 in *Humor: Theory, History, Applications* (Bloomington, IN: iUniverse, 1988).
4. Patrick F. Houlihan, *Wit and Humour in Ancient Egypt* (Oakville, Ontario: Rubicon, 2001).
5. Mikhail Bakhtin, *Rabelais and His World*, trans. Hélène Iswolsky (Bloomington: Indiana University Press, 1984).
6. Samuel Noah Kramer, *From the Tablets of Sumer* (Indian Hills, CO: Falcon's Wing Press, 1956), 154.
7. See Wilfred G. E. Watson and Nicolas Wyatt, *Handbook of Ugaritic Studies* (Leiden: Brill, 1999), 185.
8. Vidyākara, *Sanskrit Poetry from Vidyākara's "Treasury,"* trans. Daniel H. H. Ingalls (Cambridge, MA: Harvard University Press, 1965), 822.
9. Christopher Rea, *The Age of Irreverence: A New History of Laughter in China* (Oakland: University of California Press, 2015), 5.
10. See Artemis Preeshl, *Shakespeare and Commedia dell'Arte: Play by Play* (New York: Routledge, 2017) and Amy Drake, *Unmasking Shakespeare: Commedia Dell'Arte in Shakespearean Plays* (Riga: Lambert Academic Publishing, 2016).
11. Ben Jonson, *Every Man Out of His Humour*, ed. Helen Ostovich (Manchester: Manchester University Press, 2008), 118.
12. Armando Martins Janeira, "The Picaresque Novel," in *Japanese and Western Literature: A Comparative Study* (London: Charles E. Tuttle, 1970).
13. George Meredith, "An Essay on Comedy" in *Comedy*, ed. Wylie Sypher (Garden City, NY: Doubleday, 1956).
14. Ralph Mueller, "History of Humor: Modern and Contemporary Europe," in *Encyclopedia of Humor Studies*, ed. Salvatore Attardo (Los Angeles: Sage, 2014), 304–308.
15. Martin Esslin, *The Theatre of the Absurd* (New York: Anchor Books, 1961), xix.
16. See Joel R. Cohn, *Studies in the Comic Spirit in Modern Japanese Fiction* (Cambridge, MA: Harvard University Asia Center, 1998).
17. Cohn, *Studies in the Comic Spirit*, 18.

5

Technique and Style

If comedy has its own theories, forms, archetypes, and histories, it also favors certain methods for provoking humor. Scholars have analyzed the vast literature of laughter to discover patterns, the time-honored ploys and strategies of mirth. Comedy consultants have written how-to books for writers, particularly scriptwriters: advice derived from the world's most successful stage plays and movie comedies. A few comedy practitioners, like Woody Allen and John Cleese, have discussed their own funny business in biographies and interviews. This chapter offers a glimpse into their styles and techniques: the art and craft of making people laugh.

Let's begin with a moment from the movies. The scene is from *Waking Ned Divine* (1998), a British Indie film directed by Kirk Jones and set in a tiny Irish fishing village where everyone knows everybody else and nothing much ever happens to anyone. When the scene begins, two villagers, husband and wife, are at home. Jackie (Ian Bannen), seated in his armchair and wearing a striped shirt, has rolled up his sleeves to watch the national lottery drawing on television. He calls out to his wife, who is sitting in the kitchen, to bring him some dessert. "Annie, bring me me apple tart, will you? The lottery's started" (Figure 5.1a). Annie (Fionnula Flanagan) replies from the kitchen with her mouth half full, "Fetch it yourself" (Figure 5.1b). But while the lottery drum spins (Figure 5.1c), Jackie grows more animated as each number is called. "Jeepers, Annie. Will you believe it? I've got the second (Figure 5.1d). The third (Figure 5.1e)!" When he announces that he's got the first four numbers, Annie looks up from her plate (Figure 5.1f). By the fifth number, her indifference turns to astonishment. She joins him in the living room. "Jesus, Jackie," she says, "that's five" (Figure 5.1g). Annie looks down at her husband, who is grinning broadly as the final number falls. "Yes! Yes, Yes!" he cries, and in his excitement he begins ripping up the ticket (Figure 5.1h). "Have we won?" she asks (Figure 5.1i). Bewildered, she looks at the torn scraps of paper. His answer clinches the scene: "No," he chuckles, wolfing down a forkful of pie, "but it got me apple tart brought in now, didn't it?" (Figure 5.1j).

It's a simple joke, a prank played on Annie and the audience. Like many jokes, it hinges on surprise. The scene's logic seems to be headed up one path, winning the lottery, only to turn abruptly in another direction at the end. But the effect is skillfully achieved, a masterstroke of cinematic comedy. Watching the

When the World Laughs. William V. Costanzo, Oxford University Press (2020). Oxford University Press
DOI: 10.1093/oso/9780190924997.001.0001

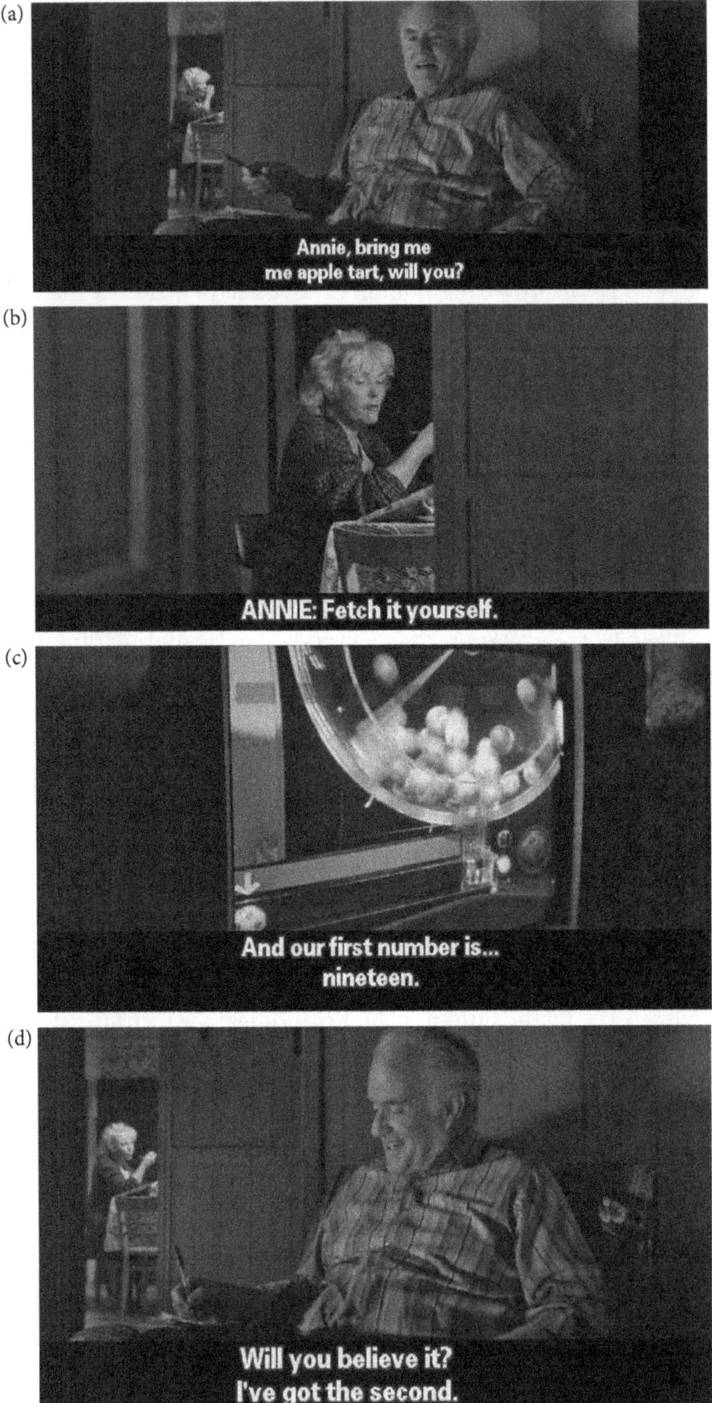

Figure 5.1 Setting up a joke on film. The lottery scene in *Waking Ned Divine* (1998).

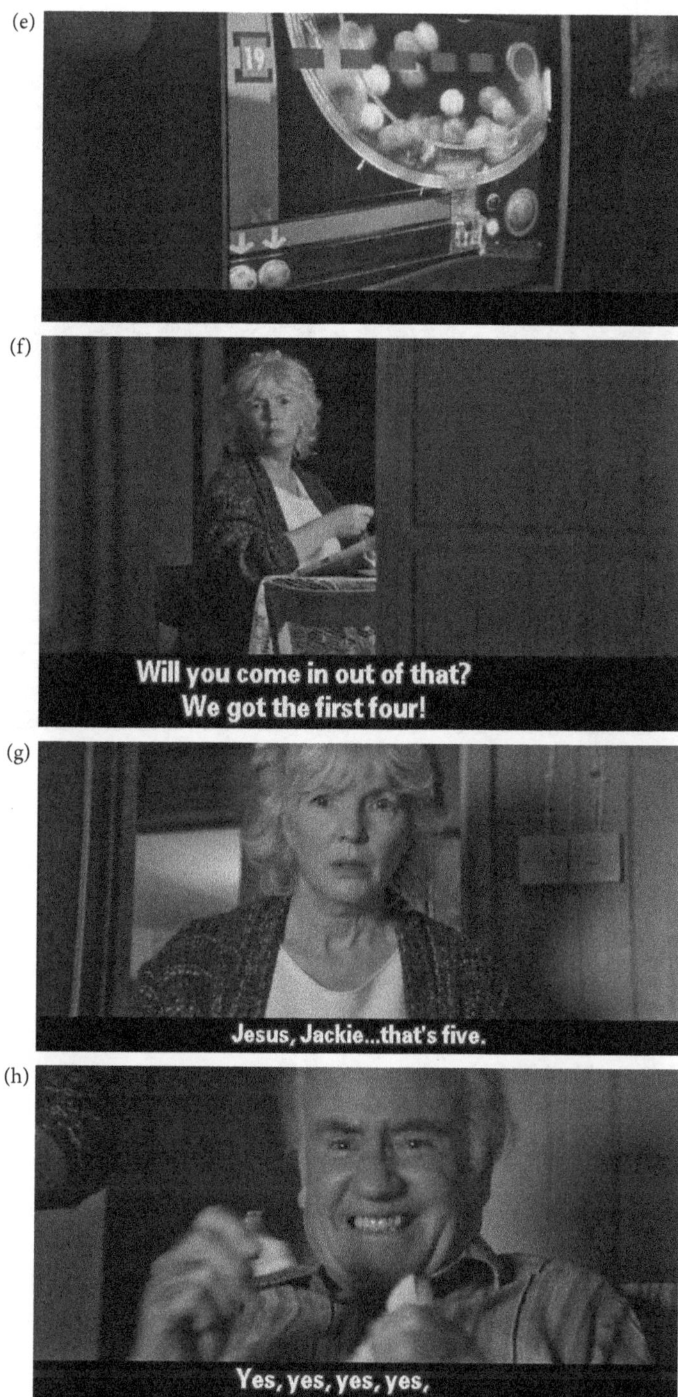

Figure 5.1 *continued*

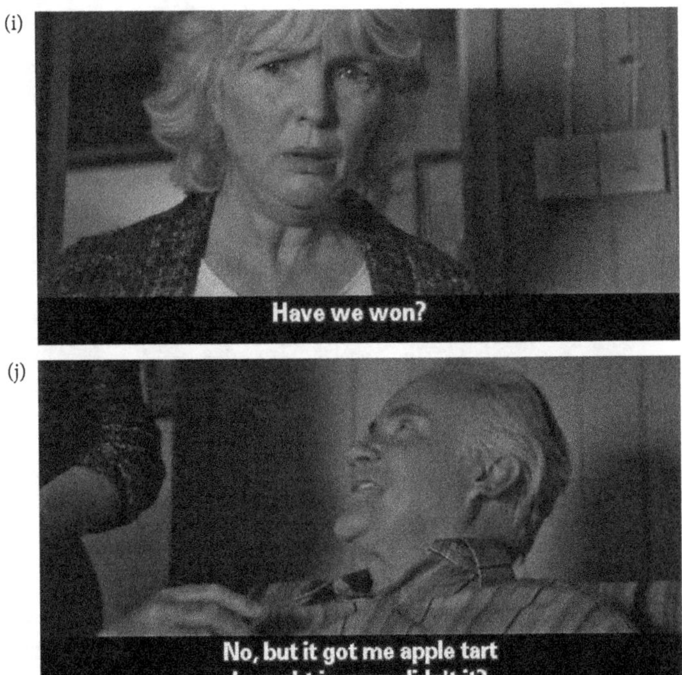

Figure 5.1 *continued*

scene again, we begin to notice how the tools of filmmaking—camera placement, lighting, music, editing—all contribute to the gag. The first shot of the couple places Jackie in the foreground, large and lively, while Annie is glimpsed through a doorway on the left, a smaller figure barely moving in the background. The lighting here is dim, as if capturing the gloom of a household that has lost its former vitality, at least for Annie. Seated alone in the kitchen with a plain, brown robe over her white shift, she seems steeped in boredom and fatigue, while her husband leans back contentedly in his colorful shirt and comfy chair. In just a few seconds, we learn all we need to know about these characters and their relationship. The camera shifts between the couple and the television screen, slowly zooming in on the lottery drum as each number falls into place. The background music rises. When Jackie calls out, "We got the first four!" the soundtrack becomes portentous and we see her rise, with her plate, to stand near Jackie. Now the camera shifts back and forth between the two of them in close-up, moving in deliberately to show each face as the final numbers roll out of the drum. The music mounts to a crescendo as Jackie calls out a stream of enthusiastic yesses. "Finally, our bonus number!" The lighting, too, has risen from low-key to a brighter focus on the faces. When Jackie gets his apple tart, he beams in triumph while his wife looks on, clearly not amused. Is she the butt of his little joke? Has she been used yet again?

An analysis of gender roles in this little scene might highlight the use of male humor to keep women in their place. A cultural analysis might reference the long history of Irish wit. But if we focus solely on technique, we may notice how the scene works on the viewer. For although the camera identifies more closely with Jackie in visual terms (he is closer, larger, more animated), it keeps us as ignorant of his scheme as Annie is. The close-ups of the lottery machine, the suspenseful music, and Jackie's excited cries as the television announcer calls each number one by one all lead us to believe, as she does, that he holds the winning ticket in his hand. When he tears it up, seemingly beside himself, we may think the joke's on him. But whatever mirth, anxiety, or shock we may feel at his unwitting destruction of the couple's one big chance at prosperity soon shifts when we realize it's a ploy, part of his childish trick, a prank at the expense of someone else, and a filmmaker's joke on us.

Time and again in this book we have noticed how so many jokes are in-jokes. The setup in the lottery scene doesn't let us in on the gag until the end. More often, though, movies give us cues that make us feel more like insiders. Mike Leigh's *Mr. Turner* (2014) is more of a dramatic biopic of the English painter's life than it is a comedy, but it has moments of strong humor drawn from the British stage. At one point, Turner is invited to the home of John Ruskin, the leading art critic of the day. The scene is set in Ruskin's living room, an elaborately furnished showplace of sophisticated antiques and ostentatious artwork. Ruskin's mother and six gentlemen in formal attire are engaged in polite conversation. Their talk is of gooseberry and rhubarb. "My dear late mother," one man begins, "always insisted that both the gooseberry and the rhubarb favor the colder climes of our victorious isles" (Figure 5.2a). Picking up the thread, the other men add their own opinions on environmental preferences, with fastidious allusions to "empirical evidence" and "the more vigorous specimens." The scene's décor, the vacuous topic of discussion, the decidedly affected upper-class accents and lame gestures at verbal wit let us know that we are in a comedy of manners. Turner's lengthy silence and the honesty of his working-class accent when he does speak place us squarely on his side. From his point of view, and the film's perspective itself, the self-satisfied pretensions of Victorian society appear ridiculous.

Later in the film, Turner surreptitiously attends a music-hall performance. On stage, the performers are discussing a new painting up for sale. "It is the latest thing in art," proclaims one actor. "It looks like bits of old jam tart," quips another. The painted scenery, exaggerated gestures, and doggerel rhymes of vaudeville are played for laughs, which are supplied in abundance by the on-screen theater audience. Onto the stage walks the cartoonish figure of a wealthy businessman. He has made his fortune selling coffee, tea, and slaves, and he wants the painting for his mantelpiece because—because it is by J. M. W. Turner. "Though ignorant of art and taste, I'm filled with boundless glee," he sings, "for what's good enough for Turner is good enough for me" (Figure 5.2b). The audience roars while the real Turner, hidden in the shadows of the balcony, steals away, grimacing with humiliation. This moment contrasts sharply with the drawing-room scene. The working-class comedy of vaudeville is, in a sense, the polar opposite of comedy of manners. More significantly, the humor here works against the grain. While we may laugh freely at Ruskin and his ilk, we are apt to catch ourselves from laughing with the music-hall crowd because we sympathize with Turner, the object of their joke. Who we laugh with or at depends in good measure on how we are positioned in the story and the way a comic scene is played. It is largely a matter of timing and film staging, of technique.

(a)

(b)

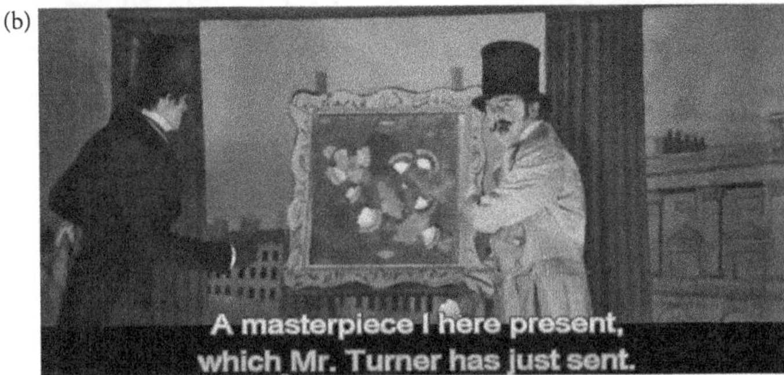

Figure 5.2 Two comic scenes from *Mr. Turner* (2014). (a) Ruskin's drawing room provides the setting for a sophisticated comedy of manners. (b) A stage parody evokes the working-class humor of vaudeville.

Scholarly Advice from the Academy

Academics who study comic practices come from different disciplines. L. J. Potts, a professor of English, approaches humor from the perspective of British literature. Taking writers like Chaucer, Shakespeare, Henry Fielding, and Jane Austen as his starting point, he concludes that comedy is "a safety-valve for disorderly passions."[1] In contrast to tragedy, which binds men to their destiny, Potts believes that comedy sets men free. Comic writers, then, should release readers from their anxieties, leaving them relaxed and open to their natural feelings. They may indulge spontaneous emotions as Fielding does in *Tom Jones*,[2] "sport with human follies" like Ben Jonson,[3] or liberate their characters from the shackles of fate, as Shakespeare does by placing them in imaginary worlds.[4] Potts asserts that the best comedy is precise; "the finest shades of character should stand revealed, and the situation must be clear."[5] Citing a scene from Shakespeare's *A Midsummer Night's Dream*, he points out how a few lines of dialog can run the gamut of humor. In Act III, Scene I, Titania awakes under the spell of a love potion when the first person she sees is Bottom wearing an ass's head. Instantly, she begins to declare her love for him in the most extravagant language. The incongruous sight of a man with a donkey's head is funny enough, but that a high-born creature like the Queen of the Fairies should sing amorous praises to a common weaver is ludicrously absurd, a delightful instance of social incongruity. We laugh at Bottom's simplicity and his unwitting wit ("in truth, reason and love keep little company together nowadays," he says) and at Titania's haughty self-regard getting a comeuppance. When she responds to Bottom, "Thou art as wise as thou art beautiful," her words are literally—and unintentionally—true. High and low comedy meet as the dialog throws these two characters into sharp relief. Shakespeare has given us physical, social, psychological, and linguistic incongruity all in one uproarious scene. In the very next scene, he reaches to the very heart of comedy when Puck declares, "Lord, what fools these mortals be!"

William Indick, a psychology professor, applies theories from the work of Sigmund Freud, Eric Erikson, Carl Jung, Alfred Adler, and Rollo May to a range of classic and contemporary movie comedies. He links body-switching films like *Big* (1988) and *Freaky Friday* (2003) to Freud's Oedipal complex and role-reversal fantasies.[6] He finds examples of Jung's archetypes in trickster figures like Bart and the Waco Kid in *Blazing Saddles* (1974) and in shapeshifters like Bud in *Wall Street* (1987). Indick regards their elusive identities as symbolic of the ever-changing Self.[7] His advice to screenwriters is to build characters and stories around the insights from psychology, to write scripts that exploit our natural tendencies to dissemble, regress, and rationalize inappropriate behavior—mental mechanisms repurposed as techniques for achieving comic relief.

Scott Weems approaches humor from both academic and artistic points of view. A former research scientist with degrees in neuroscience and creative writing, he maintains that "humor isn't just about being funny; it's also about how we deal with complex and contradictory messages."[8] Like many cognitive psychologists, Weems highlights the role of incongruity in jokes, how punchlines take us by surprise: "We laugh at what forces us to integrate incompatible goals or ideas that lead to confusions, doubt, and embarrassment."[9] As an example, he offers the one-liner, "Other than that, how did you like the play, Mrs. Lincoln?" Here our anticipated sympathy for Lincoln's widow is undercut by a very different frame of reference, one that may elicit some anxiety along with laughter with its unexpectedly mean-spirited viewpoint. For another example, Weems recalls an ironic anecdote once told by the American standup comedian Steven Wright: "There was a power outage at a department store yesterday and twenty people were trapped on the escalator."[10] In this case the usual concerns associated with a power outage turn out to be misplaced. Instead of feeling worried for the "trapped shoppers," we're more inclined to laugh at their self-imposed catastrophe. More broadly, we may snicker at the ironies of modern life that make us helplessly dependent on our own mechanical servants. What fools these modern mortals be. Writers who read Weems for insight and instruction learn not only why people laugh and what purposes are served by humor, but also how to construct successful jokes: how setups create expectations, how punchlines reverse them and laugh-provoking jab lines establish rhythm.

Arthur Asa Berger, a professor of broadcast and electronic arts, took yet another tack. He conducted an extensive content analysis of movie comedies as well as joke books, plays, comic books, and novels. From these, he distilled forty-five basic techniques, arguing that "every humorous work uses these techniques in various permutations and combinations."[11] Berger divided these forty-five devices into four main categories (identity, language, logic, and action/visual phenomena), illustrating each with examples. He found instances of absurdity (a tactic of logic) in Ionesco's *The Bald Soprano*, of allusion (language) in Tom Stoppard's *Travesties*, of caricature (identity) in Jonson's *Volpone*, and of chase scenes (action) in Buster Keaton's *Cops* (1922). While invaluable to scholars, Berger's anatomy of humor was intended chiefly for writers, as a "repertoire of techniques" to use in their work.[12]

Advice from the Comedy Industry

Advice from the industry itself comes in different forms. For decades, fledgling screenwriters have learned the basics from step-by-step guides like Syd Field's *Screenplay: The Foundations of Screenwriting*[13] and Robert McKee's *Story: Style,*

Structure, Substance and the Principles of Screenwriting.[14] More recently, a cluster of guidebooks has focused more specifically on creating comedy scripts. Some of these are written in a breezy style, like Greg DePaul's *Bring the Funny: The Essential Companion for the Comedy Screenwriter.*[15] DePaul begins with flippant answers to his initial questions—What's the Funny? ("Honestly, I have no idea") and Do I have the Funny? ("I sure hope so")—but he soon gets down to business with some technical instruction and examples. Writers should include a number of set pieces, ideally six per comedy, that play out a single funny concept in one place, like the police Taser sequence in *Meet the Fockers* (2004) or the touch football game in *Wedding Crashers* (2005). These scenes should "set up a great comic situation in one location, squeeze every drop of funny out of it, and leave it in a shambles when you're done."[16] DePaul is even more prescriptive about structure. He calls for three decisive breaks, around pages 25, 75, and 100 in a 100-page script. Each break should fall like a heavy curtain at the end of an act.[17] He also calls for a strong "inciting incident" between pages five and ten, to let the audience know what kind of movie it is watching, like the moment in *Parental Guidance* (2012) when the parents mention the idea of asking grandma and grandpa to watch the kids. But for all his rules, he acknowledges that comedies may still rely on the subtleties of subtext, which "rewards the intelligent viewer who enjoys the challenge of discerning the true intentions of characters in a dramatic story."[18] For this reason, DePaul notes, writers should give every character an agenda and put obstacles between them and their goals.

Andrew Horton—an accomplished writer, producer, and professor of film and video studies—has distilled his deep knowledge and broad experience in *Laughing out Loud: Writing the Comedy-Centered Screenplay.*[19] Horton begins with a long view, mindful of the extensive, rich tradition that embraces Dante and Shakespeare as well as *Blazing Saddles, M*A*S*H* (1970), and *Forrest Gump* (1994). He points out that the hilarious scene when Chaplin eats his boot in *The Gold Rush* (1925) builds on the same *lazzi* (comic set piece) that practitioners of *commedia dell'arte* used in 1622 when a stage clown would devour his shoe to show that he was starving. From the insightful overview of Part II, Horton zooms in to examples from film and television (Part III), then gets to the practical business of writing and selling comedy (Part IV). Throughout the book, he presents comedy as a perspective (rather than a genre), a playful state of mind that celebrates personal imagination and public celebration in the life-affirming spirit of Carnival. Whether driven by character (*Annie Hall*, 1977), by situation (*Mars Attacks*, 1996), or by "climate" (the anarchic atmosphere of the Marx Brothers; the satiric tone of *Being There* [1979]; the farcical flavor of *Dumb and Dumber* [1994]), all comedy is a kind of game that people play. Creating comedy, then, involves an understanding of the game's rules, how devices like disguise, misunderstanding, and inversion help to keep the lively game in play.

Scott Sedita, a Hollywood consultant who teaches comedy classes for writers and actors, focuses his lessons squarely on character. In *The Eight Characters of Comedy: A Guide to Sitcom Acting and Writing*, he explains why we find the Lovable Loser, the Neurotic, the Logical Smart One, the Dumb One, and other comic types so enduringly funny. Sedita also shows how to analyze a comedy script and deliver different kinds of jokes with precise attention to timing and tone.[20]

Steve Kaplan places a similar emphasis on character. He considers characters, not jokes, to be the most important element in comedy. Kaplan, who has worked in the comedy industry from California to New York, boils down what he has learned about the business into a single "comic equation": "Comedy is about an ordinary guy or gal struggling against insurmountable odds without many of the required skills and tools with which to win yet never giving up hope."[21] Expanding on this pithy formula, he proposes a humanistic definition of comedy as "the art of telling the truth about what it is to be human."[22] But for the truth to provoke laughter, it needs to be all too human. If Hamlet farts, the drama becomes comedy.[23] Kaplan's inquiry into character and comedy is far-ranging and insightful. "The genius of comedy is that it loves humanity without necessarily forgiving it."[24] It gives a character permission to win, by whatever means, without the guarantee of winning or the skills to win.[25] The good news for scriptwriters is that they don't have to invent conflict, because people are naturally conflicted; writers need only trust their characters, be clear about who they are and what they want. Put Felix and Oscar in an apartment and let them act like a married couple. Introduce Bloom to Bialystok and watch them behave like father and son. "Your characters have to be the master of their own disaster, the cause of everything bad that happens to them, just like they're the cause of everything good," Kaplan observes. Otherwise, they're victims, better subjects for a drama.[26] Kaplan offers much additional advice—about laying out implausible premises, about straight and wavy lines of action, about maintaining momentum and keeping one focus at a time—all helpful for a screenwriter or anyone seriously interested in how comedy works.

One of the most precise and practical guides is Judy Carter's *The Comedy Bible*. A self-described "comedy coach," Carter uses the technical language of setups, callbacks, and story arcs to prepare students for writing and performing comedy. Her chapters on joke structure advise that the setup should be serious and authentic to capture an audience's empathy; then the funny part, usually a surprise punchline, will make them laugh. While most of Carter's coaching is about standup comedy, she devotes part of the book to sitcoms as well, reminding readers that many film and television comedians (Robin Williams, Jim Carey, and Eddie Murphy among others) began by doing standup. Writing sitcoms is similar to writing jokes. Each sitcom has a topic (what the episode is about, usually some commonplace event) and a premise (the story's synopsis, called a log line, specifies how the hero gets into trouble when some conflict arises). Like jokes, sitcoms involve attitude (the particular way each character responds to a situation), act-out (the dialog), and a mix (which creates the situation by introducing conflict with the characters). But since sitcoms are stories, not jokes, good ones follow the guidelines of successful narrative. Carter's story arc follows six beats: It sets up a problem, adds complications as the problem escalates, introduces an unexpected twist, takes a new turn when the characters form a plan, builds to a big scene as things get worse, and ends with a happy resolution, lesson learned.[27] *The Comedy Bible* is a hefty volume filled with examples, exercises, and quotes from practicing comedians. It is meant to be studied and frequently consulted rather than read straight through. For outsiders, it affords a fascinating look into the professional world of funny business.

Many of these how-to books are rooted in Hollywood practice, with most of the examples coming from American movies and television sitcoms. Marc Blake's *Writing the Comedy Movie* follows this tendency, but it also includes a chapter on worldwide comedy. Noting that "the twenty-first-century comedy writer is no longer restricted by international boundaries," Blake offers some insights into what audiences expect abroad. He mentions Britain's tradition of class-based humor and its partiality for droll eccentricity as well as the marketing challenge of appealing to English speakers overseas. "The paradox in writing a British comedy," he points out, "is that it must centre on the individual (or ensemble cast or quirky types), but in order to sell it must have universality."[28] Blake links recent Irish comedies to two traditions of native wit: *The Commitments* (1991) and *The Van* (1996) to the light humor of George Bernard Shaw and Oscar Wilde, and *In Bruges* (2008) and *The Guard* (2011) to the dark absurdities of Jonathan Swift and Samuel Beckett. In Australia, he finds a preference for fish-out-of-water plots, citing *Muriel's Wedding* (1994) and *The Adventures of Priscilla, Queen of the Desert* (1994) as variations on *Crocodile Dundee* (1986), the Outback hero amusingly placed out of his element. Blake's comments extend to comedies from Mexico, Brazil, and Asia. His single chapter can hardly do justice to the vast panoply of world comedy, but as the film industry becomes more globally interdependent, perhaps more guidebooks on comedy will take note of the various comedic practices in use around the world.

The Comedians Speak Up

What do actors and directors themselves have to say about the experience of doing comedy? Comedians often speak of a compulsion to make people laugh. Tom Hanks refers to this addictive quality as if comedy were a drug. Some, like

Bobby Cannavale, tell stories of their childhood when they used gags to get attention at the dinner table.[29] Others learned to make fun of themselves as a kind of preemptive therapy. Joan Rivers turned her childhood weight problem into jokes: "I was my own buddy in camp," she liked to quip. "In my class picture, I was the whole front row." Gilda Radner depicted herself as "a cutup" at home and at school: "I just never let go of my child self."[30] Woody Allen described his technophobia and neurotic persona as largely autobiographical "and yet so exaggerated and distorted it reads to me like fiction."[31] He liked to sum up this relationship between real life and its comic payoff with a trademark joke: "My view of reality is that it has always been a grim place to be, but it's the only place you can get Chinese food."[32]

Comedians also draw inspiration from each other, and many speak freely about those who influenced them most. Woody Allen acknowledges Bob Hope as an important role model: "Sometimes it's everything I can do to not actually mimic him."[33] Jackie Chan remembers watching old silent movies with Buster Keaton and Harold Lloyd: "It made me think it would be good to use physical stunts in my movies—to combine action with comedy."[34] For Hong Kong's Stephen Chow, the holy grail of comedy was Charlie Chaplin.[35] Meanwhile, Jacques Tati distinguished Chaplin's humor from his own. Tati observed that Monsieur Hulot, the character who made his movies famous, relies on contrast rather than identity for effect. "People find Chaplin great because his Tramp invents ingenious ways to cope, but Hulot never invents anything unusual, just gets on with his normal life. . . . It's not Hulot who makes us laugh, but the world is made comical because he is not."[36]

While Tati's humor has precedents in the classic Hollywood clowns, much of its flavor is distinctly French, evoking a wry sense of the mindlessly collective comportment of the bourgeoisie. This lineage runs from René Clair and Jean Renoir through Gérard Oury to Michael Hazanavicius. Italian humor has its own national peculiarities—the dark strain of humor in Mario Monicelli's *Big Deal on Madonna Street* (*I soliti ignoti*, 1958), with its inept crew of unemployed working-class thieves, and *The Great War* (*La grande guerra*, 1959), with its decidedly unheroic soldiers. In both pictures, Monicelli treated previously serious subjects in a lighthearted manner, preparing the way for two decades of "comedy Italian style." He has been quoted as saying that "all Italian comedy is dramatic. The situation is always dramatic, often tragic, but it's treated in a humorous way. People die in it; there's no happy ending. That's just what people like about it. It deals with death, hunger, poverty, illness."[37]

Time and again in this book, we will encounter films that are considered comedies in other countries but that puzzle many audiences in the United States. It may be that Americans are used to the kind of humor served up by Mel Brooks, who warns, "You can't cheat an audience. You promise them comedy, you have to give them that magic carpet that'll lift them up over their own problems into giggles, laughs, and belly-laughs."[38] Contrast this with England's John Cleese, who believes, "Comedy always works best when it is mean-spirited."[39]

When it comes to the specifics of technique, actors and directors have less to say. Roberto Benigni may note that comedies rarely use close-ups ("because the face of the comedian is frightening")[40] or Lewis Black may suggest how to use silence, "the root of all comedy."[41] Only rarely does a comedian write an entire how-to manual, as Steve Allen did in *How to Be Funny: Discovering the Comic in You*. While Allen admits there are no fixed rules about humor, he offers lots of guidelines with examples, including a whole chapter on constructing jokes.[42]

The Comedy Bible Meets *A Brand New Testament*

How well do these descriptions and prescriptions of comedy techniques apply to actual movies?

Reviewing the excerpt from *Waking Ned Divine* with Rod Martin or Scott Weems in mind, it is easy to see how the lottery scene follows standard joke structure. It sets up an ordinary situation that creates a set of expectations, then suddenly shifts the ground with a surprising punchline. Focusing more closely on character as Scott Sedita and Steve Kaplan ask us to do, we notice how much of the humor comes from the interaction between Jackie and Annie, whose portraits are drawn so economically. Their body language and the way they're dressed, their placement within the frame, the set design and soundtrack all help to establish the conditions of their domestic life, building up to the joke's payoff and giving it emotional resonance.

What if we tried to correlate the guidelines discussed in this chapter with an entire film? To what extent would it prove to follow conventional advice or break the rules? For this purpose, I have chosen *The Brand New Testament* (*Le tout nouveau testament*), a Belgian comedy written, produced, and directed by Jaco Van Dormael. On its release in 2015, it was described as "a wickedly amusing religious satire,"[43] "a lighthearted/darkhearted romp through modern misery,"[44] and "a highly moral film."[45] Reviewers found instances of wit and whimsy, absurdist farce and zany slapstick, cartoonish fantasy and moments of touching sadness. Such a wide range of terms would seem to affirm the capacity for handling "complex and contradictory messages" claimed by Weems. In contrast to the straightforward trajectory of much drama, *The Brand New Testament* follows an intricately layered, zigzag course.

Von Dormael says that the idea originated with a Woody Allen quote: "If God exists, I hope he has a good excuse."[46] The film's premise is that God is indeed alive and living in a Brussels high-rise. He sits in his pajamas at a home computer devising methods to torment humanity. Far from being omniscient and all-powerful, this god (as played by Benoît Poelvoorde) is petty, tyrannical, and deeply flawed. Von Dormael gives him a family. The wife (Yolande Moreau) is a browbeaten, meekly dutiful spouse who cleans house all day when she is not collecting baseball cards or dusting off the statue of her late son Jesus. God's eleven-year-old daughter, Ea (Pili Groyne), is another matter. She's resentful and rebellious. When Ea sneaks into Daddy's office and discovers the disasters he's been inventing for his creatures, she decides to intervene.

This setup has all the hallmarks of conceptual comedy. Like Woody Allen's early films, it is based on a set of wacky ideas. What if God were a misanthropic Belgian patriarch (Figure 5.3a)? What if Jesus had a sister (Figure 5.3b)? What if everybody knew exactly when they'd die (Figure 5.3c)? This last idea is set in motion when Ea downloads a database of death dates from Papa's computer to the world. Suddenly, the entire population is getting text messages with the date, hour, and second of their own demise. The news media call this DeathLeaks, giving daily reports on how people are coping with the unexpected facts of death.

How people respond to the news drives much of the film's momentum and its comedy (Figures 5.3d and 5.3e). One man, texting while driving, reads that he has 0 seconds left to live. The next shot shows a truck smashing into his car with a terrific bang. Another man, named Kevin, sees that he's been granted sixty-two more years. He starts jumping out of windows, off bridges, even out of airplanes just because he can. Kevin reappears through the movie, each time with more bandages, always with the same goofy laugh. This kind of gallows humor, which Indick links to Freudian psychology, runs throughout the story.

If we search for Scott Sedita's eight characters of comedy in this film, we don't have far to look. God is an example of "the Bastard": mean, insensitive, insecure, never apologetic. His wife is "the Dumb One," gullible, naïve, literally dumb because she never speaks. Ea is "the Logical Smart One," stable and responsible. As the film's voiceover narrator, she is more of a straight man than the object of laughter. But she finds plenty of foolish characters when, advised by her brother's statue, she goes out into the world in search of her own apostles. She chooses six, all losers. We're reminded of Kaplan's observation that "comedy is about an ordinary guy or gal struggling against insurmountable odds without many of the required skills and tools with which to win yet never giving up hope." Jean-Claude, a former adventurer now stuck in a dead-end job; François, an angry man obsessed with homicidal fantasies; Martine, a middle-aged housewife caught in a loveless marriage; and the other three have all given up hope, making them seem more like victims in a melodrama. Then Ea intervenes, restoring hope, which is when the laughs begin. Jean-Claude follows a flock of dancing birds to the Arctic, François becomes a sniper firing at passersby with impunity ("If it's not their time, I'll miss"), Martine (Catherine Deneuve!) takes up with a gorilla from the zoo.

Von Dormael says that the story's construction interested him the most. He likened its episodic structure to *Alice in Wonderland*, where "from moment to moment, you don't know where you're going."[47] While this may seem true for viewers, the film does appear to follow the shape of Judy Carter's story arc. The opening ten minutes set up the comic *premise*, the Genesis of God's malevolent creation as narrated by his defiant daughter. The *conflict* begins (about 13 minutes into the 111-minute film) when she discovers his computer, and it *escalates* through a series of *complications* as she escapes and begins assembling the apostles to help her write a *Brand New Testament* with God in hot pursuit. Ea introduces an unexpected *twist* when she releases the death dates to the human race. Later, after the apostles *form a plan* to deal with their impending doom, a huge crowd gathers on the beach with armbands, black for those whose final day has come, white for their companions. Suddenly an airline appears overhead and starts to descend rapidly, threatening to crash into them. This is the *big scene*, the climactic moment of chaos that comes before the story's final *resolution* (Figure 5.3f). Moreover, the film supports the idea that comedy favors freedom. In the end, Jean-Claude is free to quit his job, François is free to be a serial killer, and Martine is free to live in harmony with the primate of her choice (Figure 5.3g).

It is Kaplan who points out that comedy is "the art of telling the truth about what it is to be human." For all its wacky characters and madcap moments, Von Dormael's comedy has this ring of truth. It also has what Kaplan calls a subtext. All of Ea's apostles appear as ordinary people living little lives of desperation in the shadows of society. But Ea knows that each one has an "inner music," a concerto or a symphony that proclaims their true magnificence. One by one, she reveals the melody confined within, allowing them to break free. The message here aligns with one of the most acknowledged features of comedy, its liberating voice. As J. L. Potts observes, classical tragedy presents life as fated while comedy opens doors to freedom. In Shakespeare's *King Lear*, Gloucester complains, "As flies to wanton boys are we to th' gods. They kill us for their sport." Von Dormael's God derives the same sadistic pleasure from torturing humanity, until his daughter rebels and his wife pulls the plug on his computer (inadvertently, so she can plug in her vacuum cleaner). So the film's deeper subtext is about power, power in religion and in the family. It's the women who reboot the world order, replacing the patriarchal Old Testament with a new one based on liberty and love. Seated at the keyboard, God's wife gets to choose a new floral pattern for the sky, while God, without the proper Belgian documents, is deported with the illegal immigrants to Uzbekistan.

Van Dormael says he wrote *The Brand New Testament* as a surrealistic fable—"funny and offbeat, never very far from slapstick but with a poetic style"—as counterpoint to its more serious content.[48] What keeps it light is a certain playful state of mind, what Andrew Horton calls the "comedy perspective," a

Figure 5.3 Developing a comic premise in *The Brand New Testament* (2015). (a) What if God were a misanthropic Belgian patriarch?; (b) What if Jesus had a sister? (c) What if everybody knew exactly when they'd die?; (d) How would some people react?; (e) How would others react? (f) Chaotic climax. (g) Happy ending.

Figure 5.3 *continued*

Carnivalesque affirmation of life. We see this in the film's big final scene, when everyone gathers on the shore. It looks as if that plane will smash into the crowd, killing them all. But in this story, death is a liberating force. The airliner and the movie take an unexpected turn that sends the crowd into cheers of jubilation, reminding us that comedy is also a collective experience, a celebration of our common humanity, even in Belgium.

Notes

1. L. J. Potts, *The Theories, Styles, and Development of Comedy from Chaucer to Shaw* (Los Angeles: Capricorn, 1957), 52.
2. Potts, *Theories, Styles, and Development*, 133.

3. Potts, *Theories, Styles, and Development*, 118–119.
4. Potts, *Theories, Styles, and Development*, 129.
5. Potts, *Theories, Styles, and Development*, 129.
6. William Indick, *Psychology for Screenwriters: Building Conflict in Your Script* (San Francisco: Michael Wiese, 2004), 10.
7. Indick, *Psychology for Screenwriters*, 127.
8. Scott Weems, *Ha! The Science of When We Laugh and Why* (New York: Basic Books, 2014), 14.
9. Weems, *Ha! The Science of When We Laugh and Why*, 14.
10. Weems, *Ha! The Science of When We Laugh and Why*, 120.
11. Arthur Asa Berger, *The Art of Comedy Writing* (New Brunswick, NJ: Transaction, 1997), 4.
12. Berger, *The Art of Comedy Writing*, chap. 1.
13. Syd Field, *Screenplay: The Foundations of Screenwriting* (New York: Delta, 1984, revised 2005).
14. Robert McKee, *Story: Style, Structure, Substance and the Principles of Screenwriting* (New York: Regan–HarperCollins, 1997).
15. Greg DePaul, *Bring the Funny: The Essential Companion for the Comedy Screenwriter* (New York: Routledge, 2017).
16. DePaul, *Bring the Funny*, 144.
17. DePaul, *Bring the Funny*, 139.
18. DePaul, *Bring the Funny*, 139.
19. Andrew Horton, *Laughing Out Loud: Writing the Comedy-Centered Screenplay* (Berkeley: University of California Press, 2000).
20. Scott Sedita, *The Eight Characters of Comedy: A Guide to Sitcom Acting and Writing*, 2nd ed. (Los Angeles: Atides Publishing, 2014).
21. Steve Kaplan, *The Hidden Tools of Comedy: The Serious Business of Being Funny* (San Francisco: Michael Wiese Productions, 2013), 27.
22. Kaplan, *Hidden Tools*, 14.
23. Kaplan, *Hidden Tools*, 21.
24. Kaplan, *Hidden Tools*, 22.
25. Kaplan, *Hidden Tools*, 38–45.
26. Kaplan, *Hidden Tools*, 137–138.
27. Judy Carter, *The Comedy Bible: From Stand-up to Sitcom—The Comedy Writer's Ultimate How-To Guide* (New York: Fireside–Simon & Schuster, 2001), 228, 233.
28. Marc Blake, *Writing the Comedy Movie* (London: Bloomsbury, 2015), chap. 21.
29. *Misery Loves Company*, documentary film, directed by Kevin Pollak (New York: Tribeca Films, 2015), DVD.
30. Mary Unterbrink, *Funny Women. American Comediennes, 1860–1985* (Jefferson, NC: McFarland, 1987), 131, 163.
31. Eric Lax, *Conversations with Woody Allen: His Films, the Movies, and Moviemaking* (New York: Knopf, 2007).
32. Lax, *Conversations*, 19.
33. Lax, *Conversations*, 63.

34. Jeff Rowin and Kathy Tracy, *The Essential Jackie Chan Source Book* (New York: Pocket Books, 1997).
35. Anwar Brett, "Stephen Chow: *King Fu Hustle*" (BBC interview online, September 24, 2014), http://www.bbc.co.uk/films/2005/06/20/stephen_chow_kung_fu_hustle_interview.shtml
36. "'Comedy Belongs to Everybody': An Interview with Jacques Tati," in *World Directors in Dialogue: Conversations on Cinema*, ed. Bert Cardullo (Lanham, MD: Scarecrow Press, 2011), 39–58.
37. Qtd. in Deborah Young, "Poverty, Misery, War and Other Comic Material: An Interview with Mario Monicelli," *Cineaste* 9, no. 4 (2004): 36–40.
38. James Parish, *It's Good to Be the King: The Seriously Funny Life of Mel Brooks* (Oxford: Wiley, 2007), 3.
39. In Simon Paige, *The Gospel According to John Cleese: Quotes from the Comic Messiah* (Ben Berger, 2014), introduction.
40. In Carlo Celli, *The Divine Comic: The Cinema of Roberto Benigni* (Lanham, MD: Scarecrow Press, 2001), 139.
41. Brian Contreras, "Lewis Black Navigates Politics, Prayer and Profanity through Comedy," *Chautaquan Daily*, July 31, 2017. http://chqdaily.com/2017/07/lewis-black-navigates-politics-prayer-profanity-comedy/.
42. Steve Allen, *How to Be Funny: Discovering the Comic in You* (Amherst, NY: Prometheus Books, 1998).
43. Stephen Holden, "Review: God Is Alive and Crabby, According to '*The Brand New Testament*,'" *New York Times*, December 8, 2016. https://www.nytimes.com/2016/12/08/movies/the-brand-new-testament-review.html.
44. Matthew Lickona, "*The Brand New Testament (Le tout nouveau testament)*," *San Diego Reader*, 2015. https://www.sandiegoreader.com/mo"vies/the-brand-new-testament-le-tout-nouveau-testament/#.
45. Jordan Hoffman, "*The Brand New Testament* Review—God's Not Dead, Just Useless, in a Sweet and Blasphemous Satire," *Guardian*, May 19, 2015. https://www.theguardian.com/film/2015/may/19/the-brand-new-testament-review-cannes-film-festival-2015.
46. "Interview with Director Jaco Van Dormael," *The Brand New Testament* (Chicago: Music Box Films, 2017), DVD.
47. Interview with Jaco Van Dormael.
48. Interview with Jaco Van Dormael.

SECTION TWO
LOCAL AND GLOBAL CONTEXTS

6
British Film Comedy

What makes English humor *humourous*, besides the spelling? When Brits share a round of jokes at their favorite pub, are they drawing on a common source of native wit? Why do some of their comedians and comedies have such universal appeal while others seem distinctively, even restrictively British?

When Americans think of British comedians, they're likely to come up with names like Peter Sellers, Alec Guinness, John Cleese, Benny Hill, or Rowan Atkinson. Sellers is still remembered on both sides of the Atlantic for his performances as the inept Inspector Clouseau in the Pink Panther films. Guinness is known for his wily roles in postwar Ealing comedies like *Kind Hearts and Coronets* (1949) and *The Ladykillers* (1955). Cleese, a founding member of Monty Python's Flying Circus, gave the world some of its most enduring laughs with his Dead Parrot sketch and Ministry of Silly Walks. Benny Hill's reputation owes much to the clever wordplay and goofy sketches in his long-running, internationally broadcast television show. And Atkinson's creation, the peculiar Mr. Bean, still delights audiences in more than 200 TV territories from Iran to China, making him a global phenomenon and one of the country's most successful cultural exports.

Defining British Humour

What makes these screen clowns so funny and so British? Atkinson described his Mr. Bean character as "a child in a grown man's body." This London loner, blissfully unaware of how the world works, manages to solve the simplest of life's problems by coming up with solutions that are novel, elaborate, and typically absurd. Dressed primly in a tweed jacket and thin red tie, Bean rarely speaks, and his disregard for others sometimes reveals a nasty streak, but he is endlessly amusing, fascinating to watch.

In one famous skit, he's sitting on a park bench near a gentleman who's eating a proper white-bread sandwich. The man regards him quizzically as Bean lifts a huge lump of bread from the pocket of his vest and proceeds to snip off one end with a pair of scissors. Pointedly ignoring his neighbor, Bean tosses this heel of bread (across the other man's knees) into a trash can, then cuts out two rounded pieces, clipping the rough end like a barber trimming hair. With an air

When the World Laughs. William V. Costanzo, Oxford University Press (2020). Oxford University Press
DOI: 10.1093/oso/9780190924997.001.0001

of smug self-satisfaction, Bean pulls a block of butter from his vest pocket and begins to smear some on each slice with a credit card. Next, out from the jacket comes a leaf of lettuce, which he rinses in the nearby drinking fountain and dries by twirling it around in his right sock. Then he retrieves two canned herrings, which he smacks against the armrest to make sure they're dead, and a handful of peppercorns, which he grinds in a neatly folded napkin with several hammer blows of his shoe. All this time, we're watching the astonished gentleman watch him. There seems to be some kind of rivalry going on. When the other man begins to sip his lukewarm tea, Bean leaves no doubt about his competitive advantage by dipping *his* teabag ostentatiously into a large rubber hot-water bag (Figure 6.1). But the final joke is on him. Before he can enjoy his masterpiece, a sudden sneeze sends the overloaded sandwich flying, and Bean must humbly accept his neighbor's offer: the other half of the white-bread sandwich.[1]

Bean reveals some traits we've seen in other movie clowns, especially those from the silent era. He's resourceful and surprising, an outsider competing with the establishment, the little guy taking on the status quo. Yet there is something oddly off-putting about him. He has a nasty streak that we don't find in Charlie Chaplin's "Little Tramp," a sly drollery that's missing in Buster Keaton's stoic

Figure 6.1 Mr. Bean prepares a spot of tea—his way. An episode from the *Mr. Bean* TV series (1992).

"Great Stone Face." Are British comedians less interested in being liked than in being funny, in contrast, say, to their American counterparts?

Likeable or not, Sellers, Cleese, and Atkinson indulge a British fondness for eccentricity. Sellers's droll mannerisms, Cleese's quirky tics, and Atkinson's oddball antics set them apart from stereotypes of British conformity like the upstanding constable, the courteous couple, or the gentleman discreetly nibbling his white-bread sandwich on the bench.

While Brits certainly enjoy their share of silliness and slapstick, they are probably better known for a drier, reserved variety of humor, a form more likely to provoke wry smiles than belly laughs. But what does it mean for humor to be "dry"? Let's listen in on a brief exchange between Bertie Wooster and Reginald Jeeves, that twittering son of the idle rich and his shrewdly condescending valet (Figure 6.2):

Jeeves: Pardon me for asking, sir, but are you proposing to appear in public in those garments?

Bertie Wooster: Well, certainly, Jeeves. What—a bit vivid, do you think?

Jeeves: Not necessarily, sir. I am told that Mr. Freddie "He's a Riot" Flowerdew often appears on the music-hall stage in comparable attire.[2]

Figure 6.2 "Pardon me for asking, sir, but are you proposing to appear in public in those garments?" An episode from the *Jeeves and Wooster* TV series (1991).

With a few deft lines of dialog, the script defines the characters and their relationship. Jeeves is deferential ("Pardon me for asking") but clearly disapproving of his master's sartorial judgment ("in public, in those garments?"). Wooster's casual attempt to shrug off the criticism ("Well, certainly, Jeeves") belies his recognition that Jeeves might have a point ("a bit vivid, do you think?"). We don't need to see the clothes or the men's expressions; Jeeves's verbal comeback is visual enough. His comparisons to Mr. Freddie "He's a Riot" Flowerdew and the music hall tell us all we need to know about the outfit Wooster, lamentably, has chosen to wear.

The odd couple of Jeeves and Wooster was created by P. G. Wodehouse as a caricature of prewar British society. His popular stories, written between 1915 and 1974, were adapted for British television in the 1990s, catapulting Stephen Fry (as Jeeves) and Hugh Laurie (as Wooster) to international celebrity. Audiences loved the types they represent. Wooster, ever the good-natured but dim-witted offshoot of the privileged upper class, keeps entangling himself in quandaries that can only be undone by Jeeves's superior intelligence and wit. It's an old formula. The routine of clueless master/clever servant goes back to classical Roman comedy, but Wodehouse's characters are distinctly British. So is the humor, which in contrast to the broadly slapstick antics in Plautus and Terence, is characteristically subtle, understated, dry. Much British comedy, as we shall see, is based on centuries of class distinctions and a long history of class conflict. This may help explain why audiences without this history often fail to get the joke.

Some expressions of British humor don't travel well beyond the English Channel for other reasons. Consider this scene from *Carry on Spying* (1964), a Cold War parody. A bumbling agent of the British Secret Service and his three ill-prepared trainees have just been captured by the enemy, the Society for the Total Extinction of Non-Conforming Humans, aka STENCH. The four agents are led at gunpoint to an outhouse, which turns out to be the secret entrance to an underground hideaway. "All right, in you go," says the gunman, dropping a coin in the slot marked "vacant." "I don't want to go," protests the lead agent. But his assistant, Agent Daphne Honeybutt, is more compliant. "When you got to go, you got to go," she quips in a Cockney accent. Once below, at level 50, they are met by dozens of armed women dressed like Soviet guards from a James Bond film. "This must be their headquarters," Agent Honeybutt observes. Noticing the guards' prominent posteriors, one of the trainees titters, "Looks more like their hindquarters" (Figure 6.3).

This unsophisticated form of parody and bawdy innuendo may seem far from the quaint drolleries of Mr. Bean, even farther from the detached humor of Jeeves and Wooster, but it is no less British. *Carry on Spying* belonged to one of largest and longest-running film series in the United Kingdom. From 1958 to 1992, England produced thirty-one Carry On films, poking fun at national institutions like the Army (*Carry On Sergeant*, 1958), the National Health Service (*Carry On*

Figure 6.3 "Headquarters? Looks more like their hindquarters." A moment of rib-nudging ribaldry from *Carry on Spying* (1994).

Nurse, 1959), the Royal Air Force (*Carry On Flying*, 1962), and the monarchy (*Carry On Henry*, 1971). Yet, while the series was immensely popular at home, especially with working-class audiences, it never had much appeal abroad. Perhaps the targets were too specifically British. Perhaps the mildly naughty jokes lost some of their charm for less proudly prudish cultures. The British stage farce *No Sex Please, We're British* played to full houses in London from 1971 to 1987 but flopped on Broadway after only sixteen performances.

Whatever uniquely native or universal qualities may be found in British film comedies, their evolution is closely intertwined with British history and culture. As they evolved, these movies followed discernible trends, producing cycles of popular subgenres. The regional vaudeville comedians of the 1930s gave way after World War II to the Ealing comedies and the satirical Carry On franchise. The wacky youth comedies of the 1960s and 1970s (*A Hard Day's Night*, 1964; *Monty Python and the Holy Grail*, 1975) were followed by edgier comic commentaries on multicultural England (*My Beautiful Launderette*, 1986; *East Is East*, 1999). After the Hollywood success of *Pretty Woman* in 1989, England produced its own cycle of exportable romantic comedies (*Four Weddings and a Funeral*, 1994; *Notting Hill*, 1999) while developing its own brand of working-class humor (*Brassed Off*, 1996; *The Full Monty*, 1997) and regional comedy, including *The Englishman Who Went Up a Hill But Came Down a Mountain* (1995) and *Waking Ned Divine* (1998). Each cycle reflected its time, giving British audiences the license to laugh at or with the issues confronting them at the moment.

Early Comedies and Ealing Studios

British film comedy was a late bloomer. While French and American studios set audiences laughing right from the start, few seriously funny pictures were made in the United Kingdom during the silent era. Two of England's best comic actors, Charles Chaplin and Stan Laurel, had to jumpstart their careers in the United States. All this changed in the 1930s with the coming of sound. Now that actors could say their lines aloud and give lengthier performances, the new multi-reel features could sustain a complex plot. This freed British filmmakers to draw on two established comic traditions.

One source was the plot-based formula of theatrical farce, with its cascading complications and confusions. A repertoire of successful stage plays from the Aldwych Theatre was adapted for the screen. This tradition favored narrative over character, appealing largely to the middle-class audiences who enjoyed the lightly literary qualities of Italian-style opera buffa and French-style farce. The other major source of comedy was the music hall, with its eclectic variety of physical gags, groan-generating puns, and lowbrow characters. This tradition of clown-based comedy stressed performance over story. It drew popular stars from vaudeville like George Formby, Gracie Fields, and Max Miller, whose regional accents and "little guy" personas appealed more to the working class. It also unleashed the zany antics of the Crazy Gang, Britain's answer to the Marx Brothers, at a time when the London film industry was struggling to wean local audiences away from Hollywood exports.

Hollywood was a major factor in the direction taken by British comedy. By the end of World War I, Hollywood had come to dominate most global markets. Its efficient studio system and polished products were especially difficult to compete with in an English-speaking country. Churchill's quip that England and America were two countries divided by a common language highlights the problem. While the French or Italian industry might be partly protected by a language barrier, British studios had to find other ways to distinguish their films from American competitors. Using home-grown talent speaking local dialects—the Formbys, Fields, and Millers of the 1930s—was one successful strategy. Another was an emphasis on shared experience. Many British films sought to draw British audiences into a circle of common history and familiar institutions, not unlike the music-hall routines that spectators knew so well that they could recite all the words along with the performers. The heart of familiarity is family.

Passport to Pimlico (1948) centers on the shared experience of Londoners during and immediately after World War II. Having survived the ferocious bombings of their city by the German Blitz, having endured the wartime hardships with a "stiff upper lip," the people of London found themselves facing yet more privations after the Allied victory. With their streets still pocked by craters, their neighborhoods strewn with rubble, and both food and clothing in short supply, they were tired of rations and official regulations, weary of slogans bucking up their spirits. The movie's plot begins with a bang and a fantasy. When some children playing near a crater accidentally detonate an unexploded bomb, the blast reveals a buried treasure and a document attesting that the Pimlico district of London belongs to Burgundy by royal decree. The locals embrace this opportunity to free themselves from the government's restrictive rules. With cockeyed logic, they proclaim their independence from Great Britain. "We always were English and we'll always be English," declares a woman from her window. "And it's just because we are English that we're sticking up for our right to be Burgundians." The people of Pimlico immediately dispense with rationing and taxes. Shoppers flow in from the rest of London to take advantage of the lower prices. So does a flood of entrepreneurs and black market opportunists. The British government responds angrily by closing the frontier and imposing a blockade. But the new Burgundians fight back. They stop passengers on the Underground, asking to see passports and checking hand luggage for cotton goods and livestock, making a general mockery of bureaucracy. While Parliament debates the issues and headlines scream them out in print ("Anglo-Burgundian Talks Open," "Burgundy. No Appeasement"), sympathizers airlift in supplies. A rescue helicopter hovers overhead while a grocer draws milk through two long hoses. A parachuted pig descends (Figure 6.4). A skywriter emblazons "Stick it out" across the sky while thousands cheer below. It's a Carnivalesque moment. The Battle of Burgundy recycles the imagery of Britain's finest hour in a comic mode, turning authority on its head, spoofing the nation's reputation for wartime solidarity and bulldog tenacity. But like Carnival itself, it's only a moment. In the end, when Big Ben strikes the hour of reconciliation, Pimlico returns to London and the status quo in a shower of good English rain.

Passport to Pimlico follows a familiar comic formula, a simple idea pushed to absurd extremes. What makes the joke resonate with Britons is how loudly the absurdities ring true. The government's response to the Pimlico crisis is recognizably officious and repressive. The average citizens—clever shopkeepers, Cockney barmaids, cocky kids, dutiful constables, and frumpy old ladies—display familiar patterns of self-serving opportunism, preposterous self-importance, genuine selflessness, and courageous solidarity. Historically, the joke reveals much about the prevailing outlook of the time. After years of wartime sacrifice and dogged tenacity, the populace expected change. Speaking for his countrymen, one of the film's characters shouts back at the government's overbearing loudspeaker announcements: "We're sick and tired of your voice in this country!" Michael Balcon, the head of Ealing Studios, put this defiant attitude into an historical context: "The country was tired of regulations and regimentation, and there was a mild anarchy in the air. In a sense our comedies were a reflection of

Figure 6.4 Besieged Londoners accept provisions from above in *Passport to Pimlico* (1948).

this mood . . . a safety valve for our more anti-social impulses."[3] In July 1945, the Labor Party won a landslide victory, sweeping conservative leaders like Churchill out of office; enacting social welfare legislation; and nationalizing the Bank of England, hospitals, railways, power, and much else.

Other Ealing comedies reflected the nation's ambivalent attitudes toward change during this era. In *Whiskey Galore!* (1949), a community of Scottish islanders conspire to hide a shipload of whiskey from officials soon after the war. The film pokes fun at pompous authority figures like Captain Wagget, the British officer who views Scots as "unsporting." In *The Man in the White Suit* (1951), Alec Guinness appears as an idealistic, naïve chemist who invents an everlasting textile. Dressed in his white suit like a knight in shining armor, he is chased down by the combined forces of capital and labor, who see his invention as a threat to continuing profits and employment. When they finally realize that his fiber is flawed, they grab handfuls from his suit, leaving him disrobed and as vulnerable as a plucked chicken. As he walks off down the cobblestone street alone, we hear the comically offbeat sound effects that represent his wacky invention. The movie's zany plot manages to lampoon major British institutions while both celebrating and critiquing the nation's progress toward material abundance and consumerism.

Carrying On with Parody

While the Ealing comedies combined cinematic realism with far-fetched plots to satirize British society and institutions, later films used parody to take on many of the same targets. Parody plays with the conventions of a genre. Much of the fun in watching parodies comes from being familiar with a movie genre. Think of the way Mel Brooks made fun of American Westerns, horror films, and sci-fi in *Blazing Saddles* (1974), *Young Frankenstein* (1974), and *Spaceballs* (1987). In England, Guy Ritchie did the same with crime films in *Lock, Stock and Two Smoking Barrels* (1998). More recently, Edgar Wright parodied zombie films in *Shaun of the Dead* (2004) and action films in *Hot Fuzz* (2007).

It was the Carry On film franchise that gave British parody its big boost. *Carry On Spying* is a parody of spy films. It spoofs Cold War spy movies like *The Third Man* (1949) and the James Bond series, with their cloak-and-dagger villains, sexy femme fatales, and secret hideouts. *Carry On Up the Khyber* (1968) is a parody of serious army films like *Zulu* (1964) and their nostalgic view of British imperialism. Parody can be a disarmingly effective weapon against the status quo. This may partly explain the long-lived popularity of the Carry On series with working-class audiences from 1958 to 1992, a period that overlaps the breakdown of Britain's rigid class structure. It may also help to explain the extraordinary success of Monty Python in the 1960s and 1970s, when youth culture became a national focus.

Young people have a special affinity for parody, which invokes the creative spirit of rebellion. More than other forms of comedy, parody gives them a chance to make fun of their elders while playing with traditional forms. They get to enjoy the irreverent vitality of Carnival within the safely framed borders of cinema. The Monty Python team understood all this. Two of them (Terry Jones and Michael Palin) had performed together as undergraduates with the Oxford Revue. Three (Graham Chapman, John Cleese, and later Eric Idle) had toured with the Cambridge University Footlights Revue. Terry Gilliam, an American, signed on as the team's animator and soon became a full-fledged member of the troupe. The six young men were united in their vision for *Monty Python's Flying Circus*, the television series that first aired on BBC in 1969. The Flying Circus soon went global, and within a few years, its wacky brand of humor was headed for the movie screen.

Monty Python and the Holy Grail took on the story of King Arthur at a time when it was being celebrated or condemned by other film directors, including Joshua Logan (*Camelot*, 1967) and Robert Bresson (*Lancelot du Lac*, 1974). The Python crew leavened the legend with their own brand of ironic humor. Anyone who has seen *Holy Grail* will remember the way its characters pretend to ride horses through the film (a budget constraint converted to comedy), flee from a killer bunny, or fail to breach the enemy castle with a Trojan rabbit (they forget to enter the twenty-foot wooden statue before leaving it at the gate). Nor are viewers likely to forget the duel between Arthur and the Black Knight. The proud knight defends his post with perverse perseverance, continuing to harangue Arthur even after the king chops off one arm ("I've had worse"), then another ("just a flesh wound"), at which point the Black Knight resorts to kicking Arthur until both legs are hacked off. Reduced to a limbless torso, he finally exclaims, "All right, we'll call it a draw." The scene is both silly and grotesquely bloody, a parody of medieval fight scenes pushed to ludicrous extremes. Throughout his quest, Arthur remains unreasonably British, meeting all manner of adversity with level-headed equanimity, even enduring a barrage of insults from his French foes with gracious politesse, until they bombard him with a salvo of vegetables and catapulted cows.

One of the running gags in *Monty Python and the Holy Grail* is about the role of class in medieval England. Witness this scene when Arthur encounters a couple of ragged peasants digging in the field (Figure 6.5):

Arthur: How do you do, good lady? I'm Arthur, King of the Britons. Whose castle is that?
Female Peasant: King of the who?
Arthur: The Britons.
Female Peasant: Who are the Britons?
Arthur: Well, we all are. We are all Britons, and I am your king.

Figure 6.5 Class warfare in *Monty Python and the Holy Grail* (1975).

Female Peasant: Didn't know we had a king. I thought we were an autonomous collective.
Male Peasant: You're fooling yourself. We're living in a dictatorship, a self-perpetuating autocracy in which the working classes . . .
Female Peasant: There you go, bringing class into it again.
Male Peasant: That's what it's all about. If only people would . . .
Arthur: Please good people, I am in haste.

The peasants continue to berate the ruling class with political rhetoric worthy of Karl Marx. The man rambles on about his anarcho-syndict commune and its democratic rules, and when the woman asks how Arthur became king, the King of the Britons becomes rhapsodic:

> The Lady of the Lake, her arm clad in the purest shimmering samite held aloft Excalibur from the bosom of the water, signifying by divine providence that I, Arthur, was to carry Excalibur. THAT is why I am your king.

After the success of *Monty Python and the Holy Grail*, the Python team turned their university wit on another popular genre, the biblical epic. Set in Judea soon after the death of Christ, *Monty Python's Life of Brian* (1979) featured a clueless contemporary of Jesus who gains a fanatic following in spite of himself. Like *The Holy Grail*, it has as much to say about contemporary life as it does about earlier times. Among its targets are the self-important leaders at the top (in this case, the Roman emperor and his centurion army), the bickering rebels at the bottom (the Judean People's Front vying for power with the People's Front of Judea), and the mindless masses in the middle (zealots who are all too ready to follow any fool as their messiah).

While *The Holy Grail* was, and continues to be, the most popular Monty Python film among Americans, *Life of Brian* resonated more deeply with the British public. Some of its humor comes from the English public-school tradition with its elitist focus on classical education. When Brian is caught writing "Romans Go Home" on a wall, a Roman soldier berates him, not for his anti-Roman sentiments but for his bad Latin grammar. The soldier drills him like a schoolmaster on the Latin declensions of proper nouns and the conjugations of "to go." As punishment, Brian has to write the phrase correctly a hundred times, filling the forum with his revolutionary graffiti while the soldier smugly retires from the scene. Many of the film's jabs are directed at the kind of left-wing radical groups that vexed Britain in the 1970s. In *Life of Brian*, we see this when a team of underground terrorists sets out to abduct Pontius Pilate's wife. Emerging from a tunnel (just beneath the fig leaf of a naked figure painted on the palace floor), they run into a rival group on the same mission. Soon the two groups are squabbling and killing each other off while a couple of perplexed centurions look on in disbelief. The film ridicules ordinary citizens as well. In a climate of fanatic idol worship, the Judeans hail Brian as the Messiah, despite his protests to the contrary. They flock to his window, demanding to hear his words of wisdom, until Brian's mother opens the shutter and tries to set them straight: "He's not a Messiah, but a very naughty boy."

The Monty Python parodies use the conventions of genre—the stock characters, settings, scenes, and cinematic styles of biblical epics and medieval romance—to prop up their targets. Their goal is to undermine the pretense of epic grandeur, to deflate the romance. Their chief method is ironic juxtaposition. The dramatic lighting and music of the tunnel scene is at odds with the silly slapstick antics of the would-be terrorists. King Arthur's lofty language is undercut by the sight of two peasants reciting socialist rhetoric in the mud. These incongruities in style and content highlight the subversive nature of their comedy.

Later parodies seem to have an even more complex relationship with their source material. The parody in *Lock, Stock and Two Smoking Barrels* and *Shaun of the Dead* feels more respectful of its source material: part sendup, part homage. That is because these films are closer to the spirit of postmodernism. Postmodern art is famously self-conscious, self-reflexive: Its painted canvases quote popular ads and comic strips, its buildings seem to plagiarize earlier architectural monuments, its films and novels mimic other films and novels. All forms appear to merge into one indistinguishable stream of intertextuality, blending boundaries among art forms, genres, high art and low. Linda Hutcheon finds a parodic element in postmodernism that both confirms and destabilizes the conventions and ideologies of the dominant culture. She points out that postmodern art works are really about other works of art, conversations in "an interart discourse."[4] From this perspective, postmodern parody turns out to be more about the way texts work than what they say. So while the author of an epic, play, or novel may profess to hold the mirror up to nature, the mirror of postmodern parody reflects only mirrors. Its true content is style.

This may sound bewildering, but postmodern viewers understand it instinctively. Their pleasure in watching *The Simpsons* or *The Big Lebowksi* (1998) is partly the joy of recognition, of catching allusions to the stream of media texts and messages that constitute their world. Edgar Wright's *Shaun of the Dead* belongs to this postmodern trend. (▶ See "Case Study for Chapter 6: *Shaun of the Dead*" on the website.) So does his *Hot Fuzz* (2007), in which he indulged his passion for parody with countless allusions to Hollywood action films. Wright reportedly watched more than a hundred police movies while working on the script, turning their clichés into a rowdy mixture of mockery and tribute. The big shootout at the end is so drawn out, so overloaded with outsize weaponry, that

Figure 6.6 New cop in town. Action movie parody in *Hot Fuzz* (2007).

some of the comic spirit gets lost in the director's efforts to outdo the clichés he's making fun of with their own artillery (Figure 6.6).

Multicultural Comedy: National Pride and Prejudices

Whatever image we may have of "the typical Englishman," the island we call Britain has always been a mixing bowl of various ethnic groups. Well before the eleventh century, the people living there included Celts, Romans, Anglo-Saxons, Vikings, and Normans. More recently, large groups of immigrants have come from former colonies, particularly Africa, Southeast Asia, and the West Indies. By the 1970s, the changing faces of Great Britain were being prominently mirrored in the movies along with the anxieties that accompany a changing population.

Humor has a curious way of handling such anxieties. Like many ethnic jokes, a multiethnic comedy can cut two ways, ridiculing those who stereotype ethnicities while simultaneously perpetuating the stereotypes. As Howard Jacobson observes in *Seriously Funny*, "the hyperbole of hate makes an instant ass of intolerance, while not denying you the extravagant pleasure of indulging in it."[5] One of the most popular American sitcoms of the 1970s was *All in the Family*, which revolved around an outspoken bigot named Archie Bunker. An uneducated blue-collar worker living in Queens, New York, Archie was intolerant of anyone who differed from himself, a heterosexual white Anglo-Saxon Protestant male born in the United States. From 1971 to 1979, the show brought social issues to mainstream television, but Archie's irascibly endearing character encouraged some viewers to identify with him and his views.

If Archie had a British cousin, it would be Alf Garnett, the central character of *Till Death Us Do Part*, a 1968 film based on a popular television sitcom that aired on BBC from 1965 to 1975. Alf is a dockworker living in London's East End. He is a patriarchal bully and a blatant racist. He constantly intimidates his patient wife and rips his daughter's Labour Party poster from her room, exclaiming, "It might be a free country outside, but not in here." When a neighbor complains about a stomachache, Alf blames it on a bug: "Probably come off the boat. It's the bloody coloureds that bring them in." Later he dreams of advising the prime minister: "Too many foreigners . . . chuck 'em all out, especially the black ones." Alf is patriotic to the point of chauvinism. In one wry scene, he snaps to attention when the radio broadcasts the national anthem, and the camera pulls back to show him standing fully naked in his bathtub (Figure 6.7). While moments like this were clearly meant to ridicule Alf's character, newspapers reported that theater audiences were laughing with him rather than at him.[6] So pervasive was this phenomenon of celebrating the character intended for satire that it was dubbed "the Alfie Effect."[7]

One of Alf's heroes in the movie is Enoch Powell, a real-life, right-wing politician who aggressively opposed immigration. When Powell ran for Parliament, he became known as "the Right Hon. Alf Garnett," an association he apparently embraced.[8] Powell figures prominently in another British satire about racism, *East Is East*, set in the 1970s but made in 1999. The father figure in this film is another patriarch with deep-rooted ethnic biases, except that he is a Pakistani immigrant. George Khan's main concern is that his children are losing their

Figure 6.7 Reactionary patriotism in *Till Death Us Do Part* (1969).

Asian identity. Rebelling against his Muslim teachings and arranged marriage plans, they prefer to think and act like their British peers. He drives them to the neighboring town of Bradford, where most of the townspeople wear turbans and shop in Pakistani-style markets. Someone has painted over the sign so that it reads "Welcome to Bradistan." He would be happy here, but his family has other ideas. As the conflict between George and his family intensifies, the film's humor grows more caustic. One day, as George is walking home, the figure of Enoch Powell raises its menacing head in the form of posters lining the wall across the street. George's anti-immigration neighbor, Mr. Moorehouse, has put them up to support a petition for repatriation. "Send the buggers home," he shouts to every passerby, then points to George. "See, there's one of them now." George is silent, face to face with a mirror of his prejudices, unable to speak. It's Moorehouse's young grandson who does speak, cutting through the wall of bigotry with a child's simple open-mindedness. "Saalam-Alacum, Mr. Khan," he says enthusiastically. To which his grandfather replies, "Shut up, you little bastard!"

The years between *Till Death Us Do Part* and *East Is East* saw a succession of films that dissect multicultural Britain with various degrees of humor. In *My Beautiful Launderette*, Stephen Frears dramatized tensions between white and Asian communities in London during the Thatcher era. In *Bhaji on the Beach* (1994), Gurinder Chadha followed a group of Indian women on a seaside holiday to Blackpool. In *Secrets & Lies* (1996), Mike Leigh took on the uneasy relationships between whites and blacks. In *Leon the Pig Farmer* (1992), Gary Sinyor and Vadim Jean followed a Jewish Englishman from Surrey to Yorkshire in search of his real father. If the tone changes from film to film and even scene to scene, it may be that the serious issues they deal with call for a variety of narrative tools, alternately applied with a light hand or a heavy blow.

Havoc in the Hinterlands: Workers and Farmers Unite

In 1997, a modest British comedy with an unlikely premise became the United Kingdom's biggest box-office hit and one of England's most successful exports. Made for only $3.5 million, *The Full Monty* grossed over $250 million and was nominated for four Academy Awards, winning an Oscar for Best Original Music Score. The plot features a group of unemployed steelworkers in the northern city of Sheffield who stage a strip show in order to raise money and restore their lost pride. One year earlier, British audiences had seen another film about workers in the North: *Brassed Off* (1996) centers on a group of Yorkshire miners who try to keep the mines open and their spirits up by playing in a brass band. Paul Dave calls these movies postindustrial "elegies," stories that indulge a nostalgic longing for the bygone days when working-class men could take pride in their labor.[9] Both films rely on the familiar formula of putting on a show, but they are firmly rooted in contemporary politics. After a long period of Conservatism under Margaret Thatcher, who served as prime minister from 1979 to 1990, the United Kingdom was feeling the effects of privatization and austerity. On the one hand, her supporters pointed to improvements in the national economy during Thatcher's rule. On the other hand, opponents in the Labour Party pointed to the tens of thousands of workers, and their families, who had lost their jobs and a good deal more when mines and factories were shut down.

The Full Monty provides some background with an opening credit sequence from a 1971 documentary, *Sheffield—City on the Move*. Originally intended as a promotional film to highlight the city's thriving steel industry, its appearance in the 1997 feature is pointedly ironic. The contrast between past promise and present reality becomes immediately clear when the film shifts to a scene "25 years later." Two men are trying to remove a rusty girder from the factory, now locked and deserted. Their efforts to maneuver the huge beam through a jumble of broken pillars and decaying pavement are played for laughs, but the political message behind their antics is not lost in the comedy: These former factory employees have been reduced to stealing scrap metal for a living. As the film proceeds, the story concentrates more on personal relationships than on politics, building up to the climactic big performance when the men must dance naked on the town stage (Figure 6.8). Their practice sessions are occasions for self-discovery and male bonding as the macho workers overcome anger, embarrassment, and prejudice. Ultimately, they turn economic necessity into a triumph of uproarious performance.

In his detailed analysis of the film, Nigel Mather notes its allusions to *Flashdance* (1983), the Hollywood musical romance about an American

Figure 6.8 "Leave your hat on!" Putting on a show in *The Full Monty* (1997).

steelworker named Alex who wants to be a dancer. Gaz and Dave, the two North-of-England scrap-metal thieves, watch a stolen video of *Flashdance* to learn some dance moves, but Dave is more focused on Alex's welding technique than on her dancing. Mather's comparison of the two movies is instructive. While *The Full Monty* owes much of its production technique and commercial success to the Hollywood model, it remains distinctively British in its regional authenticity and focus on working-class concerns.

In some ways, *Brassed Off* is even more British, which may help to explain why it was less successful abroad. Set around 1992, some ten years after the devastating national miners' strike of 1984–85, it too explores the impact of major events on individual lives. An early scene shows two housewives chatting across the backyard fence, a moment familiar from countless British films and television sitcoms. One of the women is pulling her wash from the clothesline. The other holds a teacup and a cigarette, with a pair of bras hanging on the line behind her.

"It's a sad old day when it's finally come to this," laments Ida in a Yorkshire accent. "Your Jim and my Ernie packing in the band."

Bea's response is philosophical: "Well, no point in carrying on, is there. If the pit goes, the band will go the same way . . . but they'll have bugger all to do."

It's an economical way to summarize the movie's backstory, to link the band's future to the closing of the pit mine, and to get us wondering what "bugger all" will happen next. But then comes a surprise, a close-up shot of a middle-aged man reading a newspaper. "You get used to it," he says curtly before the camera pulls back to show us that he's sitting in a tiny backyard plot between the two women. They have been ignoring him, speaking as if he weren't there. It's a joke, of course, but one that underscores the way unemployed men in this movie have lost their social status, have become invisible in the community.

The 1990s also spawned a series of regional comedies celebrating rural communities. *The Englishman Who Went Up a Hill But Came Down a Mountain* (1995) is set in South Wales. *In the Black Midwinter* (1995) centers on an amateur production of *Hamlet* in the south of England. *Up 'n' Under* (1998) is about an aging rugby team in Yorkshire. *Waking Ned Divine* takes place in Southern Ireland, where someone in a tiny village wins the lottery.

The Englishman Who Went up a Hill But Came Down a Mountain has a very long title and a very simple plot. To get their village back on the British survey map, a group of Welsh villagers need to raise the height of their land. This seems like much ado about nothing, but as the voice-over narrator patiently explains in a lilting accent, "The Welsh were created by mountains. Where the mountains start, there starts Wales." It's a matter of ethnic pride. If their land doesn't qualify to be counted as mountain, the surveyors "might just as well redraw the border and put us all in England . . . God forbid." *The Englishman Who Went up a Hill* is a gently comic film in which a local community pulls together in a show of solidarity reminiscent of the Ealing comedies, marking a similar shift in government from Conservative to Labour.

Aside from *The Full Monty*, none of these regional comedies attracted much attention outside of Britain, but a few years later the subgenre spawned another global hit. *Calendar Girls* (2003) took some lessons from the Sheffield men and applied them to a largely female cast, headed by Helen Mirren and Julie Walters. Based on an actual group of Yorkshire women who produced a nude calendar to raise money for charity, the film plays on the national reputation for prudery, contrasting the women's modesty with the matter-of-fact commercialism of American media when they travel to Los Angeles to appear on *The Jay Leno Show*. The Hollywood sequence is credited with some of the film's overseas success.

Romantic Comedy, British Style

The British film industry had learned some lessons since its early days of competition with the Hollywood studios: If you can't lick them, make them allies. The British romantic comedy revival is another case in point. In 1989, Hollywood scored a triumph with *Pretty Woman*. Originally conceived as a dark morality tale about class and gender inequality, it was recast as a Cinderella story featuring Julia Roberts as a Los Angeles hooker and Richard Gere as a wealthy businessman. The combination of star power, humorous tone, and happy ending proved to be a promising recipe for ticket sales on both sides of the Atlantic. The next few years saw a succession of popular British rom-coms, including *Four Weddings and a Funeral, Notting Hill, Bridget Jones's Diary* (2001), and *Love Actually* (2003). What these films had in common was a lighthearted romantic script by Richard Curtis and a plot based on the emotional chemistry between an appealing British actor, usually Hugh Grant, and a seductive actress, usually American.

In *Notting Hill*, Grant's character falls in love with a Hollywood superstar, played by Julia Roberts. In *Four Weddings and a Funeral*, the object of Grant's affection is played by the American actress and fashion model Andie MacDowell. It's as if the British film industry, in the guise of Grant, is courting Hollywood. *Bridget Jones's Diary* changes the formula a bit, since Grant must compete with another British actor, Colin Firth, but their amorous objective is still an American girl, this time played by a comically unglamorous Renée Zellweger. *Love Actually* juggles a large number of relationships, amorous and otherwise. This time Grant's romantic yearnings cross lines of social status rather than nationality. As the new British prime minister, he is infatuated with a member of his household staff who speaks English like Eliza Doolittle. The film explores also relationships between father and son, husband and wife, sister and brother, rock star and business partner, citizen and immigrant. In the sheer diversity of its sentimental complications, *Love Actually* aggressively courts an all-inclusive audience.

The theme of transatlantic attraction had been depicted before, in various shades of humor. In *A Fish Called Wanda* (1988), a heist comedy with romantic subplots, the actors enjoy some facetious fun by contrasting a staid Anglo couple with a zany American one. In one memorable montage, the camera crosscuts between the two couples as they prepare for bed. While Archie and Wendy Leach (John Cleese and Maria Aitken) discreetly undress on separate beds, Otto (Kevin Kline) and his girl Wanda (Jamie Lee Curtis) rip off their clothes and dive into the sack like animals, a sensual tangle of raw passion. The script, by Monty Python's Cleese and director Charles Crichton, mocks national types and cinematic styles, mixing understated Anglo acting with an over-the-top parody of Hollywood action films. (Archie's name is itself a sly reference to Archibald Leach, the English-born actor who became the screen's leading man in America under the name of Cary Grant.) But when Cleese falls for Curtis, his words sound like an earnest expression of culture envy: "Do you have any idea what it's like being English? Being so correct all the time, being stifled by this dread of doing the wrong thing . . . we're all terrified by being embarrassed. We're all so dead . . . but you're so alive!" Alive, indeed: The next moment, Kline appears on the balcony and pounces on him like Rambo.

Four Weddings and a Funeral, as the title makes clear, uses a sequence of social events as the structural device for tracking the relationship between an eligible English bachelor, Charles, and Carrie, his American inamorata. Once again, the difference between British timidity and the adventurous American spirit is couched in jokingly sexual terms. When Charles and Carrie end up in bed, at her invitation, he admits to having slept with nine people, while Carrie casually reveals that she has slept with thirty-three, six by the age of seventeen and two simultaneously. Curtis's script threads this transatlantic romance through a variety of comic forms. Rowan Atkinson's performance as a bumbling novice priest, invoking "the holy goat" and mixing up the names at the altar, plays like a comic sketch from television. Grant's best-man speech, with its rambling jokes about divorce, infidelity, and sheep, reads like classic standup. But the film's most original contribution to the genre is the funeral scene, which seems to borrow some of its unexpected gravity from the British documentary tradition.

Love Actually offers a more global view of love, with scenes in Portugal, Marseilles, and Wisconsin. It begins at the arrival gate of Heathrow Airport, where people from all over the world return to outstretched arms. As we see husbands embracing wives, girlfriends, boyfriends, and old friends, Grant's voice on the soundtrack observes that "love is everywhere . . . love is actually all around." But while the film embraces a universal view of love, it is less kind to the image of America. The US president (Billy Bob Thornton) shows up as a smug womanizer and bully who deserves the reprimand he gets from Grant's prime minister. At a press conference for the two heads of state (Figure 6.9), Grant refers to Anglo-American affairs as a "bad relationship," one that favors the big country over its smaller partner. We know that he's referring to the relationship with his secretary, but he makes the competition for her favors a metaphor for national policy. "We may be a small country," he says, "but we're a great one too—the country of Shakespeare, Churchill, the Beatles, Sean Connery, Harry Potter, David Beckham's right foot." As the laughter subsides and the music rises, he faces Thornton squarely, vowing that he won't be bullied. We can almost hear audiences applauding all over Great Britain. A few years later, the real prime minister, Tony Blair, alluded to this in his victory speech at the 2005 Labour Party Conference: "There's a bit of us that would like me to do a Hugh Grant in *Love Actually* and tell America where to get off," he quipped, then went on to call for close ties with Great Britain's American ally, acknowledging the "difference between a good film and real life."[10]

Blair also called for more cooperation with Britain's European neighbors, another running theme that finds comic expression in *Love Actually*. Colin Firth's character is smitten by his Portuguese housemaid when she dives into a lake to retrieve the scattered pages of his manuscript. He watches her disrobe in slow motion, then pulls off his own clothes and jumps in after her. The film uses subtitles to translate her words, contrasting her continental cynicism ("This stuff better be good . . . I don't want to drown saving some shit my grandmother could have written") with his testy British diffidence ("It's not worth the effort; it's not bloody Shakespeare"). This is the first of several scenes in which they try

Figure 6.9 British prime minister Hugh Grant and US president Billy Bob Thornton square off in *Love Actually* (2003).

to communicate across the language barrier, culminating in a flight across the Channel to her family's restaurant, where he proposes in broken Portuguese. Once again, in the United Kingdom of Curtis, romantic love is a metaphor for national affairs, and the medium of exchange is the universal language of comedy.

Going Forward

Richard Curtis continued to shape the course of British comedy in the coming years, experimenting with hybrid genres and a variety of narrative forms. He teamed up with Rowan Atkinson to produce *Mr. Bean's Holiday* (2007), directed a spoof on pirate radio (*The Boat that Rocked*, 2009), and mixed time travel with romantic comedy in *About Time* (2013).

Meanwhile, other filmmakers took comedy in new directions. Mike Leigh tested the limits of laughter with *Happy-Go-Lucky* (2008). Poppy (Sally Hawkins), the thirty-year-old Londoner at the film's vibrant center, is one of the most cheerful characters in cinema. High-spirited, inquisitive, open-minded, generous, always with a twinkle in her eye and a giggle in her voice, she makes buoyancy a way of life. But people with less sanguine dispositions want to strangle her at times, like the morose driving instructor whom she nearly drives mad with her immutably happy face. Poppy is no Mary Poppins, though. She has a healthy sexuality and likes to share a pint with her pals. She loves attention and enjoys teasing people who only see the darker side of life. She is open and nonjudgmental to a fault. All of this enables Leigh to give us an astute anatomy of happiness, moving freely between comedy and drama, using his improvisatory directing style to add an unsettling touch of realism.

Another independent film director, Michael Winterbottom, took on a seemingly impossible task by adapting Laurence Sterne's eighteenth-century novel, *Tristram Shandy*, a book about the failure of writing books. Winterbottom's ingenious project focuses on two British actors, Steve Coogan and Rob Brydon, playing egotistical versions of themselves, who are trying to make a movie version of Sterne's story. Their project becomes an unfinishable film within a film. Sly, ingeniously self-referential, hilariously digressive like its source material, *A Cock and Bull Story* (2005) demonstrates just how vexing the business of filmmaking can be and how riotously funny when filmmakers are willing to mock their own enterprise.

Winterbottom, Coogan, and Brydon took their self-ironic sense of humor on the road in *The Trip* (2010), which follows the two actors on a restaurant tour of northern England. As boastful, vulnerable, and self-absorbed as ever, Coogan and Brydon compete with one another throughout the trip with singing contests and celebrity impersonations. The hit-or-miss quality of their performances and

Winterbottom's unobtrusive camera give the film's comic moments a sense of spontaneity. In their 2014 sequel, *The Trip to Italy*, the odd couple sets out again, this time along the Mediterranean coast. Despite the film's light tone and impromptu gags, intimations of mortality arise during their visit to Shelley's grave in Rome and the eerie ruins of Pompeii. As in other recent films described as comedies, a darker strain runs through it, as if comedy and tragedy were always two sides of the same coin.

It's hard to imagine these movies being made outside Great Britain. In many ways, they are decidedly British, distinct from Hollywood films however much they may look to the United States for bankable ideas and paying audiences. It's not just a matter of the actors' accents or the words they use, or even the references to British history and politics. They are steeped in a tradition of humor—*humour*—that celebrates eccentricity; favors subtlety while occasionally reveling in slapstick; and extols the values of diffidence, good manners, and fortitude while self-consciously, often affectionately holding them up to ridicule.

British Comedy Filmography

Film Title	Director	Date
Sally in Our Alley	Maurice Elvey	1931
Boys Will Be Boys	William Beaudine	1935
Trouble Brewing	Anthony Kimmins	1939
The Frozen Limits	Marcel Varnel	1939
Passport to Pimlico	Henry Cornelius	1948
Whiskey Galore!	Alexander Mackendrick	1949
Kind Hearts and Coronets	Robert Hamer	1949
The Man in the White Suit	Alexander Mackendrick	1951
The Ladykillers	Alexander Mackendrick	1955
I'm All Right Jack	John Boulting	1959
Carry On Spying	Gerald Thomas	1964
A Hard Day's Night	Richard Lester	1964
Bedazzled	Stanley Donen	1967
Till Death Us Do Part	Norman Cohen	1968
Monty Python and the Holy Grail	Terry Gilliam, Terry Jones	1975
A Fish Called Wanda	John Cleese, Charles Crichton	1988
Four Weddings and a Funeral	Mike Newell	1994
The Englishman Who Went Up a Hill But Came Down a Mountain	Christopher Monger	1995
Brassed Off	Mark Herman	1996
The Full Monty	Peter Cattaneo	1997

Film Title	Director	Date
Sliding Doors	Peter Howitt	1998
East Is East	Damien O'Donnell	1998
Waking Ned Divine	Kirk Jones	1999
Calendar Girls	Nigel Cole	2003
Love Actually	Richard Curtis	2003
Shaun of the Dead	Edgar Wright	2004
A *Cock and Bull Story*	Michael Winterbottom	2005
Starter for 10	Tom Vaughan	2006
Hot Fuzz	Edgar Wright	2007
Mr. *Bean's Holiday*	Steve Bendelack	2007
Happy-Go-Lucky	Mike Leigh	2008
The Trip	Michael Winterbottom	2010
The Trip to Italy	Michael Winterbottom	2014
The Lady in the Van	Nicholas Hytner	2015

Notes

1. "The Curse of Mr. Bean," season 1, episode 3 of *Mr. Bean* TV series (1992), https://www.imdb.com/title/tt0651851/?ref_=ttep_ep3.
2. "Tuppy and the Terrier," season 1, episode 2 of *Jeeves and Wooster* TV series (1991), https://www.imdb.com/title/tt0614716/?ref_=ttep_ep2.
3. Sarah Barrow and John White, eds., *Fifty Key British Films* (New York: Routledge, 2008), 73.
4. Linda Hutcheon, *A Theory of Parody: The Teachings of Twentieth-Century Art Forms* (New York: Methuen, 1985), 104.
5. Nigel Mather, *Tears of Laughter: Comedy-Drama in 1990s British Cinema* (Manchester: Manchester University Press, 2006), 94.
6. Mather, 76.
7. Sharon Lockyer, ed., *Reading* Little Britain: *Comedy Matters on Contemporary Television* (London: Taurus, 2010), 101.
8. Christina von Hodenberg, *Television's Moment: Sitcom Audiences and the Sixties Cultural Revolution* (New York: Berghahn, 2013), 221.
9. Paul Dave, *Visions of England: Class and Culture in Contemporary Cinema* (Oxford: Berg, 2006), 62.
10. "Full text of Tony Blair's speech," BBC News, September 27, 2005, http://news.bbc.co.uk/2/hi/uk_news/politics/4287370.stm.

7
French Film Comedy

When asked to name a couple of French films, few of us outside of France are likely to come up with titles like *The Visitors* (*Les visiteurs*, 1993), *Asterix and Obelix Meet Cleopatra* (*Astérix & Obélix: Mission Cléopâtre*, 2002), *The Great Stroll* (*La grande vadrouille*, 1966), *The Intouchables* (*Intouchables*, 2011), or *Welcome to the Sticks* (*Bienvenue chez les Ch'tis*, 2008), let alone the relatively unknown directors of these films. Yet this short list represents the five highest-grossing French films of all time, and what they all have in common is the fact that they are comedies. Drilling even further down the list to number fourteen (*The Dinner Game* [*Le dîner de cons*], 1998) confirms the genre's extraordinary popularity: Eleven of the top fourteen box-office hits in France have been comedies.[1] And this trend is not a new one. French film scholar Rémy Fournier Lanzoni estimates that half the movies made before World War I could be classified as comedies.[2] Historically, he concludes, comedy has been "the financial backbone of the entire French film industry."[3]

Why this gap between the genre's high importance to French cinema and its relative obscurity beyond French borders? The mismatch may be partly a matter of distribution practices. Few comedies from any country win international awards, and it is the winners that get shown abroad. Another reason may be a perception that French humor doesn't travel well.

In *Welcome to the Sticks*, a driver on the national highway is stopped by a policeman. "You're traveling below the speed limit," the officer complains. Philippe, the driver, offers an apology, explaining that he's just been transferred to work in the North (Figure 7.1). The trooper shakes his head, regarding him sympathetically, then tears up the ticket. "I'm sorry," he says. "Good luck." French audiences howled at the scene. Earlier, they saw Philippe's wife bundle him into a heavy-duty parka and kiss him goodbye, their son looking on with moist eyes as if the poor man were being exiled to Siberia. Though played as a sentimental moment, this parting scene drew laughter too. The joke hinges on some local perceptions. The climate in northern France is notoriously wet and colder than the rest of the country. Its inhabitants are often stereotyped as uncouth, intemperate, and unemployed. They are also thought to be impaired by a debilitating accent. Philippe's fears are confirmed in the next scene, when he encounters his first northerner. It's raining hard when Philippe bumps into Antoine on the street—literally bumps, sending the startled man flying over the hood of his car.

When the World Laughs. William V. Costanzo, Oxford University Press (2020). Oxford University Press
DOI: 10.1093/oso/9780190924997.001.0001

Rising slowly from the pavement, Antoine says, "I waved for you to shtop but you didn't she me."

"Are you all right?" asks Philippe, "You're speaking strangely."

Antoine answers, "I fell on my ash. My ash schmartz."

It takes some time before Phillipe realizes that his new acquaintance is speaking "Ch'tis," a northern dialect in which an *s* is pronounced *sh*. This ludicrous lisp, together with a barrage of local expressions, supplies an endless source of comical confusion in the film. As hard as the subtitles might try to capture these twists of the tongue, much of the fun is lost on American or English ears. (▶ See "Case Study for Chapter 7: *Welcome to the Sticks*" on the website.)

Nor is this only a matter of translation. Some observers believe that the cultural divide runs even deeper than language and location. Writing in *The Economist* in 2003, an English critic schooled in France proposed that French civilization is devoid of humor in the English sense. He begins the article with some dialog from Patrice Leconte's 1996 film *Ridicule*, set during the court of Louis XVI:

Baron, how did you find the English?
Very droll. They have a form of conversation called "humour," which makes everyone laugh a lot.
Humour—is that like wit (*esprit*)?
No, not really.
But then how do you translate it?
Well, I can't. We in France don't have a word for it.
Any talk that causes laughter must be a form of wit.
No, not really. It's not exactly "wit." We've no word for it.
Then give us an example.

Figure 7.1 Phillipe gets a ticket for driving too slowly on his way to the North in *Welcome to the Sticks* (2008).

Well, I asked Twickenham how many mistresses he had. He answered impassively: "How many constitute *several*?" [no response]

Ridicule is a wicked satire of eighteenth-century upper-class society and its grueling dependence on a certain kind of wit (*ridicule*). To thrive at Versailles, even to survive, one must make clever jokes at someone else's expense. Wordplay is a form of dueling, a lethal game of skewering others with verbal barbs before they skewer you. *The Economist* critic notes that French comedy abounds in witty satire, farce, and all kinds of buffoonery but lacks the detachment of Anglo-Saxon humor. He concludes that French wit, *esprit*, thrives on Cartesian logic, the rigorously rational foundation of *ridicule*. It is also famously *engagé*, like the political gibes of *Charlie Hebdo*.[4]

Is this also different from American humor? Hollywood seems to think so, judging from the number of times it has appropriated French comedies, translating the jokes into American idioms and giving them to characters with American names. This is a phenomenon that we'll return to when we look at movies like *The Man With One Red Shoe* (1985), *Three Men and a Baby* (1986), *Down and Out in Beverly Hills* (1986), and *The Bird Cage* (1996), all remakes of popular French comedies. Perhaps they offer a clue to why the American comedian Jerry Lewis is so beloved in France.

To speak of these films as if they were cut from one cloth, however, is to miss the rich variety of styles, themes, and sub-genres embraced within its folds. The wardrobe of French film comedy runs the gamut from haute couture to run-of-the-mill knockoffs, including slapstick (*The Mad Adventures of Rabbi Jacob* [*Les aventures de Rabbi Jacob*], 1973), farce (*The Italian Straw Hat* [*Un chapeau de paille d'Italie*], 1928), parody (*OSS 117: Cario, Nest of Spies* [*OSS 117: Le Caire, nid d'espions*], 2006), satire (*Mr. Hulot's Holiday* [*Les vacances de Monsieur Hulot*], 1953), romantic comedy (*A Taste of Others* [*Le goût des autres*], 2000), and comedy of manners (*Boudu Saved from Drowning* [*Boudu sauvé des eaux*], 1932). What, if anything, makes these movies particularly French? What can they tell us about French history and culture? When we laugh along with them, are we laughing at the same things?

1902–1931: Silent Comedy in France—Stage Farce and Camera Tricks

Comedy was there at the beginning. The first public screenings of French films, of any films, date back to 1895 when the Lumière Brothers opened their cinématograph salon in Paris. Among the short films projected in their theater was *The Sprinkler Sprinkled* (*L'arroseur arrosé*), usually credited as the first film comedy. The plot couldn't be simpler. While a gardener stands watering his plants, a teenage boy sneaks up from behind and steps on the hose. When the gardener looks into the nozzle to see why the water flow has stopped, the boy lifts his foot and the gardener gets a face full of spray (Figure 7.2). A chase ensues, ending in a spanking for the mischievous boy. The whole scene takes only forty-nine seconds, and the camera never moves, but this silent, one-reel joke set precedents for countless comedies to come. It offers slapstick (the spray knocks off the gardener's hat), a chase (to the edge of the screen), and moral resolution (the gardener gets the last laugh). It also tells a story, unlike most of the Lumière films from the same year that simply document everyday events (like *Feeding Baby* and *Workers Leaving the Lumière Factory*). Following the classic formula for drama, *The Sprinkler Sprinkled* begins with a stable situation (the gardener at work), introduces the boy antagonist, creates a complication, builds to a high point, resolves the conflict with a literal dénouement (untying of the hose), and ends with the status quo (the gardener returns to his work while the boy walks off screen holding his bruised behind). Arguably, the first film comedy is also the first fictional narrative on film.

Figure 7.2 *The Sprinkler Sprinkled* (1895) may be the world's first movie comedy.

In the timeline of French history, the movies were invented during the Belle Époque, an era of technological progress and economic prosperity that flourished between the end of the Franco-Prussian War (1871) and the outbreak of World War I (1914). For many, it was a golden age. The Eiffel Tower, built as the gateway to the Paris World's Fair, expressed an optimistic outlook for the future. The Moulin Rouge cabaret and the Folies Bergère were icons of a new form of entertainment for the masses, a spirit captured in the post-Impressionist paintings of Toulouse-Lautrec and the symbolist poems of Charles Baudelaire. These and other artists also found a certain decadence in the spirit of the age, for not everyone shared in the prosperity. Socialists and anarchists railed against class disparities. The Dreyfus affair exposed an ugly streak of anti-Semitism in French society.

Later, the Belle Époque would become a nostalgic returning point for comedies like *Elena and Her Men* (*Elena et les hommes*, 1956). Directed by Jean Renoir, the renowned Impressionist painter's son, *Elena* recreates the period as a Technicolor farce. A handsome stranger (Mel Ferrer) enlists the charms of a lovely Polish princess (Ingrid Bergman) to persuade the famous General Rollan (Jean Marais) to take over the government. In the tradition of French farce popularized by the plays of Georges Feydeau (1862–1921), Renoir's film is a frothy potpourri of physical humor, witticisms, mishaps, and stylized nonsense, much of it revolving around Bergman's guileless performance as a man magnet. Renoir imparts a French flavor to the time-honored theme of love conquers all, concluding with a scene in which a wave of amorous sentiment flows through the nation's capital, trumping politics and power plays. Renoir also brings to the story what Feydeau could never do on stage: He populates the screen with hundreds of Parisian citizens, making the masses a major player in the drama. The crowd is there at the beginning, joyfully celebrating Bastille Day in the streets, and it is there at the conclusion, protecting General Rollan from the government police. In one animated street scene, a tipsy Elena finds herself among the rowdy celebrants dancing with someone's baby (Figure 7.3). Oblivious of the bundle in her arms, she's pushed further and further from the child's distracted mother by an equally inebriated crowd. The baby gets passed around from one person to another, miraculously ending up in its mother's arms—a hilarious feat of wordless humor and comic timing. In the movie's final scene, when the crowd sees the general's silhouette embracing Elena in the window of a brothel, everyone begins kissing husbands, wives, and lovers in the street.

For all its robust fun and good-natured absurdities, *Elena and Her Men* may also have been commenting on French politics. The character of Rollan was loosely based on General Boulanger, a popular figure during the Third Republic who was urged to assume the role of dictator in 1889. Rollan's military background and political ambitions also suggest parallels to General Charles de

Figure 7.3 The rowdy Bastille Day celebration from *Elena and Her Men* (1956).

Gaulle, who replaced the weak parliamentary government of the Fourth Republic in 1958, becoming president of the Fifth Republic and ruling with a strong hand until 1969.

By 1902, the Lumières had stopped making movies, leaving the field open to Georges Méliès and two startup companies, Pathé Frères and Gaumont. Méliès, a magician, soon learned to use the magic of special effects to create popular fantasies like *A Trip to the Moon* (1902). The same tricks that made actors disappear on screen and cranked up their actions to a frantic pace proved ideal for comedy. Many of the sight gags he invented still make audiences laugh today. It was Méliès who gave Max Linder his first movie role in 1904. Linder, who had won prizes for stage comedy and tragedy as a young actor, saw great potential in the new medium. He developed the screen persona of "Max," an elegant upper-class dandy, appearing in dozens of short comedies for Pathé before moving on to other French studios and even Hollywood, eventually becoming the most popular film actor of his time. It was Max Linder, a comedian, who created the first international star persona, a position later usurped by Charlie Chaplin, who modeled much of his "Little Tramp" on Max.

Linder's career came to end with World War I. The devastation of mass warfare broke the buoyant spirit of the Belle Époque, doing massive damage to the country, its people, and its outlook. But by the 1920s, France had joined in the postwar madness known as the Roaring Twenties. The French called this hyperactive era *les années folles*, the Crazy Years, a never-again reaction to the war that erupted in a dynamic burst of jazz music, flapper fashions, and Art Deco design. While French intellectuals gathered in the cafés of Montmartre to talk about surrealism and the avant-garde, the working class found amusement in the music hall. Variously known as burlesque or vaudeville, this light, inexpensive entertainment featured dancers, singers, magicians, jugglers, trained animals, and comic skits, all on stage.

While vaudeville provided comic actors for the screen, it also supplied comic material for the silent cinema. René Clair based his 1928 film *The Italian Straw Hat* on a vaudeville farce by Eugène Labiche. The story begins when Fadinard's horse takes a bite from a hat lying near the roadside. It turns out that the hat belongs to a lady who is hiding in the bushes with her lover. This is most inconvenient for the lady, who is married. Fadinard is obliged to find a replacement so she can return home to her jealous husband. Clair's ingenuity lies in his ability to translate Labiche's verbal wit into visual jokes. He does this partly by assigning comic roles to objects. A missing white glove, a problematic eyepiece, two identical clocks, and a pair of ill-fitting borrowed shoes all become running sight gags. Humanity's animated struggle with the world of inanimate things is an unending source of wordless humor. There is little need for intertitles when the lady with the sliding pince-nez keeps trying to signal her husband to straighten his disobliging tie during the wedding. Misinterpreting her silent gesture, he manages to nudge people off the pew, and by the scene's end, everyone is checking their ties, including the preacher. It's a sidesplitting exercise in wordless acting. In another scene, Fadinard imagines his furniture being destroyed by the married lady's angry lover, a subjective sequence that escalates into the total destruction of his home. But Clair does more than invent visual jokes. He transforms a lighthearted bedroom farce into a biting satire of bourgeois decorum during the Belle Époque. The all-too-human emotions of jealousy, lust, and greed are hypocritically suspended whenever someone knocks on the door, then ludicrously resumed after the visitor leaves. Clair even manages to parody his source material. When Fadinard tells his story to the cuckolded husband, his self-serving version is visualized as an overacted nineteenth-century stage play.

Clair's partiality for silent comedy continued well into the 1930s during the early days of sound. At first, he considered talkies to be a threat to the new medium. "The cinema must remain visual at all costs," he announced just before releasing his first sound film, *Under the Roofs of Paris* (*Sous les toits de Paris*, 1930).[5] After his second sound film, *Le Million* (1931), he elaborated on his belief that sound and music were "the worst enemies of the cinematic movement" even before the introduction of recorded speech.[6] Only in the theater, he argued, do people speak to each other one after another, on cue. Clair had his actors learn their character instead of memorizing lines so that their performance would seem more natural. He used music to complement the action, not to stop it for a spectacle.

Clair's most political film, arguably his masterpiece, is *Freedom for Us* (*À nous la liberté*, 1931). The Great Depression of the 1930s had already begun to take its toll on France. Reduced salaries provoked a wave of painful strikes. Men forced out of work sought shelter in the Métro and spent their nights on park benches. By the mid-1930s, Socialists and Communists had formed the Popular Front, electing Léon Blum as the nation's first Jewish prime minister, a pointed response to the Dreyfus affair. As if anticipating these events, *Freedom for Us* centers on two men doing time in a prison workhouse. The resourceful Louis escapes and becomes the owner of a factory. Emile, a free-spirited everyman, serves his sentence and ends up in Louis's factory. Although primarily a comedy, a musical comedy at that, Clair's film offers an acerbic critique of mechanized labor and a system that treats workers as prisoners. In the celebrated assembly-line scene, uniformed prisoners are adding screws and bolts to the row of boxes passing on the conveyor belt. Emile's preoccupation with a lady's handkerchief upsets the regimen, creating a domino effect among the workers (Figure 7.4). Someone tosses the handkerchief out the window, where it becomes the object of a manic hunt. Guards and prisoners fall over one another while Emile runs outside as he

Figure 7.4 A lady's handkerchief creates havoc on the assembly line in *Freedom for Us* (1931).

and his pursuers upset the neat line of workers being marched around the yard. The prison's Art Deco exterior, a vast amalgam of faceless geometric forms, adds to the film's critique of modern life. The little man's humanity is swallowed up in a world of anonymous abstraction, automated labor, and tedious routine. Still, while some of Clair's message may seem heavy-handed, he lightens the effect with clever touches here and there. The monotony of the conveyer belt is represented on the soundtrack by a playful melody of saxophones and xylophones, and the whole scene devolves into a comic chase played for laughs.

Clair's artful use of comedy set standards for years to come. Anyone who has seen Chaplin's *Modern Times* (1936) will notice parallels to *Freedom for Us*, not only in the way Chaplin represents modernity as a conveyor belt, but also in his approach to dialog. Although *Modern Times* was billed as a sound film, it pointedly avoids synchronized speech. The big boss's threats come to the workers over a speaker system as a disembodied voice. When poor Charlie is forced to demonstrate an automatic feeding machine, with disastrous results, the machine's supposed advantages are extolled through a phonograph recording. This asynchronous detachment of sound from image underscores the disconnection between reality and the utopian vision of modern times that Chaplin, like Clair, sought to question. It was a skepticism shared by a later master of nonverbal comedy, Jacques Tati, who continued using similar techniques well into the 1950s.

1930s–1960s: Funny Talk and the Postwar Buddy Comedies

Not everyone resisted the new ability of "talkies" to talk; Marcel Pagnol heartily embraced it. Immensely popular in his day as a novelist and playwright, Pagnol encouraged adaptations of his work to the new medium and even formed his own production company. Although many of these adaptations were directed by others, like Alexander Korda's *Marius* (1931) and Marc Allégret's *Fanny* (1932), Pagnol insisted that the real author of these movies was the playwright. He considered film to be a "minor art," a mere extension of the theater. In striking contrast to Clair, he favored dialog as the chief means of discourse, elevating actors and their lines above cinematic elements like framing, movement, editing, or music. This theory of "filmed theater" resulted in long stretches of dialog in front of immobile cameras, like the twenty-minute take in *Fanny* that he much admired.[7] Pagnol's earthy characters and their provincial lives entertained audiences throughout his lifetime and continue to charm moviegoers today. Moreover, Pagnol set precedents for a grand tradition of Gallic comedy that followed, a comedy based largely on character relationships, on local accents, on details of location and history. The talky humor of directors like Eric Rohmer or

Agnès Jaoui, as well as the place-based, accented jokes of films like *Welcome to the Sticks*, later served as test cases for how much of French comedy gets passed on or lost in translation.

Renoir's *Boudu Saved from Drowning* (1932), although adapted from a stage play, opens the fourth wall and moves much of the story out into the natural world, giving this comedy of manners—bad manners, since the central character is an incorrigible vagabond—a naturalistic feel and theme. Michel Simon plays Boudu, the shaggy vagrant who wreaks havoc in the bourgeois household of Eduard Lestingois. Eduard spots him through his spyglass from the window, "a perfect tramp," but gasps when the man suddenly jumps into the Seine. After a valiant rescue, Eduard adopts him in an extravagant act of noblesse oblige, but Boudu is not happy to be saved. Nor does he prove to be particularly grateful. Scorning the conventions of middle-class etiquette, he responds to shows of benevolence with sarcasm, wipes his nose with the family linen, trashes the furniture, seduces Eduard's wife, and runs off with the maid (Figure 7.5). Worst of all, he spits on Eduard's copy of Balzac. In short, he follows his animal instincts, exposing the complacency and hypocrisy of his hosts. In the final scene, Boudu floats down the river, following the current to his freedom.

If Michel Simon plays the clown as triumphant anarchist, Fernandel learned to play the clown as idiot savant. Migrating from vaudeville to cinema during

Figure 7.5 Marital mischief in *Boudu Saved From Drowning* (1932).

the early days of sound, he began his film career in 1930 and went on to become France's most popular comic actor for more than forty years, starring in some 150 films. The character that he invented, in contrast to Linder's stylish Max, was distinctly lower class: a common soldier or a simple farmer with a southern French accent who somehow manages to get the better of his social superiors. In Pagnol's *Le schpountz* (1938), known in English as *Heartbeat* but more aptly translated as "the village idiot," we first see Fernandel as a chatty country bumpkin. His long face, ill-suited mustache, flamboyant gestures, and goofy smile mark him as a ludicrous figure, earnest but overly dramatic. This last point is appropriate since the film is a sendup of the film industry. Later, when he tries out for a movie role, the Parisian film crew decides to have some fun with this pretentious rube. They stand him before the camera, watching in mock approval while Fernandel proposes to demonstrate his skill with a single line: "He who is sentenced to death shall be beheaded." "It's all in the delivery," he announces grandly, and offers several variations of the line: first serious (accompanied by an earnest stare), then pity (wiping his eyes), affirmative (nodding, eyes wide), and pensive (hand on chin). When he gets to comical, he flashes his white teeth, giggles, shakes his head, and breaks into a round of contagious laughter. The crew's skepticism turns to admiration as they all join in. Fernandel's stylized stabs at drama may obliquely ridicule the stagey acting of the day, but his performance of comedy is genuine and effective. Near the film's finale, this point is driven home when what he thinks is a tragic role turns out to be a comic success. Fernandel's long-lived success owed much to his flexibility. After World War II, as more Frenchmen migrated from the country to the cities, he lost his regional identity and became an urbanite, but still the clown who gets the final laugh.

Hitler's Wehrmacht invaded Paris in June 1940, quickly occupying northern France. A pro-German French government, headed by Marshal Pétain, was seated in Vichy near the country's geographic center. Although nominally independent, the Vichy Regime was largely a figurehead with influence only in the southern part of France not occupied by Germany. From 1940 to 1944, France was an uneasy site of occupation, collaboration, and resistance, and the dividing line was not always clear. Evelyn Ehrlich's study of this period concludes that the films made during this time were not particularly notable, but they kept the French film industry alive—and the most popular genre sustaining its life was comedy.[8] Not surprisingly, laughter is a popular antidote at times of stress.

To be sure, the Germans sought to use French screens to wage their propaganda war, especially against Jews. In 1940, Veit Harlan's infamously anti-Semitic *Jud Süss* (1940) was released in French as *Le juif Süss* (*Süss the Jew*). The next year, when Maurice Tourneur directed a French version of Ben Jonson's Restoration comedy *Volpone*, he was obliged to turn its sly Venetian villain into a Jew. Yet some Jewish filmmakers managed to survive through uncredited work. One of these, using his mother's maiden name of Le Chanois, wrote a screenplay for one of Tourneur productions.[9] Jean-Paul Dreyfus, his real name, survived the Occupation by working incognito at its very center, going on to direct his own films after the war. Sly indeed.

While no French comedies about the war were made during those years, several appeared after the liberation. Claude Autant-Lara's *The Trip Across Paris* (*La traverseé de Paris*, 1956) follows two unlikely companions as they smuggle four suitcases of contraband pork across the nation's capital on foot. Marcel Martin (played by André Bourvil) is an unemployed taxi driver who scrapes together a living delivering black-market goods. Grandgil (Jean Gabin) is a temperamental painter unable to sell his work. When Martin first sees Grandgil's paintings, he moves one hand up and down as if painting a house. "Oh, I thought you were a painter," he exclaims. His new friend corrects him with a delicate turn of the wrist. "No . . . painter," says Grandgil, completing his brushstroke with a flourish of the pinky. Much of the fun comes from watching this odd couple—a working-class "little man" trying to survive and a bourgeois artist motivated by cynical curiosity—trying to handle situations beyond their capability. But Autant-Lara also gives his comedy a sharp satirical edge. While earlier films about the Occupation highlighted French heroism, there is little evidence of the Resistance in this film. The trip across Paris reveals a city awash in police informants and war profiteers. For this unflattering depiction, French critics generally panned the film, with one notable exception. Although François Truffaut generally disliked the "roughness, vulgarity, and outrage" in Autant-Lara's work, he thought this one hit the mark. "Don't laugh too loudly when you see *La traverseé de Paris,*" he wrote in his review, "first of all so your neighbors can hear the dialogue—but even more because Martin and Grandgil could be you and me."[10]

Three years later, director Henri Verneuil revisited the war years from a very different point of view. *The Cow and I* (*La vache et le prisonnier*, 1959) follows Charlie, a hapless French prisoner of war (played by Fernandel), trying to escape through Germany accompanied by Marguerite, his cow. With the cow on one hand and a milk can in the other, Charlie goes from farm to farm, encountering sympathetic peasants, bargaining with Russian POWs, and doing his best to avoid the hostile SS troops. At one point, when Charlie and his bovine companion attempt to cross a military bridge, he tells the Germans on the other side that Marguerite is a *Deutsches vache*, a German cow. The Germans are obliged to march past them in single file. The barriers of language are a constant source of humor, but the ease with which people exchange clothes (at one point, Charlie meets Nazi soldiers who turn out to be Frenchmen in German uniforms) suggests a common humanity beneath them. Though the film deals with serious issues, Verneuil's brand of comedy is lighter than Autant-Lara's—and more optimistic. By 1959, the bitterness of the 1940s had waned. The two countries and their leaders, Charles de Gaulle and Konrad Adenauer, had arrived at a respectful rapprochement. Comedy, it seemed, can be a gentle healer.

The Cow and I was a popular success, Fernandel's biggest hit of the year, but not as popular as Gérard Oury's *The Great Stroll*, released in the United States as *Don't Look Now . . . We're Being Shot At!* With more than 17 million tickets sold in France, Oury's war comedy set a box-office record, a distinction it held for nearly forty years. *The Great Stroll* combines many features of its predecessors. A road movie and a buddy film set during the Occupation, it yokes together two reluctant travelers and sends them off on a madcap journey from occupied Paris to the southern "free zone." Augustin Bouvet, a naïve house painter, is played by Boruvil, who specialized in well-meaning, dull-witted foils (like the taxi driver from *The Trip Across Paris*). Stanislas Lefort, the peevish conductor of the National Opera, is played by Louis de Funès, a master of comic body language. The film begins like an action movie when a British bomber is hit by German flak. The navigator thinks they're near Calais, but when the clouds clear, the Eiffel Tower rises below. The Brits bail out, one landing on Bouvet's painting rig above a German military review. Another airman ends up on the rooftop of the opera house where Lefort is rehearsing. Thanks to a can of falling white paint, a parachute in the conductor's dressing room, and a few other sight gags, the two Frenchmen become entangled in a great escape. Oury's lighthearted version of the war years is far from Autant-Lara's caustic critique. The Brits are merrily unflappable, the Germans become butts of endless visual jokes, and the whole French population seems to be part of the Resistance. A Parisian couple stalls the German pursuers, stagehands at the opera conspire to demolish the Wehrmacht's box seats, and a monastery filled with Catholic nuns helps to hide the fugitives. There is no serious violence, only a series of funny mishaps, witty tricks, and buffoonery. In one scene, the English refugees procure civilian clothes from the red-light district. As one airman poses as a streetwalker, the others pluck unsuspecting clients through a manhole from below, stripping off their suits and using them for new disguises (Figure 7.6). Once more, comedy acts as a great leveler.

1950s–1980s: The New Prosperity and Its Ludicrous Discontents

The optimistic spirit of *The Great Stroll* was consistent with President de Gaulle's vision of French men and women acting in unison to rebuild a strong nation, pro-Gaullists dedicated to restoring "the grandeur of France." Under de Gaulle's leadership from 1958 to 1969, the ship of state sailed through the loss of former colonies and a divisive war in Algeria toward global prominence, prosperity, and modernity. But not everyone was on board. During

Figure 7.6 The French Underground in action. A scene from *The Great Stroll*, a military comedy from 1966.

the postwar years from 1945 to 1975, the so-called Glorious Thirty (*trente glorieuses*), one of cinema's greatest skeptics of the hasty rush to a new future was Jacques Tati. Like Clair and Chaplin, Tati used the resources of wordless comedy to question trends of modern life, but he was not opposed to modernity per se. What he questioned, what he lampooned with affectionate humor in his films, was a mindless embrace of consumerism and technology over traditional human values. In *Mr. Hulot's Holiday*, he plays the title character himself, an amiable if awkward Frenchman who follows the holiday crowd to a seaside resort. With his pipe and umbrella, he tries to join a busload of vacationers, all identically dressed. There is hardly room for all the hats and luggage (Figure 7.7). Amid the mass commotion, two men lose their umbrellas as the hooked handles get tangled up, and someone's suitcase gets caught in the door. When the driver finally turns to start the engine, he stops short: A little boy is looking at him with adorable big eyes, his tiny head caught between the spokes of the steering wheel. An earlier scene at the train station opens with a loudspeaker announcement. Since the voice is unintelligible, we can only guess why the crowd entering the platform suddenly turns and rushes down the stairs, emerging on another platform with their luggage and fishing gear. But the train arrives on yet another platform, and by the time they get there it's too late. These images of people at the mercy of their own mechanical behavior are familiar and uproarious. They remind us of Henri Bergson's theory that laughter is provoked by humans acting like machines. They also demonstrate why Tati is considered such a genius of comic timing. He continued his experiments in acting and directing with films like *My Uncle* (*Mon oncle*, 1958), *Play Time* (1967), and *Traffic* (*Trafic*, 1971), setting his satires in department stores, glass cities, and the modern highway.

Figure 7.7 Mass commotion in *Mr. Hulot's Holiday* (1953).

What one historian has called France's "schizophrenia about change and modernism"[11] contributed to the "Events of May," the series of paralyzing strikes by students and workers in 1968 that ended the Gaullist government. The new president, Georges Pompidou, noted for modernizing Paris with freeways and bold new architecture, died in 1974. He was succeeded by Valéry Giscard d'Estaing, a conservative with aristocratic manners who managed to implement social and economic reforms before he was replaced, in 1981, by the Socialist government of François Mitterrand. Some comedy in the seventies and eighties took the form of parody, like Yves Robert's *The Tall Blond Man with One Black Shoe* (*Le grand blond avec une chaussure noire*, 1972), a lively takeoff on spy films that kept its unwitting hero moving in an endless chase. Patrice Leconte's *French Fried Vacation* (*Les bronzés*, 1978), a sendup of Cub Med, was followed by *French Fried Vacation* 2 (*Les bronzés font du ski*, 1979). French comedies were becoming more successfully commercial. Yet much of the most popular comedy of this time dealt with social topics, such as racism (Oury's *The Mad Adventures of Rabbi Jacob*), homosexuality (Édouard Molinaro's *La cage aux folles*, 1978), and gender roles (Coline Serreau's *Three Men and a Cradle* [*3 hommes et un couffin*], 1985). All three films were major international hits, and two were remade by Hollywood.

Oury, who was Jewish, uses the formidable talents of Louis de Funès to present a bigoted Frenchman who winds up impersonating a rabbi to save his life. In the best tradition of a Keystone Cops romp, the film is a nonstop chase through a bubblegum factory and a Jewish wedding, with the French police and a group of Arab assassins in hot pursuit. The de Funès character, a rich industrialist named Victor Pivert, is a shameless racist. Stuck in a traffic jam, he weaves in and out of line while ranting against the English, German, and Belgian drivers in his way. He takes perverse pleasure in passing them until he comes to a beat-up Citroën 2CV. The cigar-chomping driver flings back a string of insults in fluent French: "Idiot! Moron! Cuckold! Dummy!" Delighted, Pivert applauds the man's French spirit. Near the film's conclusion, Pivert arrives at a provincial Jewish town disguised as the beloved Rabbi Jacob. His reluctance to join the dancing in the street turns from awkward imitation to joyful ease. "It's a miracle," he says. Through the miracle of comedy, the anti-Semite has become one of them.

La cage aux folles, a French–Italian coproduction, plunges us into the frenzied lives of a middle-aged gay couple. Renato (played by the Italian comic actor Ugo Tognazzi) manages a transvestite nightclub in Saint-Tropez. His life companion, Albin (Michel Serrault), is also his star performer, a high-strung drama queen whose hysterical behavior contrasts with Renato's levelheaded personality. Their household is an outrageous collage of kitsch décor, with Jacob (Benny Luke) in high heels and a wig acting as the maid. An average day in their lives provides enough hilarity for several comedies. One of the funniest moments takes place in a bar where Renato is giving his partner a lesson in masculinity. They're both seated at a table set with tea and toast. Renato is dressed in a pastel peach jacket and white tie; Albin wears a silver chain necklace over a sequined blouse. "Don't lift your pinky finger when you drink," Renato instructs him, "and grasp your toast firmly like a man" (Figure 7.8). Albin's grip is so tight that pieces fly all over Renato's jacket. Renato is exasperated. Albin is all sniffles and whines. Standing to freshen up, Albin sashays with studied indignation toward the door. "No, no, no," protests Renato. "You have to walk like John Wayne, not John Wayne's daughter." To demonstrate, Renato tosses his napkin aside, straightens up, lifts his shoulders, and strides through the swinging doors—right into a room filled with homophobic men.

The conventions of burlesque require stereotypes, and this film abounds in caricature, not only of the gay world but of straight families too. When Renato's son decides to marry the daughter of an ultraconservative senator, the burlesque foams over the top. Senator Charrier is a pompous patriarch. His home is decorated like a mausoleum, its cold, lifeless interiors contrasting with Renato's crazy, animated household. To make a good impression on the senator, Renato hides his outlandish sculptures and replaces the kitsch furniture. Albin, pretending to be Renato's demure, old-fashioned wife, is so convincing that the senator is charmed, even makes a pass at her. This is a film about performance, everybody playing roles, sometimes double roles. Tognazzi, a straight actor, assumes the role of a gay character trying to act straight. Serrault, who once studied for the

Figure 7.8 A lesson in manliness from *La cage aux folles (*1978).

priesthood, plays a female impersonator pretending to be the most conventional of wives. There are no threatening depictions of gay sex, none of the solemnity of a social problem picture. The whole film is played as high-camp comedy, but the immense international success of *La cage aux folles* helped bring gay life out of the celluloid closet and into the bright light of global comedy. It was followed by two French sequels (1980, 1985), a Broadway musical (1983), and a Hollywood remake (1996).

Films like these reflected the liberal atmosphere of tolerance that characterized d'Estaing's presidency, an openness to groups and lifestyles previously spurned or condemned. In the movies, racist jokes gave way to jokes about racism. The victims of bigotry became entertaining figures in their own right. Comedy could accomplish this without sermons. It could turn the tables on the anti-Semite, the homophobic patriarch, or the womanizing chauvinist, leaving us laughing at them, not with them.

1990–2020: Testing the Limits of Globalism

Some theorists have argued that comedy is inherently conservative, that it laughs at deviant behavior to preserve the status quo. Others make a case for the reverse: that comedy is fundamentally subversive, that it has always held those in power up to ridicule and questioned social norms. At the end of the millennium and well into the next, it is possible to find evidence for both claims, often in the same movie. Once such film is Jean-Marie Poiré's *The Visitors*, a time-travel comedy in which a medieval knight and his servant are transported to modern-day France. Released near the end of François Mitterrand's Socialist government (1981–1995), a few years before the country swerved to the right with Jacques Chirac (1995–2007) and Nicolas Sarkozy (2007–2011), *The Visitors* found enthusiastic viewers on both sides of the political divide. Communists saw it as a comic critique of the class system, pointing to the serf as a champion of the common people. Traditionalists focused on the knight as an icon of France's noble heritage and former glory, defending the time-honored values of the nation.[12] Either way, it soon became the most popular French film of the decade.

While Poiré's comedy is often crude and derivative—a galloping romp through the clichés of slapstick, burlesque, one-liners, and Monty Python gags—it is firmly rooted in national history and culture. Godefroy, the noble Count of Montmirail, and his servant, the wily Jacquouille la Fripouille, are the story's odd couple. We first encounter them in the twelfth century, when Godefroy, dressed in tights, proudly sporting a beribboned crimson codpiece and ridiculously pointy shoes, is about to marry the duke's beautiful daughter, Frénégonde de Pouille. Thanks to the machinations of an evil witch, Godefroy shoots the duke through the forehead with his crossbow, thinking him a bear, thus dampening his hopes for the wedding. Trying to repair his error by going back in time, he seeks the help of a wizard, who accidentally sends the knight and his servant forward to the year 1993.

The comic collision of old and new begins on the road. The visitors' first encounter with modern France is a yellow postal service truck driven by a black man, which they mistake for a devil's chariot and a Saracen (Figure 7.9). The spectacle of two emissaries from the Middle Ages raging against a dark-skinned

Figure 7.9 Medieval France confronts modernity in *The Visitors* (1993).

postal worker as the enemy of France still resonates with French audiences today. Poiré misses no opportunity for relevant anachronisms. Some of these are technological. Godefroy and Jacquouille are amazed and dumbfounded by the conveniences of a modern home. They keep playing with the lights, turning night into day and back again. In the bathroom, they mistake the toilet for a magic fountain and pour their host's entire supply of soaps and costly Chanel No. 5 perfume into the bathtub, which they enter fully clothed. At the dinner table, Godefroy tosses leftovers to his vassal, who grovels on the floor as if he were back home and roasts large hunks of meat in the dining-room fireplace using an umbrella as a spit.

Other time-travel jokes are cultural. "In my house, we all eat at the table," insists the modern host, bringing a chair for Jacquouille. Godefroy is horrified by this breach of class distinctions. He is even more disturbed to learn that his hostess, Béatrice, lives in a humble house while a *nouveau riche* named Jacquard now owns the family castle. It seems that peasant stock like Jacquard took over the country after the French Revolution. Béatrice, Godefroy's descendant, has exchanged social ranks with Jacquard, an offspring of Jacquouille. Jean Reno's performance gives a certain dignity to Godefroy's indignation. He is so genuinely courteous to the ladies and defends his outmoded mores with such fervent courage that we almost admire his simple faith in right and wrong. Neither side is safe from ridicule, however. Valérie Lemercier plays Béatrice as an effete, fast-talking nincompoop. Christian Clavier plays both Jacquouille and Jacquard, sometimes in the same scene, with sidesplitting jocularity.

Ginette's linguistic arsenal includes crude forms of argot, Verlan (a game of inverted syllables, like the term itself, an inversion of the word *l'envers*), and aggressively bad grammar. In a country once dominated by the *Académie française* and its pride in linguistic purity, Ginette's speech represents another offshoot of the democratic revolution. Linguistic anachronisms and verbal jokes run throughout the film. While Godefroy speaks in high-toned, courtly platitudes, Jacquouille brays in the coarse language of medieval *fabliaux* and Rabelais. In fact, many of the movie's comical coinages merged into common usage: French people began using words like *fillotes* for *filles* (girls), *charriotes* for *voitures* (cars), and *Sarasins* (Moors) for nonwhites.[13]

The Visitors set records at the box office and was followed by two sequels, *The Visitors II: The Corridors of Time* (*Les visiteurs 2: Les couloirs du temps*, 1998) and *The Visitors: Bastille Day* (*Les Visiteurs: La Révolution*, 2016). In 2008, Dany Boon's *Welcome to the Sticks* became an even greater hit. But while these moneymakers affirmed the financial viability of comedy in France, their reliance on jokes about regional dialects and history limited their circulation. Olivier Nakache and Éric Toledano were able to reach a larger audience abroad with *The Intouchables* (2011), which took an entertainingly lighthearted look at class and race divisions, topics with worldwide relevance. Their next film, *Samba* (2014), confronted the international issue of illegal immigration with some humor but more bite. Both features are part of the trend to make movies with global appeal.

A good way to test the limits of exportability is to compare English-language remakes to their French originals (see "Hollywood Remakes" in this chapter's filmography). Gallic comedies have been altered and reissued for American audiences with varying degrees of success. In 2001, Gaumont Studios hired the director of *The Visitors* to recast the film entirely in English, using the same two leading actors but simplifying their names and sending them to 2001 Chicago instead of 1993 Paris. *Just Visiting* retains much of the zany slapstick and lavatory humor. The French knight and his serf still do battle with a modern van (this time a red SUV) as if it were a dragon and drink from a toilet as if it were a magic fountain. Other gags are tailored to life in the United States. In one scene, the knight rides his horse through city traffic and up the stairs to the L train. Later, the serf announces he will remain in the present, where he can "eat doughnuts and wear exciting men's fashions at rock-bottom prices." Some reviewers noted a certain shift in tone. Roger Ebert found the remake "brighter and sprightlier" than the original.[14] Dave Kehr described the humor as "sanitized a bit compared with the darker, more grotesque comedy of the French original."[15]

Despite these changes, or maybe because of them, *Just Visiting* did not do well on either side of the Atlantic. The main reason for this failure may well be historical. In a country with no medieval past or sustained tradition of class warfare, the cultural undercurrents that gave heft to the story's goofy time-travel gags for French viewers had little resonance for Americans. Perhaps that's why Hollywood based *Back to the Future* (1985) and its offshoots on a more short-term cultural memory.

Compare this with another popular French comedy, *The Dinner Game* (1998), and the Hollywood version, *Dinner for Schmucks* (2010). The French film was written and directed by Francis Veber, based on his successful play. Its premise is a mean-spirited prank played by a group of wealthy men on unsuspecting dinner guests. Every Wednesday, the men invite someone they consider stupid, a "con," so they can ridicule him behind his back in a kind of competition. Whoever brings the biggest fool wins. When the Parisian publisher Pierre Brochant meets François Pignon on the bullet train, he thinks he's found the perfect dupe. Pignon's hobby is building models from matchsticks. A fat little bald man with the goofy grin of a circus clown, Pignon is eager to show off his handiwork: the Eiffel Tower, the Place de la Concorde, a chateau, a suspension bridge—all constructed out of matchsticks, every stick meticulously counted (Figure 7.10a). Brochant grins to himself; he thinks he has a world-champion idiot for next Wednesday. While Pignon is made to seem pathetic at first (his hobby fills a void left by his unfaithful wife), his cluelessness actually gives him the upper hand. As the film swerves between slapstick and farce, the idiot's missteps and misunderstandings wreak havoc with the ordered life of his social superior. Pignon mistakes Brochant's former mistress for his wife and inadvertently leads the tax inspector to the rich man's trove of hidden artwork. It's a classic case of the goose beating the fox at its own game.

The Dinner Game won three César awards and was a sensation with French viewers. It was remade in Hindi, Kannada, Malayalam, and Mandarin as well as English. *Dinner for Schmucks* translates the French slang word for fool (*con* originally referred to the female genitalia) into its Yiddish counterpart (distinctively male), one of many cultural conversions. Brochant becomes Tim Conrad, an ambitious financial analyst in California (played by Paul Rudd). Pignon becomes Barry Speck (Steve Carell), a goofy-minded government employee who is also an amateur taxidermist. They meet not on a high-speed train to Paris but on the streets of Los Angeles when Tim bumps into Barry by accident with his car. Tim is texting while driving, so he doesn't see Barry, who lands on his hood, his contorted face pressed against the windshield, before sliding off onto the street like a cartoon character. When Barry exclaims that he's been hit by a Porsche, Tim assumes he's hinting at a lawsuit. "What would it take to keep the lawyers out?" asks Tim. Barry's first answer is "five," by which he means five dollars, then keeps raising the amount while Tim looks on in disbelief because, it turns out, Barry thinks he's the one who will be sued. Any further doubts about Barry's mental disconnect are dispelled when he shows Tim his scrapbook of taxidermic art. He has stuffed dozens of dead mice and mounted them in the poses of great paintings: in a rocking chair like Whistler's mother, with paws raised like Edvard Munch's "The Scream." There is a cubist mouse, a Mousa Lisa, even a 3D diorama of "The Last Supper" (Figure 7.10b). These "mouseterpieces" are hilariously offbeat, much more so than Pignon's matchstick creations. In many ways, director Jay Roach ramps up the physical humor in *Dinner for Schmucks*, making Barry's gestures and antics more inane, transforming secondary characters like Pignon's tax-inspector friend into a maniacal mind-control freak (author of *Your Mind Is My Puppet*) and Brochant's former rival into an outrageously lecherous, narcissistic artist who resembles a satyr ("I'm just a goat halfway through eating itself"). The American film also adds a gallery of cartoonish characters, including a blind swordsman, a ventriloquist married to his potty-mouthed dummy, and a pet medium who communicates with the departed spirit of her lobster dinner. At the same time, it softens the French film's nasty tone. Rudd's Tim is less arrogant, more sympathetic than Brochant; he doesn't really enjoy humiliating his social inferiors, just wants to please his boss, move up in the firm, and marry the girl of his dreams. This adds a touch of romance to his American dream. And as if Americans had little patience for talky, stagy scenes, Roach continually breaks through the confines of Tim's apartment with energetic, action-oriented moments that include a raunchy seduction and a smashed-up sports car. While *The Dinner Game* ends before dinner, *Dinner for Schmucks* carries the expectation raised by the title through to a lengthy dinner scene that ends in unbridled mayhem worthy of the Marx Brothers. After this anarchic release of energy, the American film leaves us with a happy ending. While the French script concludes on a note of comic ambiguity, Hollywood ties up all the loose ends, gives each character what he or she deserves, and adds a feel-good, sugar-coated moral.

In some ways, *The Dinner Game* returns to the humor of *Ridicule*. The smug arrogance of Brochant and his elite fellowship in modern Paris has much in common with the mean-spirited wit that drove the courtiers of King Louis to mock their social inferiors for pleasure and personal advancement. Proponents of the superiority theory, that people laugh at those they consider to be different and inferior, will find examples in both films as well as in a good deal of French comedy. Those who see a consistently intellectual strain in French films, and throughout French culture, will find much to laugh at in Pignon's routines,

Figure 7.10 Inane hobbies. Comparing scenes from a French comedy and its Hollywood remake. (a) Pignon's matchstick model in *The Dinner Game* (1998). (b) Barry's "mouseterpiece" in *Dinner for Schmucks* (2010).

which depend on wordplay, precise timing, and ludicrous lapses in logic. When Brochant wants to know if his wife has gone to her former lover, Just Leblanc, Pignon offers to help by calling the man on the phone. He poses as a Belgian film producer interested in buying the movie rights to a book that Leblanc once wrote with Brochant's wife. At first the name confuses him: "Just Leblanc, doesn't he have a first name?"

Brochant tries to explain that Just is the man's first name, just as François is his: "Your first name is François; his is Just [just right]."

Pignon just looks at him dumbly. When Pignon gets Leblanc on the phone, he improvises an outrageous Belgian accent, getting so caught up in the accent and the pretense of negotiation that he completely forgets to ask about Brochant's wife.

"There! We have the movie rights," he shouts triumphantly after hanging up the phone. Now it's Brochant who looks dumbfounded. This kind of cognitive dissonance, what incongruity theorists explain as a sudden shift from one frame of reference to another, abounds in French comedy, from the postwar odd-couple films to the existential absurdities of *Waiting for Godot*.

As we've seen, the French also enjoy laughing with Bergson (along with René Clair and Jacques Tati) at the mechanical nature of modern life, and they find pleasure, with Freud (as well as Gérard Oury and Jean-Marie Poiré) in the release of socially suppressed impulses. Their taste in humor runs the gamut from sophisticated satire to mindless slapstick. Yet if we ask their critics and philosophers to explain the national fascination with Jerry Lewis, they are apt to do so in intellectual terms. In *Why the French Love Jerry Lewis*, Rae Beth Gordon traces this phenomenon back through Walter Benjamin, Charles Baudelaire, Henri Bergson, Alfred Binet, and Jean-Martin Charcot to theatrical performances of hysteria during the Belle Époque. Lewis, it seems, is not just doing slapstick; he's acting out the frenetic "shock of modernity."[16]

French Comedy Filmography

English Title	Original Title	Director	Date
The Sprinkler Sprinkled	*L'arroseur arrosé*	Louis Lumière	1895
The Italian Straw Hat	*Un chapeau de paille d'Italie*	René Clair	1928
Freedom for Us	*À nous la liberté*	René Clair	1931
Boudu Saved from Drowning	*Boudu sauvé des eaux*	Jean Renoir	1932
Heartbeat	*Le schpountz*	Marcel Pagnol	1938

English Title	Original Title	Director	Date
Mr. *Hulot's Holiday*	*Les vacances de Monsieur Hulot*	Jacques Tati	1953
The Trip Across Paris	*La traverseé de Paris*	Claude Autant-Lara	1956
Elena and Her Men	*Elena et les hommes*	Jean Renoir	1956
The Cow and I	*La vache et le prisonnier*	Henri Verneuil	1959
Yo-yo	*Yoyo*	Pierre Étaix	1965
The Great Stroll	*La grande vadrouille*	Gérard Oury	1966
The Tall Blond Man with One Black Shoe	*Le grand blond avec une chaussure noire*	Yves Robert	1972
The Mad Adventures of Rabbi Jacob	*Les aventures de Rabbi Jacob*	Gérard Oury	1973
	La cage aux folles	Édouard Molinaro	1978
Santa Claus Is a Stinker	*Le père Noël est une ordure*	Jean-Marie Poiré	1982
Three Men and a Cradle	*3 hommes et un couffin*	Coline Serreau	1985
The Visitors	*Les visiteurs*	Jean-Marie Poiré	1993
Would I Lie to You?	*La vérité si je mens!*	Thomas Gilou	1997
The Taste of Others	*Le goût des autres*	Agnès Jaoui	2000
The Spanish Apartment	*L'auberge espagnole*	Cédric Klapisch	2002
OSS 117: Cairo, Nest of Spies	*OSS 117: Le Caire, nid d'espions*	Michel Hazanavicius	2006
Avenue Montaigne	*Fauteuils d'orchestre*	Danièle Thompson	2006
My Best Friend	*Mon meilleur ami*	Patrice Leconte	2006
Welcome to the Sticks	*Bienvenue chez les Ch'tis*	Dany Boon	2008
The Dinner Game	*Le dîner de cons*	Francis Veber	2008
LOL	*LOL (Laughing Out Loud)*	Lisa Azuelos	2008
Micmacs	*Micmacs à tire-larigot*	Jean-Pierre Jeunet	2009
The Concert	*Le concert*	Radu Mihaileanu	2009
The Names of Love	*Le nom des gens*	Michel Leclerc	2010
The Women on the 6th Floor	*Les femmes du 6ème étage*	Philippe le Guay	2010
The Intouchables	*Intouchables*	Olivier Nakache, Éric Toledano	2011

Hollywood Remakes

The Man with One Red Shoe	Hollywood remake of *The Tall Blond Man with One Black Shoe (Le Grand Blond avec une chaussure noire)*	Stan Dragoti	1985
Three Men and a Baby	Remake of *Trois hommes et un couffin (3 hommes et un couffin*, 1985)	Leonard Nimoy	1986
Down and Out in Beverly Hills	Remake of *Boudu Saved from Drowning (Boudu sauvé des eaux*, 1932)	Paul Mazursky	1986
Mixed Nuts	Remake of *Santa Claus Is a Stinker (Le père Noël est une ordure*, 1982)	Nora Ephron	1994
The Birdcage	US remake of *La cage aux folles* (1978)	Mike Nichols	1996
Just Visiting	US remake of *The Visitors (Les visiteurs*, 1993)	Jean-Marie Poiré	2001
Dinner for Schmucks	Hollywood remake of *Dinner for Schmucks (Le dîner de cons*, 2008)	Jay Roach	2010
LOL	Hollywood remake of *LOL (LOL: Laughing Out Loud*, 2008)	Lisa Azuelos	2012

Notes

1. "Top 250 Tous les temps aux États-Unis," JP's Box-Office, http://www.jpbox-office.com/top100.php?variable=France.
2. Rémi Fournier Lanzoni, *French Comedy on Screen: A Cinematic History* (New York: Palgrave Macmillan, 2014), 2.
3. Lanzoni, *French Comedy on Screen*, 1.
4. "The French Have Jokes, But Do They Have a Sense of Humour?" *The Economist*, December 18, 2003, https://www.daumier.org/2004/02/02/the-french-have-jokes-but-do-they-have-a-sense-of-humour/.
5. René Clair, "Talkie versus Talkie (1929)," in *French Film Theory and Criticism: A History/Anthology, 1907–1939*, vol. 2, ed. Richard Abel (Princeton, NJ: Princeton University Press, 1988), 39–40.

6. René Clair, "Le Million 1931," in *French Film Theory and Criticism: A History/Anthology, 1907–1939*, vol. 2, ed. Richard Abel (Princeton, NJ: Princeton University Press, 1988), 73–74.
7. Richard Abel, "The Transition to Sound," in *French Film Theory and Criticism: A History/Anthology, 1907–1939*, vol. 2, ed. Richard Abel (Princeton, NJ: Princeton University Press, 1988), 17.
8. Evelyn Ehrlich, *Cinema of Paradox: French Filmmaking under the German Occupation* (New York: Columbia University Press, 1985), 88.
9. Ehrlich, *Cinema of Paradox*, 70.
10. In François Truffaut, *The Films in My Life*, trans. Leonard Mayhew (New York: Simon & Schuster, 1975), 171–172.
11. Wayne Thompson, *Western Europe*. The World Today Series (Lanham, MD: Rowman & Littlefield, 2012), 121.
12. Anne Jäckel, "*Les Visiteurs*: A Feelgood Movie for Uncertain Times," in *France on Film: Reflections on Popular French Cinema*, ed. Lucy Mazdon (London: Wallflower, 2001), 42–43.
13. Jäckel, *Les Visiteurs*, 45.
14. Roger Ebert, "Review of *Just Visiting*," August 6, 2001, https://www.rogerebert.com/reviews/just-visiting-2001.
15. Dave Kehr, "Film in Review: 'Just Visiting,'" *New York Times*, April 6, 2001, 64. https://www.nytimes.com/2001/04/06/movies/film-in-review-just-visiting.html.
16. Rae Beth Gordon, *Why the French Love Jerry Lewis: From Cabaret to Early Cinema* (Stanford, CA: Stanford University Press, 2000), 8.

8
Italian Film Comedy

Not surprisingly, the land that gave the world *The Divine Comedy* also gave us forms of comedy considerably more profane. Dante's masterpiece was guided by a vision of humanity that embraced the best, the worst, and everything between. His title used the word *comedy* in the original sense defined by *Webster's New World Dictionary*, as "a drama or narrative with a happy ending or non-tragic theme." For the poet, or at least for his dramatic persona, the great poem ends happily in paradise. As we'll see, this is not necessarily the path taken by many Italian film comedies. Some, especially the earliest, are full of old-fashioned pie-in-the-face humor, simple gags with no thematic strings attached, designed to make us laugh and leave the theater in a buoyant mood. Others, though, acquire a derisive or melancholy cast, troubled by the sting of social satire or a deep cynicism about life. When the curtain comes down, there may be bodies on the stage, and we're left in an uneasy darkness.

The shadier form of comedy was particularly prevalent in the 1960s and 1970s, when it acquired the label of *commedia all'italiana*, "comedy Italian style." What makes this dark strain all the more intriguing is that it coincided with Italy's "economic miracle," a period of extraordinary progress and prosperity. Film historian Peter Bondanella argues that the decade spanning 1958 to 1968 was "the golden age of Italian cinema," when the Italian film industry reached a peak of artistic quality and commercial success.[1] Auteur directors like Federico Fellini, Michelangelo Antonioni, and Luchino Visconti were winning prizes at all the prestigious film festivals. At the same time, when Hollywood was losing its grip on the global market, Italian genre films proved especially competitive. Spaghetti Westerns and gruesome *giallo* horror films were gaining huge cult followings, but the most resilient genre was comedy.

Writing in the 1980s, Bondanella observed that "film comedy continues to provide the most popular form of cinematic entertainment in Italy today."[2] Yet, as in other countries, Italian comedy has gone through phases, each phase mirroring the time, its preoccupations, and its moods. This chapter tracks some of these changes. Given their broad scope and many variations, we'll consider the degree to which comedy in Italy is a separate genre or something else: more like a mode, a vision, a dialect, perhaps one of several hues on a director's emotional palette for capturing the human drama on film—offering us witty glimpses of paradise, purgatory, and hell.

When the World Laughs. William V. Costanzo, Oxford University Press (2020). Oxford University Press
DOI: 10.1093/oso/9780190924997.001.0001

Commedia dell'Arte and Other Precursors of Italian Comedy

Like so much of Italian culture, Italian comedy can be traced back to ancient Roman times. Writing for a Latin-speaking audience, Plautus and Terrence tailored an even earlier Greek tradition to Roman tastes, delighting the populace with boisterously comic plays. Their ludicrous plots were based on everyday life and peppered with colloquial idioms. They featured stock characters like the braggart soldier, the quack doctor, the surly servant, and the lecherous old man—figures we still recognize and laugh at today. During the Renaissance, when classical literature burst forth again after centuries of medieval neglect, these robust figures of fun gained new life. For some three hundred years, beginning in the 1500s, they animated a lively form of theatrical entertainment known as *commedia dell'arte*, or "comedy of craft."

The practitioners of *commedia dell'arte* performed outdoors, sporting masks and colorful costumes in the spirit of Carnival. They freely improvised the antics of their cartoonish character types, relying more on individual style and regional taste than on given scripts. In time, these caricatures acquired local habitations and a repertoire of names. The comic servant, a spirited trickster who regularly outfoxed his master with feats of cunning and quick wit, became the *Zani* (a Venetian term for Gianni [John] and the prototype for much zany behavior). He was joined by the *Arlecchino* (or Harlequin, wearing the multicolored costume of the jester) and the *Pulcinella* (a name that may derive from the Italian word *pulcino*, or chick), a stock character in Neapolitan puppetry. Also in the mix were the unscrupulous brigand from Bergama, the bombastic solider (*miles gloriousus*) from Naples, and the miserly old merchant (*Pantalone*), irreverently named after the patron saint of Venice, Saint Pantaleon.

These characters never died out but evolved into different forms as they migrated throughout Europe. In England, they helped to shape a tradition of pantomime and Punch-and-Judy puppet shows. In France, under the name of Comédie-Italienne, their broad brand of humor flourished under royal patronage, eventually acquiring a more elevated status as it merged with comic opera and influenced playwrights like Molière and Mirabeau. Lope de Vega borrowed freely from them for his Spanish plays. In Italy, which was then more like a confederation of city-states than a unified nation, each character in the repertoire acquired regional traits. It was great fun to recognize the charlatan from Bologna, the bombastic mercenary from Naples, the self-dramatizing lovers from Florence. Then, as now, Italians liked to laugh at provincial peculiarities.

Centuries later, with the invention of movies, the spirit of *commedia dell'arte* would find its way into *commedia all'italiana*. Mario Monicelli's *Big Deal on Madonna Street* (*I soliti ignoti*) is considered to have launched the trend in 1958. In one of the film's funniest scenes, a motley crew of would-be thieves break into an apartment for an easy haul, only to be defeated by their own incompetence. Each character has a distinct personality and a regional accent. Roman, Neapolitan, Sicilian, Venetian and Bolognese, Abruzzese and Barese: Their speech is a linguistic atlas of the country. Together, their clumsy antics, ludicrous expressions, and crude language all contribute to the humor of the situation. After weeks of preparation and a long ordeal of stumbling over rooftops, crawling through windows, and drilling through walls, they end up in the wrong room of the wrong apartment, where they raid the refrigerator as compensation for their trouble (Figure 8.1). Later, the headlines read, "Persons Unknown Bore Hole to Steal Pasta and Beans"—a fitting finale for a *commedia all'italiana*.

But this particular style of comedy arrived in movie theaters only after Italian cinema had moved through several earlier forms. During the silent period, popular comedians from the variety stage adapted their slapstick gags and burlesque routines to the new medium, often with a bone-breaking heavy hand. During the 1930s, with the arrival of sound, Mussolini founded Cinecittà Studios in Rome, an ambitious project designed to turn out a steady stream of revenue-producing popular entertainment and Fascist propaganda. Borrowing heavily from Hollywood's successful methods and aesthetics, Cinecittà produced lavish comedies on Art Deco sets. Known as *telefoni bianchi* because

Figure 8.1 "Mama mia!" A group of bungling burglars break into the wrong room in *Big Deal on Madonna Street* (1958).

they used white telephones as status symbols, these films all had uniformly happy endings and reflected the conservative values of Mussolini's regime. Few are watched today. In stark contrast, the neorealist movies made after World War II were produced on small budgets, filmed in the streets on grainy film with mostly nonprofessional actors. Although neorealist films like Roberto Rossellini's *Rome, Open City* (*Roma, città aperta*, 1946) and Vittorio De Sica's *The Bicycle Thieves* (*Ladri di biciclette*, 1948) had moments of humor, their main focus was on realistic social commentary. The *neorealismo* movement was hugely influential outside the country but relatively short-lived in Italy itself, where it soon took on the lighter, brighter tones of *neorealismo rosa* (pink realism), a sentimental blend of comedy and romance less interested in realism or social issues than in amusing the masses. Luigi Comencini's *Bread, Love and Jealousy* (*Pane, amore e gelosia*, 1954) introduced a busty Gina Lollobrigida and the "pinkish" preoccupation with sex to Italians and the world. De Sica's lighthearted anthology film *The Gold of Naples* (*L'oro di Napoli*, 1954) featured comic performances by four Italian stars (Sophia Loren, Silvana Mangano, Totò, and De Sica himself), demonstrating to the world that Neapolitans are all born actors (Figure 8.2). Each of the four vignettes offers a variation on the theme of love and sex, each tinted with a lusty shade of pink. Some two decades later, such forays into bawdy comedy would take a more erotic turn with a subgenre known as *commedia sexy all'italiana*.

Figure 8.2 Sophia Loren and Vittorio De Sica rob unwary bus riders while Marcello Mastroianni looks on in *Too Bad She's Bad* (1955).

The Economic Miracle and *Commedia all'Italiana*

Meanwhile, Italy itself was on the verge of a major transformation. It began in the 1950s with a sudden boom in the country's economy. Largely financed by the Marshall Plan and fueled by Italy's huge labor force, an extraordinary surge of productive energy yanked Italy out of the wartime rubble and into the modern age. Millions of workers migrated from the rural south to find jobs in the industrial north. The urban centers exploded. New highways and railways were built. Between 1950 and 1960, the national gross domestic product doubled. From 1951 to 1971, the average income rose by 300%. Families that had been dirt-poor now clamored for consumer goods as a profusion of cheap washing machines, televisions, and automobiles swamped the market. Such booms had erupted elsewhere in the world before, and they would happen again later in places like Japan, Korea, and China.

But one of history's lessons is sadly commonplace: What goes up must usually come down.In Italy, the bust came in the late 1960s. By then, the miracle had spent itself, leaving an uneasy legacy of displacement, disruption, and distress. The new prosperity had not favored everyone equally. Two decades of frantic mobility had uprooted families, disrupted age-old traditions, and strained familiar values to the breaking point. Waves of student protests, worker strikes, and terrorist abductions spread across the country, continuing into the 1980s. Italians called this period the *anni di piombo*, "years of lead."

Not surprisingly, the golden age of *commedia all'italiana* coincides with the boom years. There was more money to make movies and a growing audience eager to watch them. An appetite for comedy seemed to fit the upbeat mood of the times. But what makes "comedy Italian style" different from earlier forms is a dark strain of cynicism running through so many of the films. It's there at the start, in *Big Deal on Madonna Street*. Beyond the obvious parody of heist films, beneath the slapstick shenanigans of the inept crew of aspiring small-time thieves are moments of disturbing bleakness. One man is attacked and crippled; another man dies in a bungled robbery. Instead of a conventional happy ending, the adventure ends miserably for most of the group.

The irony is even darker in Monicelli's next film, *The Great War* (*La grande guerra*, 1959), in which two reluctant soldiers blunder through a series of misadventures during World War I. Neither Oreste, a Roman, nor Giovanni, from Milan, is particularly fond of patriotism or courage. Like many of the characters in Italian comedy, their main goal is survival, *l'arte di arrangiarsi*, the art of getting by. After months of scheming and conniving to avoid combat, they volunteer as messengers, thinking this ploy safer than the trenches. It isn't. In the end, the two kindred antiheroes do the right thing not out of devotion to their nation but because they dislike the enemy officer's arrogance.

Their final act is a triumph of self-pride over pride in country. While the film was officially condemned as unpatriotic, many reviewers praised it as groundbreaking, the first Italian depiction of World War I to be free of propaganda, undercutting the myth of "a grand and glorious war" with the hacksaw of sardonic comedy.[3]

The Great War shared the top prize at the Venice Film Festival with Rossellini's *General Della Rovere*, set during World War II and starring Vittorio De Sica, one icon of neorealism directing another. Film historian Andrea Bini sees this divided honor as a symbolic moment: The baton of Italian filmmaking was passing from neorealism to *commedia all'italiana*.[4] Monicelli seemed to be aware of this shift as well as another triumph for his brand of comedy, its challenge to Hollywood. Not only was his *Big Deal on Madonna Street* a sendup of the traditional Hollywood caper film, but its gritty, realistic style was also a putdown of Hollywood production values. In one of the film's funniest scenes, a member of the gang shows the others some 16-mm footage that he took with a small camera on the roof. This home movie is intended as burglary reconnaissance, to show them the heavy safe across the street that they're supposed to crack.

His companions comment on the film's poor quality. "It's moving. It's all blurred," they complain.

"Uffa," he retorts, "I was setting up the shot. The camera is old. The lens is old. This ain't Hollywood, you know."

The rest of the footage is interspersed with pictures of his baby and obscured by a parade of underpants hanging on the clothesline. The projector skips and jumps. But it gives Dante, the safe expert, all the information needed for the break-in. All this is an apt analogy to comedy Italian style. The storyline may be irregular, interrupted by unexpected turns and amusing touches from ordinary life, and the photography may not be polished to a glossy fantasy, but it does the job.

Monicelli and his followers did the job of revealing defects in the economic miracle, exposing the limitations and inequities that led to the years of lead. Instead of raising the living standards of the lower classes, the boom only widened the disparity between rich and poor. For many, the promise of a better life seemed to recede farther and farther beyond their grasp.[5] In his analysis of *Big Deal on Madonna Street*, Rémi Fournier Lanzoni describes the film as a turning point in Italian comedy, signaling "an abrupt, radical shift into social criticism, a stance that no other comedy filmmaker had taken before Monicelli."[6] Peter Bondanella makes an even broader claim for *commedia all'italiana*: "Perhaps no other nation's popular cinema so consistently dared to display its worst features and to subject them to such hearty laughter."[7] Bondanella lists some targets of this laughter—"fawning respect for established authority, vilification of subordinates, sexual obsessions, cynicism, intellectual shallowness, skepticism, and emotional immaturity."[8] For a better look at these and other targets, we move on to the films of Monicelli's *compadri* and fellow satirists.

Love and Marriage Italian Style

Pietro Germi came to comedy by an unexpected path. For sixteen years, he had directed serious social issue films in the neorealist vein. Then, while adapting Giovanni Arpino's novel *Crime of Honor* to the screen, he realized that if he pushed its deeply tragic premise far enough, "beyond the boundaries of paradox," it could become a comedy.[9] It was a stroke of genius. Germi's *Divorce Italian Style* (*Divorzio all'italiana*, 1961) became one of the most uncomfortably funny highlights of *commedia all'italiana*. In fact, Germi's film is credited with lending its name to the entire cycle of "Italian style" comedy.[10]

Its premise is based on Article 587 of the penal code, still in effect in Sicily when the movie was made. In a land where divorce was illegal, this relic of feudal law allowed anyone to kill an unfaithful spouse and receive a relatively light sentence. The local population understood such murders to be matters of honor. Enter Ferdinando Cefalù (Marcello Mastroianni), a forty-something member of the declining nobility who must share the faded splendor of his family's palace to pay the bills. Fefè, as he is called by everyone who knows him, lives in close quarters with his parents, his wife Rosalia (Daniela Rocca), and his noxious uncle's family. Rosalia's cloying devotion annoys him. On stifling summer days, she turns off his desk fan and serves hot tea, then pleads with him to sip some from his cup (Figure 8.3). In this environment of claustrophobia and relentless

Figure 8.3 Fefè and his cloying wife in *Divorce Italian Style* (1961).

lethargy, Fefè's only refuge is the family bathroom, where he can be alone and watch from the window his young niece Angela, asleep in her light negligee. Angela (Stefania Sandrelli) is young, beautiful, and out of reach. He becomes obsessed with longing. But first, he must get rid of his wife.

Fefè's plan is a matter of Sicilian logic. First, he has to find a lover for Rosalia, then catch them in the act of *flagrante delicto* so he can shoot them, serve a short prison term, and be free to marry the angel of his dreams. Much of the film's comedy comes from watching him carry out this plan through a zigzag plot of calculated moves, ludicrous mishaps, and genuine surprises. He fantasizes a scene in which his wife falls into a cauldron of homemade soap, another in which she drowns in quicksand, a third when she's shot into orbit in a rocket ship. He imagines the impassioned speech of his attorney defending his wounded honor to the jury. Meanwhile, he pursues his purpose with a single-minded, cool detachment, occasionally glancing in the mirror at his calm demeanor: the slick black hair, full moustache, and elongated cigarette holder of a stage villain.

Germi casts his actors with an eye for caricature. Fefè is a cartoonish sendup of the world-weary aristocrat, Rosalia a travesty of the oppressively sugary wife. The attorney's performance is a masterwork of parody, filled with overblown language and excessive gestures that have more to do with opera than the law. Germi uses black-and-white photography to accentuate the grotesque, in the manner of Francisco Goya's charcoal *Caprichos*, at the same time that it captures a neorealist sense of time and place. The women seem to be fixed in the gloomy garb of perpetual mourning, an austerity reflected in the grim Sicilian landscape. Each scene is awash in the monochromatic tones of satire. Among his targets are the courtroom, the Catholic Church, the Communist Party, the family, and the street. More pointedly he's aiming at the people who pay lip service to these institutions, who attend church one day but cram into the local theater to watch *La Dolce Vita* the next, who show up at the party's social dances but equate women's rights with harlotry, who smile politely to their neighbor but laugh at him behind his back. Germi offers these two-faced contradictions some sixty years after Pirandello identified a binary "feeling of the opposite" at the heart of humor. It's another potent example of incongruity theory in action.

Germi followed *Divorce Italian Style* with *Seduced and Abandoned* (*Sedotta e abbandonata*, 1964) and *The Birds, the Bees and the Italians* (*Signore & signori*, 1966), establishing a successful formula for sex and comedy Italian style. In the former, he exposes another absurdity of Sicilian thought: A man who seduces the sister of his fiancée refuses to marry the girl because she's not a virgin. In the latter, set in northern Italy, he assumes a lighter tone, playing with the themes of impotence, jealousy, and promiscuity that have amused Italian audiences and their ancestors for ages.

Of course, this kind of humor was not limited to the Italian peninsula, which partly explains its popularity abroad. Nor was Germi the only neorealist to turn his camera to the new genre. Three years after *Divorce Italian Style*, Vittorio De Sica directed *Marriage Italian Style* (*Matrimonio all'italiana*, 1964). Featuring vigorous performances by Mastroianni and Sophia Loren, it was a big hit in Italy and abroad, especially in the United States, where it was nominated at the Academy Awards for Best Foreign Language Film and Best Actress in a Leading Role. Mastroianni plays Domenico, a wealthy businessman who refuses to marry his mistress, Filomena (Loren), even after she has given her best years to caring for him and his ailing mother. Filomena tricks him into marriage by feigning illness. Believing she will soon be dead, he makes his wedding vow before a bedside priest. Moments later, on the phone with a younger woman, he's shocked to find his new wife standing behind him, laughing sarcastically and very much alive. Dumfounded and livid, he follows her to the kitchen, where she grabs a plate of pasta from the fridge. While he carries on, screaming at everyone and threatening to get his gun, she eats her pasta, replying with the composure of a wife who knows her man: "It's in the dresser. Don't make a mess. I just ironed your shirts" (Figure 8.4). Her Neapolitan accent seems to add a touch of class to her composure.

No account of Italian comedy in this era would be complete without some mention of Federico Fellini, Italy's most famous film director. Although his name is associated with serious art cinema, it was his aptitude for comedy that jumpstarted his career. As a poor student in the 1930s, Fellini earned extra

Figure 8.4 The wife recovers from her deathbed wedding in *Marriage Italian Style* (1964).

cash by sketching people's faces in Roman cafés, a talent he would tap again after the war when he opened his Funny Face Shop and sold drawings to American soldiers. This knack for comic caricature would later find expression in the grotesques that he cast and filmed in many of his movies. In the 1940s, Fellini found employment with a biweekly humor magazine. Here he hobnobbed with gagmen and scriptwriters who would later become some of Italy's leading actors (Aldo Fabrizi), directors (Ettore Scola), and scriptwriters (Cesare Zavattini). By the end of the decade, he was writing his own gags and contributing to scripts, and soon he was in the director's chair himself, turning out light comedies like *Variety Lights* (*Luci del varietà*, 1950) and neorealist dramas like *La Strada* (*La strada*, 1953). Many of his later films combine comedy and drama in ways that are uniquely Felliniesque. The garish types that parade through the nostalgic mood of *Amarcord* (1973) include a parasitic brother-in-law with his ludicrous hairnet, a bean-seller smiling through his few black teeth, and a plump midget emir draped in jewels, surrounded by a harem. In *8½* (*Otto e mezzo*, 1963), another semi-autobiographical film, the gigantic figure of la Saraghina, a local prostitute who dances on the beach for Fellini and his boyhood friends, is both alarming and amusing. The key to these comic grotesques may be found in the director's quasi-documentary, *The Clown* (*I clowns*, 1970). Fellini narrates his "investigation" in a sentimental voice: "The clowns of my childhood, where are they today? That terrifying, comic violence . . . that noisy exhilaration? . . . They frightened me. Those chalky faces, those enigmatic expressions, those twisted, drunken masks . . . they all reminded me of other strange and troubled characters who roam around every country village." What makes these figures funny are their exaggerated features and behavior. What makes them scary is their resemblance to the real world. But it's those masklike faces that make them as universal as the riotous spirit of Carnival and the circus clown.

From Gold to Lead

If Germi, De Sica, and Fellini moved back and forth between comedy and drama, Alberto Lattuada plunged his audience abruptly from one genre to the other in *Mafioso* (1962). The film's first half gets us laughing with the expansive antics of Nino (Alberto Sordi), a southerner employed in an automobile assembly plant in the North. Nino is a hardworking, fast-talking, lovable Sicilian who has found a piece of the economic miracle in Milan. His wife, Marta, is a pretty blonde; his two young daughters are well behaved; his comfortable home has all the modern conveniences. So when he returns home on vacation with his family after eight years "up there," Marta is understandably uneasy. As they pass through the

Straits of Messina on the ferry toward the island of Sicily, she looks back at "Italy moving away."

The homecoming scene is a riot of chaotic goodwill. Nino is all voluble energy and hugs: "Cousin Carmine, you look the same . . . handsome Tony, strong as an oak! . . . Auntie Nifa, you still with us?" Then he turns to greet his Mama. She's standing with two other women, identically dressed in black and weeping into handkerchiefs. They look so much alike that he kisses the wrong one. This is only one of many sight gags based on regional stereotypes. A chicken sleeps under the bed. His sister has a moustache. All the women over fifty are in mourning. After soup and salad, a huge piece of fish is slapped on Marta's plate, then hunks of meat, then eggplant—and that's just the antipasti (Figure 8.5). With her petite figure and fashionable clothes, Marta is distinctly out of place.

But this comic contrast between two cultures is not the central focus of the film, nor its abiding tone. In the second half, Nino learns that he is obligated to commit a murder for the Mafia. Suddenly, he's in a violent gangster movie. The grim details, carefully arranged in advance, proceed with chilling precision. Nino becomes an unwilling but compliant cog in the machinery of feudal justice. The unwritten law of *omertà* binds him to obedient silence, and he will never be the same again.

Lattuada's judgment of Sicilian society is more troubling than Germi's because it lacks the comic relief of *Divorce Italian Style* or *Seduced and Abandoned*. The second half of *Mafioso* is relentlessly bleak. It's as if Dante's progress from hell to paradise has been reversed. There is a similar movement in Dino Risi's masterpiece, *This Easy Life* (*Il sorpasso*, 1962), which begins with the amusing antics

Figure 8.5 Homecoming dinner in *Mafioso* (1962).

of a free-spirited young man and ends in a tragic death. Bruno is the gregarious Italian male, self-centered and unscrupulous, a hedonist who uses his charms on everyone he meets. When he encounters a shy law student named Roberto (Jean-Louis Trintignant), he takes the anxious man away from his studies on a picaresque road trip from Rome to Tuscany. Bruno and his classy convertible represent Italy's new materialism and mobility, changes that threaten the country's authentic values in a new age of instant affluence.

Mafioso and *This Easy* Life were cautionary tales, premonitions of catastrophe made during the peak of Italy's prosperity. In the 1970s, as the golden age turned into the years of lead, the problems lurking beneath the boom grew more pronounced. In Franco Brusati's *Bread and Chocolate* (*Pane e cioccolata*, 1974), an Italian immigrant comes to Switzerland in search of a better life. The film opens in an idyllic Swiss park. A string quartet is playing soothing music on the lawn. Sweet, blond children carry fruit-laden baskets to a picnic. Nino Garofalo (Nino Manfredi) sits against a tree enjoying a sandwich on his day off. After tossing the wrapper aside, he reconsiders this un-Swiss behavior and deposits his trash properly in a wastebasket. But when he starts to chew noisily on his crusty bread, the music stops and everybody stares (Figure 8.6). This amusing credit sequence is a preview of the next antisocial act that gets him into serious trouble. He relieves himself against a wall. As commonplace as this might be in Italy, it costs Nino his job and sets him on a picaresque series of misadventures while trying to survive in the new land. He makes friends with a Greek refugee who has married a sour-faced Swiss official just to maintain her legal status. He competes for a waiter's job

Figure 8.6 Nino disturbs the Swiss peace with his crusty Italian bread in *Bread and Chocolate* (1974).

with a Turk who is so desperate to keep his position that he blisters his hands on a hot plate so as not to interrupt his work. Nino even dyes his hair blond, trying to pass as a German, but he gives himself away when he instinctively roots for the Italian team in a Swiss café.

A busboy asks him, "Why do foreigners treat Italians so badly?" Nino has asked himself the same question. "If the Pope picks them as his guards, they must have some good qualities." But to the busboy, he says ironically, "Go see how they treat Southern Italians in Milan." Later, Nino visits with a group of Neapolitans reduced to living in a chicken coop. At a makeshift table, they treat him to a hearty meal and high-spirited Italian comradery. But the picture of his countrymen covered with chicken feathers disturbs him. He is even more upset when they suddenly interrupt the meal to watch the owner's children bathing in the pond nearby. In rapt silence, they all peer through the chicken wire at these carefree blond Swiss youth, awed by a life of beauty and serenity that will always be beyond their reach. It is a glimpse of paradise from the netherworld.

Italy's low economic status in Europe, the Southern Italian's inferior rank in his own country, the sad-sack everyman just trying to survive, the age-old battle of the sexes: these staples of Italian comedy continued to preoccupy directors of the 1970s. In Luigi Commencini's *The Scientific Card Players* (*Lo scopone scientifico*, 1972), the disparity in status takes the form of a card game between a poor Italian (Alberto Sordi) and a rich American (Bette Davis). In Monicelli's *An Average Little Man* (*Un Borghese piccolo piccolo*, 1977), the everyman is a modest white-collar worker (Sordi again) trying to provide for his family. Again and again, Italian comedy depicts a people struggling to adapt to whatever life throws their way. After World War II, the heroes are replaced by cowards, scoundrels, and opportunists: the average Italian little man. The focus shifts from societal issues to individuals, from solidarity to social fragmentation. In many cases, the humor itself grows more discordant and more ambivalent.

Ambivalence and discord have long been considered hallmarks of humor not just in Italy but around the globe. As we saw in Chapter 1, the dominant theory to explain what makes us laugh is based on principles of incongruity, a kind of cognitive dissonance between two competing points of view. This general theory was given a local interpretation by Italy's great playwright and philosopher, Luigi Pirandello. In his 1908 essay *On Humor*, Pirandello distinguished between comedy and humor. When we see an older woman trying to look young, we laugh. Our initial awareness of incongruity, the gap between her age and her unsuitably youthful clothes, is a "perception of the opposite," which he called comic. But then we feel sympathy for her, a kind of compassion or "feeling of the opposite," which he called humor.[11] Pirandello's seemingly simple distinction caps a profound understanding of modern life. For him, all life is movement, change, flux. Pirandello sees a fundamental contradiction between this incessant mobility of life and the abstract, rigid forms in which we try to fix it to make sense of its disorder. In an age when our belief in reason has collapsed along with our confidence in systematic thought and institutions, humor is an existential choice. In opposition to those artists who create orderly images and plots, the humorist "deconstructs" the order, pulls the mask from the façade, exposing the absurdities and ambiguities.[12] The image of unmasking connects Pirandello's insights back to the Carnivals of Venice and the *commedia dell'arte* as well as forward to the theater of the absurd, which often used masks as instruments of satire. In another metaphor, he describes humor as a special kind of mirror, not of glass but of icy water. The flames of feeling are not only reflected in this mirror, but they also extinguish themselves, releasing vapor in the form of laughter. Laughter dissipates the pain. In a third metaphor, he compares humor to a shadow following close behind the body of ordinary feeling: "The ordinary artist pays attention only to the body; the humorist pays attention to both, and sometime more to the shadow than to the body: he notices all the tricks of the shadow, the way it sometimes grows longer and sometimes short and squat, almost as if to mimic the body, which meanwhile is indifferent to it and does not pay any attention to it."[13] In his own poetic style, Pirandello captured the way today's scientists describe humor as a flexible state of mind quite different from the rigidities of ordinary thought, one that playfully acknowledges contradictions, allows for ambiguity, and relieves tension. His imagery suggests that the trickster figure is a kind of shadow, dogging the hero's heels, and that the dark, satiric humor of directors like Risi and Monicelli may belong to a mocking shadow world. His words could also describe the work of Lina Wertmüller and Roberto Benigni.

Lina Wertmüller: Sex and Politics Italian Style

In the films of Lina Wertmüller, the issues of "getting by," social status, and sexual politics are all rolled into a uniquely personal form of comedy created by Italy's best-known woman director. Hailed in the 1970s as a strikingly original new talent, Wertmüller shocked, provoked, and entertained audiences everywhere with her irreverent satires on sex and politics. Her films brought a brash, confrontational style to the theater of class warfare and the battle of the sexes, always pushing the limits of comedy toward increasingly outraged characters and outrageous plots. They came in quick succession. *The Seduction of Mimi* (*Mimi metallugico ferito nell'onore*, 1972) is a sardonic sendup of Sicilian machismo. In *Love & Anarchy* (*Film d'amore e d'anarchia* . . ., 1973), a young anti-Fascist's plans to assassinate Mussolini are diverted by his rocky romance with a prostitute. In *All Screwed Up* (*Tutto a posto e niente in ordine*, 1974), the tenants of a workers' commune engage in a chaotic pursuit of love, ideology, and survival. *Swept Away* (*Travolti da un insolito destino nell'azzurro mare d'agosto*, 1974) follows the frenetic romance of a rich woman (Mariangela Melato) shipwrecked on a deserted island with a working-class sailor (Giancarlo Giannini). In *Seven Beauties* (*Pasqualino Settebellezze*, 1975), a smug ladies' man finds himself in a German concentration camp where he becomes the plaything of a sexually voracious female warden.

Born in Rome in 1926, Wertmüller was raised by devoutly Roman Catholic parents of Swiss descent. Her full name attests to her aristocratic lineage: Arcangela Felice Assunta Wertmüller von Elgg Spanol von Braueich. A rebellious child, she rejected the values of her family and got herself expelled from more than a dozen Catholic schools. Instead of studying law, like her father, she enrolled in drama school and found her way into the movies, serving as an assistant director for Federico Fellini on *8½* and eventually directing her own films. In her heyday, Wertmüller enjoyed the limelight, whether she was being praised or condemned. Men criticized her as a radical misanthropist; feminists attacked her for being reactionary, even "a male chauvinist."[14] She was never interested in being politically correct.

In their short but insightful study of her work, Ernest Ferlita and John May read her films as parables, which, like those of Jesus in the Bible, are subversive stories meant "to change us, not reassure us,"[15] "to incite and provoke."[16] Her settings are visually striking, often grimly realistic, but they are also always metaphors: a brothel in Naples, a quarry in Sicily, a restaurant kitchen in Rome, a concentration camp in Germany, a deserted island off the Sardinian coast.

It is against such symbolic backdrops that Wertmüller's human comedy takes place, punctuated by extreme close-ups that often look like grotesque distortions of the human face and animated by their nonstop chattering in Italian dialects. In *Love and Anarchy*, the privileged class is represented by Fascist males while women are allied with the subjugated peasantry and working class. In *Swept Away*, the roles are reversed. Here the mantle of power is worn by a woman, Raffaella, a wealthy capitalist who indulges in arrogant diatribes against the political left. Her antagonist is Gennarino, a deckhand on her yacht, who is also a dedicated Communist. The film begins with a close-up of Gennarino lifting the hatch slightly to get a glimpse of three topless women sunbathing on deck. The focus on his scraggly beard and inquiring eyes, the light music, and the creaking sound as he slowly lowers the hatch invite us to laugh at this buffoonish peeping Tom. But in the next shot, he gains our sympathy as Raffaella toys with him, first by flirting with her eyes, then berating him behind his back. "Typical southerner, already getting sloppy," she says to her peers within his earshot (Figure 8.7). Below deck, Gennarino complains to a fellow worker, calling her a "Fascist

Figure 8.7 Raffaella toys with the hired help in *Swept Away* (1974).

bitch": "If she screws me, I'll screw her." His threat soon takes a literal turn when the two of them are marooned on a deserted island. Tired and hungry, stripped of her personal and social resources, Raffaella must now rely on Gennarino's superior strength and survival skills. With this shift in fortune comes a shift in sexual politics. Now it's his turn to look down on her, insulting her in the crudest language, forcing her to cook and clean, to call him Mr. Carunchio. Ironically, perhaps surprisingly, the more he resorts to the stereotypical machismo role, the more she finds him sexually attractive. Some critics were not amused by what they considered sadomasochism and misogyny—no laughing matters. Others regarded the film as a bold exploration of political and sexual violence. Still others, focusing on performance rather than plot or theme, praised the chemistry between Giannini and Melato. Wertmüller emerged from the storm more defiant and self-assured than ever. In a 1979 interview, she laughed, "I don't believe in the distinction of the sexes . . . I reject every distinction between man and woman."[17]

As if to demonstrate this thesis, *Seven Beauties* puts a man at the sexual disposal of a sadistic woman. The man is Pasqualino (Giannini again), a southern Italian bound by the code of machismo. The woman is a prison guard in Germany during World War II. Wertmüller maintains continuous tension between the appalling actions of her characters (honor killing, desertion, rape) and their comic treatment in the film. Pasqualino's effort to hide the body of the man he murdered is played for gruesome laughs. Having deserted his unit in Germany, he breaks into a house and tries to tell the old woman living there that he is hungry, pouring out a stream of broken German and Neapolitan Italian: "Sorry to disturb, German lady. Me Italian soldier. Sunshine, blue water, mandolins. Understand? Pizza, macaroni, *Deutschen suppen*? I'm starving." While she looks on incredulously, he helps himself to some bread, soup, and potatoes from her table. "*Danke schön, bitte schön, auf Wiedersehen . . .*" and he's gone. The comedy ends abruptly when he is caught with his mouth full by the Gestapo. They take him to a prison camp where naked prisoners crowd together in a steamy shower stall. Gaunt bodies are piled waist high; a man in prison stripes hangs from a hook. The only sound is "The Ride of the Valkyries" from Wagner's opera. For Pasqualino, it's all about survival now. The old lady's daughter, an enormous, ugly brute, places a bowl of bratwurst and sauerkraut on the floor before his cowering figure. "Eat, Naples," she commands. "Now you eat, later you fuck." In a brutal scene that amounts to rape, he is forced to have sex with her in order to survive.

All through the 1970s, Wertmüller's popularity rose as her films continued to win awards at home and abroad. But her reputation peaked with *Seven Beauties*. As the times changed, her work became less caustic, more attuned to popular tastes, although they retained some of her satirical wit. *Ciao, Professore!* (*Io speriamo che me la cavo*, 1992) is about preconceptions and points of view. The title figure is Marco Sperelli, a third-grade teacher sent to the wrong school by computer error. Instead of the well-heeled northern community of Corsano, he is assigned to Corzano, a poor, crime-ridden town in southern Italy. What he finds is not at all to his liking. Only a handful of children bother to attend his class. The rest are out on the streets selling stolen cigarettes, waiting on tables, and selling fruit, whatever they can do to help their families make ends meet. So much for the lazy southerner, observes Professor Sperelli; everyone here is working all the time. Sperelli arrives with the belief that he can knock some learning into these kids. One of his learning goals is to teach them the proper way to pronounce the name of their school, De Amicis, no easy task. The children have their own ideas about the Italian language—and much else. The professor soon discovers that much more is at stake than niceties of speech. And he has some learning to do himself. In this town where insult, intimidation, and corruption are the order of the day, he realizes that the best way to get results is to follow the regional rules. One day, his students learn that the stereo he bought from an unscrupulous merchant in Naples turned out to be a box of bricks. "Not even the Japanese would fall for that," they tell him. "Not even the Germans. Not even the Milanese." He asks what they would do in his place. Call the police? At this preposterous idea, they hold their noses in disgust. The room erupts with their suggestions. A torrent of obscene invectives and Machiavellian measures for retaliation bursts from their young lips. Eventually, he puts their street intelligence to good use. When in Corzano, do as the Corzanos do.

Roberto Benigni: Comic Duplicities

If Lina Wertmüller's star was fading through the 1980s and 1990s, Roberto Benigni's was rapidly rising. By the time he won his Oscar for *Life Is Beautiful* (*La vita è bella*, 1997), Benigni was Italy's best-known comedian: an accomplished actor, screenwriter, and director renowned in Italy for his work on television, stage, and film. (▶ See "Case Study for Chapter 8: *Life Is Beautiful*" on the website.) In a book-length study titled *The Divine Comic*, Carlo Celli described him as "one of the very few, if not the only, foreign language comedian to conquer a mass audience in the English-speaking world."[18] Like Wertmüller, Benigni was a mischievous, rebellious, gifted child. But in contrast to her aristocratic pedigree, he was born into a family of poor peasants. His father, a subsistence famer, moved the family from rural Tuscany to the textile town of Prato looking for work during the boom years. Roberto never forgot his roots in the Tuscan people and their culture. As a young man, he loved to hang out with the local *poeti a braccio*, a group of traditional troubadours, honing his talent for verbal improvisation. By the age of fourteen, he was doing regional theater, perfecting a one-man show that led to various stage roles. At twenty, he joined the avant-garde theatre in Rome, where he eventually met many of the film directors he would work with and learn from. Bernardo Bertolucci, Cesare Zavattini, Pier Paolo Pasolini, Marco Ferreri, and Federico Fellini all left imprints on his work. But Benigni's eclectic imagination drew from other sources, too. Besides the creative complexities of troubadour poetry, he was fascinated by the lusty, often obscene humor of the Etruscans, the ancient inhabitants of Tuscany who improvised lewd exchanges in verse, called *Fescennine*, during harvest festivals. Much of Benigni's lower-body humor, which may seem childish and coarse today, is thus connected to the origins of Western comedy, performed well before the tragedies of ancient Greece were written down. Yet Benigni is also well versed in the "high culture" of Dostoevsky, Rabelais, Schopenhauer, and Dante, another Tuscan. So strong is his affinity for Dante that he has devoted much time to his *Tutto Dante* tours, bringing the power and poetry of the *Divine Comedy* to millions of people around the world.

Benigni began his comic career on the far side of the divine. The character that he created in the 1970s, named Mario Cioni, is a young man of the working class preoccupied with sex, bodily functions, and politics. Benigni introduced Cioni in an extended comic monologue teeming with anger, self-loathing, and crude language, a role that he developed and performed on stage, television, and eventually film. Cioni gives voice to Tuscan peasant culture, Rabelaisian obscenity, and troubadour poetry, not to mention his diatribes against intellectuals, right-wing politics, and the Roman Catholic Church. Citing Bakhtin, Cioni argues that the film's unbridled hedonism harks back to medieval traditions of comedy that perform a "regenerative function."[19] In short, the monologue expresses the subversive spirit of the 1970s and connects it with its forebears.

Benigni brings this complex figure to the screen in his first film, *Berlinguer, I Love You* (*Berlinguer ti voglio bene*, 1977). Now Mario Cioni belongs to a band of aimless youth with misogynist leanings and rustic Tuscan names like *Ignorante* (Fool), *Buio* (Darky), and *Bozzone* (Lumpy). For ninety minutes, he vents his sexual frustration, nurses an outsize Oedipal complex, and confides in a scarecrow with the face of Enrico Berlinguer, a contemporary Communist who had lost favor with his party. Much of this humor may be lost on viewers unfamiliar with the particularities of Italian culture, but Benigni also adds a large measure of slapstick. He squat-walks like a chicken, chases his lame fiancée around a table, and dances with an oil barrel in routines reminiscent of Buster Keaton. This kind of visual clowning and innumerable sight gags give more universal appeal to his later films. In *You Bother Me* (*Tu mi turbi*, 1983), he babysits for five-year-old Jesus, who floats on his bath water and leaves an imprint on his towel like the Shroud of Turin. In *The Little Devil* (*Il piccolo diavolo*, 1988), he plays an impish demon stumbling around in an oversize suit and making mischief for a troubled priest (played by the American actor Walter Matthau).

Benigni's next two films—major hits in Italy—put the standard comic formula of mistaken identity to ingenious use. In *Johnny Stecchino* (1991), Benigni plays a bus driver named Dante who resembles a Sicilian mobster named Johnny. Things get complicated when Dante runs into Johnny's wife, Maria, or more accurately when she runs into him, with her car. At first, Maria plans to set up Dante as the fall guy for her husband, who is being hunted by rival Mafiosi killers, but then she falls for Dante and changes her plan. Part of the fun is watching Benigni play both male parts while his wife in real life, Nicoletta Braschi, plays Maria. In *The Monster* (*Il mostro*, 1994), Benigni is mistaken for a serial killer. Although his interests in the opposite sex are fairly normal by Italian standards, he keeps getting into situations that look suspicious to the police. In one hilarious scene, a lighted cigarette falls into his pants at the precise moment that an attractive woman in front of him happens to bend over to pick up some fallen groceries. The surveillance video shows Loris (Benigni) reaching to his crotch, groping for the cigarette, and breathing a sigh of relief after finally extinguishing the flames with a pitcher of water (Figure 8.8). Later, trying to escape from one of his creditors, Loris grabs the ledge of a terrace and hoists himself up out of sight—just in time to find himself facing the rear end of a buxom young woman bending over to water her plants. He starts to let himself down, but then pops up again for a better look. When the videos are screened later in the police station for a class of new recruits, they confirm his image as a voyeuristic predator. This comedy of alternate perspectives depends on two ways of looking at the same thing. It's

Figure 8.8 Benigni quenches a lit cigarette in *The Monster* (1994).

another example of the theory of comic incongruity so often discussed in humor studies, and it is at the heart of much Benigni humor.

Loris is both a victim and a perpetrator of misunderstanding. In fact, he is a consummate con artist, a natural-born trickster with a special talent for deception. One day, with Loris's rent in arrears, the landlord arrives to show his apartment to another tenant. Loris undermines the rental price by pretending to talk on the phone with a friend. While the landlord is otherwise occupied, the would-be tenant overhears him cheerfully complaining about the roaches, leaks, and constant noises he endures every day. By the time the owner returns, the new guy has left. Then there are his weekly visits to the supermarket, where he has turned shoplifting into an art. Loris foils security by slipping produce into other shoppers' pockets, bags, and baby carriages. At the checkout counters, all the alarms go off at once. Amid the mayhem of blinking lights and general confusion, Loris pays for a stick of gum and walks off in a trench coat bulging with stolen goods. In all these roles, Benigni the trickster gives special meaning to the word *duplicity*. By playing both the mobster and the fall guy, the monster and the innocent dupe, he embodies the principle of comic opposites described by Luigi Pirandello in *On Humor*. By shifting back and forth between a character and his mirror image, the body and its shadow, he stretches our experience of alternative viewpoints.

The Tradition Continues

Although Italians continue to make and enjoy local comedies, Italy has exported fewer titles in recent years. A sampling of these can serve as a barometer of national concerns and a hint to the kinds of humor that successfully crosses borders.

Mediterraneo (1991) is set on a remote Greek island, where a group of Italian soldiers is stranded and forgotten during World War II. It's a perfect setup for the national comedic formula: a cross-section of ordinary Italian men representing different parts of the country and various degrees of ineptitude. There's a battle-hardened sergeant whose bible is the army manual, a lieutenant with an eye for art, a private who befriends a donkey named Silvano. At first, the island seems to be deserted. Wary of snipers, one of the anxious men fires at a chicken, starting a chain reaction of zany mishaps that ends with a defunct radio and a dead donkey. Eventually, the islanders come out of hiding and form attachments with the soldiers. The lieutenant restores the damaged frescoes in the church; two aquaphobic brothers from the Apennines proceed to court a pretty shepherdess, who teaches them to swim; and the gawky orderly falls in love with the local prostitute. One of the film's unsubtle themes is that Greeks and Italians belong to the same Mediterranean family, "*una face, una race*." Another message, more deeply felt, is about the lunacy of war. Both the comic and more serious moments in the film emphasize the ironies of Mussolini's warriors trying to conqueror a civilization that predates the Roman Empire when they could be enjoying the shared pleasures of music, food, soccer, love, and peaceful Aegean seascapes.

Like *Mediterraneo, The Postman* (*Il postino*, 1994) uses an isolated setting to comment on the mainland. On a small island off the Italian coast, an uneducated fisherman's son named Mario dreams of a better life. Mario (Massimo Troisi, who portrays him as a lonely soul with a hangdog face) takes a job as postman, delivering mail on bicycle to the only person on the island literate enough to get letters. This is the celebrated poet Pablo Neruda, in political exile from his native Chile. Neruda (played by the French actor Phillipe Noiret) takes an interest in this guileless but curious young man, teaching him lessons about poetry, love, and politics. Mario records the sounds of waves, the wind, and his own son's heartbeat. He pays attention to church bells and the starry sky. The beauty surrounding him touches the poet in him, and a genuine friendship with Neruda blossoms. The humor here is gentle, more smiles than belly laughs, but authentically experienced and, perhaps, deepened by the fact that Troisi knew that he was facing life-threatening heart surgery once the film was shot. He died the day after its completion.

Much of the comedy in *Il postino* depends on the low-key, physical performance of Troisi, who animates his hands and facial features in the wordless tradition of Neapolitan clowns. His pursed lips, those mournful eyes, the shoulder shrugs, and the sweeping gestures of the open palm express the whole range of his emotional life. He presents himself to Neruda as a man uncomfortable with language and begs the famous love poet to help him find words to woo Beatrice, the innkeeper's niece. Neruda tells him gruffly, "Fishermen fall in love. They are able to talk to the girls they love. Your father must have spoken to your mother to get her to marry him" (Figure 8.9). Flapping his fingers dismissively like a pair of lips, Mario replies, "I don't think so. He doesn't talk much." On this island, deeds count more than words. One of the funniest scenes occurs when Beatrice's aunt confronts Neruda about Mario's advances toward her niece. "He's heated her up like an oven," she says. "A man whose only capital is the fungus between his toes! It started off innocently enough: Her smile was like a butterfly. But now he's saying her breast is like a fire with two flames." Neruda tries to explain that these are only metaphors, expressions of imagination, but she's not buying it. To her, flowery talk is a form of deceit, although her own speech is full of figurative candor. These implicit ironies—that this hardheaded woman is herself a master of metaphor, that the son of an illiterate fisherman is a poet at heart, that their whole island speaks in the rhythms of verse—ground *Il postino* in the deep soil of unspoken truths.

In retrospect, films like *Mediterraneo* and *Il postino* seem like isolated instances of popular success. If we are looking for a consistent record of achievement, a true heir to the tradition of comedy Italian style, we might turn to the works of Paolo Virzì. Between 1994 and 2016, Virzì directed more than a dozen features billed as comedies, ranging from romantic and dramatic forms to dark and grotesque. The son of a Sicilian police officer and a singer, he developed

Figure 8.9 Learning about love in *Il Postino* (1994).

an early interest in English literature, devouring the books by Charles Dickens and Mark Twain that would later influence his screenplays. After graduating from Rome's prestigious Centro Sperimentale di Cinematografia film school, he started winning awards with movies set against the backdrop of a working-class city (*Forgetting Piombino* [*Dimenticare Piombino*], 1994), Berlusconi politics (*August Vacation* [*Ferie d'agosto*], 1995), provincial society (*Kisses and Hugs* [*Baci e abbracci*], 1999), and Italian history (*Napoleon and Me* [*Io e Napoleone*], 2006). His ability to capture contemporary life in Italy demonstrates once more how comedy can be a window to a nation's soul.

Caterina in the Big City (*Caterina va in città*, 2003) is a coming-of-age story about a thirteen-year-old girl who moves to Rome from a provincial town. Fed up with his job in "hillbilly haven," Caterina's father, Giancarlo (Sergio Castellitto), finally gets a teaching job in the nation's capital, where he grew up among upwardly mobile classmates. Frustrated with his own immobility, Giancarlo enrolls his daughter in a middle school for children of the city's elite. Although her hometown of Montalto di Castro is less than a two-hour drive from Rome, the gap between small town and big city is emphasized for laughs, as it is in much Italian comedy. The first three things that Caterina finds noteworthy on crossing into Rome are a woman doing crossword puzzles on the roadside, a nun smoking a cigarette, and "some weird guy directing traffic like an orchestra conductor" (actually a vagrant with a doomsday sign). In class, she is embarrassed to say where she is from. "It's north of here, northwest, near the coast . . . ," she stammers. But the kids find her appealingly "normal," and soon she's being courted by two opposing cliques. Margherita's group are leftists. Her mother is a prominent intellectual and political writer. Daniela's group belong to wealthy, rightwing families. Her father is a minister in Berlusconi's government.

The political divide is a lively source of comedy—and implied critique. In one scene, the students accuse each other of being Communists and Fascists. "You wish there were still concentration camps," one shouts. Another one retorts, "The Communists had them too." And they go on. "The Forza Italia guy on TV said you Communists lost the election, so that's democracy." "You're a bimbo. At least I wash my hair." This muddled blend of secondhand politics and personal insult comes to a head when a teacher enters the room and asks for definitions. One boy suggests, "The Communists are rich and have lots of degrees. The Fascists are poor and ignorant." The girls interrupt him, call him ugly, but he goes on: "I think rightwing people, like me, are the normal people, the ones who work. The Communists are all executives, doctors, directors. People who don't need to work." When Caterina is asked for her point of view, she says they don't talk about these things in Montalto. For her, and for those of us who may also live outside the inner circles of Italian political debate, Virzì offers illuminating glimpses of the territory. At one point, Caterina returns to Montalto for a wedding, where

Daniela's father meets his childhood friends. They have grown up to become big shots in the Mafia. When they all stand at the reception to sing Mussolini's anthem and give the Fascist salute, the government minister is visibly embarrassed by his roots. At another point, Margherita takes Caterina to a noisy street demonstration against the immigration police. In the midst of it all, we catch a glimpse of director Roberto Benigni shouting, "Let's bomb them all!" Most of the film centers on young Caterina's struggles to claim her own identity amid the push and pull of family and new friends. Her father is obsessively ambitious, controlling, and self-destructively outspoken. Her mother is silently, timidly resentful. Margherita is far too sophisticated and rebellious for her own good. Daniella's clique, born to privilege and entitlement, spend their time preening, gossiping, and shoplifting at the mall. For all its comic moments, *Caterina in the Big City* is a shrewd work of social commentary served up on a realistic slice of modern Italian life. Virzì's films are a good way to see contemporary Italy from the inside.

Italian comedy has come a long way since Dante's medieval allegory. The *commedia dell'arte* movement of the Renaissance revived the lively spirit of Carnival, drawing on its ancient roots in Roman theater, refitting time-honored caricatures with the colorful masks of regional types. With the dawn of motion pictures, popular clowns like Totò, "prince of laughter," carried the burlesque routines of the variety stage to the silent screen, found a voice, and burst into the age of comic talkies. By the 1930s, slapstick was giving way to *telefoni bianchi* comedies of Mussolini's era, reflecting the Fascist promise of a more sophisticated, prosperous Italy. After the war, the gritty style of neorealist cinema, itself a reaction to the fabricated world of white telephones, found a lighter touch in the "pink realism" of *neorealismo rosa*. From the 1950s through the early 1960s, as the economy enjoyed a boost, directors like Fellini and De Sica reigned over the so-called golden age. At the same time, a new generation of filmmakers emerged with Monicelli and Germi, engendering a darker vision of Italian society and the economic miracle. Their brand of *commedia all'italiana* continued into the 1980s, through the troubled "years of lead" and well into our own times. Lattuada, Risi, and Brusati combined humor with a critical perspective of corruption and crass materialism, accentuating the low status of Italy in Europe and of southern Italians in their own country. Wertmüller wielded comedy as a weapon against the inequalities of social status and sexual politics. Benigni pushed the limits of laughter to the brink of man's unthinkable inhumanity to man. More recently, directors like Salvatores, Troisi, and Virzì have integrated comedy and drama to show us the various faces of contemporary Italy.

Through all these eras and their films, it is still possible to follow threads of continuity. The best Italian comedies are uncomfortably funny. They expose the flaws in Italian society and in Italians themselves, holding the church, the government, and other institutions up to ridicule, chastising ordinary people for their biases; their mistreatment of others; and their excessive appetite for food, sex, and material gain—in short, for all the cardinal sins. More particular to Italy, these films depict a people struggling to adjust to circumstance, the little guy trying to get by. More often than not, the protagonist is a clever trickster, a master of *l'arte di arrangiarsi*, the art of getting by. Whether it's Sophia Loren scheming to catch Marcello Mastroianni as a husband (in *Marriage Italian Style*) or Mastroianni plotting to get rid of his cloying wife (*Divorce Italian Style*), whether it's a pair of misfits shirking military duty (*The Great War*), an Italian guest worker in Switzerland trying to pass as a blond-haired native (*Bread and Chocolate*), or a Jewish bookseller improvising elaborate lies to protect his son from the horrors of the Holocaust (*Life Is Beautiful*), most Italians seem ready to root for the trickster. Some of the humor may be lost on viewers unfamiliar with the local details of Italian life, and a few viewers may prefer the straight and narrow path, but there always seem to be plenty of non-Italians willing to follow the twists and turns of comedy Italian style.

Italian Comedy Filmography

English Title	Original Title	Director	Date
Variety Lights	*Luci del varietà*	Federico Fellini	1950
The Gold of Naples	*L'oro di Napoli*	Vittorio De Sica	1954
Too Bad She's Bad	*Peccato che gia una canaglia*	Alessandro Blasetti	1954
It Happened in Rome	*Souvenir d'Italie*	Antonio Pietrangeli	1957
Big Deal on Madonna Street	I *soliti ignoti*	Mario Monicelli	1958
The Great War	*La grande guerra*	Mario Monicelli	1959
Divorce Italian Style	*Divorzio all'italiana*	Pietro Germi	1961
Mafioso	*Mafioso*	Alberto Lattuada	1962
The Easy Life	*Il sorpasso*	Dino Risi	1962
Yesterday, Today and Tomorrow	*Ieri, oggi, domani*	Vittorio De Sica	1963
Marriage Italian Style	*Matrimonio all'italiana*	Vittorio De Sica	1964
Seduced and Abandoned	*Sedotta e abbandonata*	Pietro Germi	1964
The Birds, the Bees and the Italians	*Signore & signori*	Pietro Germi	1966
The Clown	I *clowns*	Federico Fellini	1970

English Title	Original Title	Director	Date
Amarcord	*Amarcord*	Federico Fellini	1973
La Grande Bouffe	*La grande abbuffata*	Marco Ferreri	1973
Love & Anarchy	*Film d'amore e d'anarchia . . .*	Lina Wertmüller	1973
Bread and Chocolate	*Pane e cioccolata*	Franco Brusati	1974
Swept Away	*Travolti da un insolito destino nell'azzurro mare d'agosto*	Lina Wertmüller	1974
Seven Beauties	*Pasqualino Settebellezze*	Lina Wertmüller	1975
Berlinguer, I Love You	*Berlinguer ti voglio bene*	Roberto Benigni	1977
The Icicle Thief	*Ladri di saponette*	Maurizio Nichetti	1989
Johnny Stecchino	*Johnny Stecchino*	Roberto Benigni	1991
Mediterraneo	*Mediterraneo*	Gabriele Salvatores	1991
Ciao, Professore!	*Io speriamo che me la cavo*	Lina Wertmüller	1992
The Monster	*Il mostro*	Roberto Benigni	1994
The Postman	*Il postino*	Massimo Troisi, Michael Radford	1994
Life Is Beautiful	*La vita è bella*	Roberto Benigni	1997
Caterina in the Big City	*Caterina va in città*	Paolo Virzì	2003
Welcome to the South	*Benvenuti al Sud*	Luca Miniero	2010
Like Crazy	*La pazza giooa*	Paolo Virzì	2016
Put Granny in the Freezer	*Metti la nonna in freezer*	Giancarlo Fontana, Giuseppe Stasi	2018

Notes

1. Peter E. Bondanella, *Italian Cinema: From Neorealism to the Present* (New York: Frederick Ungar, 1983), 142.
2. Bondanella, *Italian Cinema*, 144.
3. Rémi Foumier Lanzoni, *Comedy Italian Style: The Golden Age of Italian Film Comedies* (London: Continuum, 2008), 101.

4. Andrea Bini, *Male Anxiety and Psychopathology in Film: Comedy Italian Style* (New York: Palgrave Macmillan, 2015), introduction.
5. Roberta Di Carmine, "Comedy 'Italian Style' and *I soliti ignoti (Big Deal on Madonna Street)* 1958," in *A Companion to Film Comedy*, ed. Andrew Horton and Joanna E. Rapf (Oxford: Wiley-Blackwell, 2015), 454–473.
6. Lanzoni, *Comedy Italian Style*, 41.
7. Bondanella, *Italian Cinema*, 158.
8. Bondanella, *Italian Cinema*, 158.
9. *Pietro Germi: The Man with the Cigar in His Mouth*, documentary film by critic and filmmaker Mario Sesti, special edition of double-disc set on DVD (Criterion Collection, 2003).
10. Louis Bayman, ed., *Directory of World Cinema: Italy* (Chicago: Intellect Books. 2011), 110.
11. Luigi Pirandello, "L'umorismo" (1908), in *On Humor*, trans. Antonio Illiano and Daniel P. Testa (Chapel Hill: University of North Carolina Press, 1974), 145.
12. See Daniela Bini, "Pirandello," in *Encyclopedia of Humor Studies*, ed. Salvatore Attuardo (Los Angeles: Sage Publications, 2014), 572–573.
13. In *Pirandello's Visual Philosophy: Imagination and Thought across Media*, ed. Lisa Sarti and Michael Subialka (Teaneck, NJ: Fairleigh Dickenson University Press, 2017), xiv.
14. Ernest Ferlita and John R. May, *The Parables of Lina Wertmuller* (Mahwah, NJ: Paulist Press, 1977), 12–14.
15. Ferlita and May, *Parables*, 3.
16. Ferlita and May, *Parables*, 15.
17. Ferlita and May, *Parables*, 81.
18. Carlo Celli, *The Divine Comic: The Cinema of Roberto Benigni* (Lanham, MD: Scarecrow Press, 2001), x.
19. Celli, *Divine Comic*, 26.

9
Russian Film Comedy

Russians love to laugh as much as other people, perhaps even more so during times of stress. Statistics bear this out. Between 1918 and 1991 the Soviet film industry produced nearly a thousand comedies, including four of the ten top-grossing Soviet films.[1] Since some seven thousand movies were made on the Communist Party's watch, this chapter offers a special case study in the uses and appeals of cinematic comedy. How does laughter coexist with an ideology that spans the optimistic early years of the Russian Revolution, Stalin's repressive regime, Khrushchev's temporary thaw, and the reactionary policies of the Brezhnev years? What kinds of comedy came before and after?

Well before the movie camera was invented, the long history of Russian humor revealed itself in folktales and literature. Vladimir Propp, whose methodic studies of the oral tradition paved the way for modern folklorists, reduced hundreds of stories to a handful of basic characters and plots. Some of these (the hero, the villain, the false hero, the helper, the donor, the princess prize) recur in one form or another as literary types and movie roles. Two of these are particularly important for comedy: the trickster and the dupe. Russian peasants enjoyed laughing at the fool who gets swindled, often by a clever conman who appeals to the sucker's foolish pride, avarice, or gullibility. Russian animal tales, like Aesop's, are full of cunning foxes who outwit dumb and dumber beasts. Propp set forth his findings in the influential *Morphology of the Folktale*, first published in 1928. After his death, another work came to light, his lesser-known study *On the Comic and Laughter*. Here Propp explained the fundamental concept of *odurachivianie*, or duping, that prompts so much laughter. He notes how often Russians laugh at someone who is made a fool of. Sometimes it takes a smarter character to hold another character's flaw up to ridicule. Often the fool discredits himself.[2]

Propp repeatedly refers to Nikolai Gogol (1809–1852), the Russian writer, as a master of this comic form. From his celebrated play *The Inspector General* to his classic novel *Dead Souls* and his strange short story "The Nose," Gogol's protagonists are perpetrators and/or targets of outrageous deceptions. In *Dead Souls*, Chichikov is a trickster of the first order, a charming schemer who seeks to profit from the fact that a landowner's wealth and position is related to the number of serfs (or "souls") he owns. Since the census is always years behind, Chichikov travels through the countryside trying to transfer the names of dead serfs to his own estate, thus enhancing his status as a man of privilege. The people

When the World Laughs. William V. Costanzo, Oxford University Press (2020). Oxford University Press
DOI: 10.1093/oso/9780190924997.001.0001

he meets are hilarious caricatures of ordinary Russians. Much of the fun is in exposing their human failings—and beyond that, the failings of an absurd and ailing system. In "The Nose," a barber wakes up one day to find a nose embedded in his breakfast bread. Perplexed at first, he realizes that the nose belongs to one of his customers, a minor official known as Major Kovalyov. Was he drunk when he shaved the man on Wednesday? Very likely. Meanwhile, Kovalyov looks in the mirror expecting to admire his handsome face but finds a smooth surface where his nose had been. It turns out that the missing organ has escaped and is masquerading as a gentleman of leisure. Once we accept this ludicrous premise, we observe how everyone in Petersburg behaves in their usual way, which is to say that they exhibit the same preposterous qualities that Gogol finds so worthy of satire. The barber continues toadying to his wife and the police. Kovalyov maintains his petty pretentions. A jaded newspaper clerk and a two-faced doctor reveal their hypocrisy. The nose itself, riding around town in a resplendent coach and impressive uniform, lords it over everyone, including Kovalyov, who is outranked and snubbed by his own nose. In short, Gogol's fictional fantasy gives us a cross-section of the nation's structural and human imperfections. It continues to inspire animated shorts, television films, radio plays, and even an opera.

At the other end of the Russian literary spectrum from Gogol's grotesque humor was Anton Chekhov (1860–1904), who took a more benign and subtler approach in his plays and stories. Readers who come to *The Cherry Orchard* for the first time are often puzzled to learn that the playwright called his masterpiece "a comedy in four acts." After all, its premise seems more like the stuff of tragedy: An aristocratic family faces poverty and the loss of its ancestral home. But while Chekhov paints sympathetic portraits of each character, he also exposes their weaknesses. Or rather, he lets them expose themselves through comic incongruity. Madame Ranevskaya is a charming, generous woman, but after admitting that she squanders money "like a madwoman," she gives her last gold piece to a passing stranger. Her brother Gayev, though educated and well-bred, resorts to inane pool-table talk whenever he can't face reality, which is all too often. Trofimov, the articulate, idealistic student, expresses his high-minded principles one minute ("We must move beyond the petty and illusory toward the bright star burning in the distance") and is reduced to banal chatter about the weather the next. Even old Firs, the family's faithful servant, is not immune from unintentional irony. He refers to the Emancipation, which freed serfs like himself from bondage in 1861, as "the troubles." For Chekhov, then, the comedy is highly contextual, based more on character than plot. Not much happens in *The Cherry Orchard*, and this inaction is part of the point. Instead of Gogol's grotesque caricatures, he gives us realistic sketches, people whose flaws we laugh at through a sympathetic lens. Chekhov died at the dawn of a new era, when motion pictures were beginning to assume much of the storytelling roles of Russian literature. It remained to be seen whether Russian film comedy would follow the path of Chekhov or Gogol or create new lenses of its own.

Comic Mischief on the Silent Screen

The birth of Russian cinema is commonly identified with the Russian Revolution of 1917, when Lenin's Bolsheviks came to power. The experimental silent films of Lev Kuleshov, Aleksandr Dovzhenko, and Sergei Eisenstein created striking imagery and editing techniques that were emulated around the world. Before then, during the tsar's reign, Russian theaters offered conventional film fare, frequently French, or Russian with a Parisian flavor. The first programs included comedy shorts like *The Diligent Batman* (1908), a single take in which a clumsy valet "sits on a pin, breaks a pile of dishes, eats the contents of a pot, gets shoved out the door, and comes back to do it again."[3] By 1914, Evgeny Bauer was making full-length comedies like *Cold Showers* (*Kholodnye dushi*), a carefully constructed farce about a coquette manipulating multiple suitors. The title has a secondary meaning, "frigid souls," playfully underscoring the film's preoccupation with duplicity. Bauer died in 1917 with over seventy movies to his credit, many of them well-made comedies, but also melodramas with psychologically sophisticated characters.

The young revolutionary directors made a clean break from all this. They saw themselves as pioneers. Their new hero was the masses, not individuals, and their sights were aimed high above the conventional diversions of bourgeois society. Their goal was to educate, to move the People to embrace their Communist ideals. Eisenstein's *Battleship "Potemkin"* (*Bronenosets Patyomkin*, 1925) did this through a radical use of montage, a violent clash of film shots for dramatic and political effect. Dovzhenko's "Ukraine Trilogy" glorified collectivism and vilified landowners as ruthless, greedy opportunists. These were fervent, earnest films. What many film historians fail to recognize, however, is that both directors began their film careers in comedy. Dovzhenko's first feature was *Love's Berries* (*Yagodka luubvi*, 1926), about a barber trying to get rid of his illegitimate child, his "love berry." Eisenstein's film debut, *Glumov's Diary* (1923), was a short comic piece made for a theatrical production. It featured amusing stop-motion tricks and actors making funny faces. But it was Lev Kuleshov who directed the first full-fledged Soviet comedy. *The Extraordinary Adventures of Mr. West in the Land of the Bolsheviks* (*Neobychainye priklyucheniya mistera Vesta v strane bolshevikov*, 1924) is a sly satire about American ignorance and naïveté. Mr. West, who looks like the American comedian Harold Lloyd, travels to the USSR expecting the nation of savages depicted in American magazines. He is accompanied by his cowboy friend Jeddie as protection. At first, their expectations are confirmed when his briefcase is stolen on arrival in Moscow. Pretending to be Bolsheviks, the thieves orchestrate West's abduction and fake his "rescue" for a huge ransom. Meanwhile, Jeddie goes astray, creating mayhem in the streets of Moscow with his leather chaps, six-gun, and lariat (Figure 9.1). The sophisticated Muscovites regard this incongruously uncouth figure with astonishment. West's outfit also comes in for some broad ridicule. He waves a flag crowded with far too many stripes and stars, and even his socks are miniature Yankee banners. Through a long sequence of conventional slapstick, roughhousing, and silly disguises, the thieves go to elaborate lengths to extort dollars from Mr. West. Posing as a countess, the female member of the gang tries to seduce him. She discreetly drops her garter at his foot and has him replace it on her naked leg while the rest of the gang watches through a keyhole. When this fails to work, they attempt to frighten him with death threats, conjuring images of a hooded executioner with a giant axe. They throw him in a makeshift jail, extracting thousands of dollars in installments for a secret "rescue." Of course, they could more easily just take the money and run, but then audiences would be deprived of a classic dupe. Finally, the plot is discovered by the real Bolshevik police, who release the American and jail the malefactors. All ends happily when Mr. West is taken on a tour of the thriving city, where he can witness a parade of Soviet soldiers and

Figure 9.1 An American cowboy in Moscow. *The Extraordinary Adventures of Mr. West in the Land of the Bolsheviks* (1924).

throngs of cheering citizens. He sends a radiogram back to his wife: "Burn those New York magazines, and hang up a portrait of Lenin in the study."

Throughout the 1920s, American capitalists, thieves, and chase scenes through Moscow streets continued to animate comedies like Yuri Zheliabuzhsky's *The Cigarette Girl from Mosselprom* (*Papirosnitsa ot Mossel'proma*, 1924), but increasingly the spears of satire were aimed at targets like the New Economic Policy (NEP), a form of small-scale privatization intended to reenergize an economy still reeling from the civil war. Though sponsored by the government, the NEP was unpopular with ideologically minded directors who ridiculed a range of practices antithetical to Soviet principles. In *The Girl with a Hatbox* (*Devushka s korobkoy*, 1927), Boris Barnet lampooned Western-style flappers and their un-Bolshevik behavior. In *St. Jorgen's Feast Day* (*Prazdnik sviatogo Iorgena*, 1930), Jakov Protazanov took aim at religion, skewering a church that exploited the saint's day as a moneymaking scheme. When a petty thief gets locked in the church while trying to rob it, he escapes by impersonating St. Jorgen, announcing a miracle and forgiving sins for free—to the utter dismay of the priests. Although such films were politically aligned with Soviet policies, it would be inaccurate to call them mere propaganda. Their broad appeal lay in their entertainment value, their witty use of zany disguises, romantic entanglements, comic chases, happy endings, and other conventions of the genre.[4]

Silent films continued to be made well into the 1930s, after other national cinemas had embraced sound technology. One reason for this lag was Russia's undeveloped infrastructure; another was the problem of communicating to a nation with so many spoken languages. Alexander Medvedkin found an ingenious way to meet these challenges. During the early 1930s, he toured the country on a special film train equipped for making movies and projecting them. Along the route, he filmed workers and peasants, highlighting the problems in their factories and farms, giving special screenings to audiences that had never seen a motion picture. In this way, Medvedkin got to know the Russian people. He came to understand their dreams and their tastes in movies.

Undoubtedly his best work was *Happiness* (*Schastye*, 1934), a silent comedy about rural life before and after the Revolution. *Happiness* has the look and feel of a Russian folktale. Medvedkin's black-and-white photography contributes to this effect, emulating the *Lubki* woodcuts popular among illiterate Russians in earlier times. Its plot draws on local traditions like Ivan the fool, Baba Yaga the witch, the greedy priest, and the ever-heartless landlord—characters that seem to spring from Propp's folklore research. There is also something grotesque about the story's eccentricities that are reminiscent of Gogol, a writer much admired by the director. Medvedkin combined all these qualities with the zany slapstick of a madcap Keystone Cops comedy, creating a work that is at once uniquely Russian, distinctively Soviet, and universally funny.

Happiness opens with a stooped old man in peasant boots peeking through a fence at his wealthy neighbor, who is enjoying a heaping plateful of dumplings. The food flies into the man's mouth, one morsel after another. "Sixty years I've slaved and I've never tasted *vareniki*," says the peasant, swearing that he won't die until he's tried some. At night, he climbs over the fence, entangling his white beard in the barbed spikes, and manages to slip past the guard dog but cannot open a huge padlock on the storehouse. When the neighbor appears, holding up the key in derision, the old man drops dead from fright. His beard stands up, his feet go limp, and his soul departs from between his legs in a puff of smoke. The scene is both pitiful and hilarious. Medvedkin later explained that his picaresque tale was inspired by the people he met who didn't fit into the new Soviet five-year plan. All they wanted was a little happiness. Their simple dream was expressed in an old Russian proverb, "If I were tsar, I'd eat the fat of the bacon and sleep."[5] Khmyr, the film's protagonist, is sent off on a journey in search of the Russian dream. "Go find happiness and don't come back empty-handed," his wife admonishes. On the road, he sees two religious figures fighting over someone's lost wallet, grabs it while they fight, and returns home with a horse. But the horse eats the thatch from their roof, and his wife ends up yoked to the plow while the horse looks on. Thieves steal the horse, and life goes from bad to worse. Khmyr decides to end his miserable life, but no one will let him (Figure 9.2). A priest cries "sacrilege!" A general informs him that he lacks permission. "Who will feed Russia if the peasants die?" A whole army of Cossacks, soldiers, priests, and tsarist bureaucrats arrive to prevent his unauthorized death. After sundry comic misadventures, Khmyr finds new opportunities in a *Kolkhoz*, a Bolshevik collective farm. He's duped again by thieves, who steal the harvest from under his nose, but his comrades come to the rescue, led by his ambitious wife. Later, when he's faced with fighting two fires—one in the collective's stables, another in his own homestead—he dashes between them like a dithering circus clown. He saves the horses. The final scene shows the couple entering the revolving door of a modern department store, a house of plenty, where they get new clothes. Khmyr has a hard time getting rid of his old ones—until he decides to leave them on the road for the thieves to fight over the rags.

Is *Happiness* a satire of tsarist Russia, a sendup of peasant mentality, a critique of Bolshevism, or just plain fun? Whatever the director's intentions, his film was banned from Russian theaters for thirty years as "anti-Soviet." It was rediscovered in the 1960s, screened before enthusiastic audiences, and finally brought Medvedkin global recognition as an innovative master of film comedy. In his own day, at least one major director appreciated the significance of his work for Russian humor. Responding to the firefighting scene when Khmyr chooses the general good over personal possession, Eisenstein wrote, "Today I have seen how the Bolshevik laughs."[6]

Figure 9.2 "Who gave you permission to die?" A scene from *Happiness* (1934).

Stalin and the Soviet Musical Comedy

Eisenstein would not laugh for long. Vladimir Lenin had nationalized the film industry in 1919, proclaiming cinema as "the most important of the arts." It was in this heady climate of opportunity that young pioneers of Soviet cinema like Eisenstein and Kuleshov were encouraged to experiment with bold, avant-garde techniques. Then, after Lenin's death in 1924, Joseph Stalin tightened his grip on the government and on the film industry in particular. Stalin took a personal, some would say obsessive interest in movies, often handpicking directors, reading scripts, even making changes like a Hollywood studio head. In his own private theater, he enjoyed American genre films, but for the Soviet public he wanted something else. The experimental aesthetics of the 1920s, which Stalin found too abstract and elitist, would be replaced by "socialist realism," a focus on everyday life that promoted Communist values among ordinary people. The revolutionary era was over; the Stalinist era had begun. It would last for nearly three decades.

As the country marched toward a policy of state monopoly, central planning, and firmer censorship, Stalin appointed Boris Shumyatsky to watch over the film industry and enforce his socialist realist agenda. Despite Shumyatsky's ignorance of cinema, or perhaps because of it, he was able to pursue Stalin's program with a ruthless energy for seven years, from 1930 to 1937. He led a delegation to visit major studios in the United States, introduced talking films to the Soviets, and proposed an ambitious "Cine-City" similar to Hollywood in southern Russia.

Among the delegates to Hollywood were Eisenstein and his talented collaborator, Grigori Aleksandrov. Aleksandrov had performed in Eisenstein's short comedy *Glumov's Diary* and in *Potemkin*. He went on to co-write and co-direct several silent works. But while Eisenstein continued to push the creative envelope with his brilliant innovations, incurring Stalin's deepening displeasure, Aleksandrov found a safer path. Most of Eisenstein's ambitious final projects were thwarted. Depressed and increasingly ill, he died in 1948. Meanwhile, Aleksandrov turned out a series of lighthearted musical comedies that are still popular today. He lived to 1983, winning numerous awards, including two Stalin Prizes. Even in the worst of times, comedy can be beneficial to one's health.

Meanwhile, the health of Bolshevik cinema was declining under Stalin. By 1935, production had dropped to half of its 128-title high point of 1928, and the decline continued throughout Stalin's reign.[7] Socialist realism, with its didactic messages, did little to pack the theaters. The industry needed a boost, something to lift the spirits of the proletariat—as well as box-office revenues to fill the coffers of the government. Aleksandrov's remedy was *Happy Guys* (*Vesyolye rebyata*, 1934). Sometimes translated as *Jolly Fellows* or *Moscow Laughs*, the title refers to a group of rowdy jazz musicians hell-bent on putting on a show in Moscow. The fun starts when Kostya, a shepherd on a collective farm, leads a parade of livestock into the Black Swann Hotel playing his pan flute. The animals wreak havoc and insult the wealthy bourgeoisie. These leftovers from the (now officially discredited) NEP, with their outdated Western ways, come in for a good deal of playful lampooning. The animals have foreign names and titles, including Chamberlain (a bull), Bureaucrat (a goat), Professor (another goat), English Girls (all pigs), and Swiss Girls (the cows). When someone puts a recording of the prerevolutionary crooner Vertinskii on the phonograph, the hounds howl. A rich girl with a terrible singing voice mistakes Kostya for a famous European conductor. She is disappointed when he turns out to be a mere Bolshevik. Determined to prove himself, Kostya sets out for the big city, where he eventually joins the jazz band. They are a jolly, noisy lot, always getting into scuffles, wielding their instruments like weapons at a slapstick brawl. One night, they are forced to play outside in the rain. When they perform on stage the next day, torrents of water gush from their horns, their woodwinds, even the bass drum. It's a hilariously disorderly debut (Figure 9.3). Their fortunes improve, however, when a housemaid from the hotel (played by Orlova, the director's

Figure 9.3 After a rainy night. The soggy rehearsal in *Jolly Fellows* (1934).

gifted wife) joins the group. With her sweet voice, success is ensured. All ends well, with Kostya and the pretty housemaid singing a duet, "If you sing your way through life, you'll never lose your way." Soon the theme is picked up by a rousing chorus: "We sing and laugh like children, through the unending struggle and toil . . . we'll never give up."

Aleksandrov had struck the right chord. *Jolly Fellows* was a big hit with the people, who continued to sing long after leaving the theaters. Shumyatsky saw how musical comedy could serve the party's emphasis on struggle and toil while diverting the masses from their misery. Over time, the formula was tweaked. Musical comedies became more musical than comic, more about energy than laughs. They reflected Stalin's celebrated pronouncement of 1935 that "Life has become happier." Gradually, Western elements were downplayed or belittled. *Jolly Fellows* had opened with a jokey tribute to Hollywood in the credits: "Buster Keaton, Harold Lloyd, Charlie Chaplin . . . are *not* appearing in the film," then introduced the real Russian cast. No such jokes occur in Aleksandrov's later films.

After the release of *Jolly Fellows*, Shumyatsky called for a fresh, Soviet brand of comedy. The new hero would be the simple Russian man accompanied by the new, emancipated Russian woman. His mentor would be the party leader, the villain typically a foreigner or saboteur. This formulaic cast of characters neatly replaced the stock figures of folklore described by Propp. Since so much comedy relies on conventional devices like mix-ups, funny faces, and sight gags, its neutral aesthetics could coexist with socialist realism. There was no call for the politically precarious intellectual techniques of the 1920s. Aleksandrov would put to use what he had learned in Hollywood, but his Chaplinesque clown would be a Bolshevik Everyman supporting the community and the latest five-year plan, not an American individual pursing the American dream.

His next film was *The Circus* (*Tsirk*, 1936) a hybrid musical with moments of comedy and melodrama. Orlova (now a Soviet sensation) plays Marion Dixon, an American circus artist who is run out of town by a lynch mob after giving birth to a black baby. She finds refuge in the USSR, but her life is made miserable by the German-born manager who threatens to expose her. Thanks to the heroic intervention of a handsome young Soviet engineer named Ivan, she is rescued and finds acceptance in her new home. The big spectacle begins with the human cannonball. Announced by a volley of trumpets, Ivan and Marion appear in white capes and aviator caps near the revolving propellers of an ultramodern airplane, then descend a flight of art deco stairs. Ivan is catapulted to the big top, where he flies around with outstretched wings looking like a proto-astronaut. There is a descent by parachute and, below, a revolving multilayered drum, a huge cake with Bolshevik beauties arranged on every layer. We see them from the sides and from above, with Marion perched on top singing above the chorus. Suddenly the German steps out from the shadows, holding the baby up for everyone to see. But instead of sabotaging the event, he's astonished when the people pass the child around, one comrade of the multiethnic Soviet Union tenderly passing it to another while they sing a lullaby. The lullaby was Shumyatsky's idea. So was the movie's grand finale, which merges the circus procession with footage from the May Day parade of 1935, complete with banners and a colossal image of Stalin's face (Figure 9.4).

Aleksandrov went on to make *Volga-Volga* (1938) and *The Bright Path* (*Svyetlii Put*, 1940), paving the way for more lighthearted musicals like Ivan Pyrev's *The Rich Bride* (*Bogataia nevesta*, 1937) and *Tractor Drivers* (*Traktoristy*, 1939). Soviet screens were bursting with exultant workers singing in the wheat fields and the factories. Meanwhile, life behind the screen was becoming decidedly less happy. Threatened by hostile neighbors on two fronts, Germany and Japan, and obsessed with "the enemy within," Stalin was replacing the original Bolshevik idea of world Communism for the masses with xenophobia and a cult of the strong leader. Tens of millions of peasants were forcibly displaced, millions more died in the famine of 1932–33, and by the late 1930s, Stalin had launched a frenzy of show trials, purges, and "liquidations."[8] Shumyatsky himself was arrested and shot in 1938.

Figure 9.4 The grand musical parade from *Circus* (1936).

Laughing Through the Cold War and Khrushchev's Thaw

Russians refer to World War II as "the Great Patriotic War." The war and Stalin's postwar policies took a huge toll on the population and the film industry. In the years before his death in 1953, production plummeted to fewer than ten titles a year.[9] The devastating end of the war marked the beginning of another kind of conflict, when Russia's makeshift alliance with Western Europe and the United States turned to icy hostility. The Cold War continued from 1945 to 1991, when the USSR finally lost its ironclad unity, but the Iron Curtain did not completely shut out the West during that long period. American and European movies captured by Soviet soldiers in the 1940s were stripped of their original dialog and reedited for homeland audiences. These "trophy films" filled a void. Film scholar Maya Turovskaya remembered watching them as a child. The Hollywood genre films "enthralled and captivated us more powerfully than all the later fruits of neo-Realism and the 'New Wave,'" she wrote. "America came to life in our imagination." Russian-born poet Joseph Brodsky recalled that "the four Tarzan films alone did more for de-Stalinization than all Khrushchev's speeches to the 20th Party Congress and beyond."[10]

We can feel the Hollywood touch in comedies like Pyrev's *Kuban Cossaks* (*Kubanskiye Kazaki*, 1950), set on a *kolkhoz* in southern Russia. With its folksy songs, screwball characters, and "let's put on a show" plot, it has much in common with musicals like Rodgers and Hammerstein's *State Fair* (1945), except that the main tension is between young Soviet Cossacks and a local party leader who is old-fashioned but ultimately benign. Khrushchev reportedly liked the film at first, but after he came to power and launched his anti-Stalin campaign, he criticized Pyrev for varnishing the truth about his predecessor's regime.[11] The Cold War was beginning to thaw, and movies began to reflect the new leadership's guarded openness to change. In Eldar Ryazanov's *Carnival in Moscow* (*Karnavalnaya noch*, 1956), the show is an amateur New Year's production by students, but the old party boss is an intolerant sourpuss. His name, Ogurtsov, means pickle. It was now permissible to laugh at such a figure. Ryazanov kept them laughing. He went on to make some of the most popular comedies in Soviet history, including *The Unbelievable Adventures of Italians in Russia* (*Neveroyatnye priklyucheniya italyantsev v Rossii*, 1974) and *Enjoy Your Sauna*, also known as *The Irony of Fate* (*Ironiya sudby, ili S legkim parom!*, 1975).

Comedy is a tricky business under authoritarian regimes since it is, by many accounts, inherently subversive. When everything goes topsy-turvy, existing hierarchies land on their heads, inviting chaos and threatening the status quo. One problem facing Ryazanov and other directors like him was how to satirize Soviet institutions without overstepping the line. Another was creating a protagonist who was amusing yet recognizably heroic. In *Hussar's Ballad* (*Gusarskaya ballada*, 1962), his protagonist is Poruchik Rzjevslu, a dashing cavalry officer who takes on a young woman as his comrade in arms. Ryazanov conveniently set the musical well before the Revolution during the Napoleonic wars and made him a romantic figure who delivers many of his lines in verse. The film's popular success and hefty profits kept the Soviet critics at bay. In a system where the government owned the means of production, it was the state that profited the most.

Ryazanov's contemporaries enjoyed his entertaining films, but the era's undisputed king of Soviet comedy was Leonid Gaidai. He was from a peasant family, the son of a young Bolshevik who had been imprisoned for revolutionary activities. During the Great Patriotic War, Leonid served in the Red Army and was seriously injured by a landmine. Upon recovery, he entered Moscow's Institute of Cinematography and discovered his talent for laugh-out-loud satire. One after another, his comedies broke box-office records in their time, becoming classics that are still immensely popular with Russians today. They include *The Diamond Arm* (*Brilliantovaya ruka*, 1969; the third-highest-grossing Soviet film, with 76.7 million tickets sold in the USSR alone), *Kidnapping, Caucasian Style* (*Kavkazskaya plennitsa, ili Novie priklucheniya Shurika*, 1967; in fourth place, with 76.5 million viewers), *Operation Y and Other Shurik's Adventures* (*Operatsiya 'Y' i drugie priklyucheniya Shurika*, 1965; in seventh place, with 69.6 million), and *Ivan Vasilievich: Back to the Future* (*Ivan Vasilyevich menyayet professiyu*, 1973; 60.7 million).[12]

Among Gaidai's contributions to the genre was the amiable Everyman who inadvertently gets in the way of scoundrels and prevents their petty crimes. In *Operation Y*, this is Shurik, a geeky student who foils a robbery while substituting for a neighbor as a night watchman. The foil is literal, involving an epee and a "fatal" wound that turns out to be catsup. The scene includes a skeleton, a sneezing villain, and a passing drunkard. Such visual gags, reminiscent of the silent era, abound in this and other Gaidai films. By avoiding dialog, narrative logic, and psychological realism in favor of old-fashioned mayhem, he entertained his audience and escaped the censor's hand. With each film, Gaidai pushed the boundaries of acceptable behavior. His heroes, if we can call them that, are far from perfect citizens. They drink, they're often lazy, they don't mind bending the law to make an extra ruble, but they do everything with gusto. Their shenanigans pose little ideological threat to Soviet society even when Gaidai is making fun of Soviet bureaucracy and paranoia.

In *Kidnapping, Caucasian Style, or Shurik's New Adventure*, Shurik comes to the mountainous region of the Caucasus in search of folklore material. Instead of finding native legends, he gets mixed up in a traditional bride abduction. As naïve as he is well intentioned, Shurik is plied with liquor and duped into kidnapping beautiful Nina for a corrupt official named Saakhov. With the aid of a local friend, Shurik manages to save the girl by thwarting a trio of bumbling rascals reminiscent of the Three Stooges. Saakhov ends up with a backside full of buckshot, more accurately full of salt. Although some viewers identified Saakhov with Soviet bureaucrats, the film safely presents him as the local warlord in a backward culture remote from modern Soviet life. In *The Diamond Arm*, the setting is even more remote. Here the protagonist is an "ordinary Soviet citizen" named Gorbunkov vacationing in Turkey. When he accidentally slips on a watermelon rind, injuring his arm, he shouts out "damned melon." This phrase turns out to be the code words for a smuggling ring. Mistaking Gorbunkov for their courier, a pair of inept black marketers bandage his arm and conceal a stash of diamonds in the cast. Being an honest man, Gorbunkov explains everything to the police after returning home to the USSR. They, in turn, decide to use him as bait to catch the thieves. Poor honest Gorbunkov is caught between the law and the outlaws in a series of riotous sight gags, comic skits, and musical bits with little regard to narrative continuity (Figure 9.5). Characters randomly break into song. One of the henchmen has a nervous tic. The other loses his fake mustache. Gaidai himself makes a cameo appearance as a drunkard. All this in 1968, when Soviet tanks were rolling into Prague.

Figure 9.5 An ordinary Soviet citizen gets mixed up with a smuggling ring in *The Diamond Arm* (1969).

Comedy's Conservative Agenda: 1970s–1980s

The Soviet invasion of 1968 put an end to the Prague Spring. The "First Thaw" initiated under Khrushchev was over, soon to be followed by an era of conservative regimes. From 1970 to 1982, Leonid Brezhnev presided over a long period of military expansion and economic stagnation. When Gorbachev became head of state in 1988, he announced the reforms of *perestroika*, a "restructuring" of the economy, and *glasnost*, a new "openness" to liberal policies and freedom of speech. By 1991, when Boris Yeltsin succeeded him by popular vote, the USSR was history, replaced by a smaller, weaker Russian Federation.

During the Conservative Era (1968–1985), the public's appetite for comedy never flagged. People continued to enjoy Gaidai's zany humor in films like *Twelve Chairs* (*Dvenadtsat stulev*, 1971) and *Ivan Vasilievich Changes Profession* (*Ivan Vasilyevich menyayet professiyu*, 1973), a comic sci-fi movie based on a 1935 play by Mikhail Bulgakov. Sometimes called *Ivan Vasilievich: Back to the Future* in English, it sends the title character back to the time of Ivan "the Terrible" in a time machine while the tsar is catapulted forward into Soviet Russia. (▶ See "Case Study for Chapter 9: *Ivan Vasilievich Changes Profession*" on the website.) In contrast to Gaidai's playful tone, Ryazanov's wry sense of humor pushed his later comedies further into the risky realm of satire. In *The Irony of Fate*, after a day of drinking with his friends, the film's hero stumbles home to spend New Year's Eve with his fiancée only to find himself in someone else's bed. Zhenya has come to the right address on the right street, but it's in the wrong city. He has flown to Leningrad instead of Moscow. The explanation for the poor man's confusion is shown in the movie's animated introductory sequence. On the drawing board sits a city architect's proud design for a beautiful new building (Figure

9.6a). Suddenly, three words of official criticism are scrawled across the top, and the design is forced through a series of bureaucratic changes. Off go the balconies, the porticos, and every other attractive ornament until what's left is a drab rectangle of windows (Figure 9.6b). This becomes the template for a battalion of cookie-cutter housing projects, thousands of them, which go marching across the USSR. No wonder Zhenya is confused. The layout of every apartment, the furniture, even the keys are all identical. It's a sly variation on the universal formula for bedroom farce, but with a local target: the demeaning and demoralizing results of Communist conformity where one key fits all.

Also popular was Ryazanov's fairy-tale rom-com, *Office Romance* (*Sluzhebnyy roman*, 1977), about a nerdy statistician who manages to find love and happiness in the Era of Stagnation. In true screwball fashion, the relationship between Anatoly, the statistician, and his frumpy boss, Ludmila, begins with a series of laughable missteps and hostile language, stumbling toward the inevitable happy ending. While the plot may sound like standard Hollywood fare, its Moscow setting, familiar actors, memorable songs, and satirical sketches of contemporary life made the film a big hit in its day and a favorite even today among nostalgic Russians. Ryazanov's most pointed satire of Brezhnev's social system was undoubtedly *The Garage* (*Garazh*, 1980). The Research Institute for the Protection of Animals Against the Environment has been tasked with building new garages, which are in woefully short supply. Since construction is far behind schedule, the group must decide who gets the few garages that were built. Due to a shortage of meeting space, the members convene in their exhibition hall, a room lined with prehistoric murals and stuffed animals. One comrade, Sleepy, snoozes through the whole meeting. Another, Mute, can't speak because of laryngitis. The majority votes to cut these two from the list. Their names are read out with all the solemnity of an execution. When the group is accidentally locked in for the night, the humor turns grotesque. We are increasingly aware of the skeletons and

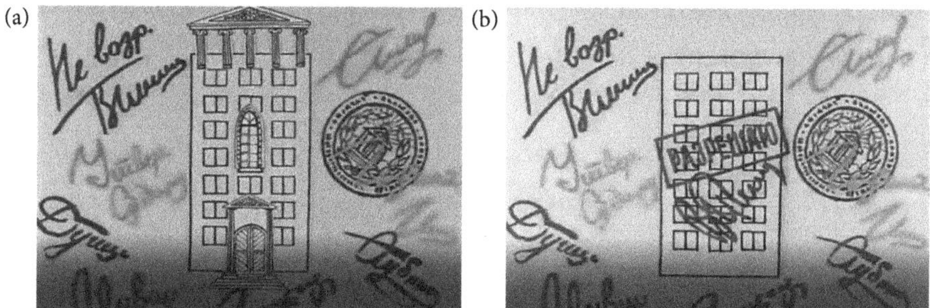

Figure 9.6 From the animated introduction to *The Irony of Fate* (1974). (a) Housing plans before official approval . . .; (b) . . . and after.

lifeless mammals in the background, which comment wordlessly, ironically, on the humans arguing over petty favors. Who are the outmoded ones? Which is the real endangered species? It turns out that Mute has swallowed all the documents, and in a society where everything depends on paperwork, the garage project no longer exists. The Institute's very survival is at stake. Up to now, Ryazanov's films were largely apolitical. There were knowing winks to the audience—a double entendre here, a musical allusion there—but always a happy ending. In *The Garage*, the ending is left open, and the conventions of social realism have been displaced by a vision as dark and fantastic as Gogol's.

Even darker and more grotesque was *Repentance* (*Pokanyaniye*, completed in 1984), a satirical film by the Georgian director Tengiz Abuladze. The plot concerns Varlam, a former town mayor whose corpse is found a day after his funeral in the garden of his son's house. The corpse is properly reburied but turns up in the garden again. An investigation begins, and we learn some truths about Varlam's regime in a series of flashbacks. At first, he appears as a genial showman. In one scene he shows up at an artist's door with flowers and a song, wearing a sheepskin coat over his uniform. He enchants the man's wife and daughter with an extravagant clown act before leaping out of the window onto a horse below. The real purpose of his visit is to enlist the artist in the state's great cause, to "enlighten the people" with his art. The artist is not fooled. After Varlam's exit, he murmurs the Russian word for buffoon, "*komedient*." In another scene, Varlam addresses a large crowd from a balcony, not unlike Mussolini, while workers wrestle with a water main break below, undercutting his Marxist rhetoric with a burst of Marx Brothers anarchy. Across the street, the artist stops his family from applauding and draws his shutters closed. With his black shirt, Hitler mustache, and bombastic oratory, Varlam is a composite image of deceitful tyranny (Figure 9.7). "We must trust no one," he declaims. "Four out of every three is an enemy." Then, invoking a Chinese adage, "It's difficult to catch a black cat in a dark room. Especially if there's no cat." *Repentance* may not fit some notions of comedy, but it does present the portrait of a dictator as a cynically self-ironic clown. The Soviet censors banned it as an allegorical critique of Stalinism. Abuladze's masterpiece was not released for another four years, under Gorbachev, when it won top honors at Cannes and the Lenin Prize in Russia.

Post-Soviet Humor

Events of the 1990s did not lead to the reforms that many hoped for. Amid the chaotic breakup of the Soviet Union, in the power vacuum left by the party's demise, there was a headlong race to privatization and an unprecedented rise in unlawful activity. By the middle of the decade, the level of corruption

Figure 9.7 A composite image of deceitful tyranny. The corrupt mayor in *Repentance* (completed in 1984).

behind closed doors and crime in the streets seemed to reach new heights. Many industries were in private hands, the old black marketeering rings were running rampant, and a new class of wealthy oligarchs had taken over. The movie industry, too, was changing. With the loss of government funding, film directors no longer had to please state censors, but they faced a new kind of dictator: commercial success. Now the kinds of films they made were dictated by the market. This, of course, was nothing new to Hollywood, so not surprisingly, many of the new Russian movies began to look more like American genre films. Others looked to Western Europe for wider audiences and financial support.

Kira Muratova's light comedy *The Sentimental Policeman* (*Chuvstvitelnyy militsioner*, 1992) is a co-production of Ukraine and France. It tells a fairy-tale story about a Russian military policeman who finds a baby in a cabbage patch and tries to adopt it. Alexandr Rogozhkin's *Peculiarities of the National Hunt in the Winter* (*Osobennosti natsionalnoy okhoty v zimniy period*, 2001) follows the unlikely adventures of a Finnish folk researcher studying the role of vodka in Russian hunting lore. Teeming with eccentric characters and wacky episodes—a drunken bear in a sauna, a cow flying in the bomb bay of a modern airplane, pineapples growing in hedgerows—Rogozhkin's comedy gives voice to English, German, French, and Finnish as well as Russian, expanding the circle of its target audience.

Yuri Mamin's *Window to Paris* (*Okno v Parizh*, 1993), a co-production of France and Russia, literally faces Europe and merits a closer look. The film's premise is based on a metaphor for St. Petersburg, built by Peter the Great as a "window to the West." When Nikolai, the hapless hero, moves into a communal apartment in St. Petersburg, he finds the previous owner's cat still fat and healthy even though the old lady died a year ago. The key to this mystery turns out to be a magic portal hidden behind the cupboard—a window opening directly on the capital of France (Figure 9.8). What he sees through that window contrasts sharply with the conditions of post-Soviet Russia. While Paris appears as a land of abundance, its street lined with fresh produce, fur coats, and liquor stores, St. Petersburg is a place of scarcity and chaos. Its once-celebrated canals stink of condoms and dead eels. Everyone waits on long lines for vodka, and when the supply runs out, the crowd breaks up, following a ragtag band of musicians down the street playing the left-wing anthem, "The Internationale," badly out of tune. At first, Nikolai's neighbors flock to the other side. They squeeze through the window and grab as many consumer goods as they can carry. But Nikolai sees that French culture has some problems, including drugs, elitism, and a soulless form of capitalism. He's from the old school. In Russia, he is out of sync with the grasping materialism of the business school where he teaches music. Its walls are lined with maxims like "Time is money" and foreign currencies framed like art. He's more interested in music than in money; he has a Russian soul. It's no wonder that he loses his job. His counterpart in France is Nicole, a highbrow

Figure 9.8 Russians find a portal to France in *Window to Paris* (1993).

Parisian artist. When Nicole chases some Russians through the portal to retrieve a stolen artwork, she finds herself in a strange land. Unable to speak the language, robbed of her silk robe, she stumbles half-naked through the streets of St. Petersburg, hungry, weak, steadily losing her humanity, indistinguishable from the vagrants and beggars. Mamin's allegory may be heavy handed at times, manically frivolous at others, but it captures a certain ambivalence toward the West at a particular time in Russian history.

Director Valery Todorovskiy's *Hipsters* (*Stilyagi*, 2008) catapults us to a different time, the 1950s, when American music and styles of dress were contentious grounds for skirmishes among young Soviets (Figure 9.9). Todorovskiy's camera takes us to Gorky Park, where clean-cut evening strollers pay a few kopeks to dance an anemic waltz. Meanwhile, in a nearby hideaway, behind closed doors, teenagers in short skirts and bright lipstick, pastel shirts, and string ties are dancing to the latest jazz. It's a scene of buoyant energy and wild abandon. Suddenly, a troop of somberly dressed youth arrives, armed with scissors, and begins snipping at ties, skirts, and stockings. We are in Moscow in 1955. Members of the Young Communist League, the righteous Komsomol, are raiding a party of "hipsters," young Russians who love Western music and fashion. The Komsomol believes "every hipster is a potential criminal," that "a saxophone is only one small step away from a switchblade."

One earnest member of the Komsomol, an athletic young man named Mels, is sent to catch a particularly elusive hipster, who easily outwits him, pushing him into a pond with the challenge, "Come spend some time with Polly on the Broadway." By Broadway she means Tverskaya Street, Moscow's central boulevard. Her hangout there is an underground nightclub called the Pompadour Club. In the hipster world, all things Russian have been given Western names. She calls herself Polly, but her given name is Pol'za

Figure 9.9 A brassy musical salute to 1950s Russia from *Hipsters* (2008).

("usefulness" in Russian), an acronym for *Pomnin Lenina Zavetsy* ("We remember Lenin's behests"). Mels (an acronym for Marx, Engels, Lenin, Stalin) will soon shorten his name to Mel.

Mel's gradual conversion from Communist to hipster is the slim narrative thread that binds this film together. Like most musicals, it is more about spectacle than story. Or rather, it's a movie in which character and plot are played out through musical performance. In one scene, Soviet life is represented in a coarsely sung number about "Man and Cat." Long tracking shots through a communal apartment show the tenants cooking, washing clothes, and brushing their teeth in cramped proximity, but with a comic mixture of resignation and élan. The camera cuts to a dark battle scene, a victory train packed with soldiers dreaming of a better life, then focuses on one returning veteran who finds his children starving at home and a stranger in bed with his wife. The scene's use of fast-paced editing and sharp color contrasts, its leaps between exaggerated close-ups and detached aerial views, are reminiscent of the cinematic styles of Busby Berkeley (*42nd Street*, 1933) and Baz Luhrmann (*Moulin Rouge!*, 2001). In terms of Russian cinema, it looks like a cross between Grigori Aleksandrov's Stalinist musicals of the 1930s and modern MTV.

As we've seen, much of the humor in Russian comedies follows the tradition of Gogol's outrageous caricatures and absurdist wit, often mixed with the visual hijinks of early Charlie Chaplin and the Keystone Cops. Chekhov's subtler forms of mockery are rarer but not entirely absent from the Russian screen. A case in point is Kira Muratova's *Chekhov's Motifs* (*Chekhovskie motivy*, 2002). Based on one of Chekhov's short stories and an unfinished play, Muratova's film centers on the dysfunctional Shnyriaev family and its problems with communication. People talk past each other, misinterpret what they hear, or fail to listen at all. Humans are continually compared to animals. At one point, the barnyard seems to be moving to a lyrical song on the soundtrack. The geese hoist their necks in sync, the turkeys wobble harmoniously, the pigs shake in unison, but when the music stops, we hear their discordant animal sounds again. Set in the era after Gorbachev, *Chekhov's Motifs* takes every opportunity to mock post-Soviet trends. At a lavishly traditional wedding, the guests seem more interested in liturgical chic than in the pieties of orthodoxy. They roll their eyes in boredom while the priest drones on. Also held up for ridicule is a fashionable trend for reviving folklore and family values. While the Shnyriaevs squabble at the dinner table, towels embroidered with proverbs like "With a loved one, you will find paradise even in a tent" line their ostentatiously decorated walls. As with the pre-Soviet aristocrats in Chekhov's *The Cherry Orchard*, the flaws of these modern Russians would be tragic if they weren't so laughably ludicrous.

Russian filmmakers have come a long way since Kuleshov and Eisenstein applied their idealism and innovative talents to the revolutionary cause or since Aleksandrov and Pyrev served the Stalinist state (and their own survival instincts) with escapist musicals a decade later. Medvedkin's extraordinary film train left the station more than eighty years ago. As the Russian people soldiered through the Great Patriotic War and experienced the chilling deprivations of a lengthy Cold War, then the brief promises of Khrushchev's Thaw and the regressive policies of Brezhnev's regime, filmmakers like Ryazanov and Gaidai adapted to the times, using laughter to amuse their audience and disarm the censors while launching spears of satire when and where they could. Although Russian art cinema may seem closer to European forms today—following the flow of international financing, transnational genres, and global themes—comedy continues to draw on the nation's great traditions of oral and literary storytelling. Gogol's grotesque distortions, Chekhov's pointed ironies, and those figures of fun that Propp found so plentiful in the country's native folklore—the wily trickster and the dupe—still animate the screen in human form. As Russia moves through the latest phase of Putin's nationalist agenda and government control, it will be instructive to watch how the people's desires and discontents are refracted through the ever-changing lens of movie comedy.

Russian Comedy Filmography

English Title	Original Title	Director	Date
Cold Showers	*Kholodnye dushi*	Yevgeny Bauer	1916
The Extraordinary Adventures of Mr. West in the Land of the Bolsheviks	*Neobychainye priklyucheniya mistera Vesta v strane bolshevikov*	Lev Kuleshov	1924
Love's Berries	*Yagodka lyubvi*	Aleksandr Dovzhenko	1926
The Girl with a Hatbox	*Devushka s korobkoy*	Boris Barnet	1927
St. *Jorgen's Feast Day*	*Prazdnik svyatogo Yorgena*	Yakov Protazanov	1930
Jolly Fellows	*Vesyolye rebyata*	Grigory Aleksandrov	1934
Happiness	*Schaste*	Aleksandr Medvedkin	1935
The Circus	*Tsirk*	Grigory Aleksandrov	1936

English Title	Original Title	Director	Date
Volga Volga	*Volga-Volga*	Grigory Aleksandrov	1938
Tractor Drivers	*Traktoristy*	Ivan Pyrev	1939
Cossacks of the Kuban	*Kubanskiye Kazaki*	Ivan Pyrev	1950
Carnival in Moscow	*Karnavalnaya noch*	Eldar Ryazanov	1956
Kidnapping, Caucasian Style, or Shurik's New Adventures	*Kavkazskaya plennitsa, ili Novie priklucheniya Shurika*	Leonid Gaidai	1967
The Diamond Arm	*Brilliantovaya ruka*	Leonid Gaidai	1969
Twelve Chairs	*12 stulev*	Leonid Gaidai	1971
Ivan Vasilievich: Back to the Future	*Ivan Vasilyevich menyayet professiyu*	Leonid Gaidai	1973
The Irony of Fate, or Enjoy Your Banya!	*Ironiya sudby, ili S lyegkim parom!*	Eldar Ryazanov	1976
Office Romance	*Sluzhebnyy roman*	Eldar Ryazanov	1977
Moscow Does Not Believe in Tears	*Moskva slezam ne verit*	Vladimir Menshov	1980
The Garage	*Garazh*	Eldar Ryazanov	1980
Repentance	*Monanieba*	Tengiz Abuladze	1984
A Man from Boulevard des Capuchines	*Chelovek s bulvara Kaputsinov*	Alla Surikova	1987
Heart of a Dog	*Sobache serdtse*	Vladimir Bortko	1988
The Sentimental Policeman	*Chuvstvitelnyy militsioner*	Kira Muratova	1992
Window to Paris	*Okno v Parizh*	Yuri Mamin	1993
Peculiarities of the National Hunt in the Winter	*Osobennosti natsionalnoy okhoty v zimniy period*	Alexandr Rogozhkin	2001
Chekhov's Motifs	*Chekhovskie motivy*	Kira Muratova	2002
Hipsters	*Stilyagi*	Valery Todorovskiy	2008
Kiss Them All!	*Gorko!*	Zhora Kryzhovnikov	2013
The Office Party	*Korporativ*	Oleg Assadulin	2014

Notes

1. Birgit Beumers, ed., *A Companion to Russian Cinema* (Oxford: Wiley Blackwell, 2016), 158.
2. Vladimir Propp, *On the Comic and Laughter*, trans. and ed. Jean-Patrick Debbèche and Paul Perron (Toronto: University of Toronto Press, 2009), chap. 15.
3. Denise Youngblood, *The Magic Mirror: Moviemaking in Russia, 1908–1918* (Madison: University of Wisconsin Press, 1999), 108.
4. See Birgit Beumers, ed., *Directory of World Cinema Russia* (Chicago: Intellect, 2011), 118–122.
5. "Medvedkin on the Train," video interview on two-disc DVD set, *The Last Bolshevik/Happiness* (released by Icarus Films, 2008). See also Emma Widdis, *Alexander Medvedkin, KINOfiles Filmmakers' Companion 2* (London: Tauris, 2005), 35–56.
6. Widdis, *Alexander Medvedkin*, 52.
7. Maria Belodubrovskaya, "Soviet Hollywood: The Culture Industry that Wasn't," *Cinema Journal* 53, no. 3 (Spring 2014): 100–122.
8. Rimgaila Salys, *The Musical Comedy Films of Gigori Aleksandrov: Laughing Matters* (Chicago: Intellect, 2009), 6.
9. Belodubrovskaya, "Soviet Hollywood," 100–122.
10. In Maya Turovskaya, "Hollywood in Moscow, or Soviet and American Cinema in the Thirties and Forties," *Kinokultura* 46 (2014), http://kinokultura.com/2014/46-turovskaya.shtml.
11. Rimgaila Salys, "Kuban Cossacks," in Beumers, *Directory of World Cinema Russia*, 130.
12. See Beumers, *Companion to Russian Cinema*, 519–542.

10
Film Comedy in Africa

To speak of African cinema instantly raises the specter of sweeping generalities. Unlike China or India, Africa is not a country but a continent. It is, in fact, an immensely large continent, large enough to fit China and India—along with Europe, the United States, Argentina, and New Zealand—within the compass of its 30.4 million square miles. Inside the outline of Africa's familiar shape are some fifty separate countries, one-quarter of the entire membership of the United Nations. Africa's 1.2 billion people speak some two thousand languages and span a great diversity of social systems, customs, and religions. Yet there are good reasons to look broadly at African film comedy instead of, say, comedy in Senegal or Nigeria. The movies of this region, or at least the territory south of the Sahara, have much in common, reflecting values, institutions, and historical realities unique to this part of the world.

As we explore the commonalities in this chapter, we will be wary of perpetuating Western stereotypes, lumping all Africa together as if there were no differences in language, culture, history, ethnicity, or religion. At the same time, we will be mindful that many of the national boundaries are artificial constructs, often created by foreign powers, that obscure transnational relationships that connect people with shared traditions. We will also heed Achile Mbembe's warning against "Afropessimsm," the tendency to picture the continent as a land plagued by famine, drought, disease, war, and ethnic strife.[1] One value of comedy lies in its capacity for countering this gloomy, disempowering view. Africans love to laugh, and the many forms their laughter takes are captured in their films as they have been for ages in their oral tales, their written literature, and their live performances.

To simplify the task, this chapter focuses on sub-Saharan Africa, sometimes referred to as Black Africa. This excludes the North African nations of the Maghreb (Morocco, Algeria, Tunisia, Libya, and Egypt), where film industries developed more rapidly under Arab and European influences and follow their own distinct traditions. We'll consider what is special about Black African films in general and comedy in particular. We'll look closely at comic figures, like the trickster, that populated animal folktales long before they appeared as human characters in African movies. We'll trace the heritage of oral storytellers, known in West Africa as *griots*, from their time-honored roles in African communities to their transformation into modern film directors.

When the World Laughs. William V. Costanzo, Oxford University Press (2020). Oxford University Press
DOI: 10.1093/oso/9780190924997.001.0001

We will explore concepts like *négritude*, pan-Africanism, and Afropolitanism, ideas offered to explain how African beliefs and sub-Saharan cinemas differ from others in the world. We will clarify Africa's unique position in world history at the time when motion pictures were introduced and how this shaped the kinds of movies Africans produced in the postcolonial days of independence and in the years thereafter.

In most regions of the world, from Hollywood to Europe and East Asia, comedy reigns as the most popular movie genre, yet historically this has not been the case south of the Mediterranean Sea. As recently as 2006, the film scholar Roy Armes has written, "very few African filmmakers have produced out-and-out comedies."[2] Other specialists have commented on this apparent departure from the global norm. In his 2017 study of *New African Cinema*, Valérie Orlando notes that "African film . . . is never made purely for entertainment."[3] He goes on to explain that even the most popular forms of the medium, like Nigerian video films, serve the purpose of "sociopolitical critique." Esi Sutherland-Addy, the distinguished Ghanaian activist and educator, daughter of Ghana's gifted playwright Efua Sutherland, comes to a similar conclusion after analyzing some ninety-seven low-budget videos produced in her country. However glitzy or sensational these films may seem to be in their treatment of poverty, drugs, immigration, teen pregnancy, or domestic abuse, they help to raise awareness of such issues, motivated by "a passion to act as the social conscience of the nation."[4] Observations like these alert us to one major difference between comedy in African films and comedy elsewhere, the widely held view that cinema bears an obligation to teach as well as to amuse. To understand this view, we need an historical perspective.

A Brief History

Unlike the histories of China or Europe, the history of precolonial Africa is less well known, in part due to a scarcity of written records. Drawing on rich oral traditions and new technologies, modern historians are learning more about the people who lived south of the Sahara and their political configurations: the many villages, city-states, and kingdoms of West Africa; the great empires of Ghana, Mali, Fulani, and Zimbabwe; the Bantu migrations from Nigeria into central, eastern, and southern regions; the Swahili people of the eastern coast; and the vast network of trade routes that crisscrossed the continent for centuries, linking early Africans with Greeks, Romans, Arabs, and each other. What is emerging from this research is a picture of diverse peoples and cultures quite different from the stereotypes and territorial grids imposed by European conquerors beginning in the fifteenth century.

For hundreds of years, the people of Africa were subjugated and its resources plundered by the colonial ambitions of Portugal, Britain, France, Belgium, and other foreign powers. While film industries were free to develop gradually in other parts of the world over the first century of cinema, native Africans acquired the means of film production only within the last sixty years or so, after attaining political independence. In some cases, colonialists deliberately kept cameras and editing equipment beyond the reach of Africans. In other cases, they trained Africans in the technology of film production but kept a firm grip on the kinds of films that could be made. Thus, creating an independent infrastructure for the industry has been one of the great challenges facing African filmmakers. For much of the time, African directors had to send their footage to Europe for postproduction, sometimes phoning long distance to find out how their takes turned out. Exhibition and distribution have been perennial problems too. In a continent where foreign concerns have historically dominated the theaters available for public screenings, it has been difficult for independent African auteurs to reach an audience and recover the cost of their films. Thus, funding, always a great hurdle for directors, has been particularly troublesome in Africa.

Despite these obstacles, the pioneers of African cinema created a remarkably rich and powerful cinematic legacy. They set out to forge a new visual language suited to African subjects and audiences: a cinema by, about, and for Africans. For decades, Africa and its population had been represented on the screen largely by foreign filmmakers with their own agendas. Think of the typical early Hollywood productions, which used African villages, wildlife, and people as backdrops for adventure films: Tarzan, Trader Horn, and other white heroes of the 1930s and 1940s battling evil in the Dark Continent. Well into our own times, even more sophisticated films like *Out of Africa* (1985), *Sahara* (2005), and *The Legend of Tarzan* (2016) have continued to bank on the old formula of non-African protagonists afoot in an exotic setting. African filmmakers like Ousmane Sembène sought to break away from these clichés. As Sembène, probably Africa's most celebrated cinematic spokesman, put it, "The development of Africa requires among other things the production of its own images."[5]

With the notable exception of South Africa, whose film history is unique in the region (and therefore is not included in this chapter), historians of Black African films rarely speak in terms of national cinemas. It is hard to find a full-length study of, say, Malian, Ghanaian, or Angolan national cinema, in contrast to the many books on Indian or Chinese films. More typically, the early history of sub-Saharan film production is divided along the lines of Anglophone (English-speaking), Francophone (French-speaking), and Lusophone (Portuguese-speaking) cinemas, reflecting the legacies left by Europe's three most important film-producing powers in colonial Africa: Britain, France, and Portugal. These terms remind us that the boundaries of most African nations are largely European constructs. They were fixed at the Berlin Conference of 1884–85, which carved up the continent about the same time that motion pictures were invented.

In terms of consistent quality and quantity, Francophone Africa has the strongest record over time. Senegal alone accounted for more than fifty films produced between 1955 and 1974. Senegal has also produced two of Africa's most renowned and influential film satirists, Sembène and Djibril Diop Mambéty. After Senegal, Mali probably ranks second in the prominence of its feature film directors, among them Souleymane Cissé, Adama Drabo, and Cheik Oumar Sissoko. Talented filmmakers have also come from Côte d'Ivoire (Désiré Ecaré), Benin (Sylvestre Amoussou), Cameroon (Jean-Marie Teno, Jean-Pierre Bekolo), Congo (Balafu Bakupa-Kanyinda, Jean-Michel Kibushi), Mauritania (Med Hondo, Abderrahmane Sissako), Niger (Moustapha Alassane), and Zaire (Ngangura Mweze, Benoît Lamy). The most remarkable developments within the Francophone community, however, have taken place in Burkina Faso. One of the poorest countries in the world, this landlocked country of 12 million inhabitants has produced directors like Gaston Kaboré, Dani Kouyaté, Idrissa Ouedraogo, Apolline Traoré, and Fanta Régina Nakro. Moreover, the capital city of Ouagadougou hosts a training school for new filmmakers and boasts the most advanced production facilities in West Africa. The Panafrican Film and Television Festival of Ouagadougou (FESPACO), dating back to 1969, brings together African films, filmmakers, and filmgoers in remarkable numbers and diversity. Audiences in Ouagadougou are estimated to reach half a million when the festival is held, in February, every two years.

Among the Anglophone countries, only Ghana and Nigeria took serious initiatives with film production after independence. Ghana's first president, Kwame Nkrumah, nationalized both film production and distribution in 1957, making Ghanaian cinema self-sustaining. Although the government of Ghana now runs a large state television studio, the more creative initiatives in both film and television were taken largely by independent talents like Kwaw Ansah and John Akomfrah. More recently, a robust cottage industry of popular videos has emerged in Ghana, a network of self-trained filmmakers producing genre-based entertainment for an eager audience of home viewers.

In Nigeria, the most populated country in Africa, film production took a somewhat different turn. Starting with foreign capital and talent, as well as film equipment left behind by British film units, Nigerians began producing movies with an international perspective. In 1970, a Nigerian-based company produced *Kong's Harvest*, an adaptation of Wole Soyinka's play directed by the American actor Ossie Davis. Nigeria's foremost filmmaker, Ola Balogun, made a large number of critically acclaimed films that drew on native theatrical traditions and African themes. Among his other achievements, Balogun demonstrated how to reach a local audience. Many of his films were shot in the local Yoruba language and feature familiar plots involving feuding families and *juju* magic. The most significant development in Nigeria along these lines has been the proliferation of cheaply made videos for local markets, similar to those in Ghana. Frankly commercial, employing local stars and nonprofessional actors, and repackaging formulaic stories that mix Nigerian myth, music, dance, and cultic rites with Hollywood chase scenes and special effects, these family-produced videos are sold in local markets, on street corners, and abroad. So successful are these marketing strategies that Nollywood, as the phenomenon is often called, has nearly rivaled India's Bollywood in output and income.

So far, we have noted some of the special challenges of making movies in Black Africa—the persistent legacy of colonialism, the absence of national structures to support a full-fledged film industry, the scarcity of theaters and regional distribution systems. By 2017, only thirty-five viable theaters remained in all of Francophone West Africa (Benin, Burkina Faso, Côte d'Ivoire, Guinea, Mali, Mauritania, Niger, Senegal, Togo).[6] Add to this list the diversity of local languages that fractures audiences into Ibo, Hausa, or Swahili markets (to name three of the estimated two thousand languages spoken on the continent), the delayed start (most African nations achieved independence no earlier than 1960), and the ever-present, unrelenting poverty. As a result, most of the best-known films have been made by persistent individuals motivated by something important to say, auteurs with agendas, trying to maintain an independent voice in the face of foreign forces while reaching across borders toward pan-African ideals. In response to these challenges, more and more young African filmmakers are turning elsewhere, not to academic auteurism or national cinema, but to globalism as a promising path. To take one example of this trend, Cameroonian director Jean-Pierre Bekolo has enjoyed remarkable success both at home and abroad with a succession of films that combine elements of African themes, experimental methods, and Hollywood genres with his own hip cinematic style. Both playful and political, anarchic and intense, *Quartier Mozart* (1992), *Aristotle's Plot* (*Le Complot d'Aristide*, 1996), and *The Bloodettes* (*Les saignantes*, 2005) have entertained popular audiences and won awards at Cannes, Locarno, Montreal, and Ouagadougou. We will be looking more closely at the hybrid character of Bekolo's work when we focus more specifically on comedy.

Indigenous Aesthetics

When Western audiences see an African movie for the first time, especially one from the early days, their response can sometimes be bewilderment. The images of animals and buried ostrich eggs that appear near the end of Cissé's *Yeelen* (1987), for example, often puzzle viewers who are unaware of Mali totems and rituals. This is largely a matter of their unfamiliarity with the cultural content of African stories. But the Western response can also be dismissive, based on an outsider's judgment of artistic merit. Many African movies have a different visual style. In Ouedraogo's *Tilai* (1990), for example, when Koudri stabs his brother Saga, there are no reaction shots, no special effects, no augmented sounds. When characters converse, the camera remains stationary instead of shifting back and forth from one viewpoint to another. For viewers used to Hollywood aesthetics, such scenes may seem amateurish. Western film tradition has conditioned many of us to expect strong plots and sympathetic characters, invisible editing, and camerawork that draws spectators into the frame. The intricate system of techniques that has evolved in Western film traditions tends to focus on human psychology and dramatic action. In contrast, the characters in many African films may seem one-dimensional, the cinematography crude and immature. African actors typically are shown in long shots, with little emphasis on their interior development. Some viewers may be tempted to attribute such qualities to limited equipment, inexperienced technicians, and nonprofessional actors. But it is also possible to see such elements—the slow pacing, wide framing, and lengthy silences of many classic African films—as part of a purposeful methodology, consistent with aesthetic principles far older than the invention of cinema. In a culture that honors community and environment, wide framing emphasizes the individual's place within society and the natural surroundings. What counts most is not the complexity of individual portraits but the dynamics of the group. In a culture that prizes listening, silence on the soundtrack can be a positive value. In a culture where direct eye contact is discouraged, point-of-view shots make little sense. It is helpful, then, to look more deeply into the cultural foundations of African art.

One of the most eloquent spokesmen on the topic of African culture was Léopold Sédar Senghor (1906–2001), poet, theorist, and first president of Senegal. Senghor used the word *négritude* to describe "the sum of the cultural values of the black world." Together with Léon Damas and Aimé Césaire, who coined the term, Senghor helped to turn a negative expression into a positive one. He argued that Africa is not a subculture, a minor alcove on the world stage, but the foundation of all cultures. While European civilization has rested on solid matter, facts, and discursive logic since the Renaissance, African civilization has always included spirit, energy, and movement, forces that transcend the surface of reality. While European views tends to be "static, objective, dichotomic . . . founded on separation and opposition: on analysis and conflict," Africans "conceive the world, beyond the diversity of its forms, as a fundamentally mobile, yet unique, reality that seeks synthesis."[7] Senghor argued that the West can learn much from this more expansive, fluid conception of the universe and humanity's place within it. He pointed out that scientists like Heisenberg, artists like Picasso, philosophers like Gaston Bachelard, and theologians like Pierre Teilhard de Chardin have helped to bring Europe closer to an African worldview.

Senghor stressed that art in Africa is not photographic, not an attempt to represent the outside of things, but an expression of life's deepest rhythms and vitality, the dance of the cosmos. Authorities on African art often emphasize this nonrepresentational function. They also stress its connections to quotidian experience. Sculpture, masks, and textiles are not created for pedestals or museum walls; they are intended for everyday use in the life of the community. Architecture and theater, music and dance, as well, are woven into the social fabric. We should expect to see these principles at work in the latest art form to be assimilated by Africans, the art of cinema.

Griots and Tricksters: Oral Storytelling in Africa

One place to look for aesthetic continuity is the oral tradition, always strong in Africa. In West Africa, storytelling has been for centuries the province of professional poets known, in French, as *griots*. This term has been traced to the Fulani word *gaoulo* (wandering poet or praiser) and the Wolof word *gewel* (poet and musician), but it is now used more widely to refer to any traditional storyteller. Like the Celtic bards or Anglo-Saxon *scops*, griots recite their stories to a musical accompaniment, typically on the *kora*, a harplike instrument fashioned from a calabash shell, cowhide, and leather strings. They may embroider old narratives with each telling or create new ones on the fly to suit the occasion. In early times, griots often served as messengers and local historians, stitching the values and collective memory of a community into entertaining narratives. Sometimes they were visionaries, designers of the future. Sometimes they put into lofty language what their king or community wanted to hear. Occasionally, like court jesters in Europe, they enjoyed special license to insult. This is where the fun begins (Figure 10.1).

Cheik Oumar Sissoko's *Guimba, the Tyrant* (*Guimba, un tyran une époque*, 1995) presents a critical portrait of griots in earlier days. Guimba's court poet functions as the bullying tyrant's ambassador, announcing the king's intimidating policies or flattering visitors with obsequious platitudes. His voice floods the soundtrack with bombastic words, words, words while the king moves through the silent crowd on an overdressed horse in pompous dignity. But when Guimba is finally met with superior force, the poet exclaims, "Gunpowder is not for griots" and hides behind his master.

The modern griot in Sembène's short film *Borom Sarret* (1963) is another satirical profile. When the film's protagonist, a poor taxi cart driver, encounters

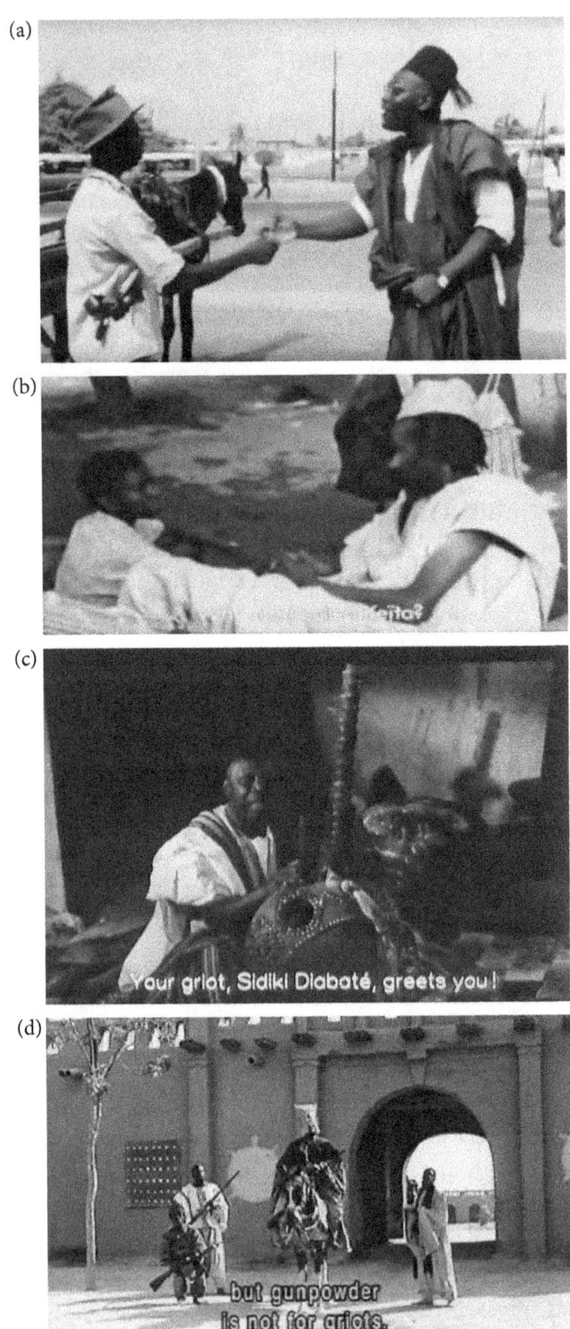

Figure 10.1 A gallery of griots. (a) *Borom Sarret* (1963). (b) *Keita: Heritage of the Griot* (1995). (c) *Skirt Power* (1997). (d) *Guimba, the Tyrant* (1995).

the griot during his journey to the city, the old storyteller spins a tale about the driver's lofty heritage. The story serves as a distraction, a momentary source of pride and hope, but offers no real help for the driver's plight in the modern world. Pocketing his fee, the haughty griot leaves a little wealthier, the driver much poorer.

More than one African director has been linked to the griot tradition. Filmmakers like Sissoko and Gaston Kaboré have described their deliberate use of oral narrative techniques like allegory, digressive flashbacks, and the teller's presence in the tale. Senegalese director Moussa Sene Absa, who comes from a family of griots, describes himself as "a modern griot using the magic of cinema" in all his work, including *Tableau ferraille* (1998), *Madame Brouette* (2002), and *Teranga Blues* (2007).

While griots can be figures of fun, more often they represent the venerable voice of oral storytelling, linking the film director to Africa's great narrative traditions. Drabo's *Skirt Power* (*Taafé Fanga*, 1997) opens with a scene in a Malian home where a group of children and adults is seated before a small television screen watching a Hollywood musical. A griot named Sidiki enters the room, turns off the television, and seats himself with his *kora* before the crowd. "Which past shall we visit tonight?" he asks. Then we see his story enacted as a lengthy flashback. (▶ See "Case Study for Chapter 10: *Skirt Power*" on the website.) In Kouyaté's *Keita! L'héritage du griot* (1995), an aged poet seeks to teach a young Burkinabe boy about his family heritage, enticing him with a story from the thirteenth-century epic *Sundjata*. The poet wants the boy to know he is descended from the royal Keitas of the epic, but the boy's mother wants him to speak French and to go to a modern school. Significantly, the role of the old poet in the movie is played by the director's father, a noted actor whose family has traditionally acted as griots for the Keita family. Even Sissoko's *Guimba*, as critical as it is of the tyrant's griot lackey, is framed as a story told by a present-day griot while playing his *kora*.

The pretentious griot is one of several comic figures that keeps popping up in African tales and films. In the older spoken stories, he is cousin to the windbag, full of bluster and smug grandiosity, whose haughty words rarely are supported by his actions. In Sembène's early films, the windbag is more often an unwitting dupe of colonialism. In *Xala* (1975), for example, El Hadji insists on speaking French even when his daughter speaks to him in local Wolof. He makes a show of drinking Evian water, even uses it to fill the radiator of his car. So proud is he of the French connection that he fails to realize how his mind has been colonized. El Hadji is also an example of the self-satisfied patriarch, the man who takes multiple wives to show off his wealth and sexual prowess. Invariably, he becomes a figure of laughter when his wives turn out to be more than he can handle. In this respect, he is related to the character of Demi-Dieu in Henri Duparc's *Dancing in the Dust* (*Bal poussière*, 1989), who decides to take a sixth wife. His plan is to sleep with each wife on a different day of the week, reserving the seventh day as a bonus. In the end, however, both El Hadji and Demi-Dieu are shown to be mere puppets, dancing foolishly on the strings of their own sexual desires.

Clowns, dupes, and buffoons abound in the animal folktales so beloved in Africa, but the most intriguing figure in these tales is probably the trickster. In Ghana and Togo, the trickster is a spider. The Ashanti people of Ghana regard Anansi, the spider, as a kind of culture hero. According to one oft-told tale, Anansi is the owner of all narratives, having tricked the gods into giving him their great hoard of stories. Always cunning, often greedy and unscrupulous, Kwaku (Uncle) Anansi is admired for his ability to outsmart everyone, animals and deities alike, sometimes even himself. Elsewhere in Africa, the trickster appears in various animal guises: a hare in Zaire, a tortoise in Nigeria, much like the raven and coyote in Native North American tales or Br'er Rabbit in the "Uncle Remus" stories collected from African American slaves. Whatever shape he takes, the trickster delights listeners of all ages with his feats of wily mischief. It isn't hard to find his human counterparts in African movies. In Mambéty's *Touki Bouki* (1973), the male protagonist devises various preposterous schemes to raise money for a trip to Paris. The film's Wolof title can be translated as "The Hyena's Journey," a reference to the shifty animal that often plays the leading role in trickster narratives. In Mambéty's other major film, *Hyenas* (*Hyènes*, 1992), the wily trickster is a woman who seeks revenge on those who wronged her, and like her famously tittering namesake, she enjoys the last laugh. Sembène's two earliest movies, *The Money Order* (*Mandabi*, 1968) and *Xala*, are also structured much like trickster tales.

Forms of Humor

What passes for comedy in African films is not always obvious to Westerners. As in any culture, much of the fun is based on wordplay, rarely translatable. Non-French-speaking audiences watching *Bal poussière* may not find the names of Demi-Dieu, Beau Gosse, or Porte-Clés particularly funny if they don't know that Demi-Dieu means "half-god" (a sly reference to his hubris), Beau Gosse means "beautiful kid" (ironic for a hunchback), or Porte-Clés means "key carrier" (he claims to open doors, hearts, and women's legs). Nor may they appreciate the snarky wit of Binta's foul-mouthed mother, who ridicules her daughter for having "legs like matchsticks" (for lighting men's fires). In addition to such verbal mischief, even some visual humor can lose something in translation. As Olivier Barlet points out, "When a film shows a well-off family grown fat from eating well, Africans laugh, whereas Westerners tend to be more saddened than anything."[8] A case in point is the scene in Sembène's *The Money Order* where the protagonist's wife removes the crying baby from her back to serve him dinner. Kneeling at his side, she picks the bones from his plate while he sits cross-legged in his undershirt, stuffing himself with handfuls of food. When he's done, her husband spits out a piece of gristle into her waiting hand, clears his throat, and belches contentedly. Americans are often troubled by the scene, particularly by the wife's obsequious role, but Africans are more inclined to accept this as a matter of custom, delighting instead in the slurping and the belching (Figure 10.2).

As elsewhere in the world, humor takes many forms in Africa. In addition to folktales and films, Africans laugh through proverbs, plays, novels, radio shows, television sitcoms, live standup, and daily banter in the village square. If humor is a measure of taste, what a society considers fair game for laughter, a few examples may help to convey the flavor of this humor and provide some insight into social norms. This is especially true in Africa, where proverbs used in daily discourse are drawn from a time-honored storehouse of community wisdom. In Congo, the Tabwa people have a saying, "To see a lion is to escape from it." There is certainly some humor here in the ironic implication: You are done for if the lion sees you first. Applied to local merchants or politicians, the proverb means, "Beware of those who sneak up on you."[9] There is also something funny in a Yoruba saying about roosters and hens (a hen knows when it is daybreak, but she allows the rooster to make the announcement).[10] Adages like these have the quality of in-jokes, a kind of knowing laughter.

Figure 10.2 Dinnertime in *The Money Order* (1968).

Scholars of African literature like Maik Nwosu have studied comic novels such as Nkem Nwankwo's *Danda* (1964) and Mongo Beti's *The Poor Christ of Bomba* (1971). Nwosu sees "a lightness of spirit" in *Danda*, which he believes to be "a fundamental aspect of the poetics of laughter."[11] Like all true clowns, the character of Danda is "movingly and palpably human, never simply funny in a one-dimensional way."[12] While *Danda* is set in a Nigerian village before independence, *The Poor Christ of Bomba* takes place in southern Cameroon during the 1930s, when a French missionary arrives to convert the natives to Catholicism. Father Drumond is a rigid, proudly pious man, condescending to the Africans whose society he fails to understand. His self-centered cook is a kind of trickster, driven only by pleasure, a master of getting others to do his work. Much of the book's comedy comes from the interaction between these characters, with Drumond and his colonial mission bearing the brunt of Beti's satire.

Television humor and standup comedy in Africa are other subjects of recent scholarly study. Charles Kebaya has applied sophisticated concepts from Mikhail Bakhtin and Andrew Horton to Kenyan sitcoms. One popular show is *Papa Shirandula*, centering on an elderly watchman who pretends to have an office job. Every morning, after leaving home in a suit, he hides behind a bush to change into a watchman's uniform; in the evening, he changes back to the keep up the deception. Papa's slapstick performance is all the funnier because it violates African norms about age and social stature. It allows urban Kenyans to laugh at their own struggles with money, community pressure, and self-respect.

Whether comedy supports change or impedes it is a matter of debate. George Orwell once wrote, "Every joke is a tiny revolution," while Joseph Stalin has been said to ask, "How many battalions does humor have?"[13] In Africa, where black filmmakers began using the medium first and foremost as a political tool, the debate has been particularly heated. The influential Tunisian screenwriter and director Férid Boughedir viewed comedy as essentially conservative, serving the status quo. Pointing to popular comedies like Henri Duparc's *Bal poussière* and Jean-Pierre Bekolo's *Quartier Mozart* (1992), he argued that such films present individuals, not institutions, as flawed, invariably returning those who stray back to the community norms.[14] In contrast, Alexie Tcheuyap views comedy as a subversive strategy. Noting that comedy typically features the lower classes, engaging them in a conspiratorial relationship against the powers that be, he argues that humor can be a "weapon of resistance." Tcheuyap finds moments of comedy in works by politically committed filmmakers like Sembène, and he traces this impulse to the postcolonial cinema of Duparc and Bekolo, when comedy becomes a full-fledged genre. Their comedies, he reasons, are not just sellouts to commercialism or mere copies of imported films. Instead, they reinforce what is specifically African in African cinemas, deploying local forms of wordplay and homegrown comic talent to mock local targets and undermine local strongholds of authority.[15]

Is humor in Black African cinema primarily conservative, subversive, or both? We'll consider this and other questions in the next few sections, where we focus on individual directors and their films.

Political Satire in the 1970s and 1980s: Sembène and Mambéty

We have already seen how Sembène used humor to satirize Africa's colonial oppressors and those who inherited the mantle of power. His path to film followed a remarkable trajectory. The son of a fisherman in Senegal, yet prone to seasickness, young Ousmane Sembène went to Dakar, where he worked for six years as a bricklayer and mechanic. During World War II, when Francophone Africans were called to serve in the French army, he was sent to an infantry unit in the colony of Niger. After the war, he migrated to France, where he worked on the docks of Marseilles and was drawn into the labor movement. It was in Marseilles that Sembène joined the French Communist Party, beginning a long career of championing the cause of workers and poor farmers and giving the voiceless a voice. He read widely, eagerly, and began to write poems, short stories, essays, and novels. His first novel, *The Black Docker*, was published in 1956. *God's Bits of Wood* (1960), a fictional account of the railroad strike in Senegal from a Marxist point of view, became his most successful novel.

Despite the success of his writing, Sembène realized that he could reach more Africans by making films. The imagery of movies appealed directly to an audience, cutting through the problems of literacy (nearly two-thirds of the people in Senegal could not read) and reflecting back to viewers the circumstances of their lives through the filter of political awareness. Yet Sembène continued to write, working on his books and movies simultaneously, so that they nourished one other. His early films show the influence of Soviet directors whom he studied at the Gorki Studios in Moscow. In his hands, the camera is primarily a teaching tool. The stories are simple, often classical in structure. The characters are more emblematic of the common man and woman, like Sergei Eisenstein's collective heroes, rather than psychologically complex. The goal is to create a critical distance, in the manner of Brecht's alienation effect, so the camerawork is often static, with long takes and few close-ups, while the editing juxtaposes opposites, in the manner of Soviet montage, enforcing a sense of ironic detachment.

We see this strategy at work in the opening sequence of *Xala*, which mocks the interchangeability of colonial and postcolonial leaders with scathing irony (Figure 10.3). A group of enthusiastic Africans is dancing in front of the

Figure 10.3 A satirical take on local politics in *Xala* (1975). (a) Before the socialist coup . . . (b) . . . and after.

Chamber of Commerce. As the crowd cheers, several dark-skinned men in traditional dress run up the steps and into the boardroom, where a group of light-skinned men in sunglasses and dark suits is seated at the table. The newcomers lift plaster busts from the mantel (one represents Marianne, emblem of the French Republic) and set them on the steps contemptuously, then drive out the white men. Meanwhile, an offscreen announcer proclaims, in French, a victorious new day: "Never before has an African occupied the presidency of our chamber. We must take what is ours, what is our right . . . We must show ourselves capable like other peoples of the world." The camera cuts back and forth between the people and their new representatives, affirming solidarity of spirit and will. But soon one of the ousted businessmen returns with a column of armed policemen, who disperse the crowd and let other Frenchmen enter while the announcer continues, with an incongruity that grows more pronounced with every shot: "We choose socialism, the only true socialism, African socialism." Inside, the old regime presents briefcases filled with money to their successors, who now all wear tuxedos. The target of this spoof is clear. The council's new president bears a noticeable likeness to Léopold Senghor, who championed the *négritude* movement in Senegal but spoke in French and remained a proud member of the *Académie Française*.

Sembène completed eleven films before he died in 2007. His satirical wit took on topics like the mistreatment of African colonial soldiers by the French (*Emitai*, 1971; *Camp de Thiaroye*, 1988), postcolonial religious conflict (*Guelwaar*, 1992), and female circumcision (*Moolaadé*, 2004). With each successive film, the production values rose, but his focus remained firmly fixed on the message. Not all Africans appreciate Sembène's work in the same way. Some consider his militant, didactic style too narrow and outdated. Moussa Sene Absa, for example, finds fault with the stilted acting and a certain lack of heart. Manthia Diawara points out that Sembène's satire often has the opposite effect on African spectators than intended; someone in the audience may see the suitcase full of bribes in *Xala* and shout out, "Hey, they got lucky!" But Sembène's legacy is still strong. He offered a vision to all Africa and, more than any of his peers, helped to bring African cinema to the world's screens.

Although born in the same country as Sembène, Djibril Diop Mambéty (1942–1998) was always worlds apart in temperament and aesthetic goals. The son of a Muslim cleric, Mambéty sought an outlet for his restless, bountifully inventive imagination in acting, but after graduating from acting school and working on the stage in Dakar, he was expelled. At the age of twenty-four, with no formal film training, he turned to movies and produced two short films in quick succession. Both films, set in Dakar, gave him a chance to experiment with the freewheeling characters, satirical style, and nonlinear narrative structure that became hallmarks of his longer works. Although unsuccessful at the box office, they drew appreciative critical attention, laying the groundwork for his lamentably brief career.

We've seen how Mambéty favors trickster figures in *Touki Bouki* and *Hyenas*. As director, he himself plays tricks with the medium and the audience. In his cunning hands, montage editing is a shape-shifting technique. The opening image of a boy riding a cow shifts to the protagonist on his motorbike, an ironic juxtaposition of tradition and modernity underscored by a set of cow horns mounted on the bike. The rider is Mory, a shallow-minded, petty thief who dreams of escaping from the tedium of Senegal to Paris, "the gateway to paradise" (Figure 10.4). His far-fetched dream, represented on the soundtrack by a sentimental French song ("Paris! Paris! Paris!") contrasts visually with the African landscape through which he rides, with its stately baobab trees, and the ancient Dogon cross on the rear of his bike. Sometimes Mambéty resorts to more conventional forms of humor, like a slapstick fight between two women at the watering place. When a man tries to break it up, the women start in on him while

Figure 10.4 Mory dreams of his triumphant return in *Touki Bouki* (1973).

the crowd laughs uproariously. In another comic scene, Mory makes a ludicrous attempt to steal the proceeds of a wrestling contest, which is earmarked for a memorial to General de Gaulle. The allusion to France's wartime hero is deliciously funny but even here, the humor turns abruptly sinister when the trunk supposedly containing the loot is opened and a human skull pops out. In contrast to Sembène's realistic narratives, Mambéty pushes the aesthetics of surrealism and magical realism into moments of ironic absurdity. In the elaborately staged fantasy sequence near the movie's end, Mory and his girlfriend return in triumph to Senegal. Smartly dressed and seated in back of a luxury Citroën, they parade past the presidential palace, handing out wads of cash to adoring crowds while a brass band celebrates the prodigal son. The couple lights cigars while the throng showers them with praise. The more outrageous the fantasy, the more devastating when Mambéty finally undercuts it.

Although more straightforward in style than *Touki Bouki, Hyenas* still bears the personal signature of its director, the griot who narrates from the heart of his imagination and writes himself into the story. We sense his presence in the camerawork and editing, the way he weaves in native images not only from Senegal, but from the entire continent: elephants from Kenya, hyenas from Uganda. Together with the monkeys, buffalo, and vultures that appear throughout the film, they function not as local color but as part of the indigenous iconography of African storytelling. Mambéty evokes them like a cinematic shaman. Although based on a Swiss play, *Hyenas* is distinctly African. Rooted in indigenous storytelling and values, it challenges Africans to resist the lure of foreign funds to rescue its people from poverty and famine. And Mambéty's inventive, hybrid style serves as a harbinger of a new direction in Black African cinema. *Touki Bouki* and *Hyenas* point the way from directors like Sembène and Cissé to a new generation of eclectic, global-minded filmmakers like Jean-Pierre Bekolo.

Into the 1990s with Parody and Social Satire: Bekolo, Alassane, and Drabo

Bekolo is a filmmaker from Cameroon whose stylish, offbeat films appeal to a generation of Africans attuned to today's global flow of pop culture. The son of a police chief, Bekolo focused his irreverent spirit and eclectic talents on the new technology of video at an early age. For two years he served as an editor in Cameroon television followed by two years of work on music videos in Paris, then turned to making his own films at the age of twenty-three. His first feature, *Quartier Mozart* (1992), spans forty-eight hours in a working-class neighborhood (the Mozart Quarter) in Yarounde, the capital of Cameroon. Things get hot when a sassy schoolgirl called "Queen of the Hood" enters the body of a suave, educated young man to experience sex and power from a male perspective. This feat is neatly accomplished with the help of Maman Thelka, a sorceress who assumes the shape of a comic trickster known as Panka. The two women are impudent and tough. They delight in turning the tables on a cast of corrupt male authorities and bullies. Made on a shoestring budget of $30,000, *Quartier Mozart* won awards at Cannes, Locarno, Montreal, and London, enabling Bekolo to advance in his career.

His second film, *Le complot d'Aristote* (*Aristotle's Plot*, 1996), was funded by the British Film Institute (BFI), which selected Bekolo to represent Africa for its high-profile celebration of cinema's centenary. If the BFI expected a sober salute to Africa's filmmaking pioneers, they got something less comfortable and more creatively complex: a comic meditation on Africa today and the meaning of cinema itself, bristling with irreverent parody, manic satire, and self-irony. The film is set in and around a rundown movie theater named Cinema Africaine. The names of the two antagonists are also self-consciously allegorical. Cineaste, a self-righteous intellectual, wants to create a genuinely African cinema. Cinema, a hooligan who has seen thousands of commercial movies, mostly Hollywood action films, just wants to watch movies all day (Figure 10.5). The policeman charged with arresting them has a limited understanding of cinema. He wants to know how a person who dies in one film can reappear living in another.

Bekolo's title alludes to the Western plot conventions that he deliberately subverts: realistic drama following a course of rising action to a climax and

Figure 10.5 "They call me cinema because I've seen ten thousand films." *Aristotle's Plot* (1966): A movie about movies.

ending in an emotionally purifying catharsis. *Aristotle's Plot* zig-ags through a series of loosely linked episodes, moving in one direction, doubling back, and continuing again in fits and starts. But he has another reason for evoking Aristotle's *Poetics*, "the bedrock of European storytelling." In an interview with Frank Ukadike, Bekolo pointed out that the Greek philosopher's analysis was limited to tragedy, a literary form that is supposed to inspire pity and fear. Bekolo linked this inadequate analysis to a limited view of Africa, in the Western imagination, as a place of continual tragedy. "I am from Cameroon," he said, where "humor and satire are basic elements of culture." What he felt was missing in the *Poetics* was comedy.[16] Bekolo's great achievement can be seen in his efforts to restore the comic imagination to African cinema.

His chief comic instruments are irony, parody, and satire, with a good deal of pointed play with names. The thugs in Cinema's gang swear like boys from the 'hood, and they use names like Cobra, Bruce Lee, Van Damme, Saddam, and Schwarzenegger, reflecting their fixation on Hollywood action heroes. They ridicule Cineaste's artistic pretensions, calling him "Silly Ass" (in the English-language version of the film, translated in the saltier French version as "*chieur-né-aste*"). Yet, when Cinema is asked by the police to identify himself, he produces a deck of ID cards with names like Djibril Diop Mambéty, Gaston Kaboré, Med Hondo, and Ousmane Sembène, the kind of African directors he finds so tedious.

Comparisons between contemporary Africa and an imaginary Hollywood run throughout the film. When forced out of Cinema Africaine, one of the gangstas is impressed by the "prehistoric" scenery he finds in the African bush. "It's like *Jurassic Park*," he says. Together, they plan to take back their theater with a stash of outsize weaponry. The sequence looks like something from a low-budget crime movie, with dark lighting, jazzy music, and corny, tough-guy dialog. The parody turns on itself when they find only one person in the audience, an African American who boasts that he has studied Swahili and wears kente cloth. He has come to learn about his roots. "If you don't know where you're coming from, how do you know where you're going?" he asks before they execute him in a *mise-en-scène* of shadow figures reminiscent of *Scarface* (1932) or *The Public Enemy* (1931). Having seized the theater, they piece it together from bits of old and new materials, rechristening it "New Africa." The wannabe Hollywood action heroes have become *actionnaires* (shareholders) in a new enterprise, screening "African Action Films."

Nine years later, Bekolo came out with *Les saignantes* (*The Bloodettes*, 2005). A satirical mélange of genres, it might be described as a futuristic, neo-noir, political horror-thriller with an attitude. The film takes place in a nameless African country in the year 2025, when the secretary general dies while in bed with a prostitute. Majolie, a feisty femme fatale, calls her best friend ChouChou to help dispose of the corpse. This starts a chain of nighttime adventures that involve corrupt government officials, a sleazy cabbie, and other men of dubious character. As in *Quartier Mozart*, women in this film call the shots. With the assistance of a mysterious female cult called the Mevoungou, the two high-rolling hookers defy the rules of politics and physics, manipulating men (who try to use them) for their own ends. Meant to entertain while it mocks the male establishment, *Les saignantes* avoids judging its protagonists, inviting viewers to interrogate the status quo of power and identity.

Bekolo's films mark a significant departure from the didactic, social realist cinema of Sembène's generation, Papa's cinema. His hybrid style is both eccentric and eclectic—a distinctly personal voice, like Mambéty's, that draws freely on American pop culture (Spike Lee) and the European avant-garde (Brecht, Godard) but always speaks to Africans about African concerns. What's more, his movies validate the importance of cinematic pleasure. He believes that films can entertain audiences and still be artistic and reflective.

Ukadike sees Bekolo as "a bridge between the pioneers and a new breed of African filmmakers now aspiring to push African cinema to a new progressive level."[17] Kenneth Harrow is more specific, arguing that current, mostly Western theories like postmodernism and postcolonial are inadequate to explain Bekolo's work, that he is "reconstituting an African postmodernism, or . . . postmodernism itself."[18] Like the young Africans in *Aristotle's Plot* who piece together their theater from fragments old and new, Bekolo constructs his version of African cinema ad hoc for a new generation. In doing so, he paves the way for filmmakers who want to reach a wider local audience by offering a blend of trendy, popular entertainment and socially conscious critique.

Popular Genres: Duparc, Ngangura, and Lamy

As early as 1978, French scholar Pierre Haffner warned that most Africans related better to popular genres like melodrama and comedy than they did to the artisanal styles and political polemics of the African film pioneers. He suggested that better models might be found in indigenous forms of entertainment like the Koteba theater of West Africa.[19] Some twenty years later, Mwezé Ngangura expressed a similar view, arguing that African art films had gained some traction abroad through the festival circuit but alienated most local audiences.[20] Ngangura is one of a growing number of filmmakers who achieved commercial success and some critical acclaim by appropriating familiar formulas like the musical and romantic comedy. The milieu of these "genre comedies" is ordinary life, highlighting the buoyant spirit and stamina of everyday Africans. The typical comic hero, like the trickster of folklore, practices *débrouillardise*, the art of being resourceful to survive, outwitting others and ridiculing authority on the way to fast money and/or sex. Almost invariably, there is music performed by popular local stars and a happy ending that restores everything to normal.

Mwezé Ngangura, a native of Zaire (formerly the Congo), teamed up with Belgian director Benoît Lamy to direct *Life Is Rosy* (*La vie est belle*) in 1987. It's a rags-to-riches story about a villager named Kourou who dreams of making it in the city as a popular musician. He hitches a ride in the back of a truck, arriving in the capital city of Kinshasa with no money, his beloved instrument having been smashed along the way. At night, he wanders through the streets, dodging cars, slinking penniless past food stands, eventually lured into a nightclub by the familiar sound of music. When he tries to join in the song, Nvouandou the club owner only mocks him. "You know nothing of music," he sneers. "You could get a job in my wife's orchestra." The joke is actually on Nvouandou since Kourou is played by Papa Wemba, the most celebrated singing star in Zaire (Figure 10.6). Nvouandou becomes the butt of other jokes. As a sendup of the haughty elite, he gets more than his share of ridicule. For all his wealth, his lavishly decorated club, and his flashy Mercedes, the man has been impotent for twenty years. This drives him to consult a local faith healer, who prescribes a regimen of silly dances and a virgin as cure. The sight of Nvouandou dancing wildly in his business suit and trying to deal with his wife's flamboyant jealousy offers a ludicrous display of incongruities, a comical contrast of arrogance and humiliation, tradition and modernity.

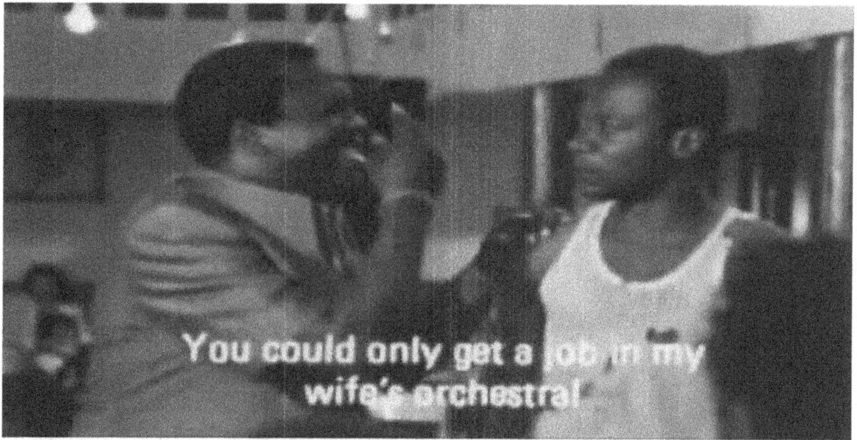

Figure 10.6 Papa Wemba auditions for a singing job in *Life Is Rosy* (1987).

The film's large cast of stock caricatures may seem reminiscent of Italy's *commedia dell'arte* but it is actually drawn more locally from African folktales, Congolese theater, and village life. In addition to the self-important bigshot and impotent husband (Nvouandou), there is the neglected first wife (Mamou), the scolding *féticheur* (faith healer), and the trickster from outside (Kourou). Ngangura and Lamy add a dwarf, who acts as a kind of narrator, not unlike a griot, passing through the film with his *chikwangue* kebabs and crying out, "Life is rosy." As Kourou schemes and hustles, piecing together a band from the untapped talent of the streets, the dwarf's cry becomes the refrain of a new song that evolves as the film advances and blossoms into a major hit. As several critics have noted, this happy ending is well earned. Ukadike called the film "commercial, but not trivial," noting how it uses music and location not merely as entertaining backdrops but as thematic elements woven into a sociologically astute study of modern Zaire and its woes.[21] Ngangura himself likened his use of comedy to a mirror that "allows people to look and laugh at themselves."[22] "If I use caricature, it is to give us the courage to look at ourselves as we really are so that we can mend our ways."[23]

In the following year, a filmmaker from Côte d'Ivoire made a popular comedy about polygamy. The arrogant male protagonist in Duparc's *Dancing in the Dust* is a wealthy farmer who calls himself Demi-Dieu (half-god) and has five wives. One day, he decides to take a young schoolgirl as his sixth wife. This way, he'll have one for each day of the week, leaving Sunday as a day of rest. Binta is smart and sexy, but her modern ideas bewilder him. She lays down the law about sex ("If I don't want any, I'll say 'I pass'"), and her sassy confidence creates mayhem in the household (Figure 10.7). Some of the wives stick to the old-fashioned ways

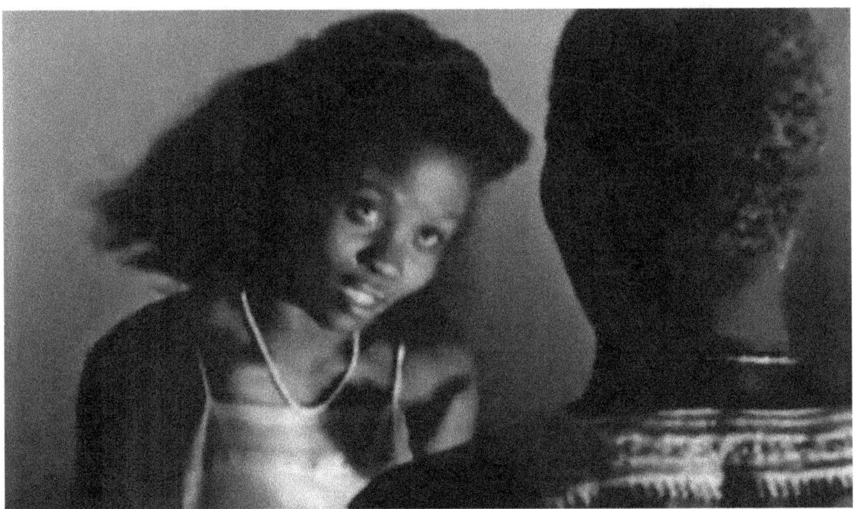

Figure 10.7 "If I don't want any, I'll say 'I pass.'" The new wife lays down the law in *Dancing in the Dust* (1988).

while others follow her example, becoming more assertive, adopting Western styles of dress—and undress. Like *Life Is Rosy*, Duparc's film employs music, dancing, and local stars, although these may seem more like gratuitous add-ons than organically thematic elements, and his humor leans toward the bawdy side. Critics like Ukadike dismissed *Dancing in the Dust* as mere amusement, not to be taken seriously,[24] but others pointed out that Duparc's lighthearted approach to social issues was a hit with ordinary Africans, paving the way for other genre-based social comedies, including his own *Rue Princesse* (1993) and *Coffee Color* (*Une Couleur Café*, 1997).[25]

Some of Africa's most successful women directors have also used the lighter touch of comedy in their work. Flora Gomes, best known for her bittersweet films about Guinea Bissau's struggles for independence, directed *My Voice* (*Nha Fala*) in 2002. The voice belongs to Vita, who loves to sing but is burdened with a family curse that threatens her with death if she does. Vita falls in love with Pierre, a Parisian musician who convinces her to join his group and helps her to defy the malediction. She returns to Cape Verde, where she organizes her own fake burial. Gomes weaves in elements of romantic comedy and the musical, but she also loads the story with symbolic details that deepen the film's political and social significance. The bond between Vita (life force?) and Pierre (rock? St. Peter?) suggests a bridge between cultures. The funeral becomes a liberating rebirth, a triumph over traditions that keep women from expressing themselves. In the final scene, a bust of the independence fighter Amilcar Cabral, whose proper place has been debated throughout the film, rises in the air and finds its own spot on a pedestal beside the sea. Another woman, Burkina Faso's Fanta Regina Nacro, directed several comic shorts in the 1990s. *Open Your Eyes* (*Puk Nini*, 1995) deals lightly but deftly with the problems of adultery, first from a male perspective, then from a female point of view. When Salif feels neglected by his wife's attention to her duties as a mother, he turns to a prostitute for his wants. Initially, we see the wife and prostitute through male eyes, as objects of need and desire. By the film's conclusion, though, the two women have formed a friendship, an alliance, and we see them making jokes about the shortcomings of men. In *Konaté's Thing* (*Le Truc de Konaté*, 1997), the title character's wife wants her womanizing husband to wear a condom as protection against AIDS. At first, the man refuses, quipping, "Have you ever seen a man enter his own house with a hat?" But Diénéba, his second wife, goes on a sex strike. What's more, she enlists Konaté's first wife and his mistress to join her. By now, Konaté is feeling impotent. He consults a diviner, who sends him on a quest to find a healing tree. This turns out to be the *hevea* plant, which produces rubber. Konaté returns enlightened, promising to use condoms in exchange for being cured. This film also ends with women laughing at the weaknesses of men. Laughter confirms their triumph and their solidarity.

Like Ngangura, Nacro embraces humor as a "means of educating the masses" without being "offputtingly didactic,"[26] a strategy adopted by African filmmakers throughout the 1990s and the following two decades. Topics range from migration (Jean Odoutan's *The Waltz of the Fat Bottoms* [*La Valse des gros derrières*], 2004; from Benin) and unplanned pregnancy (Charles Shemu Joyah's *Seasons of a Life*, 2009; Malawi) to combat (Daniel Kollo Samou's *Tasuma the Fighter* [*Tasuma le feu*], 2006; Burkina Faso) and ineffectual politics (Henri-Joseph Koumba Bididi's *The Elephant's Balls* [*Les couilles de l'éléphant*], 2002; Gabon). The titles of these films are clues to their sense of humor.

Enter Nollywood

The new focus on entertainment has given rise to one of the most astonishing phenomena in the history of African cinemas, now popularly known as Nollywood. Starting from scratch and motivated by profit, a group of resourceful Nigerian businessmen learned to harness the low-cost technologies of video to create a multimillion-dollar movie enterprise. By some accounts, Nollywood constitutes the second largest film industry in the world. With an estimated annual output of over two thousand feature video films annually by 2014, it may even be the most productive, injecting some $600 million into the national economy a year.[27]

Like the market-driven industries of Hollywood and Bollywood, Nollywood (the "N" stands for Nigeria) is a child of the entrepreneurial spirit. The street-smart vendors who began selling cheap videos in the late 1970s knew little about making movies, but they understood what people wanted and how to deliver the goods. Most Africans wanted to see themselves reflected in familiar stories on the screen. By experimenting with a fluid blend of local and foreign narrative traditions, individual producers developed vibrant cinematic formulas with mass appeal. They learned to shoot their movies quickly and efficiently on video, distributing them on VHS tapes and later on DVDs, formats that bypassed the decaying movie theaters and inadequate television stations on which celluloid films depend. Within twenty years, Nigerian video films were being sold throughout Africa and exported to the diasporic community of 100 million Africans living abroad. The Nollywood phenomenon has spread throughout the continent. In the Hausa-speaking regions of northern Nigeria, an offshoot of the video industry is known as Kannywood, based largely in the city of Kano. In the neighboring nation of Ghana, it has been labeled Ghallywood, and similar movements have sprung up in Kenya (Riverwood, based in River Road, Nairobi), Uganda (Ugawood), and Liberia (Lolliwood).

By most accounts, the first Nollywood video was *Living in Bondage*, the story of a man whose hunger for wealth involves him in a deadly cult. It was produced in 1992 by Kenneth Nnebue, a Lagos-based businessman who reportedly used the story as a way to sell off his stock of blank VHS tapes from Taiwan.[28] With little knowledge of cinema, Nnebue borrowed ideas from amateur stage recordings of traveling Yoruba troupes, establishing an early link to Nigerian theater with its colorful costumes, traditional music, and clever use of social satire, as well as characters and stories pulled from oral folklore. Scholars have also traced elements of Nollywood to the popular Onitsha Market literature of the 1960s[29]and early Nigerian filmmakers like Ola Balogun, who was trained in Paris as an auteur director but experimented with genre films during the 1970s.[30] But the eclectic storylines of these makeshift videos could as easily come from news headlines or local politics. They dramatize the power of money, love, greed, jealousy, and vengeance, mixing fantasy and reality, urban life and witchcraft in a mélange of genres that might jump from comedy to romance to action to horror in a matter of minutes. A typical plot might center on a successful businessman who gets rich through some human sacrifice and is haunted by the dead man's ghost. A sleeping family might find themselves suddenly transported from their beds to the forest or the middle of the street, victims of a vengeful spirit. Devotees of *juju* magic might turn for redemption to a Christian evangelical church. Such plots reflect what Hope Eghagha refers to as an "African world view," a kind of magical realism based on the belief that the spirit world regularly interacts with everyday reality.[31] These plots also offer versions of what some call

"Afromodernity," featuring lavish domestic sets and all-African casts, often with female stars whose physical appearance and demeanor contrast with Western models of beauty.[32]

Today's video films are more likely to have higher production values than they did in the 1990s. They make regular use of multiple media (16mm and 35mm, computer graphics and streaming video, spectacular SPFX finales), but they are still made in a hurry. Successful practitioners may boast outputs of eighty or a hundred productions, following a practical mix of assembly-line tactics and impromptu ingenuity to cast, shoot, edit, and distribute their work for a voracious market.[33] Some critics ridicule Nollywood for these slapdash practices. They deride it for glamorizing wealth and violence, for promoting glitz over substance. Others find the whole trend "ideologically bankrupt"[34] or condemn it for perpetuating Western stereotypes of the primitive African, an ignorant prey to witchcraft and self-inflicted miseries.[35] Yet as the trend receives increasingly serious attention, a number of prominent voices have highlighted its contributions, noting that Nollywood and its followers may represent a truly pan-African movement independent of foreign interests, that what appears to be apolitical melodrama actually engages people in conversations about social issues, and that it stimulates "an emergent continent-wide popular discourse about what it means to be African."[36]

The emergence in Africa of a popular, commercial, transcontinental form of video-based filmmaking—in contrast to decades of "high-brow," auteurist, nation-based, celluloid, art cinemas—has significant implications for comedy. As in Hollywood, and life, humor can be one of several emotional threads in a typical Nollywood film—all woven into the texture of a story that includes romance and drama, horror and thrills. But there are also out-and-out comedies. *Osuofia in London* is a case in point (Figure 10.8). Written and directed in 2003 by Kingsley Ogora, it stars the well-known Igbo comic Nkem Owoh as a villager from Nigeria who travels to London to claim his share of a family inheritance. Owoh often acts and dresses like a clown. Out of his element in the big city of London, he looks just like a country rube, wearing a green shirt over a blue one and a gray coat over both. At McDonald's, he tries to order pounded yam and *egusi* soup, offering to pay with Nigerian money. When he tries to cover a London girl's legs for the sake of modesty, he gets slapped in the face for being fresh. These, of course, are classic instances of culture-clash comedy, but even in his own village Owoh is a ludicrous figure. We see him hunting game, pointing his rifle at an antelope while his dutiful daughters prop him up, but the pyramid collapses and they all wind up on the ground as the quarry escapes. Later, when he first learns of his brother's death abroad, he breaks into loud wails, then stops abruptly to ask his daughters why they aren't wailing too. The slapstick and obvious pretense mark him as a familiar target of African satire,

Figure 10.8 A Nollywood success story: *Osuofia in London* (2003).

the windbag patriarch. At other times, he behaves more like a folktale trickster figure, slyly getting the better of his betters. Through a combination of audacity and street smarts, Owoh manages to outwit the unscrupulous London lawyer, an anglicized Igbo man, and his brother's cunning white wife, who set out to con him. In the end, he returns home in triumph, with the money and a trophy wife. While some critics denounce Osuofia's role as caricature, it is possible to see him as a champion of African ideals over Western values. From that perspective, a young lady's immodest public posture demonstrates a certain lack of decency, and McDonald's regimented, fast-food menu typifies the inflexibility of mass production economies. One African reading of the film interprets the story as a "postcolonial narrative of conquest—the conquest of the rationality of metropolitan European logic."[37] In this view, Osuofia reverses the historical terms of conquest, the West over Africa, perhaps not unlike recent swings in the movie industry between Hollywood and Nollywood. In any case, *Osuofia in London* set new standards for African comedy and continues to be one of the most commercially successful Nollywood films of all time.

More recent video comedies have taken local targets. The title character in Udo Igwe's *Nwa Teacher* (2003) is an overbearing pedant in an adult education school. Dressed in a short-sleeved shirt with epaulets and tie, he stands commandingly before the blackboard with a ruler in his hand. At one point, he conducts a lesson on the two-times table, using his ruler as a baton while the students recite in unison. When anyone gives a wrong answer, he threatens to "synchronize their asses." This petty tyrant meets his match, though, in the form of a local healer who appears at the back of the room. Wearing a traditional shaman's garb and body paint, the old man questions this new way of doing "math," mistaking the word math for malt. In his native language, the healer tells him, "We don't use malt, we use schnapps." Furious, the teacher calls him to the front, insults him to his face, and starts to punish him. But when he strikes the healer with the ruler, his hand recoils with pain. The whole class breaks into laughter as their schoolmaster cries like a baby. As in *Osuofia in London*, the broader target here is European culture misapplied to Africans, represented by the teacher's ill-suited clothing and the uniformity that he demands with such self-aggrandizing insistence. Tellingly, it's the native healer who cuts him down to size without lifting a finger or raising his voice.

Nollywood comedies run the gamut of topics and sub-genres. In Chico Ejiro's *Fools* (2003), two brothers bedevil their village with petty acts of thievery. Hoping to improve their lot, an uncle sends them to the city. Instead of reforming, they simply up their game, pretending to be mystics in order to swindle people seeking spiritual guidance. The film satirizes pseudo-religious groups that abound in modern Africa. Kunle Afolayan's *Phone Swap* (2012) is a romance comedy/drama set in Lagos's fashion industry. Kenneth Gyang's *Confusion Na Wa* (2013) has a darker tone, with a complicated plot involving theft, corruption, sex, drugs, and a pedestrian who gets hit while texting his girlfriend on the street.

All this demonstrates how filmmaking in Africa has both distinguished itself from other regions of the world and become part of global cinema. During the independence movement, roughly 1960 to 1979, directors like Sembène and Souleymane Cissé made socially conscious films and "allegories of resistance," movies with a message. Strongly influenced by the popular liberation ideology of "Third Cinema" in Latin America and the anticolonial rhetoric of Franz Fanon, their goal was to educate the people, to inspire them to build a future free from exploitation and oppression. Satire was a prod to awaken the masses. A few other directors, like Mambéty, were less interested in political lessons, more focused on creating a new visual language to express the felt experience of life in Africa. While Sembène worked within the bounds of Socialist realism, Mambéty explored the aesthetics of magical realism and absurdist humor to explore inner truths. By the 1980s, another wave of filmmakers like Cheik Oumar Sissoko and Idrissa Ouedraogo shifted away from the language of liberation and nation building to concentrate on African issues, on indigenous history and culture. Sometimes this new Afrocentrism advocated a "return to the source" with films set in precolonial times or rural villages. Sometimes, it turned to domestic problems like internal corruption and civil war. This Afrocentric ideology developed hand in hand with a pan-African perspective, emphasizing common causes across Black Africa, foregrounding the contributions of past African civilizations to modern Africa and stressing the responsibility of Africans to shape their own future together. By the beginning of the twenty-first century, this view widened to include the African diaspora abroad and more global film practices. Bekolo's effort to reach a broader audience is part of this. So is the Nollywood phenomenon, which has inspired video film industries in Ghana, Kenya, Liberia, and Uganda. It will be worth watching how Africa's new homegrown movie industry spreads across the continent, and the African diaspora, reflecting the interests and tastes of the growing population that it serves, including filmmakers who view themselves within a global context as "Africans of the world."

African Comedy Filmography

Country	English Title	Original Title	Director	Year
Niger	*The Return of an Adventurer*	*Le retour d'un aventurier*	Moustapha Alassane	1966
Senegal	*The Money Order*	*Mandabi*	Ousmane Sembène	1968
Niger	*Women, Home, Car, Money*	*FVVA: Femme, villa, voiture, argent*	Moustapha Alassane	1972
Senegal	*The Hyena's Journey*	*Touki Bouki*	Djibril Diop Mambéty	1973
Senegal	*Xala*	*Xala*	Ousmane Sembène	1975
South Africa	*The Gods Must Be Crazy*	*The Gods Must Be Crazy*	Jamie Uys	1980
Ghana	*Love Brewed in the African Pot*	*Love Brewed in the African Pot*	Kwaw Ansah	1981
Zaire	*Life Is Rosy*	*La vie est belle*	Benoît Lamy, Mweze Ngangura	1987
Côte d'Ivoire	*Dancing in the Dust*	*Bal poussière*	Henri Duparc	1989
Cameroon	*Quartier Mozart*	*Quartier Mozart*	Jean-Pierre Bekolo	1992
Senegal	*Hyenas*	*Hyènes*	Djibril Diop Mambéty	1992
Cameroon	*Africa, I Will Fleece You*	*Afrique, je te plumerais*	Jean-Marie Téno	1992
Cote d'Ivoire	*Rue Princesse*	*Rue princesse*	Henri Duparc	1994
Mali	*Guimba, the Tyrant*	*Guimba, un tyran une époque*	Cheik Oumar Sissoko	1995

Country	English Title	Original Title	Director	Year
Burkina Faso	*Open Your Eyes*	*Puk Nini*	Fanta Régina Nacro	1996
Cameroon	*Aristotle's Plot*	*Le complot d'Aristote*	Jean-Pierre Bekolo	1996
Congo	*The Draughtsmen Clash*	*Le damier*	Bakupa-Kanyinda Balafu	1996
Cote d'Ivoire	*Coffee Color*	*Une couleur café*	Henri Duparc	1997
Mali	*Skirt Power*	*Taafé Fanga*	Adama Drabo	1997
Senegal	*Scrap Heap*	*Tableau ferraille*	Moussa Sène Absa	1997
Burkina Faso	*Konate's Thing*	*Le truc de Konaté*	Fanta Régina Nacro	2001
Gabon	*Djogo* (also: *The Elephant's Balls*)	*Les couilles de l'éléphant*	Henri-Joseph Koumba Bididi	2002
Guinea Bissau	*My Voice*	*Nha Fala*	Flora Gomes	2002
Senegal	*Madame Brouette*	*L'extraordinaire destin de Madame Brouette*	Moussa Sène Absa	2002
Nigeria	*Osuofia in London*	*Osuofia in London*	Kingsley Ogoro	2003
Nigeria	*Nwa Teacher*	*Nwa Teacher*	Ekenna Udo Igwe	2003
Nigeria	*Fools*	*Okefe*	Chico Ejiro	2003
Burkina Faso	*Kounandi*	*Kounandi*	Apolline Traore	2004
Cameroon	*The Bloodettes*	*Les saignantes*	Jean-Pierre Bekolo	2005
Senegal	*Teranga Blues*	*Teranga Blues*	Moussa Sène Absa	2007
Chad	*Sex, Okra, and Salted Butter*	*Sexe, gombo et beurre salé*	Mahamat-Saleh Haroun	2008
South Africa	*White Wedding*	*White Wedding*	Jann Turner	2009
Nigeria	*Phone Swap*	*Phone Swap*	Kunle Afolayan	2012

Films are listed chronologically. While surnames (family names) are usually put before given names (first names) in Africa, directors' names are listed here in the Western style, with the given name before the family name. For example: Ousmane (given name) Sembène (family name).

Notes

1. Valérie K. Orlando, *New African Cinema* (Rutgers, NJ: Rutgers University Press, 2017), 87–89.
2. Roy Armes, *African Filmmaking: North and South of the Sahara* (Bloomington: Indiana University Press, 2006), 110.
3. Orlando, *New African Cinema*, 2.
4. Esi Sutherland-Addy, "The Ghanaian Feature Video Phenomenon," in *FonTomFrom: Contemporary Ghanaian Literature, Theatre and Film*, ed. Kofi Anyidoho and James Gibbs (Amsterdam: Rodopi, 2000), 265–300.
5. In Françoise Pfaff, *Focus on African Films* (Bloomington: Indiana University Press, 2006), 2.
6. Orlando, *New African Cinema*, 7.
7. Léopold Senghor, "Négritude: A Humanism of the 20th Century," in *The Africa Reader: Independent Africa*, ed. Wilfred G. Cartey and Martin Kilson (London: Vintage, 1970), 179–192.
8. Olivier Barlet, *African Cinemas: Decolonizing the Gaze* (London: Zed Books, 2000), 50.
9. Philip M. Peek and Kwesi Yankaḥp, eds., *African Folklore: An Encyclopedia* (New York: Routledge, 2004), 8.
10. Harold Courlander, *A Treasury of African Folklore: The Oral Literature, Traditions, Myths, Legends, Epics, Tales, Recollections, Wisdom, Sayings, and Humor of Africa* (New York: Crown, 1975), 130.
11. Maik Nwosu, *The Comic Imagination in Modern African Literature and Cinema: A Poetics of Laughter* (New York: Routledge, 2016), 6.
12. Nwosu, *Comic Imagination*, 30.
13. In Ebenezer Obadare, *Humor, Silence, and Civil Society in Nigeria* (Rochester, NY: University of Rochester Press, 2016), 76.
14. See Férid Boughedir, "African Cinema and Ideology: Tendencies and Evolution," in *Symbolic Narratives/African Cinema: Audiences, Theory and the Moving Image*, ed. June Givanni (London: British Film Institute, 2000), 109–121.
15. Alexie Tcheuyap, "Comedy of Power, Power of Comedy: Strategic Transformations in African Cinemas," *Journal of African Cultural Studies* 22, no. 1 (2010): 25–40.
16. Frank Ukadike, *Questioning African Cinema: Conversations with Filmmakers* (Minneapolis: University of Minnesota Press, 2002), 229.
17. Ukadike, *Questioning African Cinema*, 221.
18. Kenneth W. Harrow, *Postcolonial African Cinema: From Political Engagement to Postmodernism* (Bloomington: Indiana University Press, 2007), 152.
19. Pierre Haffner, *Essai sur les fondements du cinéma africain* (Paris: Nouvelles éditions africaines), 1978.
20. Mwezé Ngangura, "African Cinema: Militancy or Entertainment?" in *African Experiences of Cinema*, ed. Ishaq Imruh Bakari and Mbaye B. Cham (London: British Film Institute, 1996), 64.
21. Frank Ukadike, *Black African Cinema: Conversations with Filmmakers* (Minneapolis: University of Minnesota Press, 2002), 284–285.

22. In Ukadike, *Questioning African Cinema*, 148.
23. In Olivier Barlet, "Entretien avec Henri Duparc," *Africultures* 12 (November 1988): 16–17.
24. Ukadike, *Black African Cinema*, 286.
25. Melissa Thackway, *Africa Shoots Back. Alternative Perspectives in Sub-Saharan Francophone African Film* (Bloomington: Indiana University Press, 2003), 10.
26. In Thackway, *Africa Shoots Back*, 160.
27. Jake Bright, "Meet 'Nollywood': The Second Largest Movie Industry in the World," *Fortune*, June 24, 2015, http://fortune.com/2015/06/24/nollywood-movie-industry/ . See also Norimitsu Onishi, "Nigeria's Booming Film Industry Redefines African Life," *New York Times*, February 18, 2016.
28. Zina Saro-Wiwa, "No Going Back," in *Nollywood*, ed. Pieter Hugo (Munich: Prestel Publishing, 2009). Also "No Going Back" (2008), http://www.zinasarowiwa.com/wp-content/uploads/2013/03/NO-GOING-BACK-NOLLYWOOD-ESSAY.pdf.
29. Nwosu, *Comic Imagination*, chap. 4.
30. Olaf Möller, "A Homegrown Hybrid Cinema of Outrageous Schlock from Africa's Most Populous Nation," *Film Comment* 40, no. 2 (2004): 12–13.
31. Hope Eghagha, "Magical Realism and the 'Power' of Nollywood Home Video Films," *Film International* 5, no. 4 (2007): 71–76.
32. Matthias Krings and Onookome Okome, eds., *Global Nollywood: The Transnational Dimensions of an African Video Film Industry* (Bloomington: Indiana University Press, 2013), 5.
33. *Welcome to Nollywood*, DVD, directed by Jamie Meltzer, 2007 (Outpost Studios). See also *Nollywood Babylon*, DVD, directed by Ben Addelman and Samir Mallal, 2008 (Lorber HT Digital, 2009).
34. Chukwuma Okoye, "Looking at Ourselves in the Mirror: Agency, Counter-Discourse, and the Nigerian Video Film," *Film International* 5 no. 4 (2007): 20–29.
35. See Onookome Okome, "Nollywood and its Critics," in *Viewing African Cinema in the Twenty-First Century: Art Films and the Nollywood Video Revolution*, ed. Mahir Saul and Ralph Austen (Athens: Ohio University Press, 2010), 26–41.
36. John C. McCall, "The Pan-Africanism We Have: Nollywood's Invention of Africa," *Film International* 5, no. 4 (2007): 92–97, https://opensiuc.lib.siu.edu/cgi/viewcontent.cgi?referer=https://search.yahoo.com/&httpsredir=1&article=1010&context=anthro_pubs.
37. Onookome Okome, "Reversing the Filmic Gaze: Comedy and the Critique of the Postcolony in *Osuofia in London*," in Krings and Okome, *Global Nollywood*, 154.

11
Film Comedy in Scandinavia

A Swede and a Finn decide to drink together. With several bottles of vodka between them, they sit across the table from each other without a word, knocking off shot after shot. After three hours, the Swede lifts a glass and says, "*Skol*." The Finn responds with disapproval: "Did we come here to talk or to drink?"

This well-worn Swedish joke tells us a thing or two about Nordic humor. There is, of course, the focus on hard liquor, a cultural cliché of life in Scandinavia and other northern climes. Then there is the timing: long stretches of uncommunicative silence punctuated with a sudden outburst, seemingly from nowhere. The belated expression of camaraderie—*Skol* for "cheers"—may seem a little odd to us after so many shared shots, but the Finn's response seems even odder, more ironic, after so much shared silence. There may even be a hint of transnational satire, a putdown by Swedes of their Finnish neighbors.

Welcome to the peculiar world of Nordic comedy. The word "peculiar" seems apt because it's one of several terms used to describe the quality of humor in this part of the globe, along with odd, quirky, twisted, dark, and even morbid. Watch a film like *Trollhunter* (*Trolljegeren*, 2010), a gloomy fantasy in which a lone, laconic Norwegian hunter tracks down giants in the far reaches of his native land. His job is secret, solitary, and extremely dangerous, but the part he hates is filling out the paperwork required by TSS, the Troll Security Service bureaucracy. There is a form to complete for each dead troll. Or watch *The Man Without a Past* (*Mies vailla menneisyytta*, 2002), a Finnish film in which a nameless man finds refuge in a cargo container after being mugged and brutally beaten. An electrician hooks up the man's new home to the city's power supply, asking little in return. "If you see me face down in the gutter, just turn me on to my back," says the electrician with a shrug before he leaves.

Some scholars employ the Icelandic term *Gálgahúmor*, or "gallows humor," finding something peculiarly grim in films that pass for comedies in Iceland, Norway, Finland, Sweden, and Denmark, countries commonly labeled Nordic. They trace this sardonic sensibility back to the Old Norse/Icelandic sagas in which heroes laugh defiantly at their enemies or die with a sarcastic witticism on their lips ("No need to look at the leg I just chopped off. It's gone").[1] Claus Gruber, Danish ambassador to the United Kingdom, goes so far as to suggest that the British predilection for understatement and wry sarcasm is an Anglo-Saxon legacy, a gift left by the Viking invaders.[2] Other observers seek explanations for

When the World Laughs. William V. Costanzo, Oxford University Press (2020). Oxford University Press
DOI: 10.1093/oso/9780190924997.001.0001

Nordic humor in the region's weather, geography, or social issues: in its cold climate; its vast, empty spaces; its long, dark winters; its high suicide rates. While these may all be contributing factors, it will help to begin with a long view of the history, politics, and demographic facts that helped to shape the film industry in this part of the world.

The people who live here trace their ancestors back millennia to the hunter-gatherers, and later farmers, who first inhabited the northern fringe of Europe. During the Viking Age (eighth century to the middle of the eleventh century), Norwegian and Danish tribes sailed south and west, some pillaging and eventually settling in modern Britain and France. Swedish tribes traveled south and east to Finland, to the Baltic lands, and throughout Russia all the way to Constantinople, establishing important trade routes and a legendary dynasty. Separate kingdoms emerged as the area was Christianized during the tenth through thirteenth centuries. By 1397, the three kingdoms of Denmark, Norway, and Sweden were united in the Kalmar Union, a fragile merger that gave way to various divisions and regroupings under pressure from local power plays and continental conflicts, including the Protestant Reformation, Russian imperialism, Napoleon, and two world wars.

The term "Scandinavia" gained traction in the mid-1800s, originally applied to the three central kingdoms and the nations they became: Denmark, Norway, and Sweden. Later, it was loosely extended to include Finland (linked by geography, but distinguished by a different language and ethnic group) and Iceland (the island country farther west settled by Vikings in the ninth century). Today, it is more common to refer to these five nations as the Nordic countries. Those who generalize about cultural identity find common traits among the people, their traditions, and their ideas. Most dialects of Danish, Norwegian, and Swedish are mutually intelligible. Native speakers of these dialects can read each other's newspapers and understand each other's television shows. While there is a larger linguistic leap to Icelandic and a virtual gulf between these four languages and Finnish, all six Nordic nations share certain economic principles and social policies, like free-market capitalism and adherence to a welfare state. According to the *New World Encyclopedia*, they also place a high value on individual freedoms, privacy, discretion, and tolerance.[3]

Many of these values are reflected in the film traditions of the Nordic countries. Yet, as we'll see, the degree to which these films embody a homogenous cultural identity is a matter of some dispute. The editors of *Nordic National Cinemas* find a singular emphasis on individual national cinema, movies labeled as distinctly Swedish or Norwegian. Arguing that "national cinema came into existence to the extent that a nation actively attempted to construct it," they explain this national consciousness as the outgrowth of a "marginal film culture" struggling to position itself as an alternative to the dominant American film industry. These efforts were supported by government policies and the demands from festival and art-house circuits for "a corrective of sorts" to American brands.[4] A second book, *Transnational Cinema in a Global North: Nordic Cinema in Transition*, questions the national model, pointing to the increasingly interdependent global flows of talent, stories, and styles among international players. On the one hand, Nordic films borrow elements from American or Japanese genre films. On the other, Hollywood hires crossover directors like Bille August and Lasse Hallström, produces remakes of Nordic hits like *Let the Right One In* (*Låt den rätte komma in*, 2008), and incorporates features of Denmark's Dogma 95 aesthetics. The editors of *Transnational Cinema in a Global North* urge "a balanced view of the transformation of Nordic cinematic cultures" into transnational forms.[5] The contributors to *Nordic Genre Film* take another step. While they acknowledge the importance of "art" directors like Carl Dreyer or Ingmar Bergman in the early days, they propose a shift in attention toward Nordic genre films and their contributions to global popular culture: "We must focus on the history of the Nordic genre film industries and its relationship with governmental support and film institutes."[6]

The role of government is crucial in Nordic cinemas. A medium-budget movie made in Finnish or Icelandic cannot expect to recoup its full production costs from local box-office returns. One reason is the small number of native speakers. According to a recent census, the entire population of the region did not exceed 28 million in 2017, less than the state of Texas. Sweden had the most citizens (10 million), followed by Denmark (5.7 million), Finland (5.5 million), Norway (5.3 million), and Iceland (a mere 338,000).[7] With such a small market to draw on, box-office sales offer tiny yields. In 2001, for example, the combined annual returns from all five countries were less than an average Hollywood blockbuster makes in its first weekend. And Nordic films typically account for only 20% of domestic ticket sales; Hollywood takes the rest.[8] With such an uneven playing field and a strong home-field disadvantage, it's not surprising that local governments get involved.

State control of the Nordic movie industries is unique in several ways. According to some analysts, government influence is one reason why film has been considered more of an art form than a commercial product, a social force rather than mere entertainment. Under supervision from the elected guardians of culture, movies serve the same intent as Ibsen's stage plays, "to put the problems under debate." This helps to explain why so many Nordic films are based on local literature, why their protagonists so often are ordinary people rather than superheroes.[9] Not surprisingly, state funding and protective legislation come with strings attached, and it is instructive to note what different governments object to. Censorship in Finland is largely political; in Sweden it's often about violence, in Norway about sex.

Comic Sub-genres on the Northern Fringe

There is little dispute about the primacy of comedy in Nordic cinema. The experts and the data agree that "comedies have without competition been the prevalent genre in all Nordic countries,"[10] "the most popular genre throughout [Scandinavian] film history."[11] This might surprise outsiders who don't get all the jokes, especially when Norwegian or Finnish films that are marketed as "deliciously funny" or "hilarious" seem more like sober dramas. Non-Nordic viewers raised on the "pure comedies" of Jim Carrey or the Marx Brothers often fail to understand the hybrid nature of Nordic humor, how laughter can serve social and aesthetic ends.

Film historians speak of "golden ages," by which they mean classical periods of high production and global distribution, usually of genre films. In these terms, the Danish golden age dates from 1910 to 1917, when directors like Carl Dreyer, stars like Asta Nielsen, and producers like Benjamin Christensen rivaled Hollywood's silent movie talent. The Swedish golden age is usually placed between 1917 and 1924, when the works of Victor Sjöström and Mauritz Stiller were known around the world. Norway's moment arrived even later, arguably in the 1960s, when local municipalities (rather than the state) fueled initiatives in film and television projects. Yet whatever international prominence may have been achieved during these times, it is the domestic hits that tell us more about Nordic comedy and the popular tastes of native audiences.

In a study of 1930s Swedish films, Per Olov Qvist estimates that about 70% of the decade's movies were comedies, dominated by farce.[12] With its fast-paced plots of mistaken identities and other narrative snags, farce appealed to the middle classes throughout Europe. The genre's comic horseplay, ludicrous characters, and preposterous plots were easy to get and soon forget, a pleasurable evening of light entertainment. More particular to Swedish tastes was a sub-genre known as *folklustspel*, or folk comedy. Rooted in theatrical tradition and folksy tales, these films featured simple people, crude stereotypes, and lots of merriment, always ending with virtue rewarded and villainy soundly punished. The humor was unsophisticated and chaotic, so that critics—likening their artless quality to a pitcher of cheap beer—belittled them as "Pilsner films."

Another trans-Nordic sub-genre started in Denmark with Erik Balling's *The Olsen Gang* (*Olsenbanden*) series, which ran from 1968 into the early 1980s. Each of the thirteen films centers on a gang of three small-time criminals who plan the perfect crime that always goes awry. Their plots, like the crimes, follow a predictable pattern. Typically, the ringmaster emerges from prison with ideas for a new heist. First, the gang steals equipment for the heist, which might be balloons, bottle openers, or Lego blocks. Then they mobilize their contacts—lawyers, businessmen, government officials, and other white-collar types—who turn out to be even more criminal than they are. Typically, the foolproof plan ends badly because the gang has underestimated the dishonesty of people in power. Egon, the mastermind, goes back to jail, where he hatches another plan, another movie. Beyond the predictable verbal humor and slapstick gags, the fun in watching the series depends on parody and satire. The weary clichés of heist films are duly represented and lovingly lampooned, but the main target is arguably Danish authority. As Superintendent Jensen keeps saying to Inspector Holm, "The only thing the police can do when the real big criminals come by is offer them protection!"

After its big success in Denmark, the series was adopted in Norway and adapted for Norwegian audiences. These films essentially were remakes, following the same basic plots but with locally known actors speaking in Norwegian. Some remakes were shot in Denmark using the same sets to keep budgets low. But while Danish critics praised the series, it was openly scorned by the more sober, politically oriented critical establishment in Norway. Despite this condescension, or perhaps because of it, Norwegians flocked to the theatres for each installment. By the 1980s, Sweden was producing its own version, called *Jönssonligan* (the Jönsson Gang), attuned to Swedish tastes in politics and humor. Suggestively, the Swedish gang's archenemy is named Jacob Morgan Rockefeller Wall-Enberg Jr. A comparative study of these satires might reveal some of the subtle differences between the nations of Scandinavia. To take just one example, the Swedish gang distracts the guards with candy; the Danish gang uses pornography.

Sweden

"Probably no other nation of comparative population has matched the artistic success of Sweden in the cinema."[13] So mused the pioneering scholar of Scandinavian films, Peter Cowie, in 1970. Cowie was thinking of the great directors who had propelled Swedish cinema into the international limelight during its early years—Victor Sjöström, Mauritz Stiller, Ingmar Bergman—and a few who were then riding the crest of a new wave, like Bo Widerberg (*Elvira Madigan*, 1967), Mai Zetterling (*Loving Couples* [*Älskande par*], 1964), and Jan Troell (*The Emigrants* [*Utvandrarna*], 1971). For festival audiences around the globe, these names were synonymous with art cinema, serious-minded works that took psychological issues and social problems as their central concerns. But some of these same directors also ventured into comedy.

Stiller's best-known foray into the genre is *Erotikon* (1920), a sophisticated comedy of manners. Based on a 1917 stage play, the story centers on a stuffy professor of entomology whose preoccupation with the sexual life of insects blinds him to the erotic escapades around him. While he's lecturing at the podium, contrasting the red-spotted bark beetle's preference for polygamy with the monogamous violet-blue variety, his students are cavorting with his pretty niece behind the classroom door. Meanwhile, his wife, Irene, consults her datebook for the day's adventures. "Two p.m.: Teach furrier a lesson in patience. Three p.m.: Take to the skies with Baron Felix." After amusing herself with the exasperated fur merchant, she meets the baron, flying in his two-seater airplane over the Swedish countryside, while another suitor, an artist, eyes her from the ground through binoculars. Cowie dubbed *Erotikon* "an elegant pirouette of a film, sensational at the time because of its lack of inhibitions and its risqué innuendoes."[14] Despite its local source and setting, Mauritz's urbane wit feels more Viennese than Swedish. This may have something to do with the director's Russian Jewish heritage. It should come as no surprise that Ernst Lubitsch and Billy Wilder, Jews with a kindred birthright, were strongly influenced by his work.

By contrast, Bergman's humor, when it surfaces, is more in keeping with the Swedish national style. Those who know him as the director of soul-searing films like *Through a Glass Darkly* (*Såsom i en spegel*, 1961) or *Hour of the Wolf* (*Vargtimmen*, 1968) often are surprised to find a lighter-hearted Bergman in his earlier work. *A Lesson in Love* (*En lektion i kärlek*, 1954) bears the subtitle, "A Comedy for Grown-Ups." Its self-ironic jokes begin before the credits roll: "This comedy might have been a tragedy—but the gods were kind." Bergman reveals the playful, sunny side of his dark soul in films like *Summer with Monika* (*Sommaren med Monika*, 1953) and *Smiles of a Summer Night* (*Sommaranatten leende*, 1955), titles that contributed to Sweden's reputation for hedonistic romps during the height of summer.

Smiles is a roundelay of mishaps and misunderstandings spinning around the poles of love and infidelity. Fredrik Egerman and his son Henrik compete for the attention of Frederik's young second wife, Anne. Fredrik, a middle-aged lawyer, has not yet been able to consummate his marriage to the beautiful Anne, who secretly loves the twenty-year-old Henrik, a student of theology. These relationships are further complicated by the presence of a voluptuous housemaid (Petra), a lusty male servant (Frid), a former mistress (Desirée), a jealous army officer (Count Malcolm), and the officer's wife (Charlotte). Bergman's script sparkles with witty epigrams in the ironic manner of Oscar Wilde. At one point, after seeing Fredrik together with Desirée, Malcolm's current lover, the count proclaims to Charlotte, "My wife may cheat on me, but if anyone touches my mistress I become a tiger." Later, to Desirée, he says, "One can dally with my mistress, but touch my wife and I become a tiger." *Smiles of a Summer Night* combines the sophistication of boudoir comedy with the hearty merriment of *folklustpel*. On Midsummer Night, the shortest night of the year, we find Frid leaning against a tree, musing on summer love with a drink in one hand and Petra in the other (Figure 11.1). "This is the time when young lovers open their hearts and their

Figure 11.1 Time for love in a *Smiles of a Summer Night* (1955).

loins," he begins. "We invoke love, call out to it, beg for it . . . tell lies about it, but we never have it." Frid's discourse is interrupted by Henrik, who whispers something in his ear. All three rush to the barn, where Anne is waiting to run off with the young would-be clergyman. Meanwhile, watching from the shadows, Fredrik picks up the symbolic veil that the wind has blown off Charlotte during the escape. Pauline Kael considered *Smiles* to be "one of the few classics of carnal comedy, raising bedroom farce to elegance and lyric poetry."[15] What makes this all the more remarkable is that Bergman was going through a period of depression at the time. His marriage had ended, a love affair had gone awry, and two films had failed at the box office. It's another example of humor rising from the depths of despair, the kind gods turning tragedy to comedy.

Bergman's comedies were part of the revolution in mores that challenged sexual taboos after World War II. The same free-spirited impulse unleashed the American sex comedies of the 1950s and 1960s (*Gentlemen Prefer Blondes*, 1953; *Some Like It Hot*, 1959) as well as the frisky pink comedies of Italy (*Bread, Love and Jealousy* [*Pane, amore e gelosia*], 1953), but it was Swedish cinema that really stretched the boundaries with explicit pictures like Vilgot Sjöman's *I Am Curious (Yellow)* (*Jag är nyfiken—en film i gult*, 1967) and *I Am Curious (Blue)* (*Jag är nyfiken—en film I blått*, 1968). Feminism was another potent force. In *The Girls* (*Flickorna*, 1968), Mai Zetterling traced the quest of three young Swedish women for independence from the men in their lives, giving a modern twist to *Lysistrata*, the ancient Greek satire on gender relations by Aristophanes.

While Swedes enjoyed their share of local comedies during the next three decades, few of these films made it out of the country until the new millennium. By then, the optimistic flower children of the sexual revolution had lost some of their bloom. Their cynicism is reflected in Lukas Moodysson's *Together* (*Tillsammans*, 2000), a bittersweet comedy set in a 1970s commune near Stockholm. The title is ironic, since the commune members spend much of their time arguing, usually in pointlessly political terms. A woman rails against the gender coding of her children's pink and blue blankets. Men protest against doing the dishes because it is so bourgeois. This is a film in which people deliver odes to oatmeal, name their children Tet (after the North Vietnamese Tet offensive), and take turns playing "torture the Pinochet victim." The only sensible, mature members of the group seem to be the children, who parade around with signs saying, "We Want Meat" (Figure 11.2). Yet Moodysson is sympathetic to his endearingly flawed characters. *Together* is not so much a hostile satire as an amusingly nostalgic appraisal of an era.

Roy Andersson's *Songs from the Second Floor* (*Sånger från andra våningen*), released in the same year, offers a distinctly darker view of humanity. Presented as a series of loosely linked scenes, the film takes place in a nameless city through which a procession of peculiar characters moves in and out of focus. Two men chat. One stands; the other reclines, coffined in a solar tanning unit with only the soles of his feet showing. The standing man appears to be a businessman. "Life is a market," he says. "It's all about buying something so you can sell it with an extra zero." In another scene, a man with an accent is looking for someone named Allan Svensson. A group of passersby suddenly attacks him, kicking and

Figure 11.2 "We Want Meat." Swedish children learn the art of protesting in *Together* (2000).

stabbing while a line of people at a bus stop watch impassively from across the street. A few youngsters go up the street on roller skates. In a third scene, a stage magician starts to saw a man in half. His victim begins to scream. At first the magician, and the audience, think it's a gag and begin to laugh. But the victim shows up later at the hospital, shuffling in with a bandaged stomach. A fourth scene zooms in on someone in a train station crying out in pain, his hand caught in the passenger car door. A crowd has stopped to watch, some sympathetic, but the door can only be opened from the inside. Should we laugh, or weep, or leave the theater?

While Moodysson presents his characters with bemused compassion, Andersson remains distant and detached. Unmoving and unmoved, his camera captures the action in long shots. The tones are mostly blues and grays. Strange things happen, one after another, with no logical connection, as in a bad dream. If this is comedy, it is close to the absurdist comedy of Franz Kafka, the surrealist slapstick of Samuel Beckett.

Films like these can be regarded as droll comments on modern Swedish life, wry critiques of capitalism or goofy sendups of the welfare state. In *Jalla! Jalla!* (2000), a romantic comedy by Josef Fares, certain attitudes toward immigrants get their comeuppance. The film centers on two unlikely working-class buddies: a Lebanese-born immigrant (Roro) and a native-born Swede (Mans). While the movie has its share of comic mishaps and pratfalls, the funniest scenes are about reversing stereotypes. Tall, muscular, and fair-skinned Mans would normally be typecast as the strong, silent type, a ladies' man who speaks the language and knows the ways of Swedish culture. Instead, he turns out to be naïve and insecure about his sex life, the victim of erectile dysfunction. In contrast, skinny, dark-haired Roro has a satisfying physical relationship with his Swedish girlfriend and feels perfectly at home in his neighborhood. When Mans visits Roro's household, it's Mans who feels like the outsider. He doesn't understand the customs or the food. Roro's grandmother inspects his shaved head and mocks him as unmarriageable material. But eventually the two friends help each through the entanglements of family and romantic love. Fares, a Lebanese immigrant himself, gives us a happy ending in which everything works out and ethnic stereotypes cancel out each other in a cheerful multicultural resolution.

Longer life expectancy and declining birth rates create another problem in contemporary Sweden: an aging population. This topic, too, has become fair game for Swedish comedies. One of the most successful in Sweden—and an international hit—was *The Hundred-Year-Old Man Who Climbed Out the Window and Disappeared* (*Hundraåringen som klev ut genom fönstret och försvann*, 2013). Director Felix Herngren based his film on a popular Swedish novel of the same name, casting beloved comedian Robert Gustafsson in the title role of Allan Karlsson. On the day of his centenary celebration, Allan sneaks out of his nursing home in slip-ons and an open robe with no particular plan (Figure 11.3). Looking tired and confused, he steps on the pansies beneath his window and sets off down the road, accompanied by the oom-pah-pah of a tuba on the soundtrack. The offbeat sound follows him everywhere, setting a quaintly quirky tone for the entire film. Herngren follows the conventions of a road movie as the old man gathers an odd assortment of friends along the way. There is an irascible retiree, a perpetual student, an independent-minded, middle-aged woman, and a circus elephant, plus the bungling biker gang and inept policeman who are chasing them. Allan's long life is narrated intermittently in flashbacks. His lifelong passion for blowing things up leads to encounters with the world leaders of his time, not unlike Forrest Gump. We see him fighting alongside Republican revolutionaries and sharing drinks with Franco during the Spanish Civil War. He's there with Robert Oppenheimer working on the Manhattan Project, raising glasses with Harry Truman and Joseph Stalin, discussing walls with Ronald Reagan, and befriending Einstein's stupid brother Herbert. At age fifty, Gustafsson plays Allan at all stages of adulthood and old age. With his crusty voice, expressive face, and troubled eyes, he's not entirely unsympathetic, nor is he wholly loveable. In an interview, the actor explained that Swedish audiences prefer understated performances and self-ironic portraits: "We like to make fun of ourselves, to laugh at our faults and insecurities. . . . You can find comedy in Bergman if you look carefully, but it's tuned down, a matter of small gestures." The twenty-five-year-old Herngren agreed: "Comedy is more of a local genre. Scandinavian comedy is a bit twisted, dark-toned, ironic; we tend to like comedy based on our own weaknesses."[16]

Film historian Ellen Rees links this attitude to a regional style, which she calls "Nordic Quirky Feel-Good." A whole genre, she believes, has cultivated

Figure 11.3 The comic side of aging. *The Hundred-Year-Old Man Who Climbed Out the Window and Disappeared* (2013).

the perception of Scandinavians as charmingly peculiar, their odd behavior presented as a response to tragedy. This leads to a kind of emotional hybridity, combining detachment and engagement, sincerity and irony, serious drama and comic effects in the service of character development and social observation. You can have depth and still feel good. She finds these qualities in the work of Nordic auteurs like Denmark's Lars von Trier, Finland's Aki Kaurismäki, and Norway's Bent Hamer. She finds it in more commercial directors like Lukas Moodysson, Josef Fares, and Petter Næss. While Rees traces the style back to Nordic movies of the 1980s, she also acknowledges a kinship with certain European and Hollywood films. The degree to which quirky feel-good movies are a Nordic specialty or part of a transnational trend is worth considering within the context of global film comedy.[17]

Denmark

Motion pictures arrived early in the densely populated land of Denmark. Nordisk Films, founded in 1906, soon became the second largest movie studio in Europe (after France's Pathé) and still produces movies for the region and abroad, making it the oldest continuously active production company in the world. In the 1920s and well into the 1950s, Danish directors like Theodor Dreyer earned worldwide reputations for making high-quality, socially responsible dramas. Like other Nordic cinemas, however, Denmark also turned out lighter fare. During the silent period, a comic vagabond team known as Doublepatte and Patachon entertained film audiences with their slapstick shenanigans even before Laurel and Hardy. In the 1950s, a successful run of *The Red Horses* (*De røde heste*, 1950) ushered in the "genial film" (*hyggesfilm*), a low-budget, family-centered, feel-good sub-genre that thrived until the 1970s on a diet of Danish humor and local scenery. And, of course, the Olsen Gang and its clones ran rampant through Scandinavia from the 1960s to the 1980s. Danish cinema did not become truly international again until the late 1980s, when two of its films won Oscars for Best Foreign Language Film: *Babette's Feast* in 1987 and Lasse Hallström's *Pelle the Conqueror* (*Pelle erobreren*) in 1987. By then, a group of ambitious young filmmakers was hatching plans for a bold new movement known as Dogme.

The Dogme 95 Collective published its manifesto in 1995. Led by Lars von Trier and Thomas Vinterberg, the group announced a "vow of chastity" and ten commandments designed to purify their art. They pledged to restrict their work to location shooting with a handheld camera. They swore to do away with outside music, outside props, special filters, special lighting, and credits to the director. Officially, the trend began with Vinterberg's *The Celebration* (*Festen*,

1998), labeled "Dogme #1," followed by von Trier's *The Idiots* (*Idioterne*, 1998), Søren Kragh-Jacobsen's *Mifune* (*Mifunes sidste sang*, 1999), and other adherents around the world.

Almost immediately, practitioners began breaking the rules. Lone Scherfig, considered the first woman to adopt the principles of Dogme 95, violated its eighth commandment—no genre films—with *Italian for Beginners* (*Italiensk for begyndere*, 2000) (Figure 11.4a). She used handheld video cameras, stuck with natural lighting, and avoided non-diegetic music on the soundtrack. She shot all scenes on location on a tiny budget. But her film is clearly a romantic comedy. Its story centers on three men and three women, all lonely hearts in need of companionship under the gray skies of Copenhagen. What brings this thirty-something crowd together is a local class in Italian. The language's romantic appeal, with its promise of milder climes, becomes the bright spot in their lonely lives. It also becomes a catalyst for new relationships. As members of the group become involved in one another's lives, they make plans to realize a common dream: a class field trip to Venice.

Several motifs thread through the light fabric of the film. Two of the women are wrestling with the problems of ailing, difficult parents. Two of the men have difficulty communicating what they feel. All the characters are struggling with their needs for self-expression, security, and love. Each one embodies variations on the themes of sorrow, solitude, and loss. Yet there is nothing preachy or formulaic about the movie's plot. The performances themselves seem natural, often spontaneous, a consequence of Scherfig's restrained approach to directing, which stresses repetition in rehearsal to the point where performance becomes second nature. For Scherfig, Dogme was a way for a spoiled generation to discipline itself.

If any Dogme director has earned the right to be called spoiled, it would be Lars von Trier, whom critic Stephen Holden dubbed "one of the foremost tricksters of world cinema."[18] For four decades, he has courted controversy and evaded easy labels with films that play with a variety of genres, themes, and styles. His 2006 comedy, *The Boss of It All* (*Direktoren for det hele*) (Figure 11.4b) centers on a humorless protagonist, Kristoffer, an actor who takes his profession too seriously for his own good. Desperate for work, he takes a job impersonating the absentee CEO of a small technology company not knowing that the man who hires him, the real boss, has been pretending to be the onsite manager in order to hoodwink his employees. The film is a caustic critique of corporate culture and the way conniving executives like Ravn, the real boss, cheat and exploit their workers. Ravn has been sending manipulative messages from headquarters to each employee, promising marriage to one, promotion to another, confessing to be gay to a third. Meanwhile, his secret motive is to sell the company to a firm in

(a)

(b)

Figure 11.4 Two faces of Danish Dogme. (a) Romantic comedy in *Italian for Beginners* (2000). (b) Sardonic satire in *The Boss of It All* (2006).

Iceland that would take over and fire the whole lot. Finnur, the Icelandic CEO, is a nasty caricature of that country's icy pragmatism. Finnur hates the Danes and their incessant chatter, bashing Ravn with terse insults and quotes from his beloved sagas.

As if to include the audience among his targets, von Trier opens the movie with a boom shot from outside the company's headquarters, a tall glass building that reflects the camera like a mirror. On the soundtrack, we hear the director's voice. "This film won't be worth a moment's reflection. It's a comedy, and harmless as such. No preaching or swaying of opinions." How credible is this? Throughout the film, von Trier uses a new computer technique called Automavision, which allows the camera to zoom or change its angle randomly during a shot. Characters seem to mysteriously appear and disappear from view, yet one more instance of the director's trickery. His final ironic jest is addressed directly to us, the viewers. At the film's conclusion, the disembodied voice returns: "So ends our comedy. I apologize to those who wanted more, and those who wanted less; those who got what they came for—deserve it."

The shades of Danish humor darkened through the early 2000s with comedies like Anders Thomas Jensen's *Adam's Apples* (*Adams æbler*, 2005) and grew coarser with Mikkel Norgaard's *Klown* (*Klovn—The Movie*, 2010). Jensen loosely based his movie on the book of Job, one of the gloomier stories in the Bible. Adam is a skinhead on parole, a former gang leader with an anger management problem. He's sent for rehabilitation to a church run by a priest named Ivan who insists that humanity is basically good, despite all evidence to the contrary surrounding him. Ivan delivers his sermon to a nearly empty church. "If the game of chess had undergone the same development as humans, the queen would be in front, the rooks would be crooked, and the pawn would be the main piece," he says unhelpfully. An old man rises from his pew and tries to leave, but Ivan stops him. "Is the word of God boring you, Poul?" When he reminds Poul that the toilet is locked during the service for reasons of security, the man sits down. Later we learn that Poul is an old concentration camp Gestapo. The other men in rehab include Gunnar, a kleptomaniac rapist, and Khalid, a Saudi thief who robs international banks on principle. Much of the film's humor spins around this motley crew. One day, Ivan, Gunnar, and Khalid are puzzling over the church's only apple tree, which is overwhelmed by crows. Gunnar's pet cat doesn't seem to help. Then Adam approaches, pulling a pistol from behind his back and taking aim. Ivan gives his consent: "Let's try shooting them." Suddenly, Khalid produces his own weapon: "For sake of fuck, why didn't you say we could use guns?" he exclaims and proceeds to dispatch half-a-dozen birds in quick succession. For good measure, he shoots Gunnar's pet. "It was a shitty cat anyhow," says Ivan. "Let's have no accusations."

It turns out that Ivan's spirit of forgiveness and his optimistic outlook camouflage a deep depression. God has been testing him, like Job. He was a victim of child abuse, he has a large tumor in his brain, and there are worms in the apples. As things go from bad to worse, the film's sense of humor is tested too. We may well ask, what's funny about punishing a good man like Ivan even if he could rise from the dead?

Klown is punishing in another way. Based on a successful television series with the same name, it features the two star comedians from that series as mismatched buddies roaming through the Danish countryside, leaving a trail of mayhem and confusion in their wake. Both men are losers, but in different ways. Clueless about women and hopelessly inept as a potential parent, Frank (Frank Hvam) wants to prove himself to his pregnant girlfriend, but he makes a poor choice of camping buddies. His friend Caspar (Caspar Christensen) is super-confident and oversexed; the main objective of his "Tour de Pussy" is to bed as many women as he can (Figure 11.5). To complicate matters, Frank has kidnapped his timid twelve-year-old nephew and taken him along. The humor here is raunchy, sometimes shocking, often silly. In one scene, Frank arrives at

Figure 11.5 Two mismatched buddies toast their "Tour de Pussy" in *Klown* (2010).

a high-class brothel in a tux, but the head of the establishment turns him away, saying he's too ugly for admission. "Non-negotiable" is her tight-lipped verdict. The reason for this snub, it seems, is that the owner holds a grudge against Frank from their book club because Frank never read *Heart of Darkness* and, worse, he refused to take the club's humiliating schnozzle punishment as penance. For this sin, Frank pays with a bloody nose.

Marketers likened *Klown* to *The Hangover* (2009), the American sendup of loutish male behavior. Critics found elements of Dogme 95 and other links to Lars von Trier.[19] The Danish pubic loved it: One-sixth of the country's population bought tickets, making it the most successful Danish movie since *Italian for Beginners* and signaling a shift in sensibility, perhaps, from gentle romantic comedy to rowdy, high-testosterone satire.

Norway

One of the features distinguishing Norwegian cinema from others is its unique municipal system, which grants the rights for public screenings to municipal councils. Begun in 1913, this longstanding practice is based on the principle that making and showing movies are privileges that bear a responsibility to society. Other countries, including Sweden and Denmark, have exercised the power to monitor this social responsibility through state oversight, but Norway distributed this power into local hands. One result is that Norwegian films tend to be closely linked with community interests, reflecting the values of a "welfare society." Another is that filmmaking in Norway has remained relatively fragmented and weak, "a cottage industry living from hand to mouth."[20] Money from ticket sales is regularly allocated to hospitals and other public institutions instead of being reinvested in the film industry itself. When Norwegians do buy tickets, they spend eight kroners out of ten on American pictures, considerably more than their neighbors in Denmark or Sweden.[21]

It's not surprising, then, that comedy and communal issues developed side by side in Norway. The 1950s were dominated by socially conscious romantic comedies. Nils Müller's *We Are Getting Married* (*Vi gifter oss*, 1951) is about a young couple facing the postwar housing shortage. Øyvind Vennerød's *Dust on the Brain* (*Støv på hjernen*, 1959) dealt with changes in women's roles in a working-class neighborhood. For decades, most Norwegian films stayed within the country. The earliest to travel overseas were *Orion's Belt* (*Orions belte*, 1985) and *Pathfinder* (*Veiviseren*, 1987), both adventure films. It took comedy more than a decade to find international audiences with *Elling* (2001), a story about an autistic man and his sex-obsessed roommate. (▶ See "Case Study for Chapter 11: *Elling*" on the website.)

Time and again, Norwegian comedy holds the fun-house mirror up to national identity, as Bent Hamer's movies demonstrate. His *Kitchen Stories* (*Salmer fra Kjøkkenet*, 2003) is more of a two-way mirror, making fun of Swedish and Norwegian views of one another. The opening titles appear over a long shot of a desolate, wintry road. A long line of polished metal trailers shifts from the left side of the road to the right as it enters Norway from Sweden (Figure 11.6). A Swedish man gets out, complaining that he's nauseated. It's not just the disorienting feeling of driving on the wrong side of the road: Once inside the

Figure 11.6 A caravan of Swedish researchers enters Norway in *Kitchen Stories* (2003).

Norwegian border, his innards have been yanked out of place, a case of cultural vertigo. Folke Nilsson has come to study the kitchen habits of Norwegian men. The Swedes, famous for their efficiency research, want to analyze this male behavior in order to improve their kitchen products. By the rules of the research institute, Folke has to sit high up in an umpire's chair in Isak Bjørvik's kitchen and observe the man from there without saying a word. The caravan of matching vehicles, the insistence on a "scientific" study, the detached observer's seat (with its echo of Swedish neutrality during World War II)—all have their origin in Swedish history and Norwegian attitudes toward their neighbor to the southeast. Hamer's idea originated with a book on postwar research on the efficiency of Swedish housewives. Norwegians also come under comic scrutiny. When the phone rings, Isak fails to pick it up. "Why don't you answer?" Folke asks. Isak knows his neighbor has called to say that he'll be over for coffee, but he doesn't want to pay the phone bill. "Forty øre per minute; need I say more?" This stinginess is but one of his local traits. Chauvinistic skepticism is another. When Folke offers him an open-faced sandwich, he regards it suspiciously, muttering the Swedish name: "Smörgås, you Swedes sure have strange names for things." But despite the odd name (literally buttergoose, the root of *Smörgåsbord*), he eats the whole thing willingly. Gradually, Folke and Isak learn to communicate and understand each other, so two men in a kitchen overcome centuries of history and national distrust.

Hamer's next film, *O'Horten* (2007), takes up another stereotype of the Norwegian character. O'Horten is a retiring railroad engineer who lives alone. The "O" stands for his first name, Odd. It's a common boy's name in Norway, but it may also be a joke, since his behavior indeed seems odd to many viewers. Quiet and aloof, always with a pipe, O'Horten is a creature of routine. For forty years, he has conducted the same train between Oslo and Bergen in the same suit, staying at the same boardinghouse, making only small talk with the woman owner. His life is filled with silences. One of the funniest scenes is his retirement party, a comedy of contrasts. His colleagues, all identically dressed, raise a toast to his long career and award him the Silver Locomotive (Figure 11.7). They stand in unison, moving their arms like train wheels, making choo-choo sounds and a conclusive whistle. Then they play a game of Guess that Sound. "That's a 73080 Camelot." "That's the train from Trondheim to Bodø departing on Track 1." Doubtless, the ritual is hilarious for an audience of Norwegian train conductors, but it's funny enough even for an outsider. Odd meets other odd fellows along the way, including a garrulous drunk named Sissener. Sissener claims to be a diplomat, shows him a wall full of art from Africa and a meteorite older than the solar system, then convinces him that he can drive with his eyes closed. The next day, Sissener starts his car with a bag over his head and Odd in the passenger seat. Hamer's film is filled with strange surprises that contrast with Odd's predictable

Figure 11.7 The Norwegian railroad guild honors one of its own in *O'Horten* (2007).

life, making it an entertaining commentary on the reticent Nordic male. Another "quirky feel-good" film.

Equally idiosyncratic and reticent is Hans, the protagonist of *Trollhunter*. André Øvreda directed much of this film as if it were assembled from found footage, a technique made popular by movies like *The Blair Witch Project* (1999) and *Cloverfield* (2008). We are asked to believe that the shaky, badly framed digital images we see were produced by a group of student filmmakers trying to cover a story about bear poachers. The three students soon learn that Hans, the man they're following, is no poacher but an employee of the TSS, the government's clandestine Troll Security Service. Hans is a crack hunter hired to kill trolls and keep their existence secret from the public. At first, he won't speak to the students, but gradually he grows fond of their courage and persistence. He lets them tag along. They, in turn, are alternately horrified and fascinated by his work, eventually coming to regard him as an unsung national hero.

Hans is certainly an odd hero. Half hidden behind a coarse beard and bushy moustache, he seems cold and uncommunicative, focused only on his work. Nor is he particularly happy with his job. In a local eatery, wolfing down a meal of steak and eggs, he complains to the students about the paperwork (Figure 11.8). For every kill, he has to fill out a lengthy Slayed Troll Form. His matter-of-fact way of talking about trolls is part of the film's preposterous humor. He describes their single eye ("in the middle of their original head"), the function of multiple heads ("to scare other trolls and impress the females"), their low intelligence ("in the pits"), and eating habits ("How hard is it to eat rocks?") as if they were

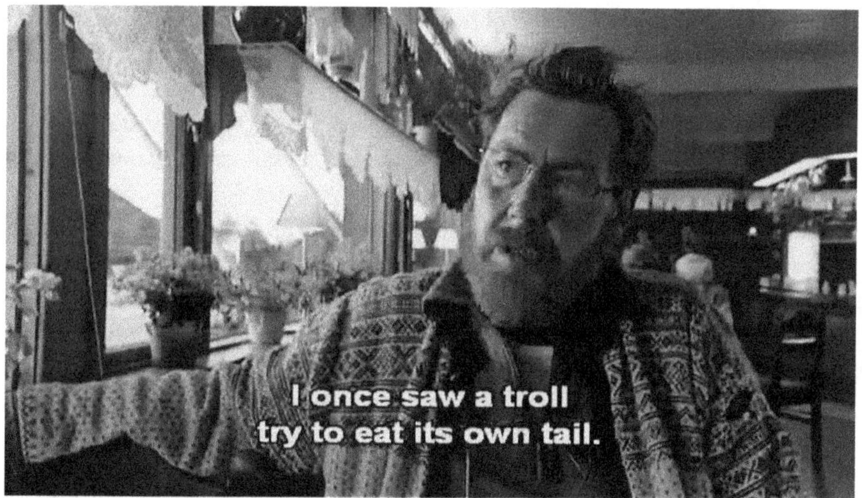

Figure 11.8 A professional troll-tracker talks about his job in *Trollhunter* (2010).

a commonplace species of game. But the hunting scenes are genuinely horrific. Trolls are immense, powerful creatures, and since they are nocturnal, they must be hunted at night. The student crew picks up strange sounds in the darkness. The camera shakes, catching only fragments of the action: heavy breathing, growling, screams, blurred images of panic. "Get the hell out of here!" someone shouts. "This is a bad joke!"

By 2010, the found-footage horror film was already a transnational genre, but Øvreda makes this one markedly Norwegian. The trolls derive from local folklore, rooted in Norse mythology, circulated through Scandinavian fairy tales, and immortalized in works like Henrik Ibsen's play, *Peer Gynt*, and Edvard Grieg's music, "In the Hall of the Mountain King." Grieg's eccentric melodies, haunted by the eerie voices of oboe and bassoon, trundle through the soundtrack. What's more, the hunter's journey northward takes us through Norway's iconic landscape, the snowcapped mountains and majestic fjords of the northwest coast. Since our only point of view is the camera's lens, we are immersed in the country's natural beauty and ferocity. There is also plenty of homegrown satire. The state-run TSS is a persistent target. An officious bureaucrat named Finn wants to disguise the fact that trolls have killed cattle in the area along with two German tourists, so he hires a Polish man to bring a dead bear as a scapegoat. He wants people to think that the bear was responsible for the deaths. Unfortunately, Pioter the Polish painter brings a Russian bear, not one from Scandinavia. It will have to do. Finn makes fake bear tracks all throughout the site, but these don't fool the locals. No bear walks like that. The fact that most immigrants in Norway are

Polish makes Pioter's accent part of the social satire: "Russian bear, Norway bear, very close, no problem." What clinches it all is the well-known fact that trolls hate Christians. In a country where few citizens consider themselves religious these days, most of the student crew feels safe. It turns out, though, that their cameraman is a closet Christian. When he's devoured by a man-eating mountain troll, he's promptly replaced by a Muslim woman.

Jens Lien's *The Bothersome Man* (*Den brysomme mannen*, 2006) stretches Scandinavian satire in a different direction, using the machinery of science fiction to comment on the welfare society. Its eponymous hero, Andreas Ramsfjell, is bothersome because he doesn't fit into a world that has been engineered for maximum happiness at the expense of genuine feeling. Everything a man could want—a stable job, a furnished apartment, a beautiful girlfriend—is provided by the state. His material needs are satisfied, but something's missing. If there is comedy in this story, and there is, it has the acerbic flavor of Franz Kafka. Andreas arrives at a decrepit gas station in a desolate landscape under a gray sky. He's the only passenger on a large bus, but there's a large welcome sign to greet him. The scene could be a deadpan joke about Norway's sparsely populated countryside. The man who greets him with a single word removes the sign and takes him by car to his new home in the city, a gleaming glass dystopia of bland conformity. Everyone goes through the motions of life without true emotions. Their favorite word is "nice." After proposing to his new girlfriend at a romantic dinner, Andreas asks if there's another man in her life, and she starts giving names. There's Lars down in reception, a guy in her building named Tom, and Jens . . . "You're nice," she says, "They're all nice. Everyone's nice." There are other signs that something is amiss. When Andreas cuts off a finger in the office paper trimmer, he howls wildly, but his bloody digit is neatly sewn back on in the hospital, good as new. We are not entirely surprised, then, when he jumps in front of an oncoming train, repeatedly run over and dragged along the tracks. So excessive is the sound of crushing blows, tearing flesh, and screams that it elicits involuntary laughter. Has the macabre gallows humor of the Vikings come to this?

There is a popular Icelandic film, *White Night Wedding* (*Brúðguminn*, 2008), that ends like many comedies with a wedding. The protagonist gets to marry the girl of his dreams, but with a notable difference: The whole wedding party winds up in the ocean, soaking wet (Figure 11.9). "If you are completely happy for more than ten minutes," the groom concludes with pointed cynicism, "you are an idiot." Maybe that's why nonstop comedy is so rare in Nordic cinemas. In a region dominated by long, dark winters and wide, sparsely populated spaces, it's reasonable to find stories in which the characters are detached and taciturn, where humor is rarified, deadpan, and often grim. Notwithstanding short-lived local genres like the Swedish *folklustpel* or the Finnish lumberjack film, with their

Figure 11.9 The semi-happy ending of *White Night Wedding* (2008).

slapstick antics and hearty comic heroes, what passes for Nordic humor in these days of global brands seems more akin to the existential sensibilities of Kafka and Beckett, as if the northern fringe of Europe were a vast theater of the absurd.

Scandinavian Comedy Filmography

Country	English Title	Original Title	Director	Date
Sweden	*Erotikon*	*Erotikon*	Mauritz Stiller	1920
Finland	*Hello, Rillumarei!*	*Hei, rillumarei!*	Armand Lohikoski	1954
Sweden	*Smiles of a Summer Night*	*Sommarnattens leende*	Ingmar Bergman	1955
Denmark	*The Olsen Gang*	*Olsen-banden*	Erik Balling	1968
Finland	*Numbskull Emptybrook in the Army*	*Uuno Turhapuro armeijan leivissä*	Ere Kokkonen	1984
Finland	*Leningrad Cowboys Go America*	*Leningrad Cowboys Go America*	Aki Kaurismäki	1989
Finland	*Zombie and the Ghost Train*	*Zombie ja Kummitusjuna*	Mika Kaurismäki	1991
Denmark	*Italian for Beginners*	*Italiensk for begyndere*	Lone Sherfig	2000
Sweden	*Songs from the Second Floor*	*Sånger från andra våningen*	Roy Andersson	2000
Sweden	*Jalla! Jalla!*	*Jalla! Jalla!*	Josef Fares	2000

Country	English Title	Original Title	Director	Date
Sweden	*Together*	*Tillsammans*	Lukas Moodysson	2000
Norway	*Elling*	*Elling*	Petter Næss	2001
Finland	*The Man Without a Past*	*Mies vailla menneisyyttä*	Aki Kaurismäki	2002
Norway	*Buddy*	*Buddy*	Mortem Tyldum	2003
Norway	*Kitchen Stories*	*Salmer fra kjøkkenet*	Bent Hamer	2003
Finland	*Producing Adults*	*Lapsia ja aikuisia—Kuinka niitä tehdään*	Aleksi Salmenperä	2004
Denmark	*Adam's Apples*	*Adams æbler*	Anders Thomas Jensen	2005
Denmark	*The Boss of It All*	*Direktøren for det hele*	Lars von Trier	2006
Norway	*The Bothersome Man*	*Den brysomme mannen*	Jens Lien	2006
Norway	*O'Horten*	*O'Horten*	Bent Hamer	2007
Sweden	*You, the Living*	*Du levanda*	Roy Andersson	2007
Denmark	*Klown*	*Klovn—The Movie*	Mikkel Nørgaard	2010
Norway	*Trollhunter*	*Trolljegeren*	André Øvredal	2010
Sweden	*The Hundred-Year-Old Man Who Climbed Out the Window and Disappeared*	*Hundraåringen som klev ut genom fönstret och försvann*	Felix Herngren	2013
Sweden	*Force Majeure*	*Turist*	Ruben Östlund	2014
Sweden	*The Square*	*The Square*	Ruben Östlund	2017

Films are arranged chronologically.

Notes

1. Jóhanna Katrín Friðriksdóttir, "Gender, Humor, and Power in Old Norse-Icelandic Literature," in *Laughter, Humor, and the (Un)making of Gender: Historical and Cultural Perspectives*, ed. Anna Foka and Jonas Liliequist (London: Palgrave Macmillan, 2015), 211–228.

2. Clair Carter, "Vikings 'Brought Sarcastic Sense of Humour to Britain,'" *Telegraph*, March 5, 2014, http://www.telegraph.co.uk/history/10677904/Vikings-brought-sarcastic-sense-of-humour-to-Britain.html.
3. "Scandinavia," *New World Encyclopedia*, http://www.newworldencyclopedia.org/entry/Scandinavia.
4. Tyutti Soila, Astrid Söderbergh Widding, and Gunnar Iversen, *Nordic National Cinemas* (New York: Routledge, 1998), 1–4.
5. Andrew K. Nestingen and Trevor Glen Elkington, eds., *Transnational Cinema in a Global North: Nordic Cinema in Transition* (Detroit, MI: Wayne State University Press, 2005), 1–10.
6. Tommy Gustafsson and Pietari Kääpä, eds., *Nordic Genre Film: Small Nation Film Cultures in the Global Marketplace* (Edinburgh: Edinburgh University Press, 2015).
7. Terri Mapes, "The Population of Nordic Countries," TripSavvy, https://www.tripsavvy.com/population-in-nordic-countries-1626872.
8. Nestingen and Elkington, *Transnational Cinema*, 6.
9. Soila et al., *Nordic National Cinemas*, 234–238.
10. Gustafsson and Kääpä, *Nordic Genre Film*, 2.
11. Soila et al., *Nordic National Cinemas*, 242.
12. Per Olov Qvist, "The 1930s' *Folklustspel* and Film Farce," in *Swedish Film: An Introduction and Reader*, ed. Mariah Larsson and Anders Marklund (Lund, Sweden: Nordic Academic Press, 2010), 119–133.
13. Peter Cowie, *Sweden 2* (New York: Barnes and Noble, 1970), 12.
14. Cowie, *Sweden 2*, 33.
15. Pauline Kael, *5001 Nights at the Movies* (New York: Henry Holt, 1982).
16. Bonus interviews, *The Hundred-Year-Old Man Who Climbed Out of the Window and Disappeared*, DVD, directed by Felix Herngren (Chicago: Music Box Films, 2014).
17. Ellen Rees, "The Nordic 'Quirky Feel-Good,'" in *Nordic Genre Film* (Edinburgh: Edinburgh University Press, 2015), 147–158.
18. Stephen Holden, "It's Not That the Boss Seems Distant. It's Just That He Doesn't Exist," *New York Times*, May 23, 2007, http://www.nytimes.com/2007/05/23/movies/23boss.html.
19. Zach Baron, "Rakes' Debauched Progress in Denmark, A Look at 'Klown,' a Raunchy Danish Comedy," *New York Times*, July 20, 2012, http://www.nytimes.com/2012/07/22/movies/a-look-at-klown-a-raunchy-danish-comedy.html>.
20. Nestingen, *Transnational Cinema in a Global North*, 262.
21. Dag Asbjørnsen and Ove Solum, "'The Best Cinema System in the World': The Municipal Cinema System in Norway: Historical and Comparative Perspectives," https://www.degruyter.com/downloadpdf/j/nor.2003.24.issue-1/nor-2017-0301/nor-2017-0301.pdf.

12
Film Comedy in South America

Ask most North Americans about their counterparts in South America and they may conjure up images of exotic landscapes: the Incan ruins of Machu Picchu high in the Andes mountains, the monumental figure of Christ stretching its wide arms above the beaches of Rio de Janeiro, the dense rain forests of the Amazon, or the windblown expanses of the Patagonian plateau. Press further and they are likely to mention the Brazilian Carnival, the Argentine tango, the economic crisis in Venezuela, drug cartels, revolutions, and military coups. An older generation may recall Hollywood's Carmen Miranda, "The Brazilian Bombshell," dancing the samba in a hat loaded with tropical fruit. Younger filmgoers are more apt to remember the edgy scenes of Brazilian street gangs in *City of God* (*Cidade de Deus*, 2002) or gritty moments from the Che Guevara road movie, *The Motorcycle Diaries* (*Diarios de motocicleta*, 2004). Some of these popular impressions come from travelogues and the US news media. Others come from feature films. The "lady in the tutti-frutti hat" was a technicolor fabrication of Twentieth-Century Fox dating back to 1943, though she still lives on in the Chiquita Banana logo. And while *City of God* and *Motorcycle Diaries* were directed by South Americans, they were made largely for export, shaped with international audiences in mind.

What images do the people of South America have of themselves? What are their day-to-day concerns, the stories that they share with one another? A good place to look for a culture's sense of self is in its comedies. As we have seen repeatedly around the world, humor is largely an assembly of in-jokes. We laugh at those who don't fit in, the guy with an odd appearance or a foreign accent. We laugh when we forget ourselves and inadvertently violate accepted rules of conduct, or we enjoy the liberating laughter when we deliberately cross the line. Understanding what people find funny or just plain fun gives us insight into their social structures and cultural beliefs. This is what makes comedy so challenging to translate, so often hard to "get," yet so crucial for gaining entry to any group.

As elsewhere, comedy is the most popular film genre throughout South America. Four out of the top ten box-office hits in Argentina have been comedies. In Chile and Brazil, the figure is seven out of ten.[1] Yet despite its obvious importance to the movie industry and to the culture at large, Latin American comedy has received relatively little serious scholarly attention. Only two books on the subject have appeared in English, both in 2018, and a sustained comparative

When the World Laughs. William V. Costanzo, Oxford University Press (2020). Oxford University Press
DOI: 10.1093/oso/9780190924997.001.0001

study of the entire region has yet to be made.[2] This chapter takes a modest step in that direction. For reasons of space, our exploration will be limited to the geographical region of South America. Regrettably, we must sidestep the important contributions to Latin American film comedy of Mexico and Cuba, for example, along with the rest of Mesoamerica and the Caribbean. Still, there is more than enough film history south of the Panama Canal to provide deep and telling insights into the people and their cultural identities.

From the northern coast of Colombia to the southern tip of Argentina, the continent of South America covers an expanse of some 6.9 million square miles, more than twice the size of the continental United States and home to roughly twice the number of inhabitants. Much like the multiethnic population of the United States, the 600 million people who live in its twelve separate nations are of mixed origin. They may trace their roots back to the ancient Mayas, Aztecs, and Incas; to the sixteenth-century Spanish and Portuguese conquistadors; to African slaves; and to more recent immigrants from Europe and Asia. The motion pictures that they make and watch naturally reflect this blend of ethnicities, its social structures, artistic traditions, and religious beliefs. Although Portuguese is the official language of only one country, the immense land mass and population of Brazil accounts for the fact that nearly as many South Americans speak Portuguese as do Spanish, with smaller enclaves speaking Dutch (in Surinam), English (in Guyana), and French (in French Guyana). Other non-Latino speakers—largely Chinese, Hindustani, German, and Italian—are scattered throughout the area, in addition to the sizeable Amerindian groups that still speak indigenous languages like Quechua, Aymara, and Guarani. The Spanish and Portuguese colonialists left a strong religious legacy (an estimated 82% are Roman Catholic today) and traces of a social hierarchy that once placed *Peninsulares* and Creoles near the top of a pyramid, Mestizos and Mulattoes in the middle, and Africans and Native Americans at the base. *Peninsulares* were born in the Iberian Peninsula. Creoles were born in the New World but were of 100% European descent, Mestizos were of mixed European and Amerindian descent, and Mulattoes were of European and African descent. All of these groups and their traditions are reflected in the multifaceted styles of art, fashion, cuisine, architecture, literature, theater, music, and dance in South America. If cinema is the most inclusive of the arts, we should be able to find most of these traditions embodied on the screen.

To understand these films in context, we also need some knowledge of local history. Well before Columbus landed in the Caribbean isles in 1492, the continent hummed with human activity. People grew chilies, beans, and potatoes as far back as 6500 BCE, adding corn, peanuts, and quinoa to their diet by 2000 BCE. They domesticated llamas and alpacas in the highlands, excavated salt from mines, spread throughout the Amazon, and populated cities that predate the great

Inca, Arawak, and Carib civilizations of the fifteenth century. By some estimates, from 20 to 30 million people lived in South America before the conquistadors and missionaries arrived with sword and cross, conquering, converting, and carrying diseases that decimated the native population. For some four hundred years, from the 1450s through the nineteenth century, European colonists dominated the region, exploiting its resources, subjugating its people, and wielding the reins of power. Then, in a succession of popular uprisings and revolts, the colonies gained independence, championed by leaders like Simón Bolivar, José de San Martín, and Bernardo O'Higgins. By 1825, most of the countries we know today had claimed independence from Europe.

But the story did not end there. Through much of the remaining century and well into the next, the political and economic picture remained unstable, roiled by border disputes, power struggles, revolution, warfare, and the exigencies of nation building. Though nominally independent, governments relied on outsiders, particularly the United States, which promoted its own national agenda through treaties, military muscle, and financial clout. The Monroe Doctrine of the 1820s, which basically opposed European control, gave way to Theodore Roosevelt's "big stick" doctrine a hundred years later, launching a period of aggressive intervention. In the 1930s and 1940s, Franklin D. Roosevelt softened the tone with his "good neighbor policy," intended to create a friendlier relationship with South American countries, an approach that encouraged ideological solidarity and trade within the Americas during World War II and later, through the Cold War with Soviet Russia. Hollywood played a major role during this era, redefining the image of Latin Americans for US audiences and vice versa.

The Cold War increased tensions between left- and right-wing groups. The 1960s and 1970s were ripe for revolution and dictatorships. In Brazil, a military coup overthrew leftist president João Goulart in 1964. In Bolivia, Hugo Banzer Suárez muscled out leftist General Juan José Torres in 1971. In Chile, Augusto Pinochet ousted democratically elected Salvador Allende in 1973, replacing him with a reactionary dictatorship lasting seventeen years. Similar events took place in Uruguay and Argentina while military forces battled leftist groups farther north in Nicaragua, Guatemala, and San Salvador. With the rise of globalization in the 1980s and 1990s, Washington maintained ties to countries in economic crisis through trade agreements and financial institutions like the World Bank and the International Monetary Fund. Still, a "pink tide" of socialist ideology continued to influence governments in Venezuela, Brazil, Paraguay, and elsewhere on the continent well into the 2000s. All of these movements and events figure in South American cinema, sometimes as a central focal point, sometimes hovering in the background or just off screen.

The cinematic history of South America has been divided by film historians into three eras.[3] From the 1920s through the 1950s, motion pictures were introduced to the region as a feature of European modernity, then developed through local industrial initiatives into a commercially successful "golden age" of genre films. From the 1960s through the 1980s, filmmakers motivated by the leftist principles of "Third Cinema" and other revolutionary movements shifted the focus from popular entertainment to political activism and awareness. Sometimes referred to as "New Latin American Cinema," this phase generated a great deal of interest among international directors and scholars, accompanied by a steep decline in production and local theatrical attendance. In contrast, a third period, from the 1990s to the present, has witnessed a resurgence of films that have enjoyed both critical and commercial success. Boosted by state funding, a widespread return to democracy, and the rise of globalism, this latest phase has been given names like the *Cinema da Retomada* in Brazil and "New Argentine Cinema" in Argentina.

Over the hundred-year-plus trajectory of film production on the continent, the films themselves sometimes seem to be distinctly national in character, like the Brazilian *chanchadas* and the Cantinflas comedies of Argentina, both creations of the "golden age." Other times seem to favor certain transcontinental trends, like the popularity of road movies near the end of the 1900s and of multinational co-production practices in more recent times. Accordingly, our attention will alternate between individual countries and more panoramic views. At the same time, we will occasionally check our bearings within a wider, global context. We will see, for example, how the early comedies in South America copied, parodied, and superseded their counterparts in Hollywood. We'll note how the ideology and aesthetics of "Third Cinema" influenced filmmaking in Africa during the 1960s and 1970s and how African directors faced similar problems when trying to preach politics to mass audiences. We will observe how current production strategies in Argentina, Uruguay, and Peru fit into a larger picture of transnational cinema, drawing talent, styles, and stories from a multicultural pool for a global audience.

Although our survey will be relatively light on theory, we will detect certain shifts in the way these movies, particularly comedies, have been filtered through various conceptual frameworks. Poblete and Suárez's *Humor in Latin American Cinema* references the standard theorists and theories of humor described in Chapter 1 of this book (Aristotle, Bergson, Bakhtin, Freud, Nietzsche, Baudelaire; superiority, incongruity, relief). Nilo Couret's *Mock Classicism*, though published in the same year, proposes a very different set of lenses (Miriam Hansen, Franco Moretti, Mariano Siskind, Laura Podalsky, Homi Bhabha, Arjun Appadurai, Gilles Deleuze; vernacular modernism, post-hegemony, cosmopolitan modernity, odographic film history, circulation theory). Perhaps most important, in this respect, is the way that comedies in general, and South American comedies in particular, are now receiving the kind of serious attention that has been long overdue.

The Golden Age of Comic Genres

It was during the arrival of the "talkies," the technology that added sound to motion pictures, that the region's two main centers of film production came into their own: Argentina and Brazil. Before then, moviegoers relied mostly on silent pictures from Europe or North America. In 1910, when three-quarters of the adults in Buenos Aires could claim a European birth, the capital of Argentina aspired to be "the Paris of the Southern Hemisphere." Within a few years, US film imports replaced European sales, and by 1926 Argentina had become the largest US market outside Europe. Sound films tipped the balance even further. People wanted to hear their own language spoken on the screen, to listen to their favorite kinds of music. Not surprisingly, Argentina's film industry began with strong connections to the tango, to local personalities from radio and vaudeville, and to Spanish-language jokes. Brazilian studios, in turn, gave birth to the *chanchada*, a form of musical comedy featuring well-known music hall and radio stars performing in the energetic spirit of Brazil's Carnival tradition.

A similar crossover from stage to screen was occurring elsewhere on the planet. In the United States; in Britain, France, Italy, and Germany; and even in Africa and Asia, the new medium of motion pictures borrowed freely from popular musical and theatrical forms of entertainment. In all these places, early movie theaters appealed to the same working-class audiences that enjoyed the music halls in England, Yoruba plays in Nigeria, or *kyogen* farce in Japan. But as Nilo Couret argues with impressive evidence and rigor, there were notable differences in Latin America. Central to his argument is the way comedians such as Argentina's Niní Marshall and Luis Sandrini used sound to get laughs. Hollywood practices and international variations of the classical Hollywood style relied on a seamless synchronicity of sound, fostering the illusion of continuous action and psychological integrity. In contrast, Marshall and Sandrini created deliberate disruptions between sound and action for comic effect.

Marshall brought her vocal talents as a radio comedian to the screen when she began making movie comedies in the 1940s. In *Hay que educar a Niní* (1941), her character takes a job as a screen double, giving voice to multiple characters through hilarious feats of ventriloquism, exploiting the humor of asynchronous sound. In *Girls Orchestra* (*Orquestra de señoritas*, 1941), she repeatedly pretends to be someone else or somewhere else by disguising her voice and mimicking background sounds, like the whistle of a train that isn't really there (Figure 12.1).

Figure 12.1 Niní Marshall in *Girls Orchestra* (1941).

As Couret points out, these gags all depend on "an incongruity of sound and source."[4]

Sandrini, a former stage and circus performer, relied on similar sound tricks in his comedies. In *Bartolo Had a Flute* (*Bartolo tenía una flauta*, 1946), he plays a poor musician trying to compose a waltz by candlelight. A wind keeps blowing out the flame and the neon advertisement outside his window flashes on and off, but in an instant of comic irony, these interruptions provide a rhythm that helps him write the song. "Who says that ads are useless?" he quips triumphantly. In *La casa de Quirós* (1937), his frustrated efforts to express himself are aided by another set of verbal accidents. Here he is Casimiro, an Argentinian merchant's son in love with the daughter of a Spanish nobleman. Distracted by amorous thoughts, he's unable to focus on his job—until his father inadvertently helps to translate his stuttering Spanish ("la . . . mi . . . fa") into the language of music and love (the melodic scale beginning la-mi-fa ends with sol, the girl's name) (Figure 12.2). Couret sees this as another example of humorous nonsynchronicity, the peculiar way that Latin American comedy dismembers sound from meaning with humorous results. The joke also illustrates how much laughter in these films is linguistic, nearly impossible to translate.

In broad terms, Couret concludes that "Latin American film comedies produce a classical mode of spectatorship different from classicism figured in Hollywood." He calls this "Mock Classicism," which he considers to be the principal mode of cinema in South America.[5] The term reminds us that film

Figure 12.2 Luis Sandrini in *Bartolo Had a Flute* (1946).

industries centered in places like Buenos Aires, Rio de Janeiro, or São Paulo have had a complex relationship to Hollywood and European culture. Whatever elements of style or story they may have copied or adapted, there has always been a robust tradition of parody. In 1930, Luiz de Barros mocked Ramon Novarro's silent romance, *The Pagan* (1929), in a Brazilian sendup titled *The Baboon* (*O Babão*). In the following decades, there were spoofs of *The Three Musketeers* (*Los Tres Mosqueteros*, 1942), *Sinbad the Sailor* (*Simbad el mareado*, 1950), *High Noon* (*Matar ou Correr*, 1954), and *Jaws* (*Codfish* [*Bacalhau*], 1975). These early mockeries of English-language genre films display a certain ambivalence toward their sources, mixing spoof and homage, coopting rival products for home markets, transforming foreign cultural goods into something local in the process.

In Brazil, a key to this transformation was the *chanchada*. The *chanchada* has been labeled as a hybrid genre: a mélange of music from Brazilian radio and vaudeville burlesque, classical Hollywood song and dance musicals, mournful *fado* tunes, lyrics from Portugal, and rhythms from Africa. All these musical ingredients were combined with strong doses of irreverent humor and served up in the festive spirit of Carnival. An early prototype was Adhemar Gonzaga's *Hello, Hello, Carnival!* (*Alô Alô Carnaval!*, 1936), featuring Carmen Miranda and her sister Aurora as well as the popular comedian known as Oscarito. During the next three decades, studios like Atlántida and Vera Cruz produced hundreds of them, mostly upbeat celebrations of Brazilian culture, some romantic, some satiric, others more inclined toward comedy of manners. The genre kept changing with the times. In the 1950s, it intersected with the politically conscious Cinema Novo movement. In the 1970s, it morphed into an erotic form known as *pornochanchada*, with titles like *Secretaries Who Do It All* (*As Secretárias . . . Que*

Fazem de Tudo, 1975) and *Clockwork Banana* (*Bananes mécaniques*, 1973)—a prolific sub-genre (more than seven hundred made in São Paolo alone[6]) comparable to pink neorealism in Italy and pink cinema in Japan.

Another key was the popularity of resident comedians. Just as the British film industry countered Hollywood's influence in the 1930s with homegrown talent speaking local dialects, the fledgling studios of Buenos Aires and São Paolo signed contracts with actors whose comic characters had been honed in radio and popular theater. Sandrini and Marshall, Amácio Mazzaropi, Oscarito, and the Grande Otelo created rustic types that aroused sympathy and laughter from a generation undergoing immigration from abroad and mass migration to the cities. By championing the little man's struggle against privilege and greed, these Brazilian and Argentinian clowns may have served political agendas. When Juan Péron came to power in 1946, he supported Argentina's film industry as a way to build his base among the poor and working classes. In Brazil, the right-wing politician Getúilo Vargas led a bloodless coup d'état in 1930, later becoming a pro-Fascist dictator during the years of World War II. He in turn was replaced in another bloodless coup that, this time, established a democratic government. Left-wing intellectuals, focused on political change and national identity, criticized *chanchadas* as cheap, low-quality, patchwork products ill suited to represent their vision for Brazil. But the genre frequently mocked Vargas's state slogans and poked fun at the elite.[7] In retrospect, the *chanchada* was reevaluated and credited with planting the seeds of social consciousness that sprouted in a new form of politically motivated cinema, the Cinema Novo.

Experiments in Social Consciousness: Cinema Novo, Third Cinema, and Tropicalism

Amid the global turbulence of the 1960s and 1970s, a fresh generation of filmmakers sought new directions for their work. The revolution in Cuba, anticolonial struggles in Africa, the war in Vietnam, racial tensions in the United States, political protests across Europe and the Americas—all contributed to a climate ripe for radical change. In Brazil, the 1964 coup established a dictatorship that would last for two decades. In Bolivia, after years of significant reform, Hugo Banzer consolidated his repressive regime in 1971. In 1973, democratic governments gave way to military rule in Uruguay and Chile. In 1974, Péron's death precipitated the brutal "dirty war" in Argentina, a period of right-wing death squads and left-wing guerrilla resistance in which some thirty thousand people reportedly "disappeared."

Politically motivated directors responded with revolutionary essays and films. Two Argentine filmmakers, Fernando Solanas and Octavio Getino, published a call for action in 1969. Their manifesto, "Toward a Third Cinema," proposed an alternative to Hollywood's entertainment model (which they called First Cinema) and the personal expressions of auteurs (Second Cinema). Grounding their proposal in Marxist ideology and drawing on the aesthetics of both British documentaries and Italian neorealism, they sought to rouse the masses from economic oppression with an innovative form of moviemaking, one that would help to combat inequalities of class, gender, and race. Their manifesto inspired activists to take up cameras throughout the Third World, in the Near East and Africa as well as Latin America. At the same time, directors like Glauber Rocha and Nelson Pereira dos Santos pursued similarly subversive goals in Brazil. Hailed as *Cinema Novo* (Portuguese for New Cinema), the Brazilian movement went through three stages. It began in 1960 with stark, angry exposés of poverty and social injustice. Then, around 1964, when it became apparent that black-and-white photography, handheld camerawork, and the grim "aesthetics of hunger" had failed to interest the masses, directors added color, middle-class protagonists, and a measure of self-criticism to soften the message. A third stage (1968–1971) ventured farther afield, inventing the bizarre sub-genre known as Tropicalism.

While Third Cinema and the first stages of Cinema Novo produced only serious films, frankly didactic and political, Tropicalism returned to comedy. Its practitioners favored kitschy colors and outrageous plots. They deliberately courted bad taste. A typical example is Nelson Pereira dos Santos's *How Tasty Was My Little Frenchman* (*Como Era Gostoso o Meu Francês*, 1971), in which the title's protagonist is captured by cannibals and eaten. In the movie, cannibalism is both literal and metaphoric.

Set in sixteenth-century Brazil, when French and Portuguese invaders used the local tribes to help fight each other, the indigenous Tupinambá people (Tupis) come across several Europeans. To identify their European nationalities, the Tupis make them say a few words in their native language. The Frenchman quotes a few lines from a contemporary travel book about naked savages. The Portuguese soldier recites a recipe for lamprey stew. Neither one seems to be conscious of the ironies involved. This film abounds in the humor of incongruity, particularly in disconnections between what is said and what is seen. During the opening credits, the narrative voice of a newsreel describes a barren land of barbarous savages, "beasts with human faces, without any knowledge of what is right and unjust," but what we actually see is something else: a tropical paradise of brave men and beautiful women living by their own scrupulous principles. The voice recounts how the French protagonist fell into the sea and drowned, but the screen shows him being pushed, in chains, and later making it to shore, where he is seized by the locals (Figure 12.3). Eventually, the Tupi chief takes the Frenchman prisoner: "I have already captured and eaten five Portuguese,"

Figure 12.3 *How Tasty Was My Little Frenchman* (1971).

he explains, "and every one of them has pretended to be French." The rest of the movie follows the unnamed Frenchman's gradual assimilation into Tupi society. He takes a wife, who tries to teach him their customs despite a series of comical misunderstandings and misjudgments. In the end, he winds up in the pot, angrily exclaiming that they will all be exterminated by his compatriots.

His prediction, of course, came true, and much of his story is based on actual historical accounts, but the film's many deliberate discrepancies suggest how records don't always match reality. In dos Santos's version, the indigenous Brazilians turn the tables on their would-be conquerors. The trope of cannibalism is reversed, so that the Europeans seeking to consume the new land and its inhabitants are themselves consumed. Michael Wintraub interprets this as a commentary on colonialism and a "cleverly disguised critique of Brazil's repressive military dictatorship."[8] Ella Shohat and Robert Stam point out that the film was also taken as a kind of manifesto: "Just as the aboriginal Tupinambá Indians devoured their enemies to appropriate their force, the modernists argued, Brazilian artists and intellectuals should digest imported cultural products and exploit them as raw material for a new synthesis."[9] It's another instance of Carnivalesque subversion.

Even more outlandish in its humor is Joaquim Pedro de Andrade's *Macunaima* (*Macunaíma*, 1969) (Figure 12.4). This film follows the misadventures of its eponymous anti-hero from his poor jungle home to the city of Rio and back again. His journey unfolds in a series of loosely linked episodes, much like a picaresque novel, embellished with elements of miracle and magic, much like a folkloric tale. The voice of an unseen narrator begins the story and returns from time to time. "Deep in the jungle, silence becomes so thick, hearing the flow of the Urariquera . . ." Suddenly, the silence is broken by a scream. An old woman is giving birth. Out from beneath her skirt plops a black man, naked and fully grown, crying like a newborn baby. This strange child (played by Grande Otello, renowned for his classic *chanchada* comedies) is given the name Macunaíma, "hero of the people." He passes his first six years without uttering a word, sleeping lazily throughout the day while his two older brothers work. Much of the time he spends sucking on a pacifier and decapitating ants. One day, his brother's light-skinned girlfriend gives him a magic cigarette, which transforms him temporarily into a handsome prince. The two go off on a wild romp in the bushes to the tune of an old Carnival march on the soundtrack. In another episode, he traps a tapir, which his family greedily dismembers and devours, giving him only the entrails to eat. Later, when a flood ravishes the land, bringing hardship and hunger, Macunaíma tries to hide a stash of fruit that he has found. As punishment for withholding food from the family, his mother takes him far from home and leaves him to fend for himself. Eventually he finds his way back and sets off for the city with his brothers in search of a better life. Along the way, they

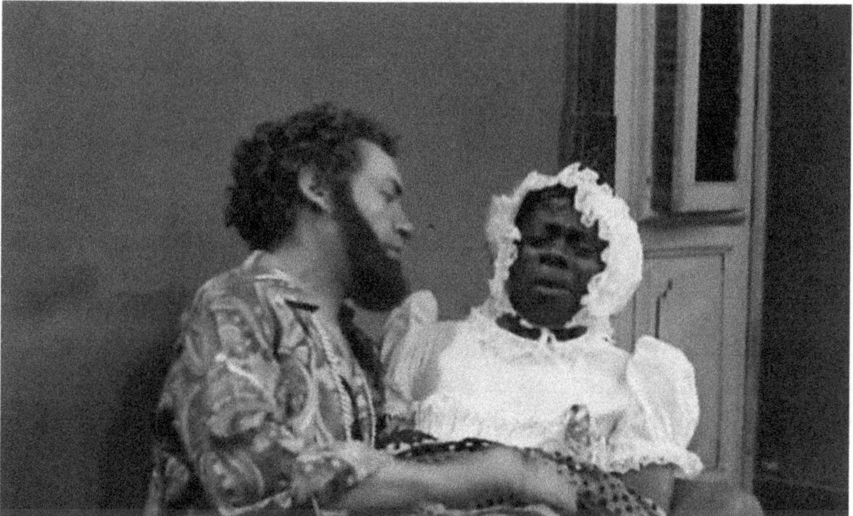

Figure 12.4 *Macunaima* (1969).

come across a magic fountain, which turns Macunaíma into a white man. While the fountain flows, the soundtrack plays "By a Waterfall," from Busby Berkeley's 1933 musical *Footlight Parade*, the Hollywood equivalent of a *chanchada*.

Once in the city, he discovers that his white skin and good looks are useful assets. Women find him irresistible. He falls in with a female revolutionary named Ci, who promises to leave him a magic stone when she dies. But the talisman falls into the hands of Venceslau Pietro Pietra, a rich industrialist who refuses to part with it, so Macunaíma hatches a plan to get it back by trickery.

Macunaíma is in fact a trickster figure. His racial alteration from black to white is one of several conversions and inversions. Sometimes he uses his wits to con people out of their possessions; sometimes he's the dupe. When a stranger shows him a goose that lays silver coins, he's quick to buy the bird only to discover that his goose lays only turds. Sometimes he is the aggressor, especially with women; at other times, he is the object of aggression. Ci dominates him entirely, using him as her sex toy. He prostitutes himself to her for money and a place to live, inverting the usual gender roles. Later, he even dresses like a woman in order to seduce Venceslau and reclaim the talisman. As they chase each other around the room, one in boxer shorts and garters, the other in ludicrous drag, the soundtrack plays an Argentine tango. In short, Macunaíma embodies black and white, man and woman, clever scammer and naïve fool, predator and prey. As Randal Johnson points out, his very name is a composite of bad (*maku*) and great (*ima*), spanning humanity's capacity for greatness and ineptitude.[10]

With de Andrade's film, we reenter the topsy-turvy world of Carnival, an arena of inversion and ambivalence. This is the comedy of incongruity, of upturned expectations and grotesque images of the body reminiscent of Rabelais. We are also in the Tropicalist realm of Antropofagia (cannibalism). In one scene, Macunaíma meets a forest ogre who offers him a slice of his own leg to eat, then tries to eat his guest. In another scene, the giant Venceslau invites the hero to a banquet of *feijoada*, the national Brazilian dish, but instead of the traditional sausage, beef, and pork, there is a pool of half-eaten bodies. The giant wants to add Macunaíma to the human stew. In the end, Macunaíma is seduced by the mermaid sorceress Uiara. After he leaps into her pond, he disappears beneath the surface and a cloud of blood rises with his green shirt. The credits roll on a field of green and gold, the colors of the Brazilian flag, before fading to black. It is the film's final image of consumption, Brazil devouring its own.

De Andrade based his movie on an avant-garde novel published by Mario de Andrade (no relation to the director) in 1928. Grounded in the author's research into indigenous culture, the book links his country's past to the Modernist movement, defining Brazilian identity in terms of its heritage. It is widely regarded as a classic: a national allegory that combines gently self-mocking humor with sharply satirical critiques of local institutions, historical events, and predatory capitalism. Even today, people in the streets jokingly refer to *o nosso lado Macunaíma*, "our Macunaíma side."[11]

Humor on the Road

In 1980, another pioneer of Cinema Novo set out to explore Brazilian identity quite differently, focusing less on the nation's past than on its uncertain future. By the end of the 1970s, Carlos Diegues had produced eight films in sixteen years, including the comic romance *Xica* (*Xica da Silvo*, 1976), continually evolving with the times. His *Bye Bye, Brazil* (*Bye Bye Brasil* in Portuguese, 1980) centers on a ragtag circus traveling from one small town to another. Calling itself the *Caravana Rolidei*, the troupe includes Gypsy Lord (its charismatic impresario who doubles as magician and clairvoyant), his dark-eyed lover (a rumba dancer who goes by the name of Salomé), and a black strongman named Swallow (Figure 12.5). Along the way, they're joined by a young accordion player, Ciço, who falls for Salomé to the dismay of his pregnant wife. The show itself is an amusingly tawdry affair, a jumble of conventional circus tricks patched together with bravado and imagination. In one number, fake snow falls inside the tent while Bing Crosby croons "White Christmas" on a phonograph—proof, boasts Gypsy Lord, that the Brazilian backlands are now part of the civilized world. The caravan's journey is both naturalistic and metaphorical, a chance to tour the country from its arid northeastern *sertão* through the lush Amazon forest to the Central

Figure 12.5 *Bye Bye, Brazil* (1980).

Plateau. Back roads and highways take them through sleepy villages and bustling cities, past bulldozers, palm groves, and armadillo road kill. In one town, a religious procession prays for rain while a traveling projectionist packs his bags, for there is no future here. So the caravan heads for Altamira, "land of plenty," where they find plenty of cinemas, music shops, Coca-Cola, traffic jams, and "fishbone" television antennas but not much for their circus. They have arrived too late, for the Trans-Amazonian Highway has already created this consumer paradise. The only way for the players to survive is to prostitute themselves. Salomé does this literally, returning with money that will transform the show into a glitzy, Hollywood version of its former self. True to its title, Diegues's film is a farewell to the old Brazil, rendered obsolete like the old caravan, superseded by industrialization, new forms of entertainment, and a voraciously consuming new world order. His filmmaking aesthetics, like the *Caravana Rolidei* and Brazilian cinema itself, have adapted to a nation in flux.

With *Bye Bye, Brazil*, Diegues blazed a trail that would be well traveled throughout the next three decades, enlivening the road movie genre with several variations of film comedy.

In 1992, another revolutionary pioneer took his camera on the road. Fernando Solanas, a champion of Third Cinema during the 1960s, chose a teenage schoolboy named Martín as the protagonist for *The Voyage* (*El viaje*). The young man leaves his home in Tierra del Fuego after an earthquake destroys his school. Portraits of the nation's leaders fall from the walls; a statue of Argentina's celebrated liberator, San Martín, topples from its base, releasing its stone horse to gallop away. This is the first of many surrealistic moments in a film where natural disasters are metaphors for historical events. The tremor signifies the political turmoil threatening Argentinian society. Later, floodwaters from Chile invade the streets of Buenos Aires, portending the inundating effects of neighboring economies. Amid the rising waters, President Frog gives an optimistic speech from the steps of the Casa Rosada. He's not worried because, as we notice from the flippers on his feet, he is amphibious (Figure 12.6).

The film's satire ranges from goofy slapstick to sardonic sniping. Martín's pompous teachers fall over themselves like clowns in the mayhem of the quake, but a later scene in the mines of Rio Turbio presents a darker vision, more akin to Dante's *Inferno*. Martín's journey covers some thirty thousand miles from the southern tip of Argentina to Mexico in the far north, taking him across a range of emblematic landscapes that evoke the grandeur and disfigurement of Latin American topography. It becomes a schoolboy's alternative lesson in the history, geography, and culture of his people. Solanas's vision of cultural diversity—a mosaic of languages, ethnicity, and race—differs sharply from the official grand narratives of national unity, a homogeneous Latino culture, and global

Figure 12.6 The amphibious mayor in *The Voyage* (1962).

convergence. By the time Martín arrives in Mexico, his view of the continent and his place within it have been transformed.

The Voyage also serves as a lesson in alternative cinema. In contrast to the Hollywood conventions of credible characters and continuity editing, Solanas offers caricature and montage construction. His episodic structure breaks the rules of a tightly plotted script. His departure from realistic storytelling is more aligned with Latin American traditions of magical realism. Recent studies of South American road movies[12] confirm that they are less often motivated by individual yearnings for freedom and adventure than the genre's North American prototype *Easy Rider* (1969). More typically, Latino protagonists take to the road for practical reasons. They carry with them a strong commitment to community, and their journeys "allude to broader economic, historical, and national frameworks."[13]

While few of these road films are full-fledged comedies, many display a sense of humor that is both local and transnational. In Pablo Trapero's *Rolling Family* (*Familia rodante*, 2004), a large extended Argentinean family piles into a homemade motor home and sets off from Buenos Aires to Missions, six hundred miles to the north (Figure 12.7). What happens on the way offers enough comedy and drama for a whole *telenovela*, the kind of television fare so popular in Latin

Figure 12.7 *Rolling Family* (2004).

America. Generational conflicts simmer, sexual tensions flare, and family feuds erupt—all within the pressure cooker confines of their tiny caravan. At one point, the engine overheats and everyone must get out and push while the flustered patriarch sweats like a pig behind the wheel. Yet in Trapero's hands, the two-day trek is much more than a traveling soap opera. His handheld camerawork, tight framing, and nonprofessional actors give the film an authentic feel, as if we were in the van witnessing each moment while it happens. At the same time, we are very much aware that the film's title is symbolic: Its rolling family embodies all the chaos and charm of Argentinean society at large.

Carlos Sorín's *Intimate Stories* (*Historias mínimas*, 2002) moves through Argentina in the opposite direction, north to south. Modest in scope and intention as its Spanish title suggests, this film interweaves the stories of three people bound for a small town in southern Patagonia. One of them, Roberto, is a fastidious traveling salesman keen to impress a pretty widow by bringing a cake in the shape of a soccer ball for her youngster's birthday. When he realizes that the child's name could be either male or female, he keeps altering the cake, changing its color, adding a head and four little legs until it becomes a unisex turtle fit for boy or girl. The humor here is based on character and the daily interactions among people in this part of the world. Sorín sets sympathetic close-ups of their faces against the windswept grandeur of the landscape, making this an intimate study of *la comedia humana* in a remote corner of the world.

A travel comedy by Diego Arsuaga unrolls not on the road but on the railroad tracks of Uruguay. *The Last Train* (*El último tren*, 2002) centers on a trio of old codgers who steal a locomotive. Their goal is to prevent its sale to Hollywood by an unscrupulous entrepreneur. There is a lot of good-natured joking about each other's age. Dante, who has a heart condition and a failing memory, has brought salami sandwiches for everyone. His friend the professor reprimands him: "Where is my fat-free cheese? At our age so much fat is not good," to which Dante responds, "At our age, everything is good." Unknown to them, a young boy has stowed away on board. When they discover him, the lad is quickly adopted as their collective grandchild. At one point, flustered by the technology of his cellphone, Dante hands it to the boy: "You're from this generation. See if you can figure it out." Much of the film's fun is watching these eccentric septuagenarians, these *locos* in motion, matching wits with the officious police chief who tries to catch them. A commando team leaps onto the train from a bridge with guns raised, but the professor threatens to set off a stick of dynamite. Mission aborted. In the end, the local community, inspired by the boy, rallies to their cause. "*El patrimonio no se vende*," reads a banner behind the locomotive. "Our heritage is not for sale" (Figure 4.9). Instead of being sold to Hollywood, the train—and the indigenous traditions that it represents—becomes a national icon, revitalizing the motion picture industry in Uruguay.

Global Trends in the New Millennium: Swindlers, Schemes, and Steamy Sexuality

Road movies gained popularity during the 1990s and early 2000s for several reasons. By taking their camera through a cross-section of their country's population, filmmakers were able to highlight issues of local importance and explore questions of national identity. Along the way, they often photographed exotic landscapes that proved good for tourism and public relations, which attracted government funding and appealed to international festivals. All these reasons aligned with the increasingly transnational character of cinema everywhere in the new millennium.

By the year 2000, the political landscape of South America looked significantly different than in previous decades. Most countries had moved away from strict military rule and state control in the direction of democracy, privatization, and free-market economics. Begun in the 1990s, these policy reforms were reflected in the governments of Carlos Menem in Argentina, Collor de Mello in Brazil, Alberto Fujimori in Peru, Luis Alberto Lacalle in Uruguay, César Gaviria in Colombia, and a series of elected presidents in Chile following Pinochet's fall from power. Increasingly, their policies favored the conservative ideology of individual enterprise and traditional family values rather than state ownership of industry and liberal standards of morality. To be sure, some governments and many activists opposed the tide. Evo Morales nationalized the gas fields of Bolivia and enacted other leftist policies after his election in 2006. Hugo Chávez followed a similar course in Venezuela, with less fortunate results. Since then, more than one popularly elected president has fallen from grace under clouds of corruption, ineptitude, and economic failure. In 2001, Argentina's President de la Rúa was brought down by galloping inflation that led to riots in the streets. His populist successors, Néstor and Cristina de Kirschner, who governed successively from 2003 to 2015, were replaced by the aggressive neoliberal programs of Mauricio Macri. In 2010, facing charges of dishonesty and an unprecedented gap between rich and poor, Brazil's "Lula" da Silva was prevented from running for a third term. His successor, Dilma Rousseff, was impeached in 2016. These changes cycle through the ever-shifting undulations of film comedy, sometimes in the form of escapist entertainment but more often by providing local topics and character types for affectionate humor or dark satirical wit.

Nine Queens (*Nueve reinas*, 2000) is a prime example of both. Director Fabián Bielinsky set the film in Buenos Aires, where two small-time conmen, Juan and Marcos, meet in a convenience store. Juan, younger and apparently less experienced, gets caught when he tries the same money-changing trick twice at the same cash register. Marcos, who is watching from the aisles, saves Juan from arrest with a clever ruse, then offers him a job as his accomplice. So begins a wobbly collaboration of tricksters bound by mutual distrust. Part of the movie's appeal is watching these two men run their ingenious scams. One trick involves a cup of coffee and a torn bill. Another begins by ringing doorbells of unsuspecting aunts. The two cons try to outdo each other with devious ploys. Marcos seems to be the knowing veteran, always on the lookout for danger and opportunities for another scam. He's willing to take money from anyone, even a little old lady, but has an eye out for bigger game. Juan, by contrast, shows some scruples and wants to follow certain rules of conduct. Their partnership is a marriage of convenience. One needs an accomplice; the other needs a teacher.

Nine Queens reminds us just how close the art of cinema can be to a con game. As moviegoers, we pay to be manipulated by a good director using actors who pretend to be what they are not. We're aware of the pretense, and we enjoy being taken in. In this respect, the film works as comic entertainment. It's a pleasure to watch its performers at work and to be caught up in the movie's witty contrivances. At times, however, it brings us uncomfortably close to the duplicities of real life. At one point in the film, Marcos shows Juan a street full of thieves, pickpockets, and swindlers who suddenly seem to be everywhere (Figure 12.8). "That's what it's all about," Marcos explains. "They are there, but they are not there. So mind your briefcase, your car, your savings." When *Nine Queens* appeared at the beginning of the new millennium, Marcos's words had special relevance in Argentina, when the whole country appeared to be awash in gamesmanship,

Figure 12.8 "They're everywhere!" The streets of Buenos Aires crawl with cons in *Nine Queens* (2000).

duplicity, and distrust. The neoliberal policies of the 1990s—with their promises of a robust economy boosted by free trade, private enterprise, and participation in the global marketplace—had failed miserably. By 2001, under pressure from the International Monetary Fund, de La Rúa's government devalued the peso, setting off a run on the banks and deadly riots. The whole economy seemed to be based on a con game. If Marcos has delusions of grandeur, his mentality mirrors a national delusion, a form of self-delusion driven by greed and abetted by corruption at every level of society.

As the worldwide popularity of *Nine Queens* suggests, the deluge of deception and suspicion was not confined to the basin of the River Platte. Nor was the figure of the small-time swindler limited to a single film from Argentina. A few years earlier, Mara Mourão directed a comedy about serial scamming in Brazil. In her *Hello?!* (*Alô?!*, 1998) everyone is running some kind of racket, rich and poor alike. A wealthy businessman and his wife rip off their fellow countrymen while they themselves are victims of extortion. A housekeeper blackmails her butcher while her nephew cons his aunt's boss, who is cheating the clients in her boutique. In contrast to the anxious paranoia of *Nine Queens*, the tone here is lighter, more naughty than nasty, much like the early *chanchadas* alluded to in Mourão's title.

Brazilian crime and caper comedies continued to appear over the next few years. Guel Arraes set *A Dog's Will* (*O Auto da Campadecida*, 2000) in the rural northeast, where two bumbling low-life bandits, João and Chicó, trick their way through a throng of rogues and fools. Their victims include a miserly baker, his adulterous wife, a pretentious landowner, and an avaricious priest. This gallery of local figures recalls the colorful stereotypes of Italian *commedia dell'arte*, and the film's episodic structure resembles the picaresque novellas from Spain. Occasionally, Arraes veers toward the surreal, adding a Monty Python twist to the homegrown aesthetics of magical realism. One of the more outrageous scenes is a courtroom contest between Satan and Jesus, who is black, in which the Virgin Mary is persuaded to tip the scales of divine justice. *A Dog's Will* was a big hit, enabling Arraes to make more ironic comedies like *Basic Sanitation, the Movie* (*Saneamento Básico, O Filme*, 2007).

Jorge Furtado's *The Man Who Copied* (*O Homem Que Copiava*, 2003) takes place in urban Brazil on a slightly higher rung in the social ladder. The man of the title is a convenience-store employee named André whose voiceover narration sounds like a how-to manual for getting rich. André begins his rise to prosperity by photocopying his boss's $50 bill, using it to buy a winning lottery ticket. This takes him through the crazy antics of a bank heist, a shopping spree, deception, and betrayal. Beneath Furtado's playful mixture of genre conventions—Hollywood's screwball romance and film noir, Brazil's *chanchada* and Cinema Novo—lies a serious indictment of the culture of wealth based on dishonesty and greed.

Borrowing the same generic types of small-time criminals, Orlando Lübbert filmed *A Cab for Three* (*Taxi para tres*, 2001) in Chile. Like Bielinsky, Araes, and Furuado, Lübbert uses comedy to explore Chile's new order, a neoliberal economy based on credit and consumption that exploits the gap between rich and poor. The cab driver is a middle-class family man struggling to pay installments on his Russian-made Lada taxi. His name, Ulises Morales, is one of many clues to the film's allegorical significance. It is an odyssey through modern Santiago in which the protagonist must make decisions with moral consequences. When his motor stalls in a bad neighborhood, he is accosted by two muggers with a knife who offer him an ultimatum: drive or trunk. He chooses to drive, chauffeuring them around town as they perform their petty robberies, but when their work is done, they want to split the cash three ways. It seems there is some honor among these thieves. The older mugger, Chavelo, is an uneducated man who speaks a crude vernacular Spanish. He has taken Coto—younger, inexperienced, orphaned, and illiterate—as his partner in crime. Ulises, with unexpected cash now in his pocket, decides to make it a three-way partnership (Figure 12.9). Soon he is improving their technique, teaching them to be more sophisticated criminals in keeping with the new millennium.

Some of the humor is familiar slapstick, comparable to Italian heist comedies like Mario Monicelli's *Big Deal on Madonna Street* (*I soliti ignoti*, 1958), with their hilarious sendups of inept, would-be burglars from the lower class. Much

Figure 12.9 Two small-time thieves recruit a third in *A Cab for Three* (2001).

of the humor, like Monicelli's, is subtly or pointedly satiric. The characters are constantly drinking Coca-Cola and eating junk food, even while they're being chased at gunpoint. When Chavelo and Coto move in with Ulises's family, much to his chagrin, they come bearing gifts—computer games, a vacuum cleaner, a sewing machine, a TV set—the same mind-numbing array of consumer goods that was targeted by *commedia all'italiana* during the boom years in Italy. As the film unreels, we begin to ask what we are laughing at. Ulises persuades his partners to stop robbing poor old ladies and cabbies like himself, to focus instead on the wealthy. But this turns out to be more dangerous: The rich have safe alarms, armed guards, and the police to protect their property. What is the root of the problem anyway? One of Ulises's acquaintances blames delinquency on the politicians. Another talks of family values and the responsibility of schools. Ulises mutters something about the distribution of wealth. But when it comes to his own skin, when the police are closing in, he makes a moral judgment that surprised many viewers, twisting the comedy into a dark indictment of the times.

The economic boom in Chile, accompanied by a rapid growth in GDP and a corresponding rise in income inequality,[14] echoed throughout other nations of the region with little or no previous film industries. Between 2000 and 2015, Uruguay, Peru, and Colombia were regularly turning out movies aimed at both local audiences and global markets. Filmmakers in Uruguay like Juan Rebella and Álvaro Brechner were aided by new film schools, government grants, and changing modes of exhibition. Peruvian directors like Francisco Lombardi and Álvero Velarde found financial support in co-productions and creative partnerships in television programming. Colombian directors like Sergio Cabrera and Felipe Martínez benefited from their country's expanding economy, which overtook Argentina's as the second largest in South America by 2014.[15] Part of this success was due in no small part to comedy, which took various forms ranging from the ambivalent emotions of absurdist humor to bubbly sex comedies and outrageous slapstick.

As in *The Last Train*, Uruguayan directors continued their focus on the older generation. Juan Pablo Rebella and Pablo Stoll's *Whisky* (2004) is about two Jewish brothers in their sixties. Jacob leads a monotonous life in Montevideo, seemingly oblivious to the way his loyal employee Marta has patiently served him for years. The film takes its time establishing his dull routines: opening his dreary sock factory day after day, turning on the machines, taking his morning tea from Marta, sorting through piles of business receipts while the machinery drones on. This may not sound much like the stuff of comedy, but scholars have found some of the dark comedic tone of Aki Kaurismäki's Finnish films or Samuel Beckett's plays in the repetitious absurdities of Jacob's existence.[16] The pace picks up when Jacob's brother Herman arrives from Brazil for their mother's gravestone ceremony. Herman is livelier, more successful in his business, which explains some of the unspoken resentment Jacob harbors for having spent years caring for their ailing mother in Herman's absence. A Jewish joke that Herman tells after dinner is a clue to the film's dry humor. Old Isaac is on his deathbed with his family gathered round. "Are you here, my dearest wife?" he asks. "Yes, my dear husband," she replies. "And you, my daughter, and my son?" When they all answer him, each in turn, Isaac exclaims in an exasperated voice: "If everybody's here, then who's minding the store?" The film's title is another clue. It seems that the word "whisky" is the Spanish equivalent of "cheese" in English. Latino photographers use it to coax a smile from their subjects, who pronounce it "weekee." Two photos are taken in *Whisky*, and there is little voluntary smiling. In the few scenes when Jacob is not at home or at work, we catch glimpses of his countrymen at the movies or a soccer match, but the seats are mostly empty. All this can be seen as a wry comment on Uruguayan culture as tight-lipped and lethargic in contrast to its neighbors to the north, to Brazil for example, where Herman's vitality and industry have flourished while his brother has languished at home. In contrast, the film itself did well. The *Historical Dictionary of South American Cinema* cites *Whisky* as "the first great global success for Uruguayan cinema," distributed in twenty countries and garnering a number of festival awards.[17]

There is a good deal of wry Jewish humor in Álvaro Brechner's *Mr. Kaplan* (2014), another Uruguayan film with an aging Jewish protagonist. Kaplan, who survived the Holocaust as a child and has lived most of his life in Montevideo, questions his accomplishments at the age of seventy-six. Comparing himself to other late achievers—Churchill, Goethe, Abraham—he decides to make a difference in the world when he learns about a German immigrant who runs a café on the nearby beach. With only a few facts to go on and his own overactive imagination, Kaplan concludes that the German is a Nazi war criminal. Thus begins the great adventure of his life. Enlisting his chauffeur as a partner, he plans to capture the fugitive from justice. What happens next is partly a comedy of errors and misunderstandings, partly a poignant tale of misguided ideals. The wiry Kaplan and his paunchy sidekick have been compared to Don Quixote and Sancho Panza chasing metaphoric windmills. Other comparisons come to mind, including the self-ironic humor of Franz Kafka and the Czech new wave. At one point, Kaplan hears the voice of God. "I Am who I Am," begins the booming voice, then continues. "And You are who You'll be. You will be who You were. If you were who You are." Looking very small under a dramatic sky, Kaplan gives a feeble, short reply, "What?" And so it goes, one man's intense determination to fulfill a destiny well beyond his grasp. Ironically, it's the formula for both the tragic hero and the clown.

These three films from Uruguay—*The Last Train, Whisky*, and *Mr. Kaplan*—are similar in characterization, theme, and style, but there is a notable shift to comedies from countries like Colombia and Peru. Movies made before 2005 tend to be more overtly political, with a strong focus on national identity. Since then, many filmmakers have moved to genre films with characters and plots that can be more readily appreciated abroad, with regional issues minimized or relegated to the background. Two comedies from Colombia illustrate this shift. Colombia has one of the largest movie audiences in South America and a long cinematic tradition obscured by the prominence of drug cartels and partisan violence in the news.[18] In the 1990s, after the death of Medellín's cartel boss Pablo Escobar and a peace agreement with antigovernment FARC guerillas, the country took significant strides toward modernity, democracy, and economic growth. In 1998, Sergio Cabrera directed *Stadium Coup* (*Golpe de estadio*), a comedy that uses soccer as a trope for recent events in Colombia. Set in 1993, when the national team is qualifying for the World Cup tournament, the film focuses on an oil tower owned by a foreign drilling company. Government troops have been sent to protect the tower from guerillas who want to blow it up. The rebels, led by a woman, are more disciplined and competent than the uniformed soldiers—a running joke throughout the film. An army helicopter pilot sent to fire at the *guerilleros* is listening to the game. He presses the trigger at the same time that a radio announcer shouts "gooool!" and his missile collides in midflight with a rebel missile headed for the tower. This humorous intersection of soccer and warfare is hinted at in the film's title, which combines the word for stadium (*estadio*) with the term for military coup d'état (*golpe de estado*). Both sides of the conflict are so excited about the game that they momentarily forget their differences and hug each other after the score, then step back uncomfortably. Claudia Guzmán has read this as Bakhtinian humor, "terror turned into something gay and comic" through the grotesque.[19] For many outsiders, Cabrera's film was seen as an antiwar satire that painted the absurdities of armed aggression with a cartoonish comicality. For those familiar with the violent history of FARC rebels in Colombia or Pinochet's use of the national stadium to detain political prisoners in Chile, Cabrera's humor had a sharper focus and a more localized sting.

There are fewer overtly political messages in *Bluff* (2007), a dark comedy directed by Simon-Olivier Fecteau and Marc-André Lavoie ten years later. Its English title introduces a noirish world of pretense and duplicity. A photographer named Nicolás tries to blackmail his boss with compromising photos because the boss is having an affair with Nico's ex-girlfriend. The would-be blackmailer's smug demeanor at the film's beginning soon changes when he realizes that he's out of his league, caught in a web of scheming and betrayal spun by masters with more money and power. While the plot has enough suspense and surprises for a serious thriller, much of it is played for laughs. Nico's amateurish efforts are ludicrous: "I've got it all worked out," he says. "I watch *CSI*!" But of course, he's wrong. Things spin out of control not only for him but also for the wealthy boss and a corrupt detective whose lust for younger women makes them both predators and prey. Fecteau and Lavoie borrow from the palette of Hollywood aesthetics that has become increasingly global in influence and appeal. They keep the movie brisk and entertaining with fast-paced editing, energetic camerawork, pop music, and touches of romance—all of which made *Bluff* an exportable commodity.

We can follow a similar trajectory toward more universal forms of comedy in Peru. Francisco Lombardi's *Captain Pantoja and the Special Services* (*Pantaleón y las visitadoras*, 1999) is based on a novel by the celebrated Peruvian writer Mario Vargas Llosa. The story's amusing premise offers an unlikely solution to a serious problem. To reduce the high incidence of rape by soldiers stationed in its jungle outposts, the army decides to build a brothel. The officer assigned to this mission is a by-the-book professional known for efficiency and discipline. Reluctant at first, Captain Pantoja dutifully applies his orderly approach to the task, calculating that ten thousand "renderings" will mollify the men, which will require 2,271 "visitations" by women working full time. When the new employees arrive, they are supplied with special uniforms sporting the army colors. On board the transport, Pantoja delivers an inspiring briefing at the "hour of truth." He appeals to the women's patriotic spirit, preparing them for "body to body combat" (Figure 12.10). All this euphemism and incongruity—military discipline applied to simmering sexuality—dominates the first half of the film. The second

Figure 12.10 The captain prepares his new recruits in *Captain Pantoja and the Special Services* (1999).

half becomes more personal, dramatic, and moralistic when Pantoja falls in love with a seductive vamp and steps out of line. As the army brass, the church, and the media form ranks to silence him and protect their public image, the jokes become more cynically satiric, turning from broad sex comedy to a pointed indictment of institutional corruption and dishonesty.

The didactic tone is missing in Alvero Velarde's *Destiny Has No Favorites* (*El destino no tiene favoritos*, 2003). The film's settings and characters are recognizably Peruvian. A television crew is shooting an episode for its popular *telenovela*. Their set is a lavish backyard garden, which they have rented from a wealthy businessman while he is away. His bored wife watches indifferently from her window while her two maids, both soap-opera fans, follow every movement of their favorite stars. The television script mirrors the class distinctions in the household and the social structure of Peru at large. Ana, the mistress of the house, belongs to the vanishing white privileged class. Her servants, resentful and rebellious, are from the indigenous lower classes (Figure 12.11). One of the clichés of the television genre is the sexy maid who aspires to marry the rich white man. When Ana's servants try out for parts in the production, fiction begins to get confounded with reality. Ana herself accepts a minor role, hiding her true identity, and soon starts changing the script. Intrigued by her ideas and her seductive femininity, the director abandons the soap's timeworn plot and his moral scruples with hilarious results. Velarde takes this opportunity to parody South America's favorite television genre, with its familiar types, well-known behaviors, wedding dresses, elaborate hairdos, and overblown dialog. Where else but in a *telenovela* can one

Figure 12.11 Class division in *Destiny Has No Favorites* (2003).

actress say to another with a straight face, "Don't tell me that you have the joy of carrying Alejandro's bastard in your womb!" At the same time, he entertains his audience with a comedy of Peruvian manners. There are few traces of local politics or history to hinder the film's exportability.

A similar strategy operates in recent films from Brazil and Argentina. With *If I Were You* (*Se Eu Fosse Você*, 2006), Brazilian director Daniel Filho turned to body-swapping comedy. The concept is familiar from Hollywood hits like *Freaky Friday* (1976) and *Big* (1988), but instead of exchanging bodies with an older person of the same gender, the husband-and-wife protagonists in *If I Were You* switch places with their spouse. Early on, we see them going through their morning routine. Helena gets up first, stretches on the bedside, gently wakes her daughter in the adjoining bedroom, draws open the curtains, and nudges Claudio awake before stumbling toward the kitchen. After breakfast, Helena takes their child to school, where she teaches music. Claudio drives off to the advertising agency where he is a partner. Despite their comfortable middle-class lifestyle, things are not all rosy. Claudio's business is in financial straits. Helena feels that her identity has been squeezed to nothing, caught between her husband, daughter, and mother. One night, after a marital spat, the couple find themselves speaking the same words simultaneously. "I'd like to see you in my place," he scolds. "If I were you . . ." she retorts (Figure 12.12). Everything they say is echoed by the other until they fall asleep. The next morning, we see them following their

Figure 12.12 Trading places in *If I Were You* (2006).

usual behaviors, but this time it is Claudio who rises first, wakes their daughter, and pulls aside the curtains. When he looks in the mirror, he realizes that something is amiss. Helena is trapped in her husband's body, and vice versa. From this point on the comedy takes off, careening between sidesplitting farce and social satire. Claudio must learn how to apply lipstick and climb stairs in high heels. Helena has to make adjustments at the public urinal. "I didn't quite get the shaking thing," she tells her husband afterwards. Their daughter notices the change. Mom is more aggressive with her students now, and Dad is more permissive. "You're just like Ozzy Osbourne," she tells him delightedly. "Only you don't play rock." How, we wonder, will they perform their new roles in bed?

The script misses no opportunity for slapstick, but it also questions the traditional roles assigned to men and women in Latin America, much as *Skirt Power* (*Taafé Fanga*, 1997) did in Africa. The African film explored gender relations beyond the realm of local culture by alluding to an ancient belief about balance in the universe. According to Dogon mythology, the social order should reflect the larger order of the cosmos. Filho makes a similar move by starting the film with an extreme long shot of the Earth from somewhere in the solar system. An unseen voice announces, "Every 7,850,00 years and 130 days, the planet is aligned with Mars and Venus. This is the day." The camera zooms in to the coast of Brazil, where we enter the bedroom of Claudio and Helena. This reference to planets and the Roman gods representing male and female principles is clearly made with tongue in cheek, but the global imagery is apt. Produced by Brazil's Globo Filmes with international funding, *If I Were You* was a major success. It was Brazil's biggest box-office hit in ten years, followed by an even more successful sequel in 2009. The comedy in both films is deliberately universal, part of the trend to market movies for global audience. It is a pattern of successes repeated in more recent South American films like Argentina's *Wild Tales* (*Relatos salvajes*, 2016). (See "Case Study for Chapter 12: *Wild Tales*" on the website.)

Sophia McClennen calls this pattern "millennial globalization," a term she uses in her study of Latin American cinema from 1900 to 2016.[20] She argues that the new trend does not abandon national politics or culture but adopts "a [greater] range of styles and aesthetics available to viewers than ever before."[21] Like Nilo Couret, McClennen calls for a new theoretical paradigm to explain the new reality, one that abandons previously held distinctions between homogeneity and heterogeneity, global and national, Hollywood hegemony and Latin American subservience. In our survey of South American comedy, we have followed the course of movies in this region from the golden age of the 1920s to the 1950s—with its popular parodies, Brazilian *chanchada* musicals, and Argentine comedies—through the highly charged political films of the 1960s to the 1980s—with their edgy realism and absurdist humor—to the more recent reliance on international genres in the 1990s to the 2010s, bringing comedy to road movies, crime and caper films, and sexually provocative romance. At each stage, the strategic response to Hollywood's historical hold on markets has shifted. What began as imitation, mockery, and clever cooption in the early days changed to defiant resistance or indifference and now seems more like alignment, not so much with a dominating US industry as with a complex sea change of global currents flowing in multiple directions. Hollywood itself continually adjusts to the changing cinematic climate, importing creative talent and ideas as it contributes to the world's evolving stock of stories, images, and sounds. In this global media environment, South American culture—with its vibrant music, lively *telenovelas*, and wide-ranging forms of comedy—has found an enduring place.

South American Comedy Filmography

Country	English Title	Original Title	Director	Date
Brazil	*Hello, Hello, Carnival!*	*Alô Alô Carnival!*	Adhemar Gonzaga	1936
Argentina	*Girls Orchestra*	*Orquestra de señoritas*	Luis César Amadori	1941
Argentina	*Bartolo Had a Flute*	*Bartolo tenía una flauta*	Antonio Botta	1946
Brazil	*Macunaima*	*Macunaíma*	Joaquim Pedro de Andrade	1969

Country	English Title	Original Title	Director	Date
Brazil	*How Tasty Was My Little Frenchman*	*Como Era Gostoso o Meu Francês*	Nelson Pereira dos Santos	1971
Brazil	*Bye Bye, Brazil*	*Bye Bye Brasil*	Carlos Diegues	1980
Colombia	*The Latin American Immigrant*	*El immigrante latino*	Gustavo Nieto Roa	1980
Argentina	*The Voyage*	*El viaje*	Fernando Solanas	1991
Brazil	*Hello?!*	*Alô?!*	Mara Mourão	1998
Colombia	*Time Out*	*Golpe de estadio*	Sergio Cabrera	1998
Peru	*Captain Pantoja and the Special Services*	*Pantaleón y las visitadoras*	Francisco Lombardi	1999
Argentina	*Nine Queens*	*Nueve reinas*	Fabián Bielinsky	2000
Brazil	A *Dog's Will*	O *Auto da Compadecida*	Guel Arraes	2000
Argentina	*The Swamp*	*La Ciénaga*	Lucrecia Martel	2001
Chile	A *Cab for Three*	*Taxi para tres*	Orlando Lübbert	2001
Argentina	*Intimate Stories*	*Historias mínimas*	Carlos Sorín	2002
Uruguay	*The Last Train*	*El último tren*	Diego Arsuaga	2002
Brazil	*The Man Who Copied*	O *Homem Que Copiava*	Jorge Furtado	2003
Peru	*Destiny Has No Favorites*	*El destino no tiene favoritos*	Alvero Velarde	2003
Argentina	*Rolling Family*	*Familia rodante*	Pablo Trapero	2004
Uruguay	*Whiskey*	*Whisky*	Juan Pablo Rebella, Pablo Stoll	2004
Brazil	*If I Were You*	*Se Eu Fosse Você*	Daniel Filho	2006
Colombia	*Bluff*	*Bluff*	Olivier Fecteau, Marc-André Lavoie	2007
Brazil	*The Man from the Future*	O *Homem do Futuro*	Cláudio Torres	2011
Brazil	*Till Luck Do Us Part*	*Até que a Sorte nos Separe*	Roberto Santucci	2012

Country	English Title	Original Title	Director	Date
Uruguay	Mr. *Kaplan*	Mr. *Kaplan*	Álvaro Brechner	2014
Argentina	*The Distinguished Citizen*	*El ciudadano ilustre*	Gastón Duprat, Mariano Cohn	2016
Argentina	*Wild Tales*	*Relatos salvages*	Damián Szifron	2016

Films are listed chronologically. Some directors' names are abbreviated.

Notes

1. Juan Poblete and Juana Suárez, eds., *Humor in Latin American Cinema* (New York: Palgrave, 2018), 1.
2. See Nilo Couret, *Mock Classicism: Latin American Film Comedy 1930–1960* (Oakland: University of California Press, 2018) as well as Poblete and Suárez, *Humor in Latin American Cinema.*
3. See John King, *Magical Reels: A History of Cinema in Latin America* (London: Verso, 1990); Timothy Barnard and Peter Fist, eds., *South American Cinema: A Critical Filmography, 1915–1994* (Austin: University of Texas Press, 1996); Stephen M. Hart, *A Companion to Latin American Film*, vol. 2, Studies of National Cinemas (Woodbridge, Suffolk, UK: Tamesis, 2004); Michael T. Martin, *New Latin American Cinema* (Detroit: Wayne State University Press, 1997); Deborah Shaw, ed., *Contemporary Latin American Cinema: Breaking into the Global Market* (Lanham, MD: Rowman & Littlefield, 2007); Cacilda Régo and Carolina Rocha, eds., *New Trends in Argentine and Brazilian Cinema* (Bristol, UK: Intellect, 2010); Juan Poblete and Juana Suárez, eds., *Humor in Latin American Cinema* (New York: Palgrave. 2018); Maria M. Delgado, Stephen M. Hart, and Randal Johnson, eds., *A Companion to Latin American Cinema* (Oxford: Wiley Blackwell, 2017).
4. Couret, *Mock Classicism*, 102.
5. Couret, *Mock Classicism*, 17, 21.
6. Poblete and Suárez, *Humor in Latin American Cinema*, 18.
7. Jens R. Hentschke, ed., *Vargas and Brazil: New Perspectives* (New York: Palgrave Macmillan, 2006), 214–217.
8. Michael Wintraub, "Cannibal Histories: Some Comments on Nelson Pereira dos Santos's *How Tasty Was My Little Frenchman*," *Fiction and Film for French Historians: A Cultural Bulletin* 8, vol. 3 (Feb–March 2018), https://h-france.net/fffh/classics/cannibal-histories-some-comments-on-nelson-pereira-dos-santoss-how-tasty-was-my-little-frenchman/.
9. Ella Shohat and Robert Stam, *Unthinking Eurocentrism: Multiculturalism and the Media* (New York: Routledge, 1994), 307.

10. Randal Johnson, "Cinema Novo and Cannibalism: Macunaíma," in *Brazilian Cinema*, ed. Randal Johnson and Robert Stam (New York: Columbia University Press, 1995), 179.
11. See Robert Stam, "Racial Representation in Brazilian Cinema and Culture," in Martin, *New Latin American Cinema*, 359.
12. See Verónica Garibotto and Jorge Pérez, *The Latin American Road Movie* (London: Palgrave Macmillan, 2016)and Nadia Lie, *The Latin American (Counter-) Road Movie and Ambivalent Modernity* (New York: Palgrave Macmillan, 2017).
13. Garibotto and Pérez, *Latin American Road Movie*, 8–10.
14. See Joanna Page, "Neoliberalism and the Politics of Affect and Self-Authorship in Contemporary Chilean Cinema," in Delgado et al., *Companion to Latin American Cinema*, 269–282.
15. Delgado et al., *Companion to Latin American Cinema*, 6.
16. See David Martin-Jones and Soledad Montañez, "Cinema in Progress: New Uruguayan Cinema" *Screen* 50, no. 3 (October 1, 2009), https://doi.org/10.1093/screen/hjp015, and Maria M. Delgado, "'Escaping from the Ordinary World into a More Epic One': An Interview with Álvaro Brechner," in *Companion to Latin American Cinema*, 446–458.
17. Peter H. Rist, *Historical Dictionary of South American Cinema* (Lanham, MD: Rowman & Littlefield, 2014), 603.
18. For a brief history of filmmaking in Colombia, see Juana Suárez. "The Reinvention of Colombian Cinema," in Delgado et al., *A Companion to Latin American Cinema*, 307–324.
19. Claudia Aburto Guzmán, "Balls and Bullets: A People's Humor as an Aesthetic Stratagem in *Golpe de Estadio* (1998)," chap. 7 in *Heroism and Gender in War Films*, ed. Karen Ritzenhoff and Jakub Kazecki (New York: Palgrave Macmillan, 2014).
20. Sophia A. McClennen, *Globalization and Latin American Cinema: Toward a New Critical Paradigm* (New York: Palgrave Macmillan, 2018), 2.
21. McClennen, *Globalization and Latin American Cinema*, 5.

13
Film Comedy in East Asia

For most Western moviegoers, East Asia is one of the most culturally remote regions on the planet. The ancient traditions of China, Japan, and Korea—their languages, histories, social institutions, and religious beliefs—are worlds apart from the Americas or Europe. It would not be surprising, then, if many Westerners are puzzled by East Asian humor, what people find funny or count as comedy in the Far East. While some forms of their comedy, like slapstick, are easy to relate to (think of Jackie Chan), other forms call for considerable explaining. It may be true that nothing kills a joke like long-winded explanations. yet to overlook East Asian humor would mean disregarding a fifth of the world's population and ignoring one of comedy's oldest, most intriguing traditions.

One way to understand the strange and unfamiliar is to relate it to what we know. Consider these two Japanese riddles:

QUESTION: In what American state is it always morning?
ANSWER: Ohio.
QUESTION: What American state is famous for its waterworks?
ANSWER: Missouri.

If the answers seem baffling, this is most probably a problem of language. To a Japanese speaker, the state name Ohio sounds like *ohayo*, the common greeting in Japan for "good morning." The state of Missouri sounds like *mizu uri*, meaning "to sell water." These jokes are examples of *nazo*, Japanese riddles based on wordplay.[1] They illustrate an important point about humor in Japan: Much of what people find funny there is based on tricks of language and therefore inaccessible to nonnative speakers. Even when a verbal joke is translated into English, it loses something in translation.

A non-English speaker from Japan might have the same problem with a knock-knock joke:

Knock, knock.
Who's there?
Canoe.
Canoe who?
Canoe come out to play with me?

When the World Laughs. William V. Costanzo, Oxford University Press (2020). Oxford University Press
DOI: 10.1093/oso/9780190924997.001.0001

Any English-speaking child might find this funny if she understands the wordplay on "Canoe" and "Can you?". Knock-knock jokes and *nazo* depend on different languages, but they are similar in form. Moreover, they illustrate the kind of childish pleasure that we take in humor, whether we're American or Japanese.

Language jokes are even more abundant in China. That's because the Chinese language lends itself so easily to puns. With a limited pool of sounds and a system in which most words are limited to one or two syllables, nearly every spoken word in Mandarin Chinese can have multiple meanings, or homophones, sometimes dozens of them. It is possible to write an entire story using a single sound, like *shi*, which may mean ten, snake, time, room, true, affair, market, is, and scores of other words in English.

A key to understanding what East Asians laugh at lies in the terms they use for "comedy" or "humor." Look up these two words in an English–Chinese dictionary and you'll find a confusing assortment of related terms. Among the most common words are *huaji* and *youmo. Huaji* is regularly translated as funny, amusing, or comical, as in "The clown gave a very funny performance," but it can also mean odd-looking, funny in appearance. This double meaning, similar to the English blending of "funny (ha-ha)" with "funny (peculiar)," points to a time when someone ugly or abnormal, the odd man out, was considered laughable, an object of derision. The first part of the term, *hua*, has a secondary meaning of slippery, cunning, or crafty, suggesting that originally *huaji* was connected to a quickness of intellect, the stock-in-trade of tricksters. As early as the Zhou dynasty (1046–256 BCE), the word described wits of the imperial court, not unlike the French courtiers of Louis XVI who used ridicule as an instrument of power. The most common Japanese terms for comedy, *kokkei* and *okashii*, have similar roots, connoting a certain slickness (*kokkei*) and disdain for nonconformity (*okashii*). In contrast, the term *youmo* refers to a more recent form of humor. If it sounds like the English word "humor," that's because it was borrowed from the English language, together with the British ideal of humor as the mark of a well-mannered individual, a sign of geniality and a balanced personality. Not surprisingly, similar loan-words exist in Japanese (*yumou*) and Korean (*yumeo*). This distinction between laughter of the head (*huaji, kokkei, okashii*) and laughter of the heart (*youmo, yumou, yumeo*) may not be consistently observed in modern uses of the terms, but it will be useful in our study of East Asian film comedy.

Laughing in East Asia—Traditions of Comedy in China, Japan, and Korea

The cultural assumptions behind such terms help to explain how historical events, religions, and social institutions of East Asia have shaped prevailing attitudes toward laughter in this part of the world. Consider, for example, the role of China's three great ethical systems: Confucianism, Daoism, and Buddhism. Generally speaking, Confucianism is a humanistic philosophy of moral principles rather than a religion. For more than 2,500 years, Confucian teachings have guided its followers to act with integrity, compassion, and self-control. In Confucian thought, laughter is an expression of delight (*le*), a natural emotion that must be tempered, like all emotions. Confucian scholars speak of an "ethics of mirth" designed to regulate humor through a code for moderate behavior.[2]

In contrast, Daoist humor is carefree and subversive. For at least as long as Confucians have been cultivating prudent conduct through social etiquette, Daoists have pursued a path of simplicity and spontaneity toward the goal of harmony with nature. If Confucian laughter is closely allied to the gentler humor of *youmo*, then Daoist laughter tends toward the witty ridicule of *huaji*. Daoists often use satire as a weapon against misguided power, "to punctuate pomposity and platitudes."[3]

Humor also plays a role in Buddhism, a relatively recent arrival in East Asia (around 100 BCE), especially in Chan Buddhism (known as Zen in Japan). Zen masters may use the humor of incongruity, or paradox, like a slap on the head, to knock their disciples into a higher state of consciousness. Conrad Hyers recounts the story of a monk who once asked his master for the Buddha's current residence, to which the monk replied, "The Buddha is in the outhouse." Hyers explains this with the analogy of a foolish boy who keeps running around in circles, wasting energy when he needs to find a toilet.[4] The expanded awareness needed to get such jokes moves the pupil closer to enlightenment. The "laughing Buddha," known as Pu-Tai in China and Hotei in Japan, is sometimes linked to this concept of humor.

We saw in Chapters 1 and 4 how the English word for humor derives from a theory of medicine dating back at least to ancient Greece. Well into Shakespeare's time, physicians in Europe believed that the human body was regulated by four basic fluids, or "humours": black bile, yellow bile, phlegm, and blood. An excess of any humour was thought to cause an imbalance in physical and mental health. Too much blood (*sanguis*) made a person sanguine; too much black bile (*melaina kholé*) produced a melancholic disposition. "Good humour," then, was linked to the body's equilibrium and a balanced temperament. There is a similar concept in Chinese medicine, which maintains that the body's vital energy or spirit (*qi*) flows throughout the body by means of channels, regulating health and mental well-being. Problems arise when *qi* is blocked. Laughter helps to free the vital spirit and restore a healthy balance. Both systems, East and West, remind us that comedy can be a liberating force, contributing to stability and health.

The notion that laughter helps to repair imbalances can extend to the body politic. Throughout the history of East Asia, as in other parts of the world, humor has served political agendas. Early scholar wits (*huaji*) told anecdotes and fables intended to amuse their lords and temper their misuses of power. One such story was about the king of Wei, who decided to build a tower halfway to the sky—against the advice of his counselors. Anyone who dared to advise the king was executed. One day, a worker arrived with a spade, saying, "I've come to do my duty." The laborer went on to make some practical calculations. The base of the proposed tower would need a base of eight thousand square *li*, bigger than the king's domain, so neighboring states would have to be conquered. Then more land would be required to store the building blocks and grow rice for the laborers, requiring more wars, more soldiers, more land. By the time the worker had completed his calculations, the king decided to call off the project.[5]

Another story was about the king of Chu, who insulted the ambassador from the neighboring state of Qi. "There must be very few people in Qi," sniped the king, "or why would they send me someone like *you* as envoy?" The ambassador replied, "We have a method for selecting envoys. If a state's leader is competent, we send a good one. If not, we send an incompetent envoy. I'm one of the most inept ambassadors in Qi, which is why I was sent to you."[6] Chinese wits used ironic comedy like this to soften their cautionary tales, much like the court jesters of Europe or the royal griots of West Africa.

Political protest often took the form of homophones. During the Nationalist anti-Communist campaign of the 1930s, a popular slogan was "Kill the pig and pluck its hair." Everyone knew that the family name of Chairman Mao can also mean "hair" and that the family name of Marshall Zhu, a high-ranking official under Mao, can mean "pig." The slogan was a code for killing Zhu and removing Mao from power. Today, political homophones are common on the internet as a means of circumventing censorship. When bloggers make playful references to "river crabs" (*hexie shehui*), how can censors prove that they were making fun of former president Hu Jintao's "harmonious society," which sounds the same as the crustacean in Mandarin?

Homophone humor also plays a big part in standup talk shows (*tuokouxiu*), comic skits (*xiaopin*), and "crosstalk" comedy (*xiangsheng*; two performers playing off each other on stage), as well as on TV—all popular forms of humor in China today. As we'll see, puns also get a lot of the laughs in Chinese movie comedies. So do traditional slapstick, chase scenes, practical jokes, and many of the other physical hijinks that entertain audiences elsewhere on the planet.

Like China, Japan has its own oral and dramatic traditions of comedy. Some three hundred years before movies were introduced to Japan in the 1890s, its people enjoyed a form of storytelling called *rakugo*. When the country was still divided into warring states, *rakugo* practitioners amused their warlords (and kept them awake for battle) with funny stories. Seated on purple cushions, they drew their tales from a stockpile of familiar stereotypes, caricatures of the lower classes. Theirs was a form of sit-down comedy. By the 1600s, well-honed comic monologues known as *karucuchi* ("idle chatter") were being passed along from one generation of raconteurs to the next. At first, they plied their trade among the street crowds of Kyoto and Osaka, then eventually moved into theaters, becoming part of vaudeville shows, university comedy clubs, and, later, television programs. The *rakugo* tradition shares comic elements with Japan's dramatic forms, like the vulgar clowning in *kabuki* theater, the mischief-making in *bunraku* puppet plays, and the short farcical skits (*kyogen*) performed between the solemn Noh dramas. The roots of laughter in Japan can be traced back even further to its Shinto myths. Since 1199, the Warai-ko ceremony has been held each year in Hofu City, where participants reenact an ancient harvest in which laughter is symbolically linked to fertility. At the conclusion of the ritual, everyone joins in a big communal laugh.[7]

All these early forms of humor contributed in one way or another to the genre of Japanese film comedy known as *kigeki*. *Kigeki* spans a broad spectrum of slapstick, burlesque, parody, irony, black comedy, comedy of pathos, and comedy of manners.

Early Film Comedies in Mainland China and Japan

For most of recorded history, China's sphere of influence has dominated the area like a large planet dominates its moons. But during the shorter span of motion pictures, roughly since 1900, the center of cinematic gravity has shifted back and forth. The 1930s was a golden age for Chinese cinema. Then filmmaking on the mainland lost much of its global appeal under Chairman Mao (1949–1976), when the industry became a propaganda agency of the People's Republic of China (PRC). By the 1970s, the generative source of Chinese-language films had moved to the tiny British protectorate of Hong Kong and, to a lesser extent, the island of Taiwan. In its heyday, Hong Kong boasted the third largest film industry in the world, becoming the East Asian hub for film production and distribution. Meanwhile, across the Taiwan Strait, Taiwan emerged from decades of insularity and Japanese control to become a creative and financial force in Chinese-language cinema. Rapid modernization and an economic boom set the stage for a new Taiwanese cinema in the 1980s. By then, conditions on the mainland had also changed. Greater creative freedom and prosperity in the PRC unleashed the extraordinary talents of the fifth-generation directors, followed by a sixth generation of younger, grittier filmmakers. By the 1990s, the film industries of the "three regions" of Taiwan, Hong Kong, and the PRC had become productively intertwined.

Japan, which had embraced the new art form from the beginning, grew into a cinematic powerhouse after World War II. The 1950s was Japan's golden age, and by the 1960s, the country's art films were regularly winning international prizes. Through the ups and down of the island nation's economic growth spurts and recessions, Japan emerged as the fourth largest box-office market in the world.[8] Meanwhile, the Republic of Korea (South Korea), with some 50 million people and the fourth largest economy in Asia, has produced a vibrant new wave of both artistic and commercial movies that continue to arouse excitement throughout Asia and around the globe.

Despite their proximity and overlapping histories, China, Japan, and Korea are distinct in many ways. Their languages, for example, are genetically unrelated, with different roots, grammars, and pronunciation. Yet through centuries of mutual influence, the people in this region have come to share many cultural affinities. This chapter charts a course through the highlights of film comedy in East Asia. But first, it will be helpful to consider the role of comedy itself within a region that evolved so differently than the West.

In his introduction to *Asia Laughs*, Roger Garcia begins with a generalization about the region's genre films:

> Like comedy elsewhere, Asian comedy foregrounds the comedian and character, usually a populist everyman (like the working-class audience), often reflecting historical struggles of nationalism or migration to cities: the "salaryman comedy" in Japan, office romantic comedy in Korea, country bumpkin comedies in Hong Kong.[9]

In our survey of East Asian comedies, parallels to comic characters and funny films in other parts of the world will be readily apparent. It is always tempting to talk about the Chinese Charlie Chaplin, the Buster Keaton of Korea, or Toho's Billy Wilder. But as we crisscross the continent or shuttle back and forth across the Sea of Japan, we will also encounter movies that are uniquely Asian, comedies steeped in native traditions and local histories.

The earliest Chinese filmmakers followed Western recipes for physical comedy, adding local flavoring. One scholar estimates that a third of the Chinese films made between 1905 and 1921 were slapstick shorts with titles like *Stealing a Roast Duck* (*Tou shaoya*, 1909) and *The Corrupt Official Returned in Glory* (1921).[10] Silent movies in Japan seem to have been less derivative and more serious, and they continued to be made well into the 1930s, after other industries adopted synchronized sound. For the next two decades, while Japan and much of China were engaged in war, Shanghai became a sanctuary for directors making entertaining genre films. This "second golden age" continued through the 1940s with popular screwball comedies like *Long Live the Wife* (*Tai wan sui*, 1947), romantic comedies like *Phony Phoenixes* (*Jia feng xu huang*, 1947), and well-regarded satires like *Crows and Sparrows* (*Wuya yu maque*, 1949). With the

Chinese Communist victory of 1949, many in the Shanghai film industry fled to Hong Kong and Taiwan. The Communist-led PRC was more interested in education than entertainment. Under Mao's leadership, the number of comic movies released on the mainland dwindled, as did the number of movies overall.

It was a different story in Japan. There, after more than a decade of military control, the film industry rose from World War II in a burst of creative energy. The 1950s gave us ghost stories like Kenji Mizoguchi's *Ugetsu* (*Ugetsu monogatari*, 1953), Yasujiro Ozu's *Tokyo Story* (*Tokyo monogatari*, 1953), monster pictures like Ishiro Honda's *Godzilla* (*Gojira*, 1954), and art films like Akira Kurosawa's *Rashomon* (1950), catapulting Japanese movies into the pantheon of world cinema. Some of these directors, like Ozu and Kurosawa, also tried their hand at comedy.

Ozu's *Good Morning* (*Ohayo*, 1959) might best be described as a comedy of manners. In a country preoccupied with etiquette, it gently ridicules the elaborate rituals of politeness while exposing the insincerity beneath them. Ozu sets the film in a small neighborhood near Tokyo, one of the modern suburbs that were springing up after the war. Their modest homes are composites of East and West, adorned with white picket fences and tatami mats. They look so much alike that, after a night of too much sake, a man can easily find himself in the wrong house. Much of the plot revolves around consumer goods. Women gossip about a neighbor who has bought a new washing machine. Children go on a silence strike for a television set so they can watch sumo wrestling at home. They refuse to talk because, as they see it, adults are always speaking pointless pleasantries like "good morning" instead of saying what they really mean. Surprisingly for viewers unfamiliar with Japanese humor, a string of flatulence jokes runs through the entire film. The schoolboys play a game based on their ability to fart on demand (Figure 13.1). One unfortunate lad, who lacks this manly skill, keeps soiling his knickers. Even adults engage in flamboyant flatulence. Every time one of the husbands lets loose, his wife asks from the next room, "Did you call me, dear?" A whimsical soundtrack underscores the joke.

In addition to this juvenile humor, beyond the picket fences and commodities Ozu gives us glimpses of a society in distress. One aging neighbor has been laid off from his job. Another has been reduced to selling housewares from door to door. This salesman tries to harass the housewives into buying his goods. If a woman shows no interest, he takes out his penknife and starts whittling his pencil to a point, a veiled threat. But Grandma knows just how to handle him. When he produces the penknife in her presence, she grabs a kitchen knife and sends him packing. This is the quality of Ozu's humor, typically subtle and refined, occasionally lowbrow, but always pointed.

While not a comedy per se, Kurosawa's *Yojimbo* (*Yojinbo*, 1961) leavens a story of feudal fighting and intrigue with moments of broad humor. Toshiro Mifune

Figure 13.1 Flatulence becomes a boy's game in *Good Morning* (1959).

plays the part of Sanjuro, a skillful swordsman who hires himself out as a bodyguard in a war between two feuding clans. Both sides are so corrupt and cowardly that he decides to play them off against each other. In one of the funniest scenes, the opposing groups approach each other, armed to the teeth and trembling with fear, while Sanjuro sits cross-legged in a tower high above the fray, smiling at his cunning handiwork. We smile too at this picture of would-be warriors wavering between fits of boastful sword rattling and craven retreats. Mifune regularly appears as a comic figure in Kurosawa's films. In *Rashomon*, he plays a boastful brigand whose claims of skill and sexual conquest are hard to take seriously whenever he scratches himself (Figure 13.2). His crude physical appearance and boorish behavior in this film have been compared to the *oni* (demonic ogres) of native folklore. For Japanese viewers, this cultural in-joke adds an extra layer of comedy. In *Seven Samurai* (*Shichinin no Samura*, 1954), Mifune assumes the role of Kikuchiyo, a buffoon claiming noble birth. His actions are apish, his sword is much too big, and his dress is ludicrously inapt. Kikuchiyo is the wildcard, the trickster, the clown—always a potential hazard in any fighting unit—but he brings the important ingredients of vitality, surprise, and jesting to the story. With his swagger and mocking humor, he marshals the farmers into troops, and he shows fearless, if imprudent, courage under fire.

While samurai movies were making a comeback and tough *yakuza* gangster films began to take over Japanese screens, a series of extremely popular feel-good

Figure 13.2 Toshiro Mifune in *Rashomon* (1950).

comedies began its long career. From 1969 to 1995, Yoji Yamada directed some forty-eight episodes about Tora-san, a hapless hero in search of the ideal woman, his "Madonna." He struck the chord with *Am I Trying* (*Otoko wa tsurai yo*, 1969) and followed the same formula in each sequel. Tora-san sets out on his quest with a small suitcase of wares to sell, traveling to a different location in Japan or abroad, and finding a new woman. He always loses her, of course, but he manages to help others along the way. Tora-san is another kind of trickster figure, pulling pranks and letting people laugh at themselves. Hailing from the blue-collar section of Tokyo, he represents the common man, but he is uncommonly free. With no steady job or family attachments, dressed in his beige checkered suit and old-fashioned wooden clogs, Tora-san evokes a pleasurable nostalgia for the good old days when life was simpler. Still much beloved in Japan, his films may be the longest-running franchise in the history of world cinema.

Hong Kong Hybridity

Generally insulated from the mainland by its status as a British protectorate until 1997, Hong Kong developed its own commercial film industry, specializing in genre films like kung fu and comedy. A fixture in many of these comedies is the Hong Kong smartass, a quick-witted, often vulgar trickster who twists words and creates chaos in the interest of self-serving anarchy. The loud-mouthed wise guy, boisterous and competitive, always trying to make an extra Hong Kong dollar, reflects some of the commotion and commercialism associated with bustling Hong Kong. Film historian Sam Ho uses the term "tricky-brain humor," tracing this tradition from the 1930s up to Stephen Chow's performance in Wong Jing's *Tricky Brains* (*Jing gu jyun ga*, 1991).[11]

Since every swindler needs a sucker, another perennial character in Hong Kong comedies is the fool. Often enough the fool is someone else's dupe, but just as often he's the victim of social ignorance. Sam Ho points to titles like Lai Bak Hoi's *Idiot's Wedding Night* (*Shazai donfang*, 1933) and Hou Yao's *The Fool Pays Respect* (*Dailao baishou*, 1933), explaining that "the Chinese simply love witnessing fools in embarrassing situations, especially in formal situations."[12] Bruce Lee often played the fool in his action films. In *The Way of the Dragon (Meng long guo jiang*, 1972), he is a simple farm boy, a rube who arrives in Rome to work for his uncle. Hungry, but ignorant of the Italian language or of big-city ways, the first thing he does is order dinner by pointing at random to items on the menu—only to find himself facing acute digestive distress when the waitress returns with a dozen different soups (Figure 13.3a). Later, heeding his mother's advice to be friendly with the natives, he smiles at a stranger, who turns out to be a local prostitute. Despite these laughable faux pas, he is still Bruce Lee and ends up defeating all the bad guys with his astounding mastery of the martial arts. Bruce

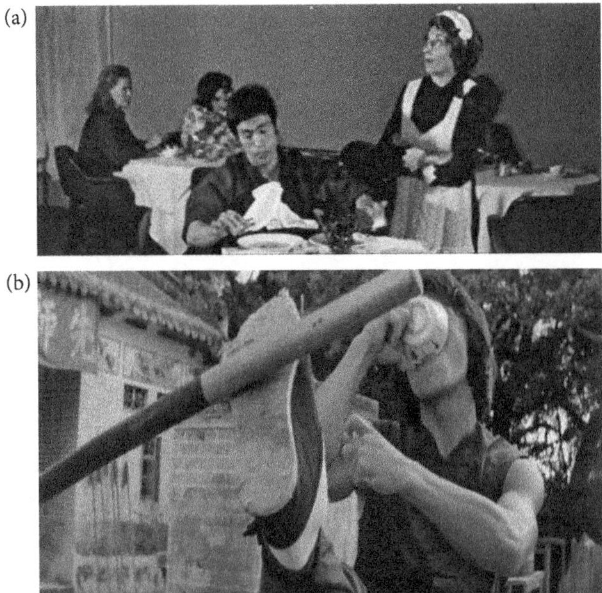

Figure 13.3 The lighter side of kung fu heroes. (b) Bruce Lee orders Italian food in *Way of the Dragon* (1972). (b) Jackie Chan gets crocked in *Drunken Master* (1978).

Lee, of course, is better known for kung fu than for comedy. Meanwhile, Hong Kong studios, dependent for their funding on box-office success rather than on government subsidies, soon learned to mix comedy with other genres. These hybrid films included martial arts comedies like Yuen Woo-ping's *Drunken Master* (*Zui quan*, 1978), action comedies like Jackie Chan's *Project A* (*'A' gai wak*, 1983), and horror spoofs like Ricky Lau's *Mr. Vampire* (*Geung si sin sang*, 1985).

Drunken Master is based on the legendary martial artist Wong fei-hung. In the movie, Wong is trained at a young age by a tough-minded master of a secret fighting style known as "drunken boxing."[13] Since fighters using this technique gain advantage by pretending to be drunk, it offers ample opportunity for physical comedy. Jackie Chan was the perfect actor to play young Wong. In real life, Chan had endured ten years of rigorous training at a Peking opera school, where students were regularly beaten as they learned music, tumbling, acrobatics, and fighting skills. In *Drunken Master*, he begins as a lazy, mischievous youth. Time and again, he is disciplined, often brutally, for disobeying orders. Time and again, he undercuts his potential talent with playful buffoonery. But once he has a clear goal, he puts everything he has into the drills until he emerges as the unbeatable hero. In one scene, he fends off an attacker's deadly stick by feigning drunkenness: twisting, turning, ducking, falling, and performing back flips on a table, all with a cup of wine in his right hand (Figure 13.3b). In another scene, he defeats a whole gang of fighters between wobbly somersaults and swigs from the bottles tossed to him by rooting bystanders. Chan's kung fu stunts are marvels of gymnastic choreography, reminding us how practice and creative timing can contribute to this kind of comedy. But the many beatings that he suffers along the way also illustrate how pain and laughter can go hand in hand.

Project A is more broadly a comic action film since it includes knives, guns, and explosives as well as kung fu's hands and fists. This time Jackie Chan is a police sergeant fighting pirates in nineteenth-century Hong Kong. He is joined in his fight against overwhelming odds by Sammo Hung. With his round face and extra girth, Hung looks more comical than fierce, but like Chan, he was trained in Peking opera and skillful in the martial arts. The film's plotline is a thin excuse for comic mayhem, a rollicking series of chases, droll faces, side-splitting stunts, and visual jokes. In one of these, Chan hangs from the hour hand of a clock tower, then falls sixty feet through a succession of striped awnings to the ground, head first, a tribute to Harold Lloyd's clock scene in *Safety Last* (1923).

Project A was a big success, as was Eric Tsang's *Aces Go Places* (*Zui jia pai dang*, 1982), a parody of James Bond films. *Aces* became a lucrative franchise (known as *Mad Mission* films in the United States). Its unlikely action heroes bumbled their way through six films and ever more outlandish escapades for another fifteen years.

Meanwhile, Sammo Hung became a director and producer, helping to create another Hong Kong sub-genre by mingling native Chinese traditions with a figure from the Western horror film. The result was the spooky *jiangshi*, or "hopping vampires." *Jiangshi* are dressed in Mandarin robes rather than capes. They advance toward their victims in standing jumps, with long purple fingernails outstretched. As reanimated corpses, they can be subdued only by Daoist spells or a red dot on the forehead. In his *Encounters of the Spooky Kind* (*Gui da gui*, 1980), Hung takes on a bet to spend the night in an abandoned house. The fun begins with an apple and a mirror. Before it's all over, the encounter has involved fifty chicken eggs, dog's blood, coffins, witches, sorcerers, and a monkey god. By the mid-1980s, the Hong Kong theatres were overrun with *jiangshi* of the spooky kind. *Mr. Vampire*, produced by Hung and directed by Ricky Lau, continued in sequels and spinoffs into the 1990s (Figure 13.4).

The Hong Kong film industry had found a formula for commercial success: Take a proven genre (action, horror), add elements of local culture (kung fu fighting, *jiangshi* ghosts), and mix with generous helpings of comedy. As we'll see, this recipe would be put to good use at the turn of the next century by a director who became Hong Kong's undisputed king of comedy, Stephen Chow.

Laughing in Taiwan

On the island of Taiwan, five decades of Japanese occupation came to an end in 1945 with the Allied victory. Four years later, the civil war between Chiang Kai-shek's Nationalists and Mao Zedong's Communists was over. Chiang evacuated

Figure 13.4 An attack of hopping corpses in *Mr. Vampire* (1985).

to Taiwan along with 1.5 million mainlanders. The first postwar comedies under Chiang's rule were "policy films" like Tang Shao-hua's *Everybody's Happy* (*Jie da huan xi*, 1951). Such films prescribed happiness by decree, with all complications resolved between song-and-dance numbers, and everybody serving society in the end—not unlike Stalinist musicals in Soviet Russia. In the 1960s, however, Taiwanese natives in search of entertainment could turn to less heavy-handed comedies in their own dialect. Among these was Hsiao Tung and Lee Hsing's *Brother Liu and Brother Wang on the Road in Taiwan* (*Wang ge Liu ge you Tai Wan*, 1959). It followed the escapades of two working-class buddies: a heavyset shoe shiner (Wang) and a scrawny rickshaw driver (Liu), who strike it rich and live it up like a Taiwanese Laurel and Hardy. The two comedians became so popular that they performed in several sequels. In 1962, Lee made *Good Neighbors* (*Liang xiang hau*), the island's first dual-dialect comedy. One neighbor is a Taiwanese-speaking local, the other a wealthy Mandarin speaker from the mainland. Their laughable struggles to understand each other reflect the island's real-life problems in accommodating two very different populations.

If Wang and Liu reminded audiences of Laurel and Hardy, Taiwan's "Little Tramp" was indisputably Hsu Pu-liao. Writing about the island's film traditions, George Chun Han Wang calls Hsu "arguably the most talented comedian in Taiwan cinema history."[14] Hsu began his career as a child performer in a circus. He was discovered by a government official and introduced to state television, where he became "one of the funniest entertainers on TV." His first film role was in *Off to Success* (*Chen gong ling shang*, 1979), a military comedy directed by Chang Pei-Cheng with major government funding. The film lampooned the boot-camp experience endured by every young man on the island and spawned a long line of sequels. Meanwhile, Hsu went on to make more movies. Unfortunately, he became the victim of his own success. Hsu got mixed up with criminal investors who supplied him with drugs and forced him to make movies, lots of them: eight in 1980, ten in 1981, thirteen in 1982. By 1985 he was dead at the age of thirty-four, leaving a legacy of sixty-four films. Most of these were comedies, ironic reminders of his stage name (Hsu Pu-liao means "to suffer endlessly") and the fact that some of the greatest comedians have the saddest lives.

Hsu's best years, 1979 to 1985, have been called the golden age of Taiwanese comedy. His principal director, Kevin Chu Yen-ping, finished out the decade with a series of blockbuster kung fu comedies bearing his distinctive brand. The 1980s also marked the start of Taiwan's New Cinema movement. While its award-winning directors were best known for their serious art films, some of them, like Hou Hsiao-hsien and Ang Lee, began their careers with comedies. What makes all these comedies uniquely Taiwanese is the rich mixture of cultures—Japanese, mainland Chinese, Hakka, and Taiwanese—woven through their stories. Part of the appeal to local viewers, notes George Wang, are the "heartwarming portrayals of underprovided individuals, their down-to-earth lives and the wonder and humor of extraordinary encounters."[15] As we will see, Taiwan's best-known director, Ang Lee, went on to master an extraordinary range of topics and genres when he moved to the United States, but he never lost touch with his Taiwanese roots.

Humor Korean Style

South Korea has enjoyed an original and vibrant movie industry in recent times. Critics have spoken of a "New Wave" in the 1980s and a "New Korean Cinema" from 1992 onwards.[16] Since then, according to scholars like Chris Berry, it has emerged as "the powerhouse cinema of East Asia."[17] Yet film-making on the Korean peninsula did not have a promising beginning, especially for film comedies: The entire Korean film industry produced only one comedy during its first thirty-five years, and no copies have survived.[18] One reason may be that Koreans had little to laugh about. Their modern history has been exceptionally violent and oppressive. Squeezed between the Chinese mainland and the island of Japan, Koreans have suffered from both sides. From 1910 to 1945, when their homeland was a Japanese colony, Japan enforced tight control on all cultural activities, including movies. Soon afterwards, from 1950 to 1953, Korea was embroiled in the brutal civil war between Communists and Nationalists. When the fighting stopped, Kim Il-song ruled the Democratic People's Republic in the North while Syngman Rhee presided over the Republic of Korea in the South. North Korea's military government has maintained an isolationist, state-based culture until today. South Korea endured a series of autocratic leaders, military coups, and uprisings until democratic elections were held in 1987. Some say it did not become a true democracy until the 1990s. Within a few short years, South Korea's image was transformed from a backward country into an industrial dynamo with the eleventh largest world economy. When the capital of Seoul hosted the Olympics in 1988, it was the fourth largest metropolis on the planet. Today, South Korea makes more than a hundred movies a year. Yet, except for a devoted cult following, South Korean films are much less well known abroad than products like Hyundai cars or Samsung mobile phones.

This is particularly true of comedies. Typically, the humor in these films sprang from local issues. With the rise of independent women in the 1950s, a spate of romantic comedies served as safety valves for releasing tension in the form of laughter. In Han Hyeong-mo's *A Female Boss* (*Yeosajang*, 1959), the lead characters meet and clash at a public payphone (Figure 13.5). Well dressed and oblivious of anyone else, she hogs the phone and feeds her dog expensive

Figure 13.5 Waiting for the public phone in *A Female Boss* (1959).

Western cookies. Impatient with her sense of entitlement, the man waiting behind her kicks the dog and tells her to hang up. The next day, this man shows up looking for a job at her magazine company, *Modern Woman*, where all the powerful positions are held by women. But for all the jokes at the man's expense, women are put in their place at the end. It's an example of Freud's release theory in action: letting off steam through laughter to maintain the ship of state. In 1960s, anxieties about changing parental roles led to a series of family comedies. More changes in Korean society produced the sex-war comedies of the 1990s and the gangster comedies of the early 2000s. As Darcy Paquet points out, "These mini-movements mark defining moments in Korean film history and reflect the culture of their times," but many of the jokes that entertained earlier generations no longer seem funny. This may be true anywhere on Earth, but Paquet observes that the rate of social change has been much greater in Korea than, than say, in the English-speaking world.[19]

The homebound nature of Korean humor is a big factor in its local appeal. Take the scene in Park Chan-wook's *Joint Security Area* (*Gongdong gyeongbi guyeok*, 2000) when a South Korean soldier finds himself in a North Korean border station during a time of military tension. Gradually, the young men on both sides become friends, playing games and sharing family photos. Non-Korean audiences could appreciate the grim humor of sworn enemies who pal around under such dangerous conditions. But they would be unlikely to know that the snapshot in the soldier's wallet is not his girlfriend, as he implies, but a famous South Korean pop star or that the hand game (which they play with bullets instead of pebbles) is really a girl's game. Outsiders, like the North Korean characters themselves, are left out of the joke. *Joint Security Area* did get positive attention at international art festivals, but in South Korea it broke all box-office records.

Eight years later, Kim Jee-won kept the focus on local issues but broadened its appeal in his hilarious parody, *The Good, the Bad, the Weird* (*Joheunnom nabbeunnom isanghannom*, 2008). The film is set in 1931, after the Japanese invasion of the Korean peninsula sent thousands of Korean refugees into the vast flatlands of Manchuria. Kim uses the landscape to evoke a familiar genre (his title plays on Sergio Leone's "spaghetti Western," *The Good, the Bad and the Ugly*, 1966), adding a train heist, hired guns, kung fu fighting, and the Japanese army for good measure. One of his three protagonists, Yoon Tae-goo (the Weird), is a goofy, small-time thief who gets caught up in a giddy chase for treasure. Yoon makes his first appearance in a padded jacket, aviator's cap, and motorcycle goggles, peddling rice cakes on a train. The camera follows him and his cakes down the aisle as mariachi music plays on the soundtrack. He moves from one car to another, past a clutch of Japanese soldiers beating a Korean nationalist, through a car filled with multiethnic passengers, steps through the baggage car, and emerges into a swanky bar car with two guns drawn: "Nobody move!" he yells, as the opening credits roll (Figure 13.6). To make his pastiche of global kitsch even more palatable to international audiences, Kim filmed an alternative version for export, one that excised many of the references to Japanese aggression and made the film more politically neutral. This shorter version is the one released for foreign markets. Either way, Kim's "kimchi Western" was a box-office hit not only in Korea but throughout East Asia.

Joint Security Area and *The Good, the Bad, the Weird* marked a shift in South Korean film production. In the 1990s, the industry was dominated by large companies, called Chaebols, which financed a series of so-called planned films. Films were designed for selected target audiences, using market surveys to help develop the script. Kim Ui-seok's *Marriage Story* (*Gyeolhon iyagi*, 1992) was a

Figure 13.6 The train robbery in *The Good, the Bad, the Weird* (*2008*).

notable example. After the financial crisis of 1997, when the International Monetary Fund forced Korea to change its business practices, the film industry shifted to venture capital. Government restrictions were relaxed, and money began pouring in from hundreds of entrepreneurs, financing a new boom in South Korean cinema. Film schools opened, new theaters were built, and a new generation of young filmmakers was encouraged to pursue new paths.[20]

This new Korean cinema bears the scars of a high-pressure society whose energy is born of deep-seated struggle and oppression. Much of the humor, when it surfaces, may seem grim or even twisted to outsiders. A case in point is Kim Sang-jin's *Attack the Gas Station!* (*Juyuso seubgyuksageun*, 1999), which struck viewers as both "ruthlessly violent" and "hysterically funny."[21] The film's central characters are four rebellious youth who take over a roadside service station and trash it "just because" they can (Figure 13.7). They decide to put on uniforms and act like attendants, but they have no idea how to pump gas. When their cocky upper-class customers insult them as ignorant clods, they lash back, capturing some as hostages and humiliating them. It is possible to view this aggression as a form of social revenge. In flashbacks, we learn that the young men are themselves victims. One was repeatedly forced by a bullying teacher into painfully bending from the hip with his head on the ground. Another quit the high-school baseball team when his corrupt coach demanded payment from the players. The service-station owner berates a third for being a disgrace to his parents, but we later learn that the youth's parents are both dead. Meanwhile, the boss has left his own young child at home alone. No wonder the gang takes pleasure in smashing patriotic signs that promise "A Great Era for the Common People" and

Figure 13.7 *Attack the Gas Station!* (1999).

"A Better Korea." Yet their behavior is far from sympathetic: They inflict pain and destruction with undisguised delight, acting more like raging psychopaths, even misogynists at times. Their victims often seem cartoonish. The boss pouts like a spoiled child when he is beaten. A "pretty" girl's face becomes a caricature of the new fashion for heavy makeup, double eyelids, and reconstructive surgery. Kim's cinematic style encourages laughter from his viewers rather than fear or outrage. He employs an MTV aesthetic, escalating the action in a series of madcap brawls toward anarchic absurdity. This lack of narrative logic has been hailed as symptomatic of a new direction in South Korean cinema, away from the familiar stories of economic development and antigovernment activism toward a less conventionally coherent rationale of *kunyang*, "just because."[22]

The thin line between pleasure and pain is often tested in the horror film, where smiles and grimaces can become indistinguishable at moments of extreme emotion. Korean horror was marketed in the West as "Asia extreme," emphasizing its reputation for extreme violence. While this violence has been read metaphorically, as a trope for historical trauma, it takes intensely graphic form in films like *Oldboy* (*Oldeuboi*, 2003), part of Park Chan-wook's "vengeance trilogy." Oh Dae-su, the main character of *Oldboy*, is imprisoned for fifteen years without knowing why or who has put him in his cell. After his release, he has five days to find his mysterious captor or the young woman he loves will be killed. His search for the man and his quest for vengeance take him on a dark journey through a web of machinations, memories, and lies involving torture, murder, and incest. Early in the film, driven to madness after only two months in solitary confinement, he kneels before the drawing of a man whose bare teeth are slightly parted in an ambiguous expression (Figure 13.8a). Dae-su's own face mirrors this strange look (Figure 13.8b). Beneath the sketch are the words, in Korean, "Laugh, and the world laughs with you. Weep, and you weep alone." Much later, near the film's finale, when he seems to be reunited with his loved

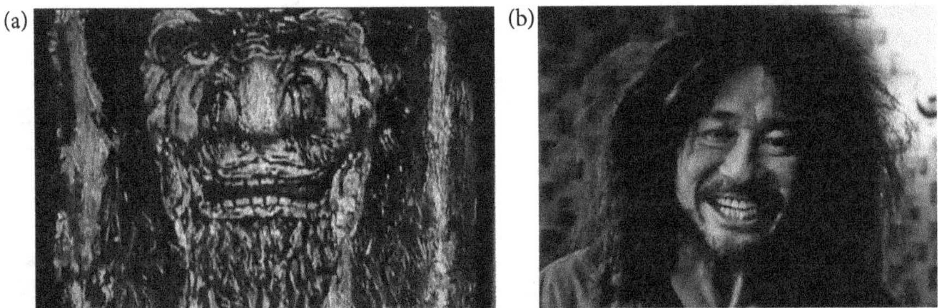

Figure 13.8 The ambiguous faces of comedy in *Oldboy* (2003): pleasure or pain? (a) The equivocal poster. (b) Dae-su's incongruous smile.

one, his lips form a brief, bright smile before melting into an agonizing scowl. It is moments like these that call the nature of laughter into question. Are we watching the laughter of derision, a scornful acknowledgment of bitter truths, release from nervous tension, or the simultaneous apprehension of two opposite emotional extremes? All three of the most influential accounts of humor in the West—superiority theory (Plato, Hobbes), relief theory (Spencer, Freud), and incongruity (Schopenhauer, Kant)—seem to apply at once.

Japan's Master Satirist: Juzo Itami

An undisputed master of Japanese comedy in recent times was Juzo Itami, whose work delighted audiences at home and abroad in the 1980s, but whose choice of targets may have led to his untimely demise. Juzo was himself the son of a bold cinematic satirist, Mansaku Itami, who made twenty-two films in the 1930s before dying at the age of forty-six. Mansaku's samurai parodies made fun of the military class that sought control of Japanese policy and much of the region at the time. Juzo did not begin directing until the age of forty-nine, after successful careers as a commercial artist, actor, writer, and television talk show host. The idea for his first film came when he was asked to conduct the funeral for his wife's father. The experience seemed so bizarre that he realized it could be a movie. In *The Funeral* (*Ososhiki*, 1984), he turns a winking eye on the elaborate Japanese rituals for observing death. The deceased party in the film, who was difficult enough to live with when alive, is an even greater inconvenience as a corpse. The dead man's son-in-law and daughter (played by Itami's wife, Nobuko Miyamoto) are a trendy, urban couple unfamiliar with the ancient rituals. To learn how to conduct themselves, they resort to an instructional video, watching in the kitchen while making whipped cream with a new electronic whisker. Over the next three days, they must choose a proper coffin, hire a Buddhist priest, work out the details of cremation, host the wake, and navigate the intricate rules of etiquette at the service itself. This proves to be particularly tricky when the son-in-law's ditsy mistress shows up drunk and insists on making love in the woods. From such incongruities of high technology and arcane customs, hilarity and grief, Itami fashions a concoction of comic contradictions. In his next film, *Tampopo* (*Tanpopo*, 1985), he targets another venerable Japanese tradition, the art of making noodles. (▶ See "Case Study for Chapter 13: *Tampopo*" on the website.)

Itami found comedy in everything, literally from death to taxes. Three years after *Funeral*, he directed *A Taxing Woman* (*Marusa no onna*, 1987). Again, Nobuko Miyamoto takes the title role as a short, freckled tax auditor named Ryoko who works for the National Tax Agency. Like other Japanese traditions, the tax system in Japan is based on principles of honor: Taxpayers are expected to report their earnings honestly. But people are people, and in the 1980s, an age of unprecedented Japanese prosperity, tax evasion had become a national pastime. Itami got the idea for a movie about taxes after the box-office receipts from his first film placed him in the highest bracket. He began studying cases of evasion, interviewing tax agents and their victims. The fruits of his research are evident in *A Taxing Woman*. As his heroine works her way up from mom-and-pop offenders to pinball operators and bigger game, we learn the most ingenious methods for hiding money from the government. We also get to watch some resourceful detective work by the tax agents and their high-tech allies (Figure 13.9). Itami's preoccupation with these obsessive details may itself seem obsessive, but it is never simply technical. Itami sees money as the "alter ego" of the individual. In a society where corporate success has replaced the values of family and state, collecting and evading taxes is an affirmation of identity. The film's biggest tax evader is Hideki Gondo, a big-time entrepreneur. He's made piles of money in crooked real estate and a string of "adult hotels." Like other Japanese investors, he feels entitled to keep his earnings, so he hides it from the government—until he meets his match in Ryoko. Gondo's greed is tinged with charm. He has a flair for life, blending his twin passions for women and cash in a lively and engaging medley. It's hard to reconcile his winning ways with his mistreatment of the poor

Figure 13.9 Staking out tax evaders in *A Taxing Woman* (1987).

and elderly. Ryoko, for her part, is as ferocious as she is straight. She climbs the bureaucratic ladder in single-minded pursuit of justice while the victims of her auditing miserably squirm. She is indeed a taxing woman. As the plot thickens, others join the fray: Gondo is reinforced by a horde of gangsters and corrupt politicians, Ryoko by a cavalry of tax inspectors. But who is the cat and who the mouse in this mad chase? Beyond the comic tribute to gangbuster films, there is a harsh edge to such scenes. They cut through the polite drapery of Japanese society to expose a level of raw fanaticism, sexism, and greed. Itami's sequel, appropriately titled *A Taxing Woman Returns* in English (*Marusa no onna 2*, 1988), was even darker.

In 1992, Itami took aim at his riskiest target, the *yakuza*, and the international crime syndicate was not amused. Three days after the release of *The Gentle Art of Japanese Extortion* (*Minbo no onna*), two members of the gang attacked the director, slicing him with knives. He recovered, but five years later his body was found on the sidewalk outside his office. The official report was suicide by jumping from the roof, but rumors of homicide persist.

Through the next few decades, Japanese directors continued to make sport of national pastimes. Masayuki Suo spoofed his countrymen's addiction to sumo wrestling with *Sumo Do, Sumo Don't* (*Shiko funjatta*, 1992). In *Shall We Dance?* (*Sharu wi dansu*?, 1996), he affectionately lampooned Japan's mania for ballroom dancing, scoring an international hit. Shinobu Yaguchi played with the fad for synchronized swimming in *Waterboys* (*Wota boizu*, 2001). Nobuhiro Yamashita took on the punk-rock trend in *Linda, Linda, Linda* (2005). In Japan, it seems that every new craze is fair game for the satirist's camera.

Hong Kong's God of Comedy: Stephen Chow

Stephen Chow is best known in the West for *Shaolin Soccer* (*Siu Lam juk kau*, 2001) and *Kung Fu Hustle* (*Gung fu*, 2004), his wacky sendups of sports mania and the martial arts. That's because these comedies depend more on physical humor and internationally familiar subjects than do other films with a large following in China, some of which feature the high-speed verbal wit known in Hong Kong as *mo lei tau* (nonsense). Chow is a master of both slapstick and double talk. Born in 1962, he began his career as a dramatic actor, working in television and even children's programming before moving to film. By 1994, he was directing as well, and within a few more years he was a pop-culture phenomenon, starring in five of the top twelve films in Hong Kong history. Sometimes, like Chaplin, he plays the scrappy "little man," struggling to make something of himself in an aggressive or indifferent environment. At other times, he presents himself as a superhero, a godlike master of soccer, fighting, cookery, or whatever niche he's chosen to prove his ostentatious superiority. Chow's proclivity for zany antics can be misleading. As with Italy's Roberto Benigni (and Rabelais himself), there is a sharp intelligence behind the penis gags and toilet jokes. Some scholars argue that his films are not just offhand, postmodern pastiche but carefully composed creations, deliberately staged and cleverly choreographed, illuminating commentaries on the relationships between local and global culture in our increasingly interdependent world.[23]

In *The God of Cookery* (*Sik san*, 1996), Chow plays a celebrated chef who judges his would-be competitors from on high. Actually, Chef Chow knows little about cooking; he's a corrupt fraud who hides his ignorance behind a façade of bravado and fancy trickery. Early in the film, when his pretensions are exposed, his culinary empire comes crashing down around him. Chow is forced to live a hand-to-mouth existence in the back streets of Hong Kong. Thoroughly humiliated and soundly thrashed by low-life thugs, he still manages to unite two rival street-food gangs by combining their signature dishes, beef balls and "pissing shrimp," into a single creation: pissing beef balls. This new success puts him on the path to cooking school and a chance to claw his way back to the top. As always with Chow's films, the plot can be read as historical allegory, in this case Hong Kong as a bustling battlefield for Western-style capitalism (the big food conglomerates) and the collectivist ideologies of the East (the street-food gangs). More simply, the food fight between competing chefs can be seen as Chow entering the fray of recent Hong Kong food film comedies like Tsui Hark's *The Chinese Feast* (*Jin yu man tang*, 1995) and Ang Lee's *Eat Drink Man Woman* (*Yin shi nan nu*, 1994).

Much of the comedy in *Kung Fu Hustle* is designed for an international audience acquainted with the martial arts movies that it fondly parodies as well as an eclectic selection from global pop culture. The film style is deliberately cartoonish, the characters are outlandish, the action is a continuous parade of goofy sight gags. Chow plays a smalltime con artist named Sing who, pretending to be a member of the notorious Axe Gang, tries to shake down the tenants in a poor neighborhood of Shanghai. Unfortunately for him, the motley tenants of Pig Alley turn out to be experts in kung fu. When Sing challenges them with a boastful threat, "Who wants to die?" they all step forward (Figure 13.10). Sing quickly modifies his challenge to single combat, selecting an old lady from the crowd. When she gives him a gut-wrenching punch in the stomach, he chooses someone else. "Hey, shorty," he shouts, not realizing that the little man in the second row is sitting on a stool. When the guy stands up, he's a towering giant. Sing retorts, "Go sit down, you're cheating." One by one, he picks and instantly dismisses his would-be opponents. The "geezer with the glasses" is built like a rock, the "kid" in the second row is even stronger, and the fat landlady with curlers in her hair turns out to be the toughest of them all. Things get even worse

Figure 13.10 *Kung Fu Hustle* (2004).

for him when the real Axe Gang shows up. Dressed in black suits and top hats, they look as if they've just stepped out of Martin Scorsese's *Gangs of New York* (2002). But it turns out that *Kung Fu Hustle* is alluding to older, more indigenous traditions. The Axe Gang and its top hats appeared in Chinese films as early as the 1970s. The tenants of Pig Alley are borrowed from a 1940s play in which the marginalized poor of Shanghai rise up to challenge the privileged class. What's more, Chow chose actors from old Cantonese kung fu films for much of his cast. Such references may be lost on outside audiences, but they enrich the experience for local viewers, planting his comic mischief deep in the soil of Hong Kong cinematic history.

In 2013, Chow dug even deeper. In *Journey to the West: Conquering the Demons* (*Xi you: Xiang mo pian*, co-directed with Chi-kin Kwok), he gives a comic interpretation of the Ming Dynasty literary classic known in the West as *Monkey*. That story, itself based on a real monk's travels to India from 629 to 646 in search of Buddhist sutras, is embroidered with fanciful tales of demons, magic weapons, and astounding battles. On his journey to enlightenment, the monk (Xuanzang in Mandarin, Tripitaka in Sanskrit) encounters a fish demon, a pig demon, and a dragon. Each demon serves the monk in some way, but his most powerful protector is the unwilling Sun Wukong, the monkey king who has been imprisoned in a cave for five hundred years for extravagant misdeeds. With Buddha's help, the monk subdues these miscreants and all four set forth on the perilous westward path.

Monkey is the ultimate Chinese trickster. Boastful, brave, willful, elusive, exceedingly clever, and endlessly mischievous—like Chow's usual screen persona—he is a constant threat to the established order. Even in heaven he creates havoc, which is why Buddha has confined him to the cave. But this troublesome, impulsive figure can also be as endearing as a child and as entertaining as a clown, the very soul of comedy.

To the five main characters Chow adds Miss Duan, a distinctly unfeminine demon slayer whose aggressive nature contrasts with the monk's naïve compassion. Sanzang (as the monk is called in the movie) is mop-haired, childlike, and totally inept in the martial arts. These deviations from expected gender roles are a constant source of comedy. When Miss Duan recognizes the bravery behind Sanzang's humble appearance, she falls in love with him. The problem is, she is too macho for his tastes. The lopsided relationship between Duan and Sanzang draws laughter throughout the film, but the most creative comedy swirls around the four outlandish CGI monsters, which are forever shifting shapes and acting badly, cartoonish caricatures of human greed, rage, hubris, and other cardinal vices.

Like Stephen Chow's other comedies, *Journey to the West* plays with genres as well as gender, combining elements of romance, martial arts, slapstick, horror, and road movies. It also merges character types, motifs, and themes familiar from Chinese storytelling: Buddhist bodhisattvas, Daoist immortals, magic books, enchanted weapons, deception, and betrayal. But Chow's inventiveness and his particular brand of humor achieve something unique. The fighting is both fantastically flamboyant and extremely violent; even children die. As Nicholas Rapold put it in his *New York Times* review, there is a "fairy-tale edge of menace" mixed in with its "childish frivolity."[24] The film's great popularity in China offers clues to what people still find funny in that part of the world.

Taiwan's Gentle Wit: Ang Lee

At the other end of the spectrum, Ang Lee offers a kinder, gentler form of humor. Born to conservative parents on the island of Taiwan in 1954, he moved to the United States at the age of twenty-four and earned a bachelor's degree from the University of Illinois and a master's degree in film production from New York University. This bicultural education influenced his approach to movies and to comedy. In contrast to Chow's emphasis on manic competition, Lee's first three films—known as the "father-knows-best trilogy—use humor as an adjunct to wisdom, more in the manner of Lin Yutang.

In *Pushing Hands* (*Tui shou*, 1992), the patriarch is an aging martial-arts teacher who has come to the United States from Beijing to live with his son's family. The problem is that Master Chu does not communicate well with his son's American wife, Martha. Although they share the same house, Master Chu and Martha are culturally worlds apart. While he practices calligraphy in one room, she sits in another room tapping out text at a computer. While he goes through the slow-motion rituals of tai chi, she tries to work in frantic silence. It doesn't help that he enjoys traditional Chinese meals rich in meat (she's a vegetarian) or that he likes cigarettes (she can't stand smoke). Nor does it help when he tries to microwave his dinner neatly wrapped in aluminum foil. The camera shows us these discrepancies in revealing close-ups: the fluid sweep of his calligraphy brush, her fingers pecking at the keys; his fried pork, her anemic health salad. At one point, we see them from outside, each framed in a separate window. The whole scene is shot without music or words, the silence underscoring their uncomfortable isolation from each other. Literally and figuratively, these two don't speak the same language. Master Chu fails to understand a good deal more about American culture than microwaves, but he also sees much with a clear eye. "Americans teach children as if they were always making a deal," he observes. From his Daoist perspective, life and death are matters of fate. "Everything is destiny." The goal is to strive for "carefree nothingness." Yet Chu's philosophy is not one of inaction or indifference. As a practitioner of tai chi, he knows how to redirect an opponent's aggressive energy back against its source. This is the secret of "pushing hands," which conceals power in the guise of quietude. By remaining centered, one throws the adversary off balance. It is a traditional Chinese principle, a matter of maintaining poise, an equilibrium between yin and yang.

In *The Wedding Banquet* (*Xi yan*, 1993), the patriarch is a retired Chinese general who comes from Taipei to America with his wife to celebrate his son's wedding. The movie's comic premise is based on the fact, unknown to the son's traditional parents, that Wai-Tung is gay and happily living with his Caucasian boyfriend in Manhattan. For years, Mother Gao has been searching Taiwan for an eligible bride, while her son has kept her at bay with a list of impossible standards. He wants a woman who is at least five foot nine inches tall, has two doctorates, sings opera, and speaks five languages. When Mom finally finds someone who fits most of these criteria, he realizes that he needs a new strategy, so he persuades one of his female tenants, a poor artist of Chinese origin named Wei-Wei, to agree to a sham wedding. In return for this deception, she will get the green card that she needs to stay in the United States. Down go the photos of male bonding; up go the pictures of Wai-Tung and his "fiancée." The walls are papered with Chinese art to please the parents. But the civil ceremony at the courthouse is a family disaster: A perfunctory official rushes through the proceedings, mispronouncing the bride's name and giving her a rubber-stamped document before hurrying on to the next couple. Mrs. Gao leaves humiliated and depressed. Chinese marriages should be grand events, a spectacle of social status and achievement, more of a celebration for the parents than for the couple. So when the chance arises for a banquet, Wai-Tung's parents embrace the opportunity. Ang Lee devotes some ten minutes to the elaborate banquet scene and another eight to the bridal-chamber pranks that follow. The evening is a raucous carnival of good-humored bad behavior, traditional solemnity turned on its head. Lee himself, appearing as one of the wedding guests, comments slyly on this bacchanalia: "We're witnessing the result of 5,000 years of sexual repression" (Figure 13.11). The banquet is a hybrid affair, a concoction of rituals and icons from both sides of the Pacific. Like the film itself, it is an uproarious blend of Western and Asian elements, of comedy and drama, designed to appeal to a wide, multicultural audience.

The father in *Eat Drink Man Woman* is another troubled patriarch, a master chef who is losing his sense of taste and his connection with his Westernized family. Every Sunday, Old Chu prepares dinner as a reassuring ritual of traditional Asian values, but the custom has become uncomfortable for his three daughters, who are each struggling with the problems of modern life in a changing Taiwan. Most of the film's funniest moments center on a fourth woman, the father's self-centered, would-be fiancée, whose mouth runs like a motor in hyperdrive. But in contrast to Chow's *God of Cookery*, where fast talk and flashy cuisine are weapons in a war of self-promotion, Lee's film pays homage to modesty and good food as ingredients for togetherness and family love.

Feng Xiaogang and Chinese New Year Comedy

A new year is cause for celebration throughout the world, a time for gathering together, for sharing cherished memories of the past and joyful expectations for the future. In China, where the lunar calendar begins in January or February, the New Year's celebration (known as the Spring Festival, or *chun jie* in Mandarin) is

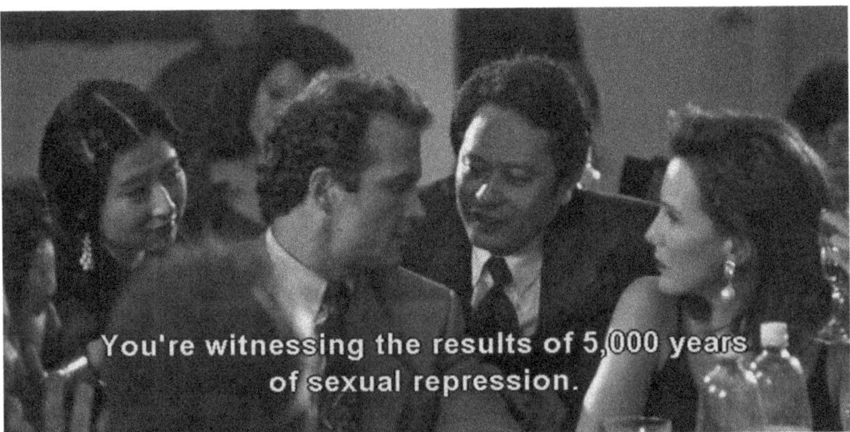

Figure 13.11 *The Wedding Banquet* (1993).

especially important. Chinese workers and students journey home for two weeks of extravagant eating, drinking, and merriment. The collective spirit of jollity, akin to Carnival, creates a perfect mood for watching movies, especially comedies. The movie industry has benefited from this happy occasion for years.

Since at least the 1950s, Chinese studios have timed their big-budget films for late-winter release, creating a special genre now marketed as "New Year's celebration movies" (*hesui pian*). Eric Tsang's madcap action film *Aces Go Places* was an early example; Stephen Chow's *King of Comedy* was another. Both were Hong Kong productions. In recent times, the genre's most successful practitioner on the mainland has been Feng Xiaogang. Feng grew up on a military base in Beijing among the "little people" who later figured so prominently in his films.[25] Although he was accepted to the prestigious Beijing Film Academy, his parents could not afford to buy him art supplies, so he joined the army before working his way into the industry, first as a television set designer, then as art director, scriptwriter, and director. His first big movie hit, *The Dream Factory* (*Jia fang yi fang*, 1997) brought the energy of *hesui pian* to the mainland and set new standards for Chinese commercial cinema. *The Dream Factory* is about four friends who form a startup company that caters to the dreams of wealthy customers. Their service enables clients to simulate the lives they wish they had using imaginary scenarios. In due course, Feng manages to satirize contemporary issues like corruption, China's aging population, and the false dichotomies between high and low culture. The film's central conceit, embodied in the title, slyly references Hollywood and Feng's own ability to appeal to popular tastes for profit.

After a successful romantic comedy (*Be There or Be Square* [*Bu jian bu san*], 1998) and two dramatic detours, Feng returned to the topic of cinema with *Big Shot's Funeral* (*Da wan*, 2001). The big shot is a famous American director named Tyler (played by Donald Sutherland) who has come to Beijing to film a remake of Bernardo Bertolucci's *The Last Emperor* (1987). His assistant, a Chinese American named Lucy (Rosamund Kwan), hires an obscure local cameraman (Ge you, nicknamed "YoYo" in the film) to shoot a short "making of" bonus video for the DVD. Lucy finds YoYo annoying, but when Tyler asks him what the ordinary Chinese think of the emperor, the director is impressed by the man's honesty, his street smarts, and the creative genius that he sees beneath YoYo's humble exterior. Speaking plainly, YoYo tells him that the emperor had lots of babes, all state-subsidized, while he himself had only one, who divorced him. "No money, no women. That's a tragedy." Much of the film's humor revolves around language and efforts to communicate over the linguistic barrier. At one point, Tyler tells Lucy that he can't complete the project because his heart isn't in it. Despite her perfect English, she fails to understand, but YoYo does. He shows this to Tyler by dropping a coin in a glass of water. Interpreting this gesture for Lucy, Tyler says, "Without the right idea at the center of the movie, you might as well piss in the ocean." Then, turning toward YoYo, he says, "See, I speak Chinese" (Figure 13.12). The two men embrace. Later, while the men are discussing funerals, YoYo explains that a good funeral is like a good comedy: Both leave people feeling satisfied. So when Tyler has a heart attack on camera, his last request is to have YoYo direct his funeral like a good comedy. To do this, YoYo finds an old acquaintance, a shamelessly greedy conniver, to promote the project. The idea takes off, with big-name brands all begging for product placements at the funeral. It turns out that YoYo has a genius for placing products. He dresses the mannequin, a stand-in for the corpse, in big-brand clothing and loads of accessories that conspicuously expose the names of sponsors. He even manages to make a plug for cigarettes, which are forbidden on TV. A sign above the casket reads "No smoking at the funeral. That includes Brand 666." Ironically, the funeral becomes a biting satire on modern China's mania for branded products and the film industry's exploitation of this trend. Feng managed to have his cake and eat it too.

Nor was he alone. Xu Zheng scored a huge hit with *Lost in Thailand* (*Ren zai jiong tu: Tai jiong*, 2012), which follows a businessman and his unwelcome, bumbling buddy through Southeast Asia in search of a new patent. After the film's release, the tourist trade from China to Thailand increased by 60%. Another enterprising director, Ning Hao, made money at the box office with *Crazy Stone* (*Feng kuang de shi tou*, 2006), a black comedy in which the bad guy is a greedy land developer. Ning's dialog is a hodgepodge of Chinese dialects, adding to the humor for local audiences. When someone crashes into a BMW, the owner shouts out "*bie mo wo*" (don't touch me), a pun on the British initials that would certainly be missed by most English-speaking viewers. Tian Yusheng's *Ex-Files* (*Qian ren gong lue*, 2014) toys with the clichés of modern romance. A popular

Figure 13.12 *Big Shot's Funeral* (2001).

young businessman attends the wedding party of an ex-girlfriend only to find himself seated at a table of her former boyfriends. Across the room is another table labeled "former girlfriends." On stage, the newlyweds ironically thank their exes for contributing to their emotional growth. It's an invitation to a fracaṣ that sets the brawl rolling for a rollicking rom-com. All these films started global trends within the context of contemporary China. To be sure, some of the comedy is culture-bound, incomprehensible to outsiders. But the rest of the world can recognize many of its own foibles in the looking glass of China's movie screens, laughing at our common missteps in doing business and making love.

It should be clear by now that the people of East Asia have a deep appreciation of humor that dates back some three thousand years and resonates with comic traditions elsewhere in the world. We have followed several strands of laughter. The witty laughter of the intellect, known as *huaji* in China and *kokkei* or *okashii* in Japan, found expression in literary works like *The Forest of Laughter* (*Xiao lin*, circa 220), in anecdotes and clever poems. It often served the moral and political purposes of satire, a challenge to abusive power and emotional excess, and it was practiced by ancient scholar wits not unlike European court jesters or African griots. A second strand, the gentler laughter of the heart variously translated as *youmo* (in Chinese), *yumou* (Japanese), and *yumeo* (Korean), is more a matter of balance. Related to the English word *humour*, with origins in medieval Western medicine, it is comparable to the Chinese belief in freeing the life force, *qi*, from bodily constrictions to restore a healthy equilibrium. The first strand is allied to the use of paradox in Daoist and Zen Buddhist thought, the second to a Confucian preference for moderation in all things. A third strand of bawdy laughter, expressed through the erotic innuendo of riddles and puns, can be traced back to Shinto fertility rites. This, too, has non-Asian correlatives in the boisterous communal spirit of Carnival and the ubiquity of crude sexual jokes abroad.

All three forms of laughter are vibrantly alive in the region's movie comedies. There is plenty of slapstick, satire, innuendo, dark humor, and decorous comedy of manners in the films of China, Korea, and Japan. We've seen how Stephen Chow harnesses the manic energies of "tricky humor" to parody Hong Kong genres and make fun of native types, how Ang Lee's cautionary comedies prod his fellow Taiwanese with an affectionate sense of humanistic humor, how Feng Xiaogang's New Year blockbusters shine the spotlight of mirth on contemporary issues in the PRC. We've seen how Juzo Itami spoofs the institutions and obsessions of modern Japan. And we've seen how the three leading Western theories of humor can be applied to South Korean films like *Old Boy* (superiority theory), *A Female Boss* (release theory), and *The Good, the Bad, the Weird* (incongruity theory). We've also noted instances of the world's most popular comic archetypes throughout East Asian cinema: comic duos like Wang and

Liu (the "Taiwanese Laurel and Hardy"), clowns like Hu Pu-liao (the Chinese "Little Tramp"), and an abundance of trickster figures, from Chow's Monkey to Mifune's seventh samurai.

At the same time, we've come up against some cultural barriers. Much of the verbal humor in East Asian movies is untranslatable, a particular problem in a region where puns are such important features of the languages. A good deal of the particularities of place, history, and local issues are also lost to outside viewers. Furthermore, some of the humor is distinctly regional in flavor. A large dose of pain is served with the laughter in films by Jackie Chan and Hsu Pu-liao. The level of violence in Chow's *Journey to the West* may be too extreme for some tastes, and what passes for humor in Korean films leaves many non-Eastern viewers totally bewildered. Finally, some concepts that Westerners take for granted, like the distinction between comedy and tragedy, simply don't apply. A plausible explanation for this is that "the tragic vision of life" described by John Morreall[26] has never taken root in this part of the world, where the trope sustaining this vision—the individual hero's fight against adversity—tends to be minimized by a culture of collectivism in which suffering is considered a natural part of life rather than something to fight against, and where the prevalent social ethos supports a community-oriented comic vision of existence.

East Asian Comedy Filmongraphy

Country	English Title	Original Title	Director	Date
PRC	*Crows and Sparrows*	*Wuya yu maque*	Junli Zheng	1949
Japan	*Good Morning*	*Ohayo*	Yasujiro Ozu	1959
South Korea	A *Female Boss*	*Yeosajang*	Hyeong-mo Han	1959
Taiwan	*Brother Liu and Brother Wang on the Road in Taiwan*	*Wang ge Liu ge you Tai Wan*	Tung Hsiao, Hsing Lee	1959
Hong Kong	*The Greatest Civil War on Earth*	*Nan bei he*	Tian-Lin Wang	1961
Japan	*Yojimbo*	*Yojinbo*	Akira Kurosawa	1961
Japan	*Am I Trying*	*Otoko wa tsurai yo*	Yoji Yamada	1969
Hong Kong	*Way of the Dragon*	*Meng long guo jiang*	Bruce Lee	1972
Taiwan	*Off to Success*	*Cheng gong ling shang*	Pei-Cheng Chang	1979
Hong Kong	*Drunken Master*	*Zui quan*	Woo-ping Yuen	1978

Country	English Title	Original Title	Director	Date
Hong Kong	*Encounters of the Spooky Kind*	*Gui da gui*	Sammo Kam-Bo Hung	1980
Hong Kong	*Aces Go Places: Mad Mission*	*Zui jia pai dang*	Eric Tsang	1982
Hong Kong	*Project A*	*'A' gai wak*	Jackie Chan	1983
Japan	*The Funeral*	*Ososhiki*	Juzo Itami	1984
Hong Kong	Mr. *Vampire*	*Geung si sin sang*	Ricky Lau	1985
Japan	*Tampopo*	*Tanpopo*	Juzo Itami	1985
Japan	A *Taxing Woman*	*Marusa no onna*	Juzo Itami	1987
Hong Kong	*God of Gamblers*	*Dou san*	Jing Wong	1989
Hong Kong	*Armour of God 2: Operation Condor*	*Fei ying gai wak*	Jackie Chan	1991
Hong Kong	*Tricky Brains*	*Jing gu jyun ga*	Jing Wong	1991
Taiwan	*Pushing Hands*	*Tui shou*	Ang Lee	1991
Japan	*Sumo Do, Sumo Don't*	*Shiko funjatta*	Masayuki Suo	1992
South Korea	*Marriage Story*	*Gyeolhon iyagi*	Ui-seok Kim	1992
Taiwan	*The Wedding Banquet*	*Xi yan*	Ang Lee	1993
Taiwan	*Eat Drink Man Woman*	*Yin shi nan nu*	Ang Lee	1994
Hong Kong	*The Chinese Feast*	*Jin yu man tang*	Hark Tsui	1995
Hong Kong	*The God of Cookery*	*Sik san*	Stephen Chow, Lik-Chi Lee	1996
Japan	*Shall We Dance?*	*Sharu wi dansu?*	Masayuki Suo	1996
PRC	*The Dream Factory*	*Jia fang yi fang*	Xiaogang Feng	1997
Hong Kong	*King of Comedy*	*Hei kek ji wong*	Stephen Chow	1999
South Korea	*Attack the Gas Station!*	*Juyuso seubgyuksageun*	Sang-jin Kim	1999
PRC	*Happy Times*	*Xing fu shi guang*	Yimou Zhang	2000
South Korea	*Joint Security Area*	*Gongdong gyeongbi guyeok*	Chan-wook Park	2000
Hong Kong	*Shaolin Soccer*	*Siu Lam juk kau*	Stephen Chow	2001
Japan	*Waterboys*	*Wota boizu*	Shinobu Yaguchi	2001

Country	English Title	Original Title	Director	Date
PRC	*Big Shot's Funeral*	*Da wan*	Xiaogang Feng	2001
South Korea	*My Sassy Girl*	*Yeopgjeogin geunyeo*	Jae-yong Kwak	2001
PRC	*Cell Phone*	*Shou ji*	Xiaogang Feng	2003
South Korea	*Oldboy*	*Oldeuboi*	Chan-wook Park	2003
Hong Kong	*Kung Fu Hustle*	*Gung fu*	Stephen Chow	2004
Japan	*Linda, Linda, Linda*	*Linda, Linda, Linda*	Nobuhiro Yamashita	2005
PRC	*Crazy Stone*	*Feng kuang de shi tou*	Hao Ning	2006
Japan	*Glasses*	*Megane*	Naoko Ogigami	2007
South Korea	*The Good, the Bad, the Weird*	*Joheunnom nabbeunnom isanghannom*	Jee-won Kim	2008
Taiwan	*Cape No. 7*	*Hai jiao qi hao*	Wei Te Shen	2008
PRC	*A Woman, a Gun and a Noodle Shop*	*San qiant pai an jing qi*	Yimou Zhang	2009
Japan	*Sawako Decides*	*Kaawa no soko kara konnichi wa*	Yuya Ishii	2010
PRC	*The Piano in a Factory*	*Gang de qin*	Men Zhang, Bo Gao	2010
PRC	*Lost in Thailand*	*Ren zai jiong tu: Tai jiong*	Zheng Xu	2012
Hong Kong	*Journey to the West: Conquering the Demons*	*Xi you: Xiang mo pian*	Stephen Chow, Chi-kin Kwok	2013
Japan	*The Great Passage*	*Fune wo amu*	Yuya Ishii	2013
PRC	*Ex-Files*	*Qian ren gong lue*	Yu-sheng Tian	2014

Films are listed chronologically, not by country. All release dates and film titles are based on imdb.com. Names of directors may differ slightly within the chapter to reflect common usage, which sometimes follows Asian conventions that place the family name first (Lee Bruce, Park Chan-wook). In this filmography, family names come last (Bruce Lee, Chan-wook Park). PRC refers to the People's Republic of China, sometimes known as Mainland China. South Korea is also known as the Republic of Korea to distinguish it from the Democratic People's Republic of Korea (North Korea).

Notes

1. "What Makes Japanese Laugh? The Art of Wordplay and Storytelling," *Asia Society* (September 1, 2016), http://asiasociety.org/what-makes-japanese-laugh.
2. Jessica Milner David and Jocelyn Chey, eds., *Humour in Chinese Life and Culture: Resistance and Control in Modern Times* (Hong Kong: Hong Kong University Press, 2013), 50.
3. Jocelyn Chey, "History of Humor: Classical and Traditional China," in *Encyclopedia of Humor Studies*, ed. Salvatore Attardo (Los Angeles: Sage, 2014), 295.
4. Chey, "History of Humor," 295
5. "A Grand Tower Base," in *Everyday Chinese: 60 Fables and Anecdotes*, ed. Zhong Qin (Beijing: New World Press, 1983), 135–136.
6. "Ambassador" [my translation], in *Everyday Chinese*, 51–52.
7. Goh Abe, "Rituals of Laughter," in *Encyclopedia of Humor Studies*, 649–650.
8. See "Film Industry," *Wikipedia*, February 5, 2018, https://en.wikipedia.org/wiki/Film_industry#Statistics.
9. Roger Garcia, ed., *Asia Laughs! A Survey of Asian Comedy Films* (Udine, Italy: Centro Expressioni Cinematografiche, 2012), 14.
10. Shaoyi Sun, "From China with a Laugh: A Perusal of Chinese Comedy Films," in Garcia, *Asia Laughs!*, 19–36.
11. Sam Ho, "Duck Cackling: Hong Kong Comedy," in Garcia, *Asia Laughs!*, 14.
12. Sam Ho, "Duck Cackling," 40.
13. Most, if not all, experts agree that Wong Fei-hung was never trained in drunken style. Despite any historical inaccuracy, this form of fighting has become associated with Wong because of the movie.
14. George Chun Han Wang, "Bringing Laughter in Changing Times: Taiwan's Comedy Cinema," in Garcia, *Asia Laughs!*, 167.
15. Wang, "Bringing Laughter," 171.
16. Chi-Yun Shin and Julian Stringer, *New Korean Cinema* (New York: New York University Press, 2005).
17. *Cinema Asia: South Korea,* DVD. Produced by Films on Demand; Films Media Group (Hamilton, NJ: Films for the Humanities & Sciences, 2007).
18. Darcy Paquet, "Korean Comedies in the 1950s and 1960s," in Garcia, *Asia Laughs!*, 103.
19. Paquet, "Korean Comedies," 2012.
20. Darcy Paquet, "The Korean Film Industry: 1992 to the Present," in *New Korean Cinema*, ed. Chi-Yun Shin and Julian Stringer (New York: New York University Press, 2005), 32–50.
21. Nancy Abelmann and Jung-ah Choi, "'Just Because': Comedy, Melodrama and Youth Violence in *Attack the Gas Station*," in Shin and Stringer, *New Korean Cinema*, 132–143.
22. Abelmann and Choi, " 'Just Because.' "

23. Vivian Lee, *Hong Kong Cinema since 1997: The Post-Nostalgic Imagination* (New York: Palgrave Macmillan, 2009), 126.
24. Nicholas Rapold, "He's Glad She Came Along," film review of *Journey to the West*, *New York Times*, March 6, 2014, https://www.nytimes.com/2014/03/07/movies/in-journey-to-the-west-hunting-demons-and-laughs.html.
25. Rui Zhang, *The Cinema of Feng Xiaogang: Commercialization and Censorship in Chinese Cinema after 1989* (Hong Kong: Hong Kong University Press, 2008), 4.
26. John Morreall, "Taoism," in *Encyclopedia of Humor Studies*, 749–751.

Postscript

When I began this project, I was motivated by a personal taste for comedy and an abiding curiosity. I knew that many of my students and colleagues shared my interests, but I had no idea just how popular comedies were around the world. I did not know what I would discover: how rich the field of humor studies had become, that questions about comedy were at the center of so many important issues of culture and history, art and science, personal and national identity.

I learned that humor serves multiple purposes. A comedy can be subversive, holding those in power and their institutions up to ridicule (like Ousmane Sembène's satires in Senegal or Jean-Pierre Bekolo's parodies in Cameroon); it can be conservative, a diversion from injustice and oppression (like Stalinist musicals of the 1930s), or a safety valve to let off steam (the Carnivalesque humor of Britain's Ealing comedies); it can be both progressive and regressive at the same time (as in France's time-travel comedy *The Visitors*, or Soviet Russia's *Ivan Vasilievich: Back to the Future*). Comedies arguably perpetuate ethnic prejudice by indulging in stereotypes (as Alf Garnett did in England or Archie Bunker in the United States), but they may also counter stereotypical thinking by exposing its absurdities and deflating its power (France's *Welcome to the Sticks*, Italy's *Welcome to the South*, Britain's *East Is East*).

As I studied hundreds of comedies from dozens of countries, I began to see how most jokes are really in-jokes, intimately shared by certain groups. What people laugh at in different places and at different times may differ widely in key respects, differences that serve as clues to understanding them and our own relationship to others. It soon became apparent that movies, especially comedies, offer glimpses of how people in Africa or Scandinavia see themselves and their daily life concerns. Furthermore, these movies provide informative historical and cultural perspectives. Tracing cinematic trends in South America across time (the *chanchadas* of Brazil's golden age; the Tropicalist movement in Argentina in the 1970s; the road movies, scam-and-swindler flicks, and cross-cultural co-productions in later eras) revealed to me the evolution of a continent. In East Asia, I noticed regional specialties like the tricky-brain comedy of Hong Kong, the dark humor of Korea, the humanistic wit of Taiwan, and the self-critical social satire of Japan. At the same time, I realized how inadequately Western theories explain the role of humor in regions that make no clear distinction between tragedy and comedy, like India, China, and the Middle East. In Africa, I saw how recent film comedy is countering the gloomy, disempowering view of "Afro-pessimism," building confidently on age-old traditions of oral storytelling and connections to the spirit world. I came to appreciate the taste for dry, eccentric *humour* in British comedy (Monty Python, Mr. Bean) and the intellectual strain of *esprit* in French comedy (in *Ridicule* and *The Dinner Game*, and even in the logical absurdities of Jacques Tati). I took careful note of the preoccupation in Italian comedies with sexual politics (*Marriage Italian Style, Divorce Italian Style, Swept Away*) and the hybrid, tragicomic forms and quirky feel-good comedies of Scandinavia (*Elling, Kitchen Stories, The Hundred-Year-Old Man Who Climbed Out the Window and Disappeared*). While I have tried to avoid the trap of essentializing an entire culture in narrow pigeonholes, I do believe that these observations contribute useful insights into our pasts and social differences.

Since film is a business as well as a cultural phenomenon, I have highlighted how the world's film industries developed, sometimes independently, but often in reaction to Hollywood's global hegemony. Early on, Britain turned to local talent and regional accents to compete. South American studios responded with clever strategies of imitation, parody, and homage. In Scandinavia and other European countries, state funding and protective policies helped to keep their national cinemas viable and culturally distinct. The Soviets appropriated the successful formulas of Broadway, applying them to musicals about the Moscow circus and the daily lives of tractor drivers. Meanwhile, Hollywood itself responded to the realities of global trends, making English-language versions of France's biggest hits, hiring foreign talent, and adapting transnational themes to its big-screen comedies. As the forces of globalism grow, as the planet moves closer to McLuhan's vision of the global village, the distance between Hollywood and other film industries seems to shrink. Increasingly, the world is laughing more and more in sync.

It was E. M. Forster who reportedly asked, "How do I know what I think until I see what I say?" Now that I have completed this book, I ask myself if there is a thesis running through the many lessons learned. A certain refrain stands out. It begins with the classical division between tragedy and comedy expressed in those twin masks of Greek theater figured in Chapter 1 (Figure 1.1a). The frowning mask reminds us that a great deal of Western literature, including movies, favors the trajectory of tragedy. That is, the canon of Western narratives still largely follows the storytelling arc described by Aristotle: a heroic course of action beginning with a complication, progressing through a series of challenges and struggles, rising in intensity and anguish until some final battle resolves the conflict, returning to an earlier state of relative stability. Most of these stories—from the *Iliad* to the epic war film *Troy*, from horror to disaster movies—are rife with negative emotions and behavior: anger, fear, humiliation, violence, injustice, vengeance, people doing stupid stuff. Some might say that film and television storytelling today has grown ever darker (literally and figuratively, if *Game of Thrones* is any indication), more explicitly libidinous, more graphically ferocious. All this has an impact on us as individuals and on our social interactions. Cultural critics have been issuing warnings for years. More recently, neuroscientists and cognitive psychologists have joined the debate, offering evidence that a steady emphasis on trauma perpetuates mental and emotional stress. The persistent trauma of drama activates our most primitive instincts. It feeds the sub-rational, autonomic portions of our brain and nervous system associated with survival, flight or fight. What researchers have learned about the mental circuitry of humor and its cultural dimensions points to a healthy alternative. As this book amply demonstrates, comedy offers diverting detours from the *agon*-driven, angst-heavy, straight-and-narrow path of Aristotle's plot. In contrast to the hero's single-minded journey, comic narratives tend to be more varied, supple, circuitous, and complex, capable of reflecting a greater range of human experience than, say, the tragedies of Sophocles or Eugene O'Neill. It turns out that the lighthearted behavior of Shakespeare's jester and the ubiquitous clown, the devious performance of African tricksters, the childishly playful shenanigans of Laurel and Hardy, Olmedo and Porcel, or Brother Wang and Brother Liu can all be powerful antidotes to stress, social repression, and the heavy hand of tyranny. Scholars and scientists, theorists and practitioners are at last acknowledging the phenomenon of humor in all its multicultural dimensions and on a global scale. As I have sought to show, the world's great movie comedies, as well as its lesser-known varieties, are an essential part of the human story. Properly understood, they can help to restore a much-needed measure of balance to our mental, emotional, and social well-being.

Recommended Reading

Theory and Humor Studies

Attardo, Salvatore, ed. *Encyclopedia of Humor Studies*. 2 vols. Los Angeles: Sage, 2014.

Bakhtin, Mikhail. *The Dialogic Imagination: Four Essays by M. M. Bakhtin*. Edited by Michael Holquist. Translated by Caryl Emerson and Michael Holquist. Austin: University of Texas Press, 1981.

Bakhtin, Mikhail. *Rabelais and His World*. Translated by Hélène Iswolsky. Bloomington: Indiana University Press, 1984.

Bassil-Morozow, Helena. *The Trickster in Contemporary Film*. New York: Routledge, 2012.

Bergson, Henri. *Laughter: An Essay on the Meaning of the Comic*. Translated by Cloudesley Brereton and Fred Rothwell. New York: Macmillan, 1914.

Charney, Maurice, ed. *Comedy: A Geographic and Historical Guide*. Vol. 1. Westport, CT: Praeger, 2005.

Foka, Anna, and Jonas Liliequist, eds. *Laughter, Humor, and the (Un)making of Gender: Historical and Cultural Perspectives*. London: Palgrave Macmillan, 2015.

Freud, Sigmund. *Jokes and Their Relation to the Unconscious*. Edited and translated by James Strachey. New York: Norton, 1960.

Frye, Northrop. *Anatomy of Criticism: Four Essays*. New York: Atheneum, 1967.

Griffin, Dustin. *Satire: A Critical Reintroduction*. Lexington: University Press of Kentucky, 1994.

Grodal, Torben. *Embodied Vision: Evolution, Emotion, Culture and Film*. Oxford: Oxford University Press, 2009.

Harries, Dan. *Film Parody*. London: British Film Institute, 2000.

Horton, Andres, and Joanna E. Rapf, eds. *A Companion to Film Comedy*. Oxford: Wiley-Blackwell, 2015.

Huizinga, Johan. *Homo Ludens: A Study of the Play-Element in Culture*. London: Routledge & Kegan Paul, 1949.

Hutcheon, Linda. *A Theory of Parody: The Teachings of Twentieth-Century Art Forms*. New York: Methuen, 1985.

Martin, Rod A. *The Psychology of Humor: An Integrative Approach*. Amsterdam: Elsevier Academic Press, 2007.

Mizejewski, Linda. *Pretty/Funny: Women Comedians and Body Politics*. Austin: University of Texas Press, 2014.

Morreall, John. *Comedy, Tragedy, and Religion*. Albany: State University of New York Press, 1999.

Pirandello, Luigi. *On Humor*. Translated by Antonio Illiano and Daniel P. Testa. Chapel Hill: University of North Carolina Press, 1974.

Solomon, William. *Slapstick Modernism: Chaplin to Kerouac to Iggy Pop*. Champaign: University of Illinois Press, 2016.

Weems, Scott. *Ha! The Science of When We Laugh and Why*. New York: Basic Books, 2014.

Writing and Performance

Berger, Arthur Asa. *The Art of Comedy Writing*. New Brunswick, NJ: Transaction, 1997.
Blake, Marc. *Writing the Comedy Movie*. London: Bloomsbury, 2015.
Carter, Judy. *The Comedy Bible: From Stand-up to Sitcom—The Comedy Writer's Ultimate How-To Guide*. New York: Simon & Schuster, 2001.
DePaul, Greg. *Bring the Funny: The Essential Companion for the Comedy Screenwriter*. New York: Routledge, 2017.
Field, Syd. *Screenplay: The Foundations of Screenwriting*. New York: Delta, 2005.
Horton, Andrew. *Laughing Out Loud: Writing the Comedy-Centered Screenplay*. Berkeley: University of California Press, 2000.
Indick, William. *Psychology for Screenwriters: Building Conflict in Your Script*. San Francisco: Michael Wiese, 2004.
Kaplan, Steve. *The Hidden Tools of Comedy: The Serious Business of Being Funny*. San Francisco: Michael Wiese Productions, 2013.
Lax, Eric. *Conversations with Woody Allen: His Films, the Movies, and Moviemaking*. New York: Knopf, 2007.
McKee, Robert. *Story: Style, Structure, Substance and the Principles of Screenwriting*. New York: HarperCollins, 1997.

National and Regional Film Comedy

British

Hunter, I. Q., and Laraine Porter, eds. *British Comedy Cinema*. New York: Routledge, 2012.
Lockyer, Sharon, ed. *Reading* Little Britain: *Comedy Matters on Contemporary Television*. London: Taurus, 2010.
Mather, Nigel. *Tears of Laughter: Comedy-Drama in 1990s British Cinema*. Manchester: Manchester University Press, 2006.

French

Abel, Richard, ed. *French Film Theory and Criticism: A History/Anthology*. 2 vols. Princeton, NJ: Princeton University Press, 1988.
Gordon, Rae Beth. *Why the French Love Jerry Lewis: From Cabaret to Early Cinema*. Stanford, CA: Stanford University Press, 2002.
Lanzoni, Rémi Fournier. *French Comedy on Screen: A Cinematic History*. New York: Palgrave Macmillan, 2014.

Italian

Bini, Andrea. *Male Anxiety and Psychopathology in Film: Comedy Italian Style*. New York: Palgrave Macmillan, 2015.
Bondanella, Peter. *A History of Italian Comedy*. New York: Continuum, 2009.
Bullaro, Grace Russo, ed. *Beyond "Life Is Beautiful": Comedy and Tragedy in the Cinema of Roberto Benigni*. Leicester: Troubador Publishing, 2005.
Celli, Carlo. *The Divine Comic: The Cinema of Roberto Benigni*. Lanham, MD: Scarecrow Press, 2001.

Ferlita, Ernest, and John R. May. *The Parables of Lina Wertmuller*. Mahwah, NJ: Paulist Press, 1977.

Lanzoni, Rémi Fourier. *Comedy Italian Style: The Golden Age of Italian Film Comedies*. New York: Continuum, 2008.

Russian

Beumers, Birgit, ed. *A Companion to Russian Cinema*. Oxford: Wiley Blackwell, 2016.

Beumers, Birgit, ed. *Directory of World Cinema Russia*. Chicago: Intellect, 2011.

Horton, Andrew, ed. *Inside Soviet Film Satire: Laughter with a Lash*. Cambridge: Cambridge University Press, 2005.

Propp, Vladimir. *On the Comic and Laughter*. Edited and translated by Jan-Patrick Debbèche and Paul Perron. Toronto: University of Toronto Press, 2009.

Salys, Rimgaila. *The Musical Comedy Films of Gigori Aleksandrov: Laughing Matters*. Chicago: Intellect, 2009.

African

Armes, Roy. *African Filmmaking: North and South of the Sahara*. Bloomington: Indiana University Press, 2006.

Bakari, Ishaq Imruh, and Mbaye B. Cham. *African Experiences of Cinema*. London: British Film Institute, 1996.

Harrow, Kenneth W. *Postcolonial African Cinema: From Political Engagement to Postmodernism*. Bloomington: Indiana University Press, 2007.

Hugo, Pieter. *Nollywood*. Munich: Prestel Publishing, 2009.

Krings, Matthias, and Onookome Okome, eds. *Global Nollywood: The Transnational Dimensions of an African Video Film Industry*. Bloomington: Indiana University Press, 2013.

Nwosu, Maik. *The Comic Imagination in Modern African Literature and Cinema: A Poetics of Laughter*. New York: Routledge, 2016.

Orlando, Valérie K. *New African Cinema*. Rutgers, NJ: Rutgers University Press, 2017.

Pfaff, Françoise. *Focus on African Films*. Bloomington: Indiana University Press, 2006.

Thackway, Melissa. *Africa Shoots Back: Alternative Perspectives in Sub-Saharan Francophone African Film*. Bloomington: Indiana University Press, 2003.

Ukadike, Frank. *Black African Cinema: Conversations with Filmmakers*. Minneapolis: University of Minnesota Press, 1994.

Ukadike, Frank. *Questioning African Cinema: Conversations with Filmmakers*. Minneapolis: University of Minnesota Press, 2002.

Scandinavian

Gustafsson, Tommy, and Pietari Kääpä, *Nordic Genre Film: Small Nation Film Cultures in the Global Marketplace*. Edinburgh: Edinburgh University Press, 2015.

Nestingen, Andrew, and Trevor Elkington, eds. *Transnational Cinema in a Global North: Nordic Cinema in Transition*. Detroit: Wayne State University Press, 2005.

Soila, Tyutti, Astrid Söderbergh Widding, and Gunnar Iversen. *Nordic National Cinemas*. New York: Routledge, 1998.

South American

Couret, Nilo. *Mock Classicism: Latin American Film Comedy 1930–1960*. Oakland: University of California Press, 2018.

Delgado, Maria M., Stephen M. Hart, and Randal Johnson, eds. *A Companion to Latin American Cinema*. Oxford: Wiley Blackwell, 2017.

Johnson, Randal, and Robert Stam, eds. *Brazilian Cinema*. New York: Columbia University Press, 1995.

King, John. *Magical Reels: A History of Cinema in Latin America*. London: Verso, 1990.

Lie, Nadia. *The Latin American (Counter-)Road Movie and Ambivalent Modernity*. New York: Palgrave Macmillan, 2017.

Martin, Michael T. *New Latin American Cinema*. Detroit: Wayne State University Press, 1997.

McClennen, Sophia A. *Globalization and Latin American Cinema: Toward a New Critical Paradigm*. New York: Palgrave Macmillan, 2018.

Pobleta, Juan, and Juana Suárez, eds. *Humor in Latin American Cinema*. New York: Palgrave Macmillan, 2016.

Rêgo, Cacilda, and Carolina Rocha, eds. *New Trends in Argentine and Brazilian Cinema*. Bristol: Intellect, 2010.

Shaw, Deborah, ed. *Contemporary Latin American Cinema: Breaking into the Global Market*. Lanham, MD: Rowman & Littlefield, 2007.

Shohat, Ella, and Robert Stam. *Unthinking Eurocentrism: Multiculturalism and the Media*. New York: Routledge, 1994.

East Asian

Cohn, Joel R. *Studies in the Comic Spirit in Modern Japanese Fiction*. Cambridge, MA: Harvard University Asia Center, 1998.

Garcia, Roger, ed. *Asia Laughs! A Survey of Asian Comedy Films*. Udine, Italy: Centro Expressioni Cinematografiche, 2012.

Lee, Vivian. *Hong Kong Cinema Since 1997: The Post-Nostalgic Imagination*. New York: Palgrave Macmillan, 2009.

Milner, Jessica Davis, and Jocelyn Chey, eds. *Humour in Chinese Life and Culture: Resistance and Control in Modern Times*. Hong Kong: Hong Kong University Press, 2013.

Rea, Christopher. *The Age of Irreverence: A New History of Laughter in China*. Oakland: University of California Press, 2015.

Shin, Chi-Yun, and Julian Stringer. *New Korean Cinema*. New York: New York University Press, 2005.

Index

Figures are indicated by *f* following the page number.

For the benefit of digital users, indexed terms that span two pages (e.g., 52–53) may, on occasion, appear on only one of those pages.